WAR
OF THE
WORLDS

WAR OF THE WORLDS

A GRAPHIC NOVEL
ADAPTED FROM THE CLASSIC TALE OF ALIEN INVASION
BY H.G. WELLS

WRITTEN BY
STEPHEN STERN

ILLUSTRATED BY
ARNE STARR

LETTERING AND SPECIAL EFFECTS
DAN COTE

ART PRODUCTION
BILL MAUS

BEST SELLERS ILLUSTRATED
Los Angeles   New York   Miami

BEST SELLERS ILLUSTRATED

Dr. Adrian Alexandru Chief Executive Officer and Publisher
Stephen Stern President
Aron Kessler Chief Creative Officer

This book is a work of fiction. The characters, incidents and dialogue are drawn from the author's imagination and are not to be construed as real. Any resemblance to actual events, institutions or persons, living or dead, is entirely coincidental.

BEST SELLERS ILLUSTRATED, 4804 Laurel Canyon Blvd., Suite 544, Valley Village, CA 91607. Tel: (800) 988-8300.

Best Sellers Illustrated may be purchased for educational, business or sales promotional use. For information write to us at the above address or info@bestsellersillustrated.com.

Library of Congress Control Number: 2004195272

ISBN: 0-9764755-0-2

FIRST EDITION

Printed in Canada

Who would have thought, in the first years of the twenty-first century, that across the gulf of space, intelligences far greater than our own regarded this Earth with envious eyes. Slowly and surely, they drew their plans against us...

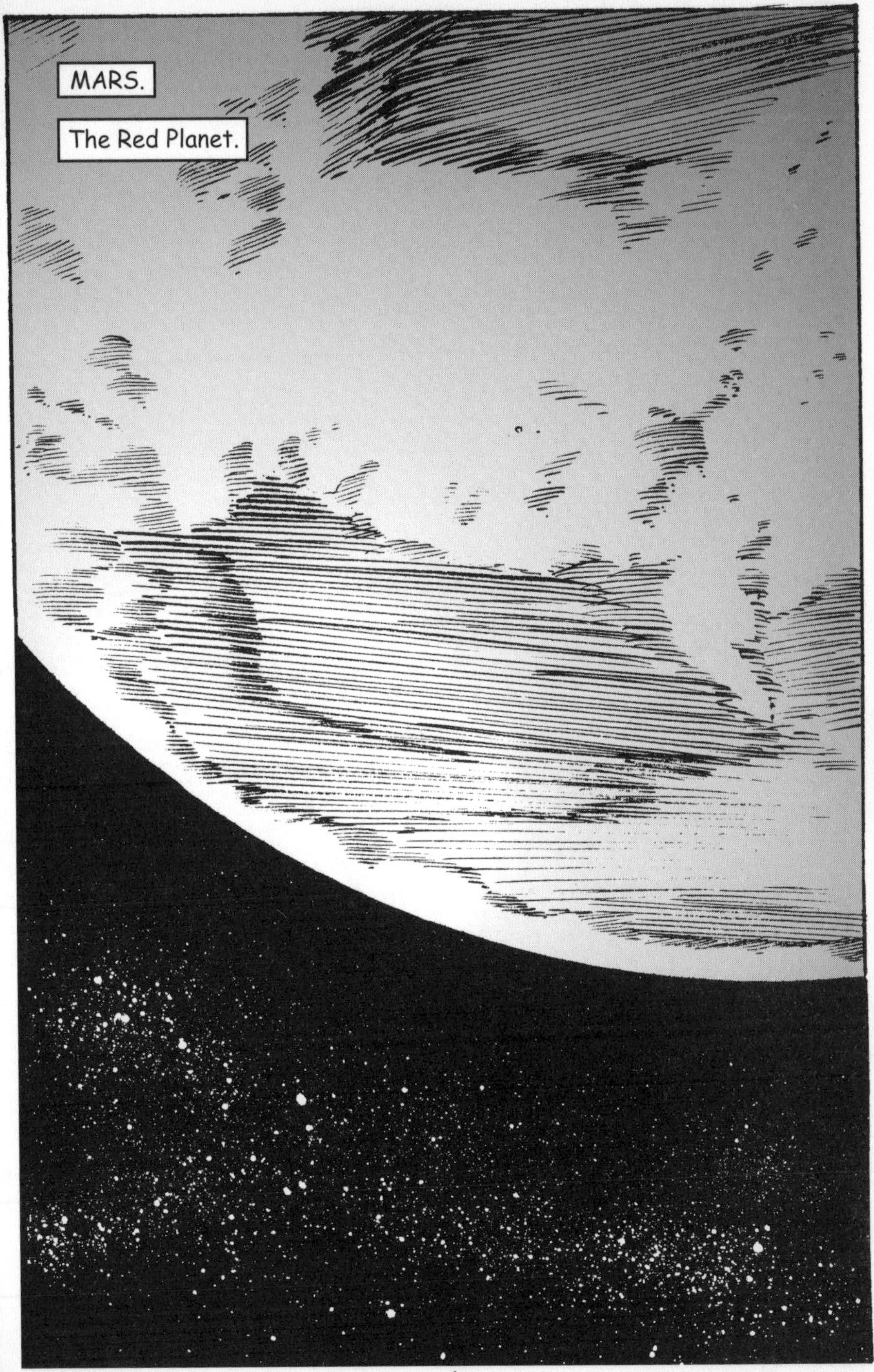
MARS.
The Red Planet.

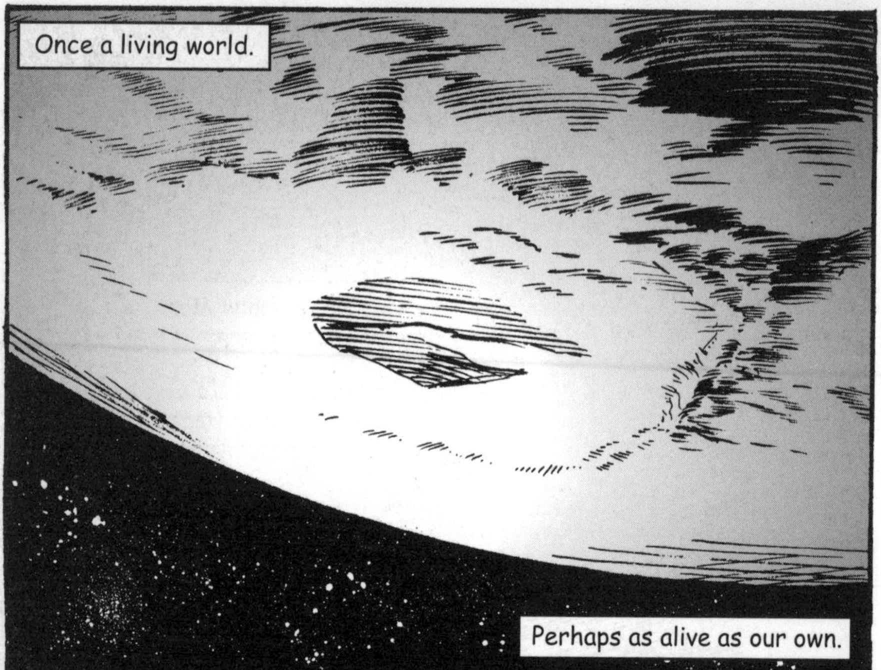
Once a living world.
Perhaps as alive as our own.

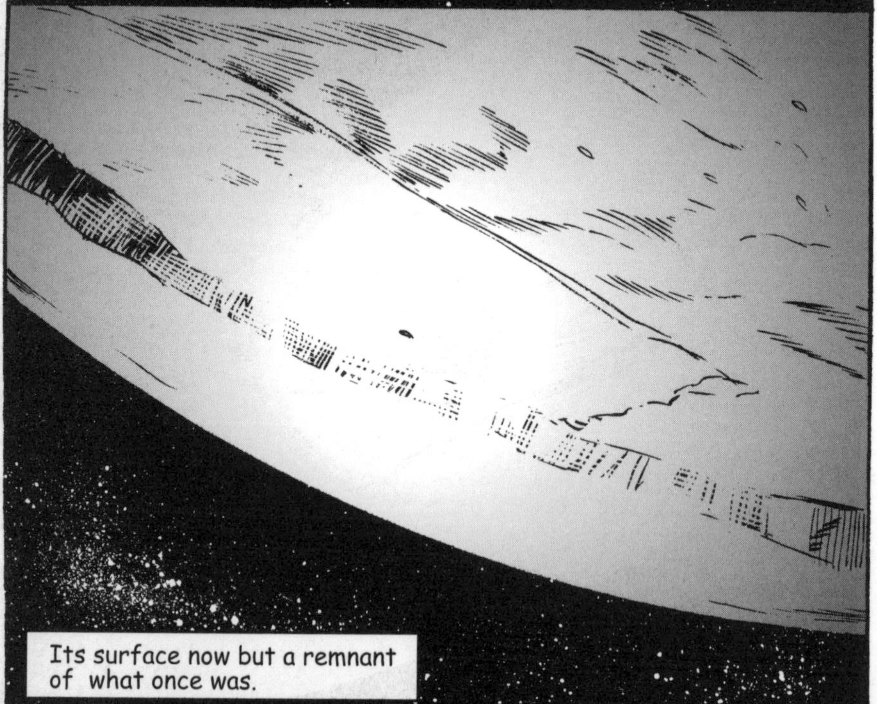
Its surface now but a remnant of what once was.

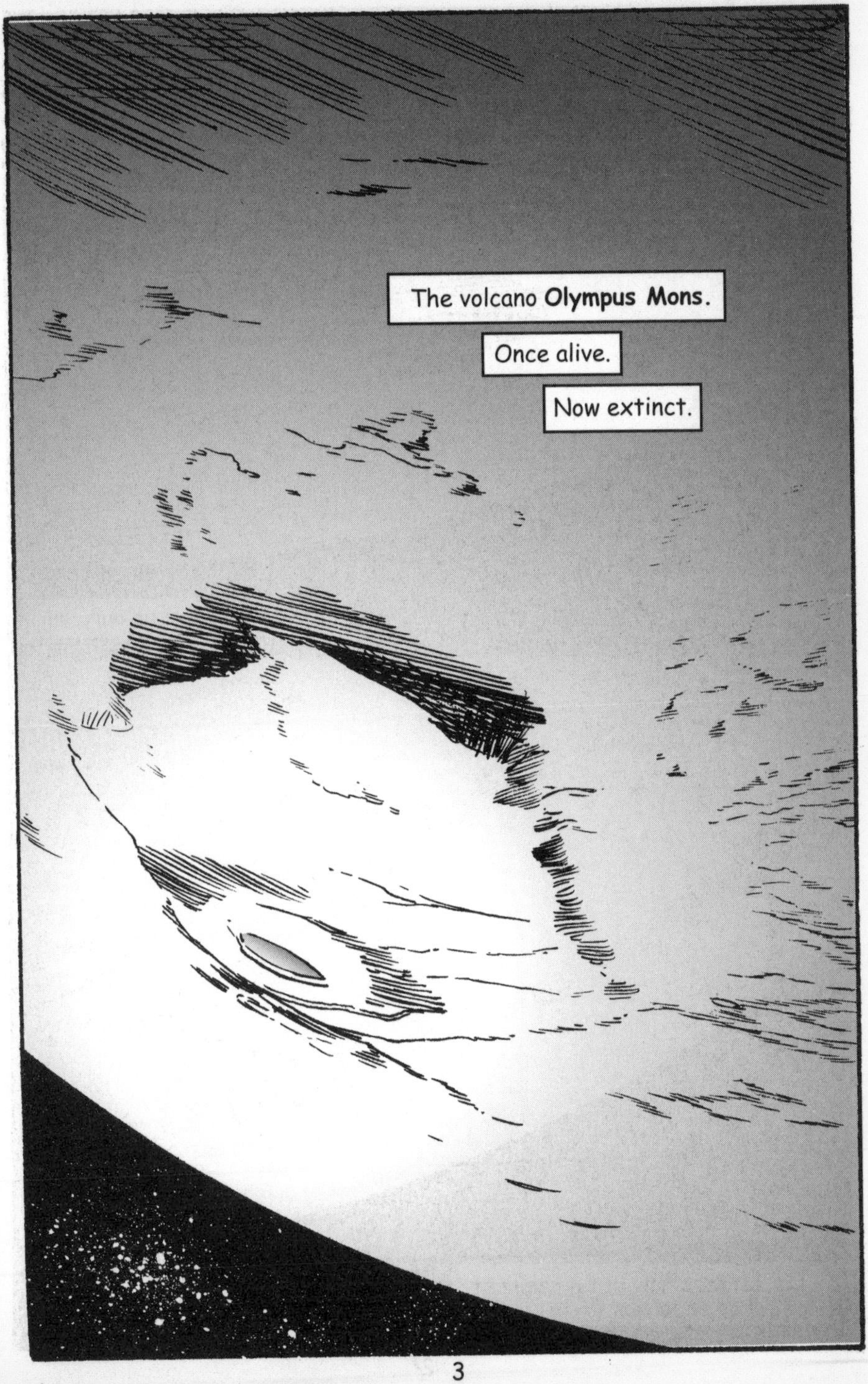
The volcano **Olympus Mons**.
Once alive.
Now extinct.

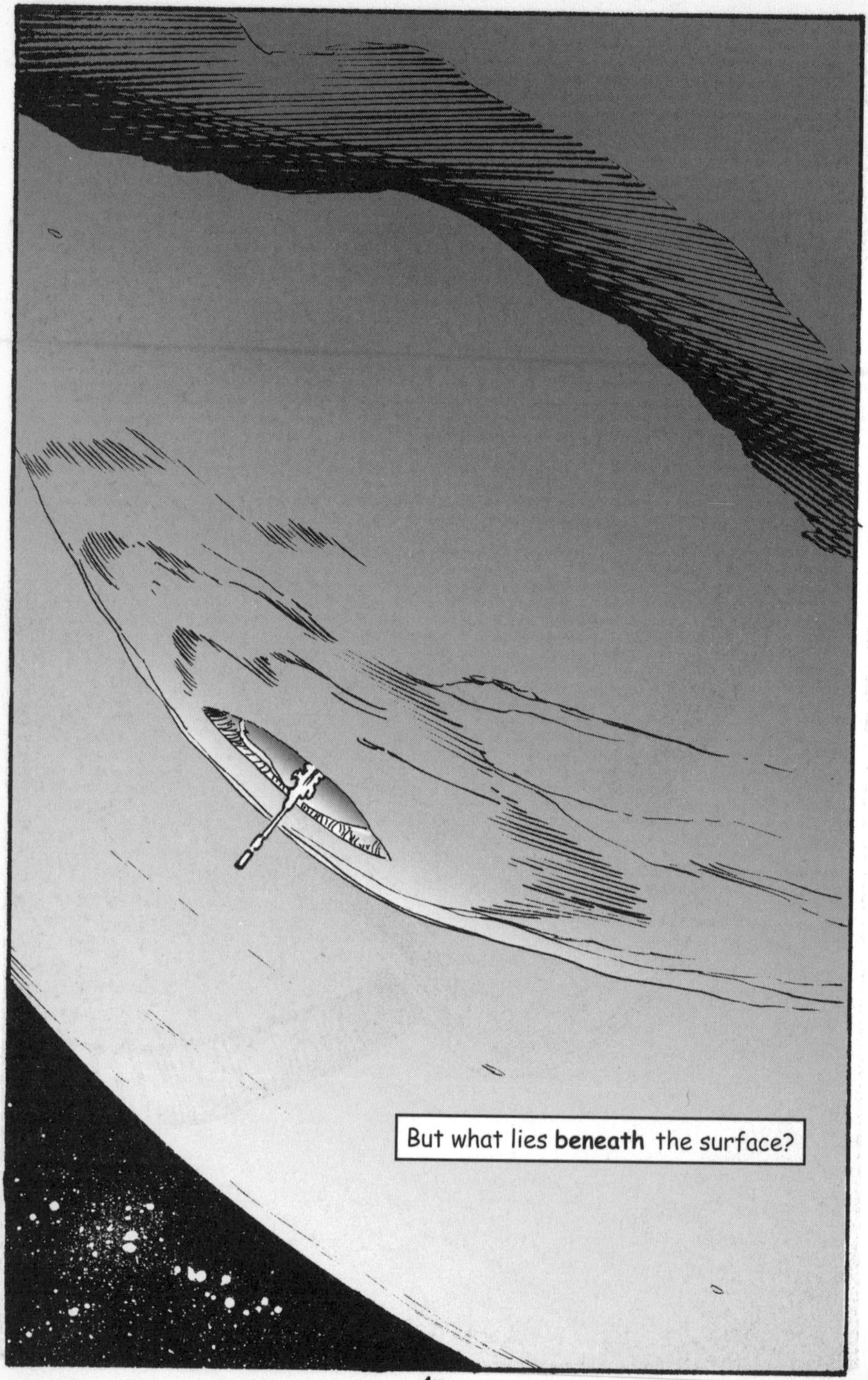
But what lies **beneath** the surface?

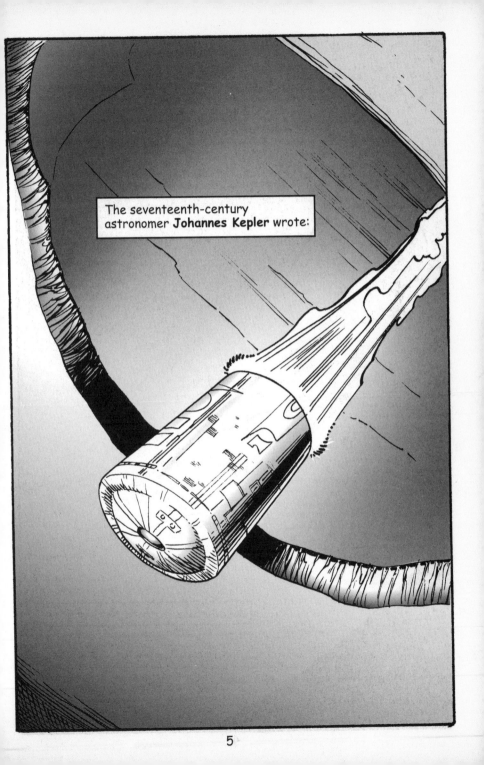

The seventeenth-century astronomer **Johannes Kepler** wrote:

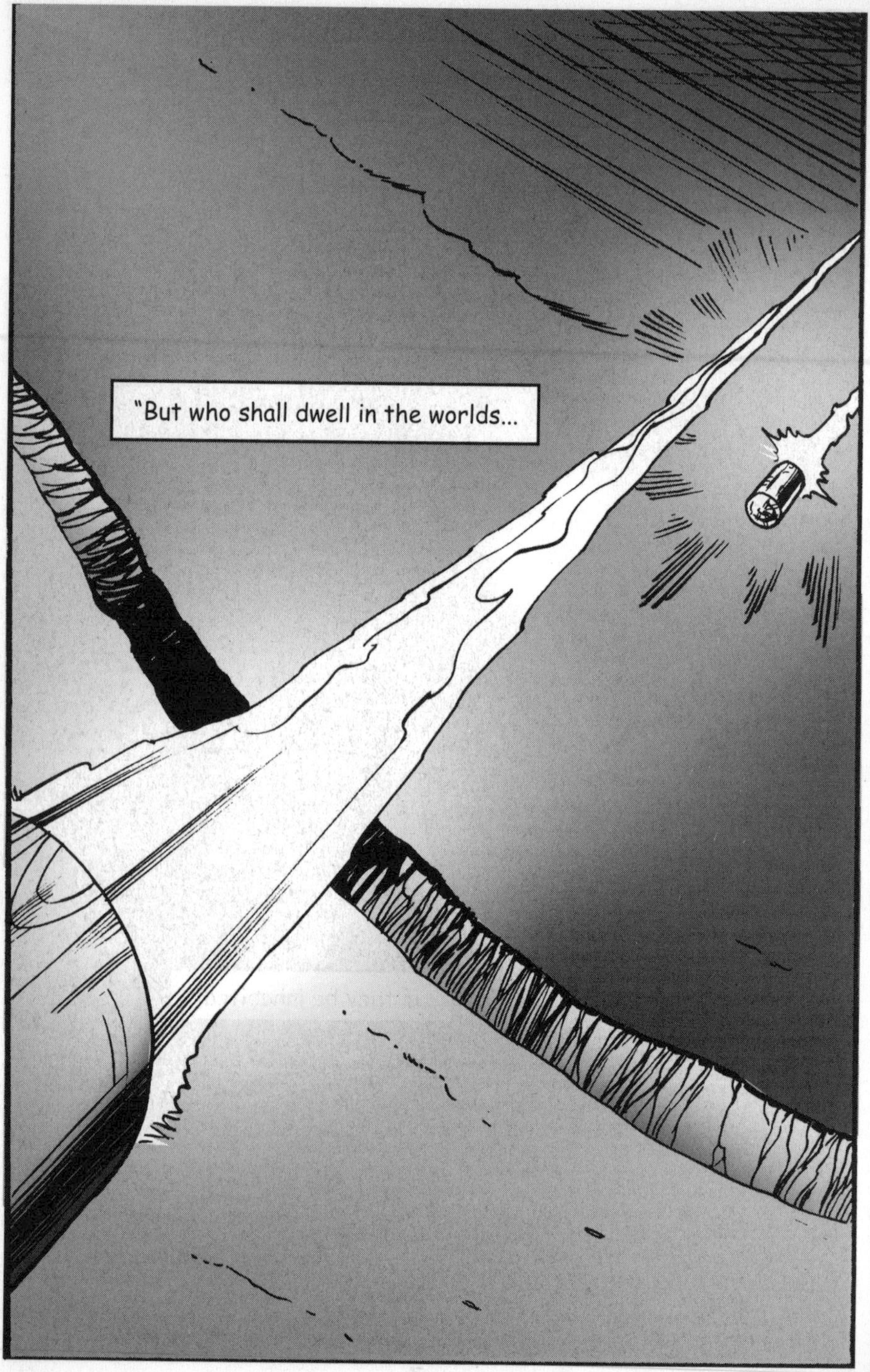
"But who shall dwell in the worlds...

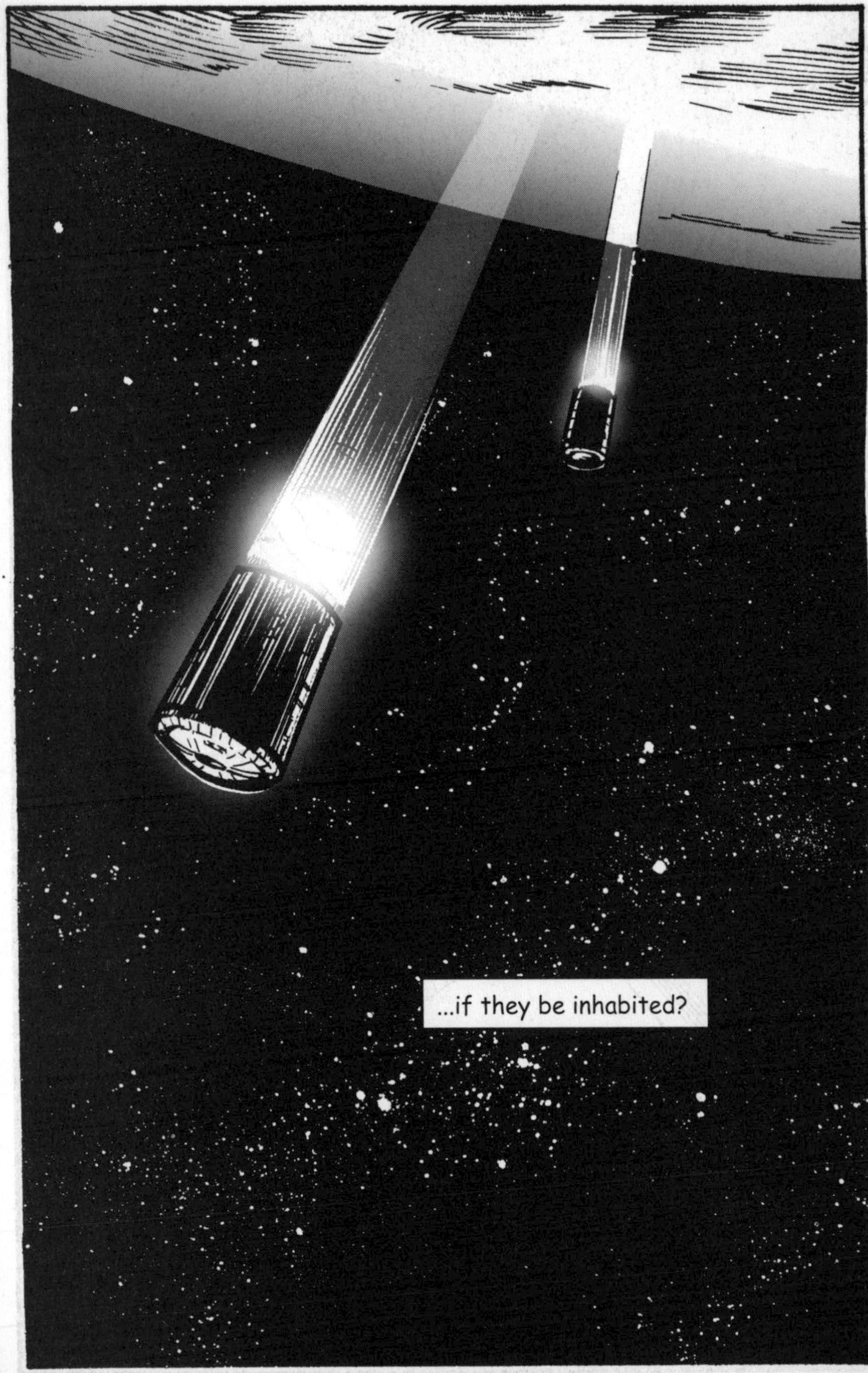
...if they be inhabited?

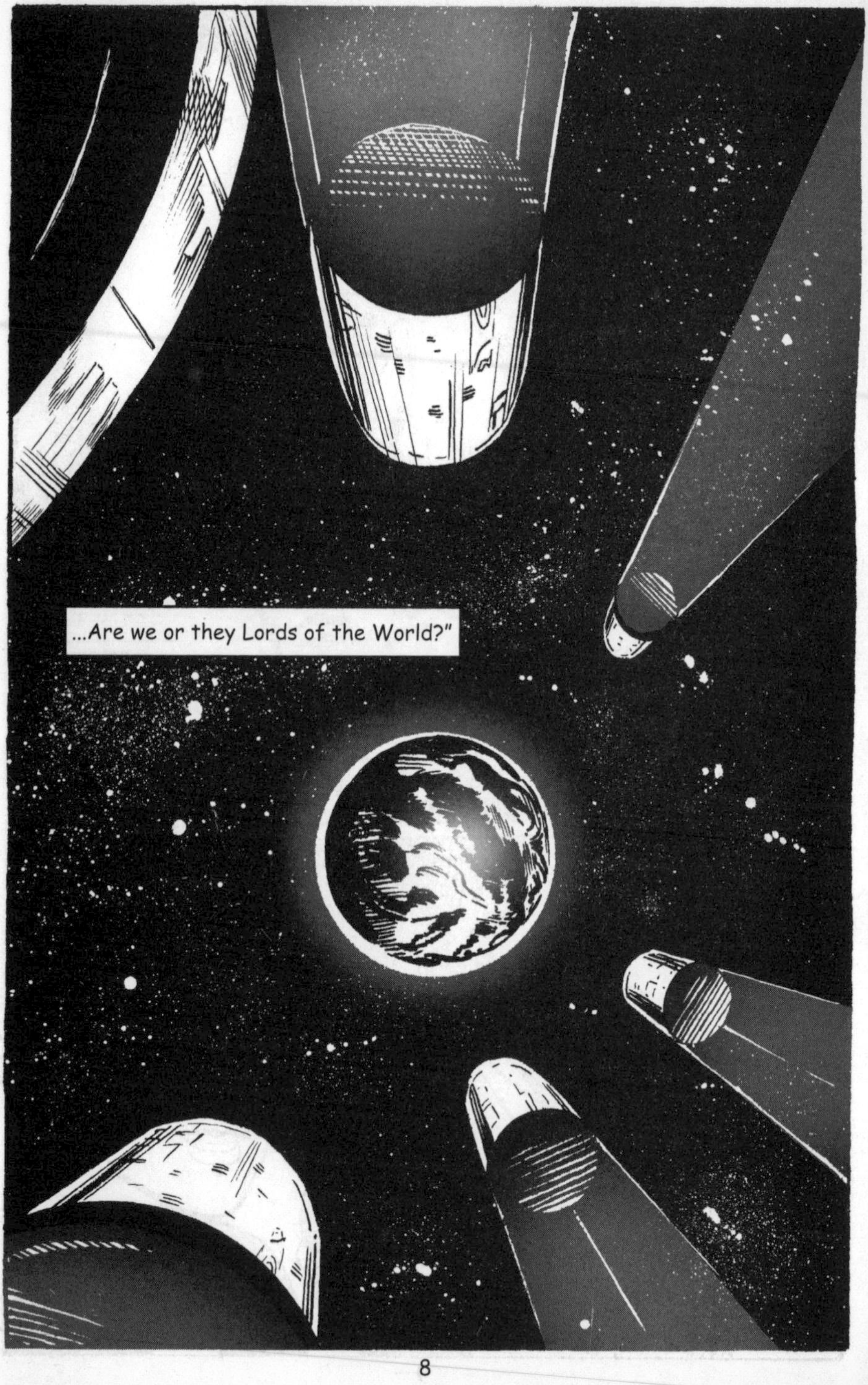
...Are we or they Lords of the World?"

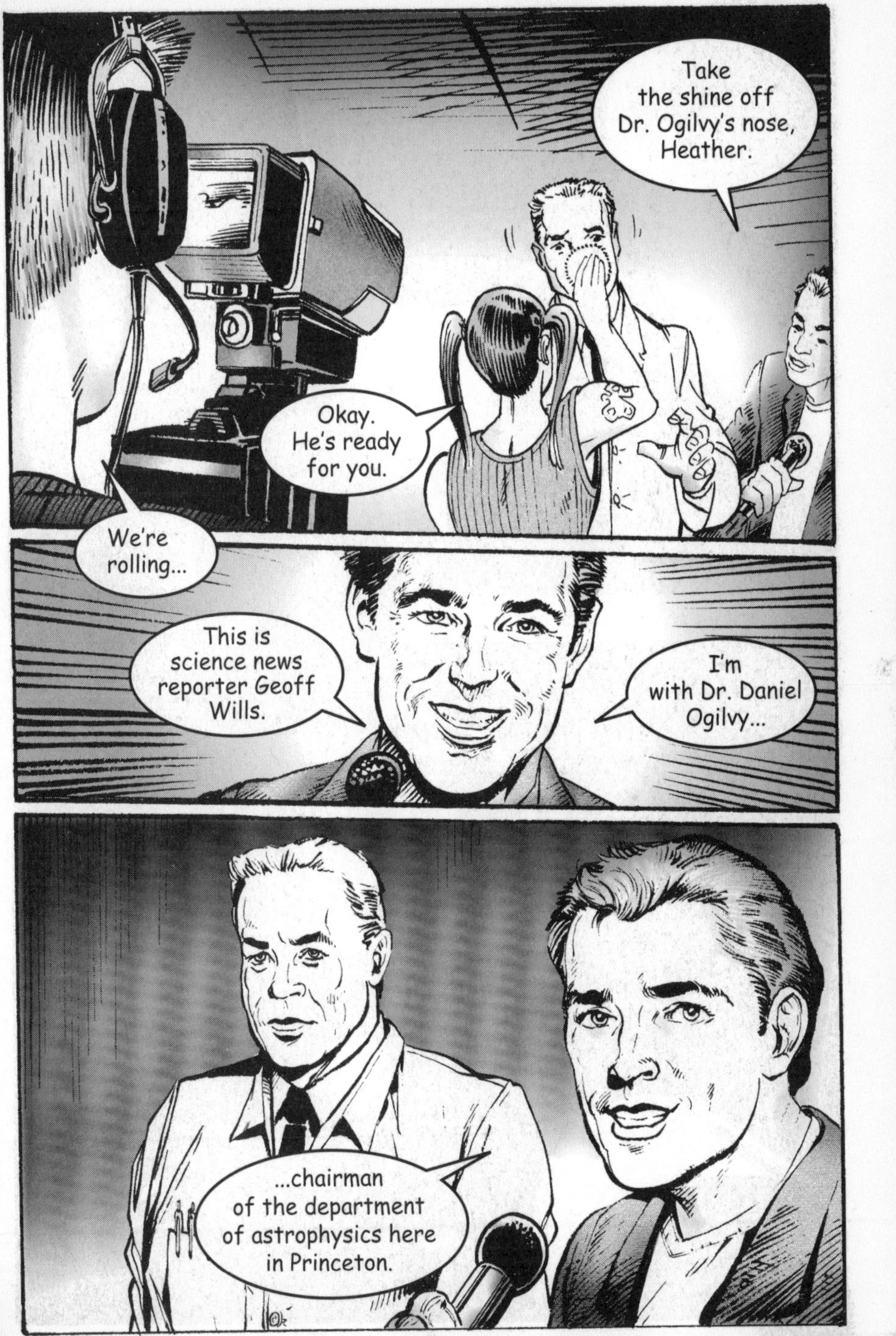
Take the shine off Dr. Ogilvy's nose, Heather.
Okay. He's ready for you.
We're rolling...
This is science news reporter Geoff Wills.
I'm with Dr. Daniel Ogilvy...
...chairman of the department of astrophysics here in Princeton.

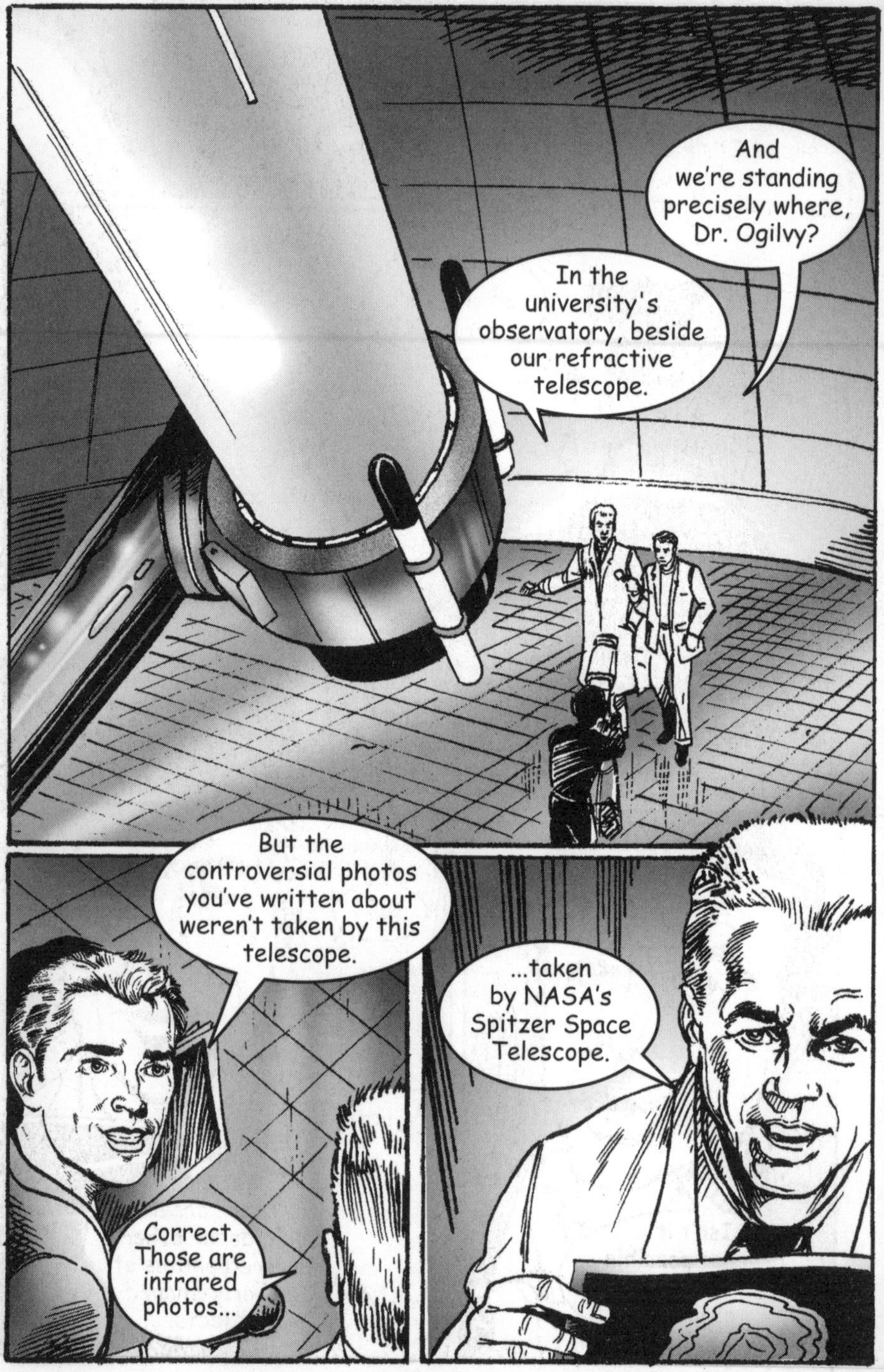
And we're standing precisely where, Dr. Ogilvy?
In the university's observatory, beside our refractive telescope.
But the controversial photos you've written about weren't taken by this telescope.
Correct. Those are infrared photos...
...taken by NASA's Spitzer Space Telescope.

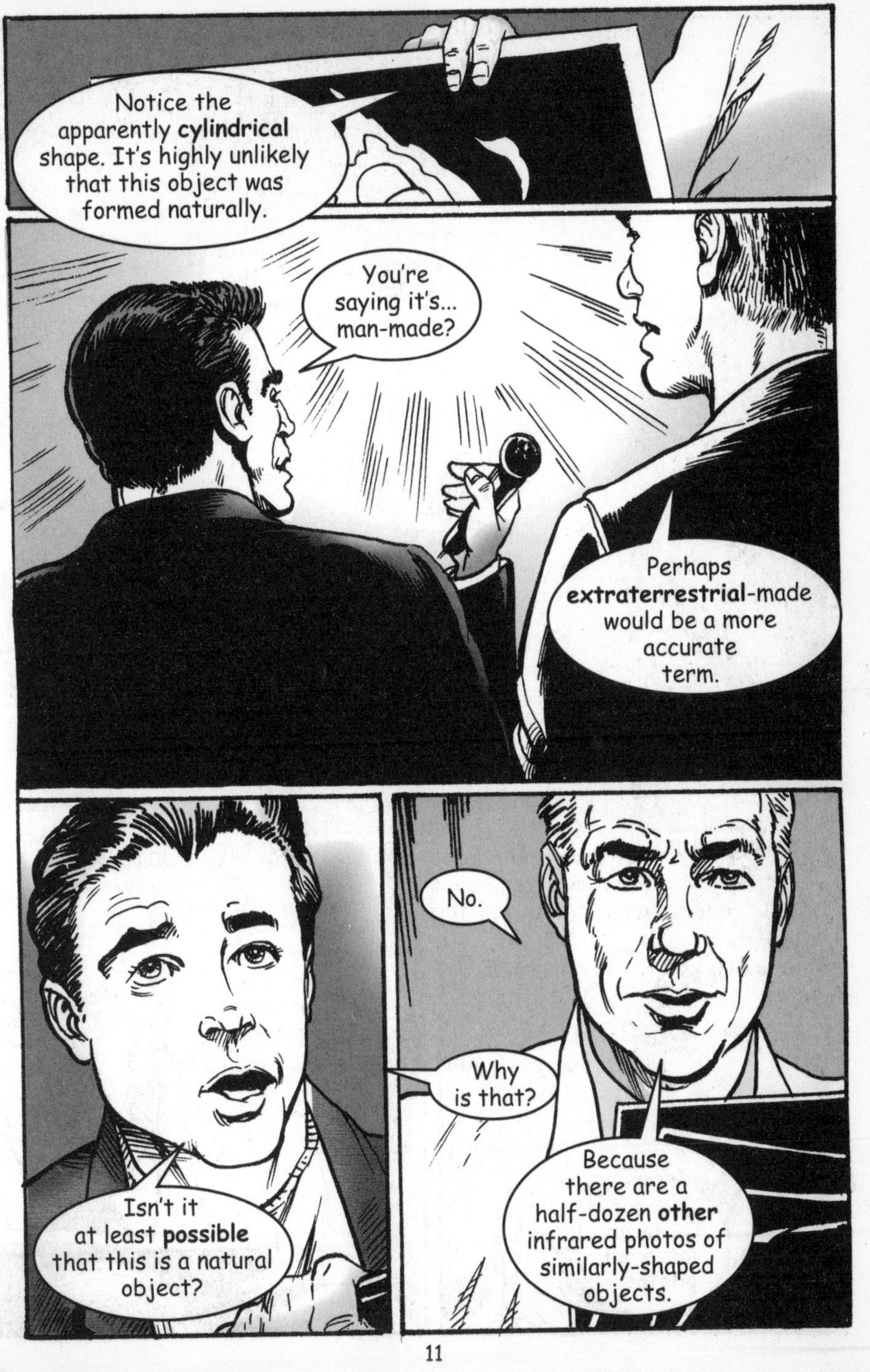
Notice the apparently **cylindrical** shape. It's highly unlikely that this object was formed naturally.
You're saying it's... man-made?
Perhaps **extraterrestrial**-made would be a more accurate term.
Isn't it at least **possible** that this is a natural object?
No.
Why is that?
Because there are a half-dozen **other** infrared photos of similarly-shaped objects.

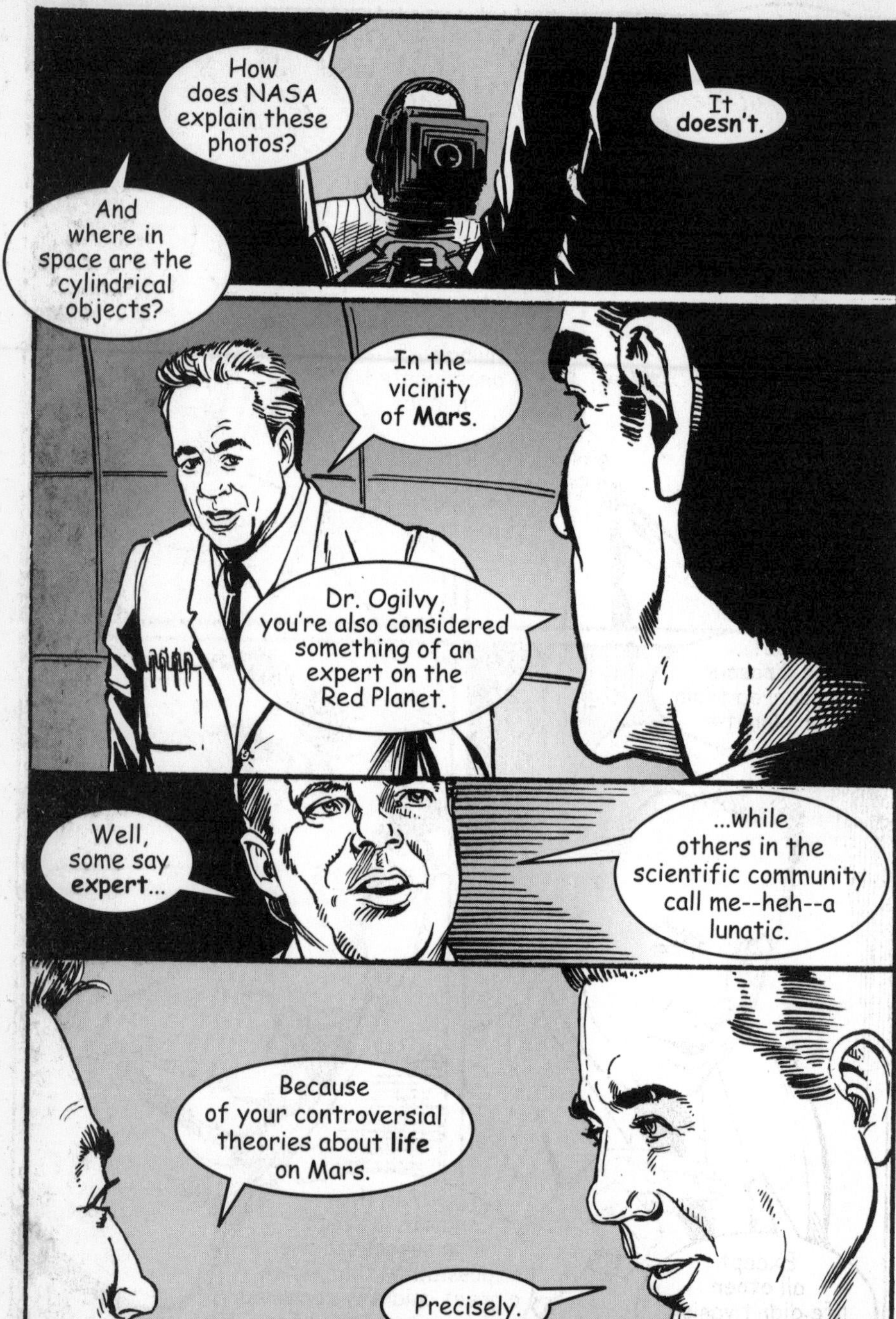
How does NASA explain these photos?
And where in space are the cylindrical objects?
It doesn't.
In the vicinity of **Mars**.
Dr. Ogilvy, you're also considered something of an expert on the Red Planet.
Well, some say **expert**...
...while others in the scientific community call me--heh--a lunatic.
Because of your controversial theories about **life** on Mars.
Precisely.

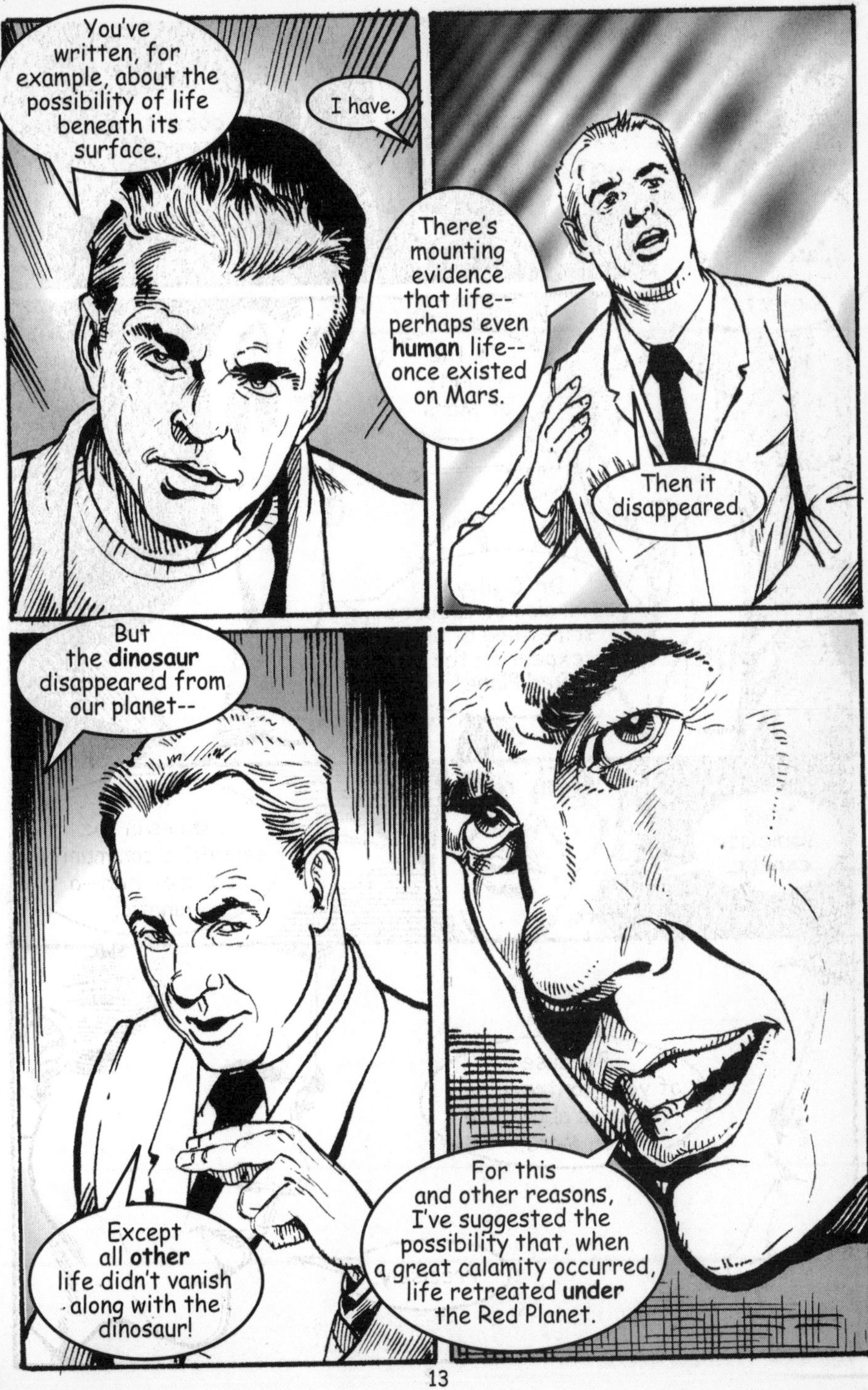
You've written, for example, about the possibility of life beneath its surface.
I have.
There's mounting evidence that life--perhaps even **human** life--once existed on Mars.
Then it disappeared.
But the **dinosaur** disappeared from our planet--
Except all **other** life didn't vanish along with the dinosaur!
For this and other reasons, I've suggested the possibility that, when a great calamity occurred, life retreated **under** the Red Planet.

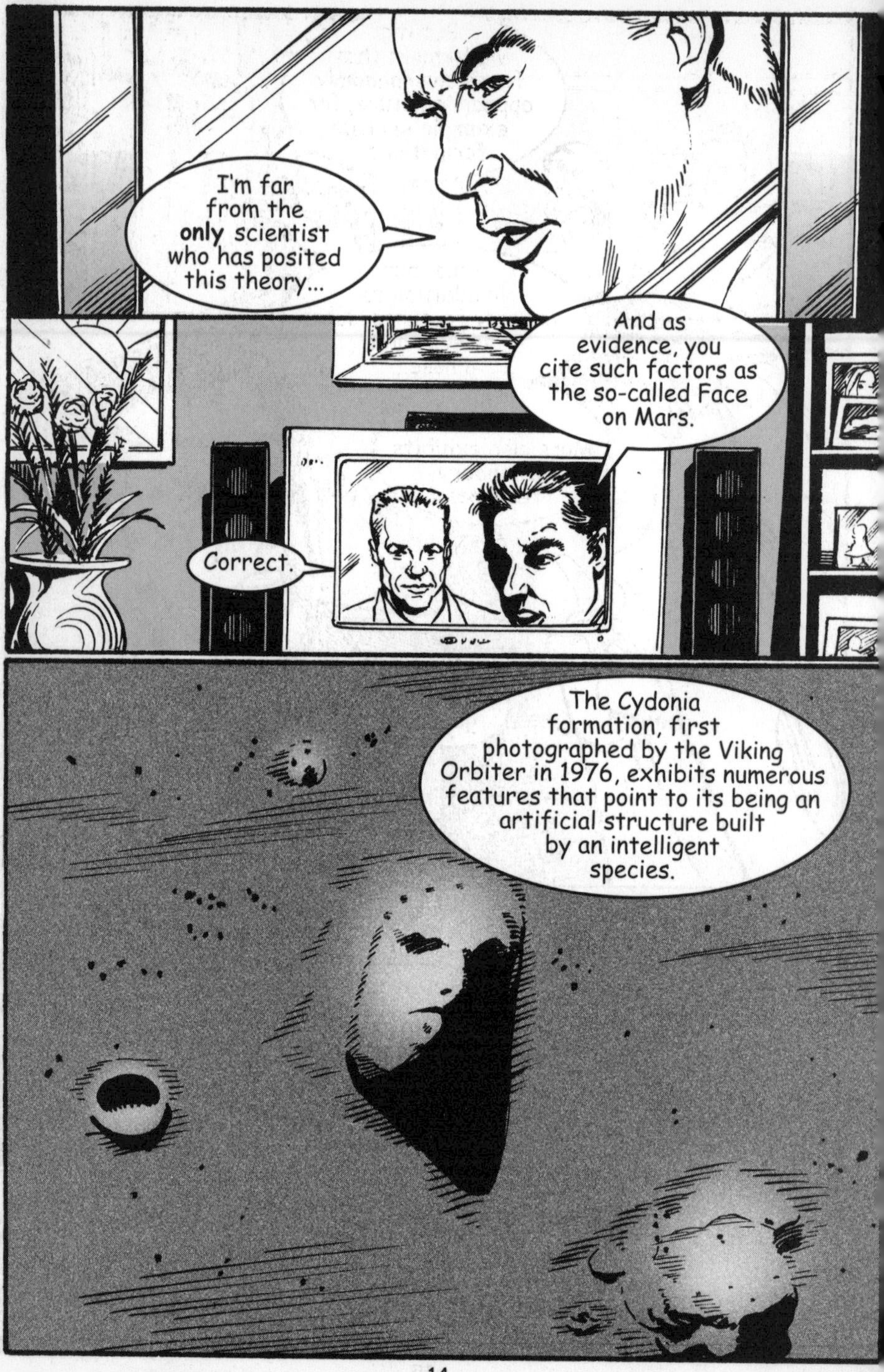
I'm far from the **only** scientist who has posited this theory...
And as evidence, you cite such factors as the so-called Face on Mars.
Correct.
The Cydonia formation, first photographed by the Viking Orbiter in 1976, exhibits numerous features that point to its being an artificial structure built by an intelligent species.

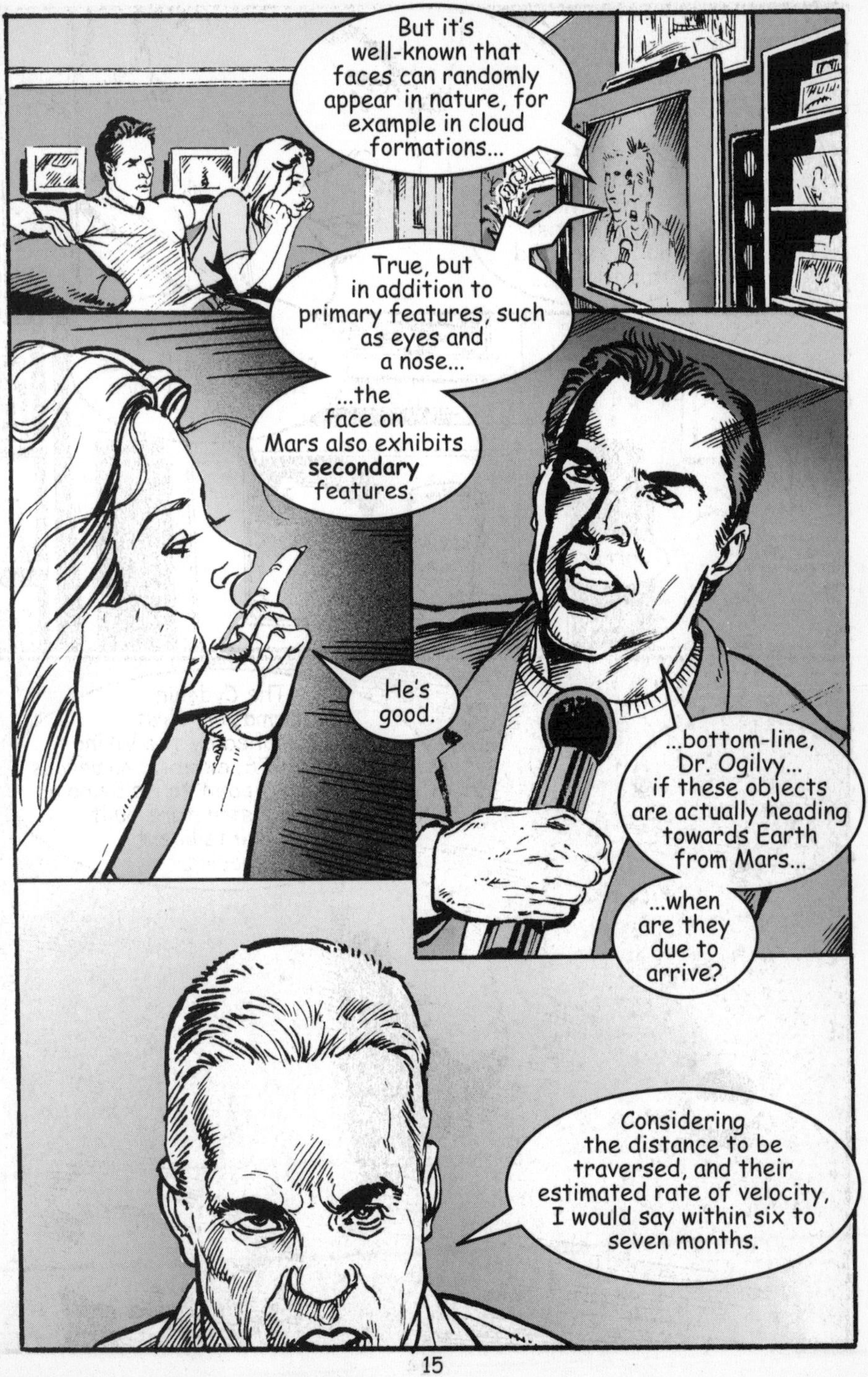
But it's well-known that faces can randomly appear in nature, for example in cloud formations...
True, but in addition to primary features, such as eyes and a nose...
...the face on Mars also exhibits **secondary** features.
He's good.
...bottom-line, Dr. Ogilvy... if these objects are actually heading towards Earth from Mars...
...when are they due to arrive?
Considering the distance to be traversed, and their estimated rate of velocity, I would say within six to seven months.

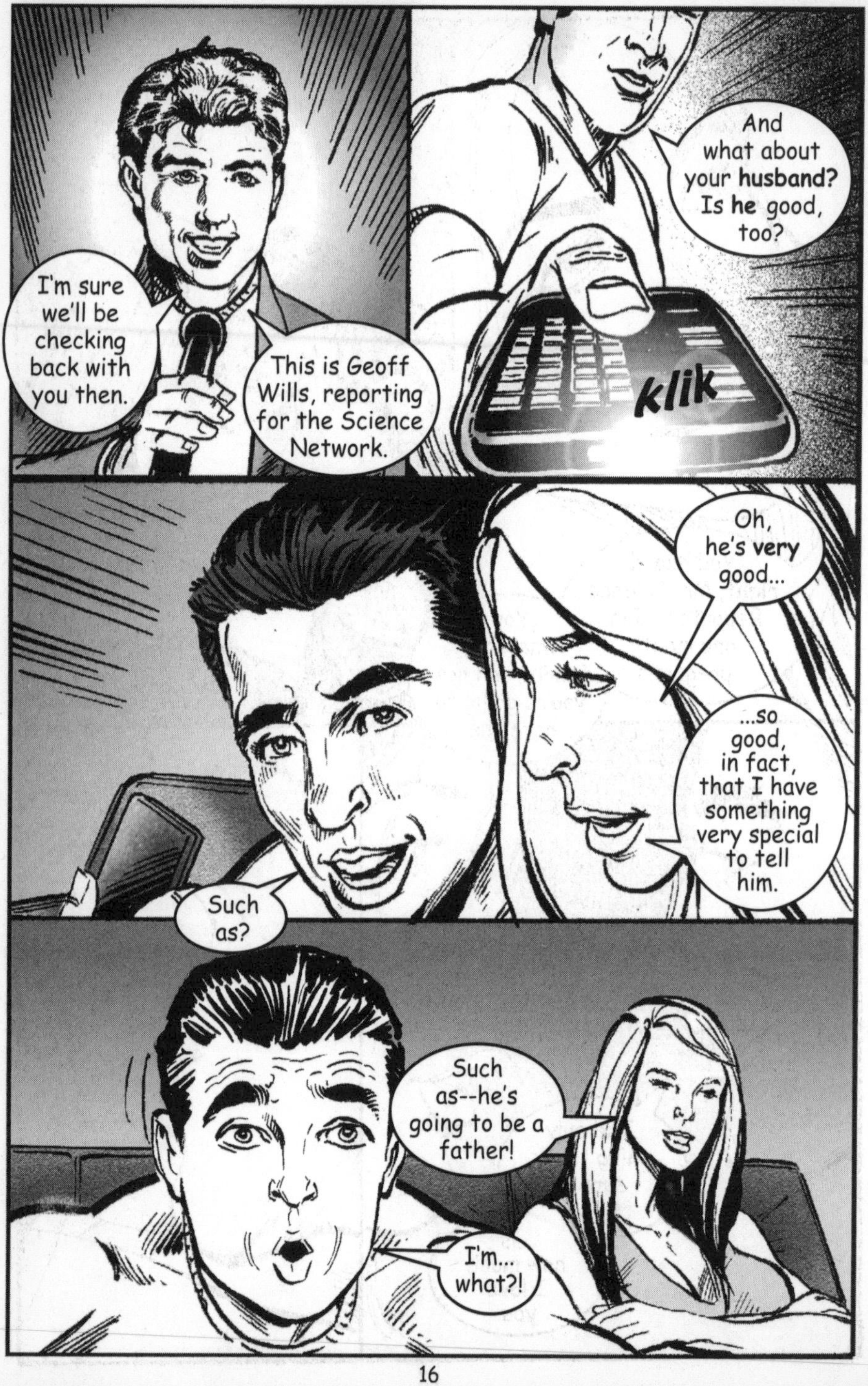
I'm sure we'll be checking back with you then.
This is Geoff Wills, reporting for the Science Network.
And what about your **husband?** Is **he** good, too?
klik
Oh, he's **very** good...
...so good, in fact, that I have something very special to tell him.
Such as?
Such as--he's going to be a father!
I'm... what?!

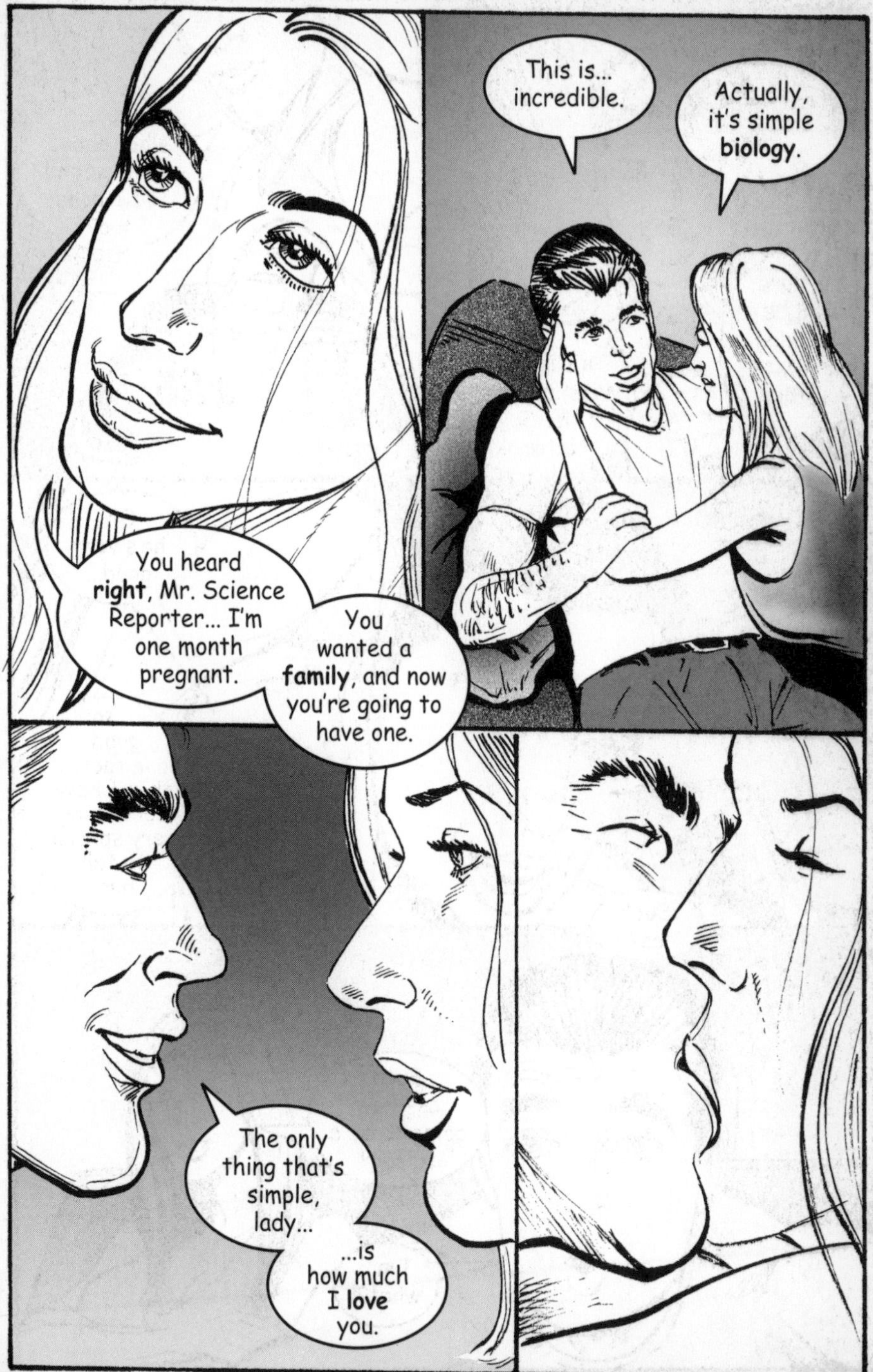
You heard right, Mr. Science Reporter... I'm one month pregnant.
You wanted a family, and now you're going to have one.
This is... incredible.
Actually, it's simple biology.
The only thing that's simple, lady...
...is how much I love you.

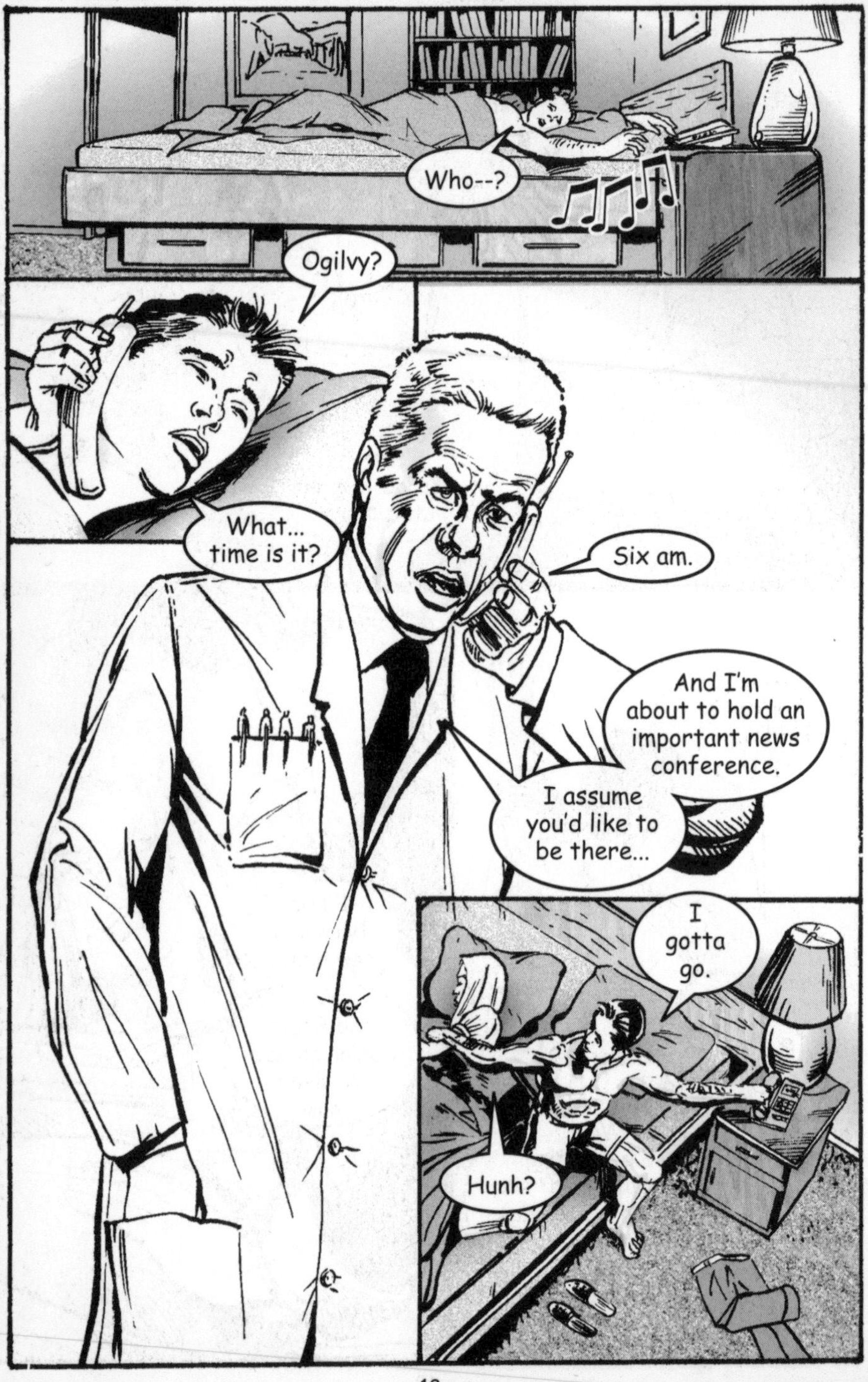
Who--?
Ogilvy?
What... time is it?
Six am.
And I'm about to hold an important news conference.
I assume you'd like to be there...
Hunh?
I gotta go.

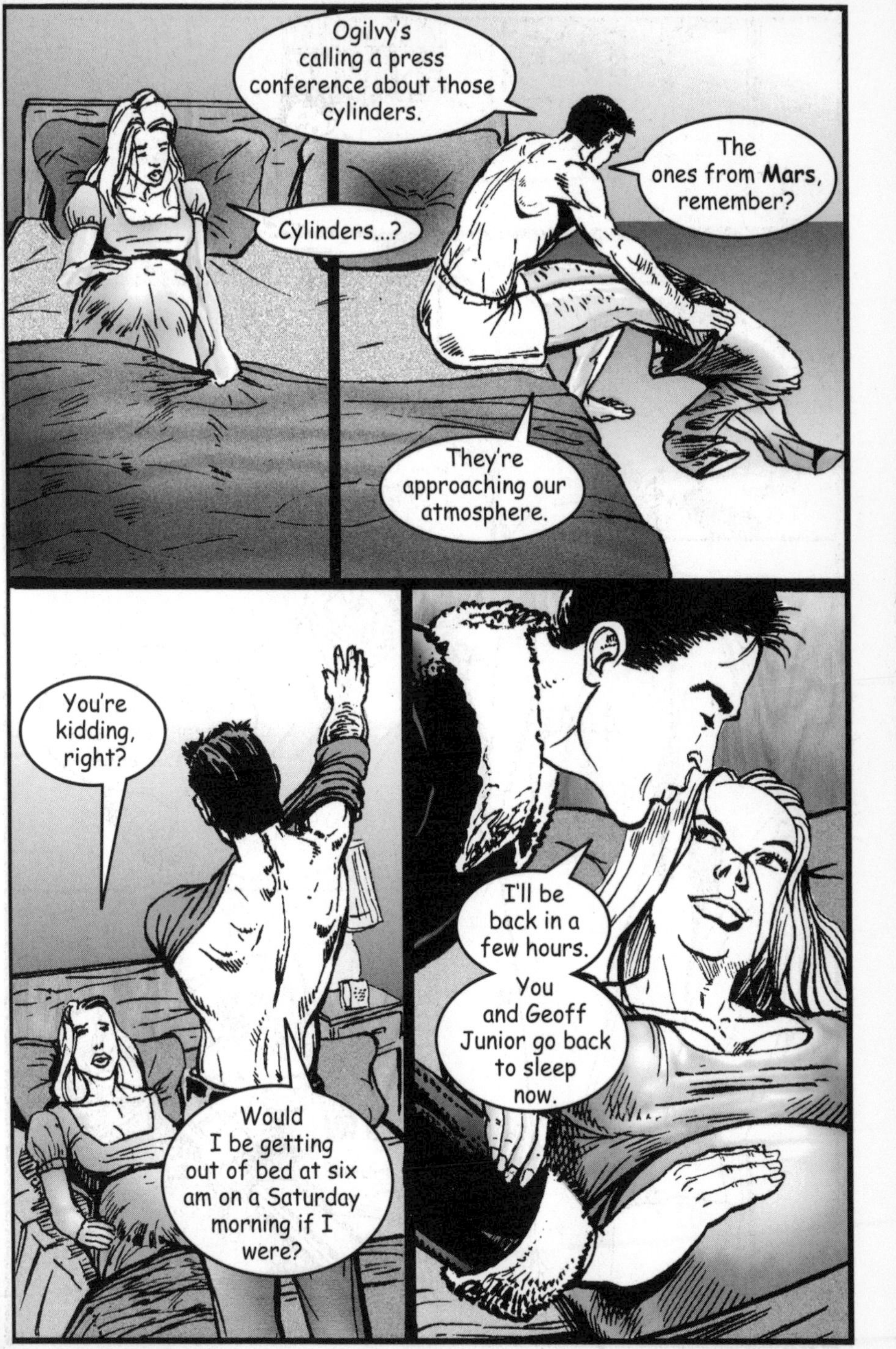
Ogilvy's calling a press conference about those cylinders.
Cylinders...?
The ones from Mars, remember?
They're approaching our atmosphere.
You're kidding, right?
Would I be getting out of bed at six am on a Saturday morning if I were?
I'll be back in a few hours.
You and Geoff Junior go back to sleep now.

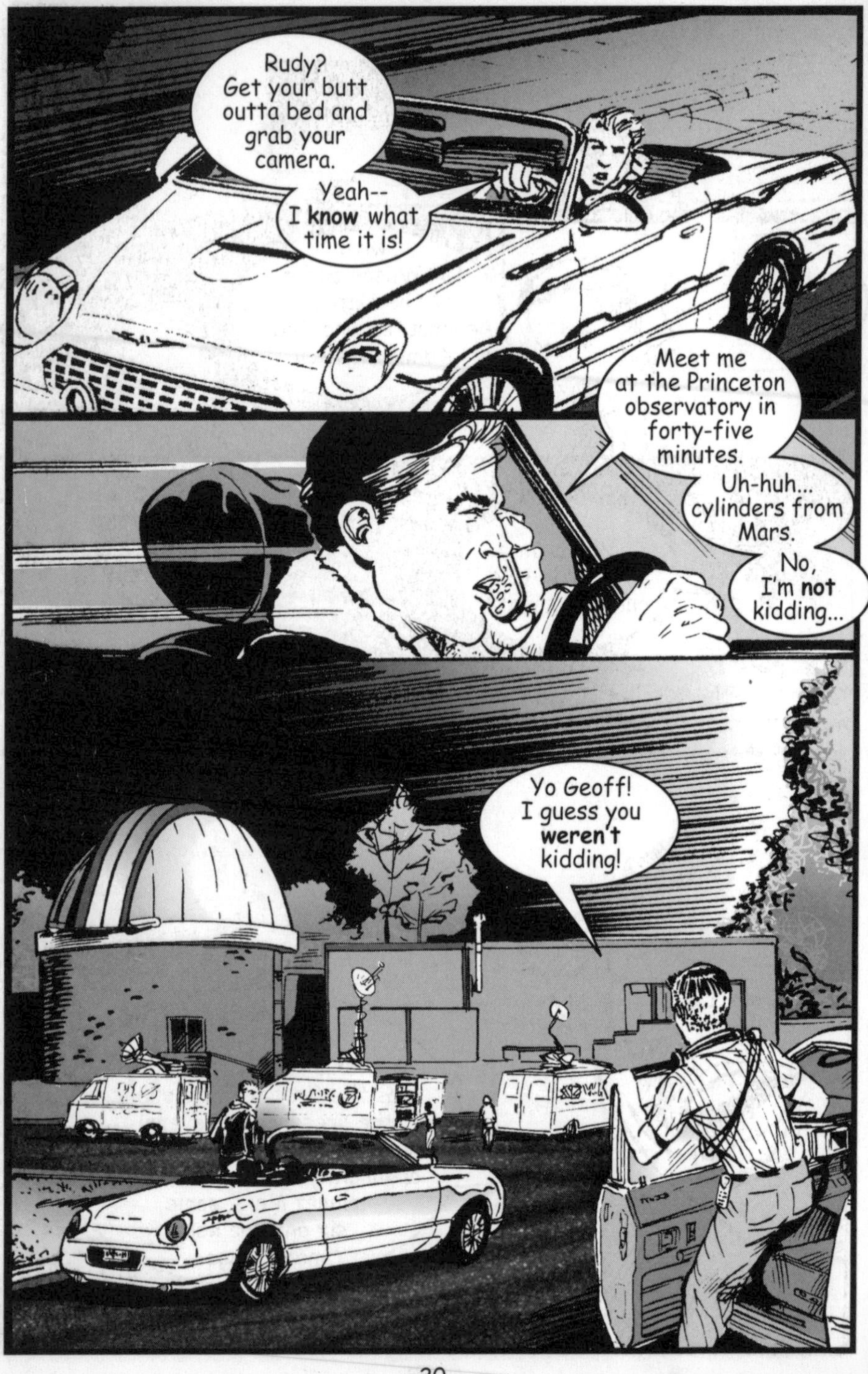
Rudy? Get your butt outta bed and grab your camera.
Yeah-- I **know** what time it is!
Meet me at the Princeton observatory in forty-five minutes.
Uh-huh... cylinders from Mars.
No, I'm **not** kidding...
Yo Geoff! I guess you **weren't** kidding!

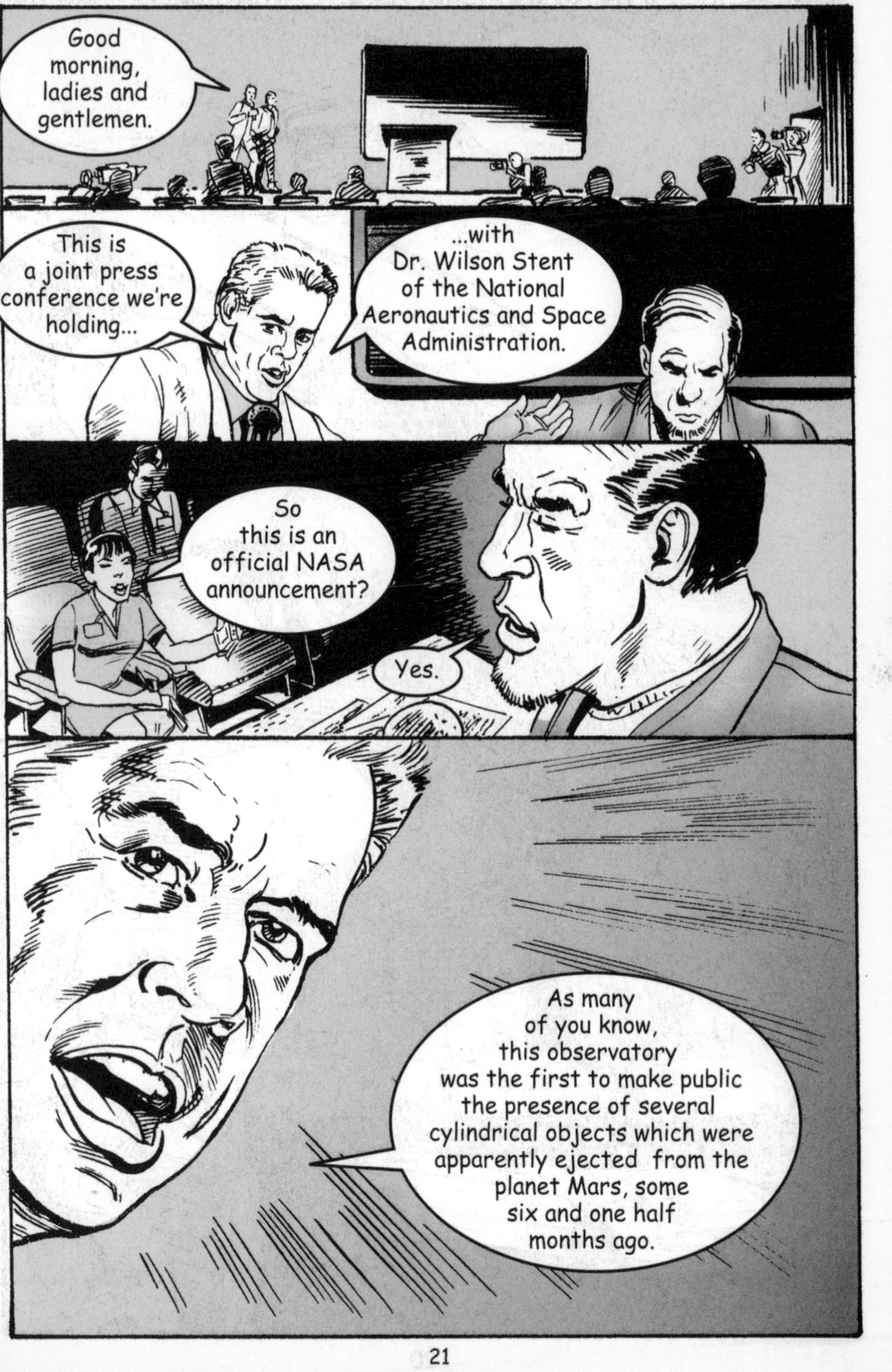
Good morning, ladies and gentlemen.
This is a joint press conference we're holding...
...with Dr. Wilson Stent of the National Aeronautics and Space Administration.
So this is an official NASA announcement?
Yes.
As many of you know, this observatory was the first to make public the presence of several cylindrical objects which were apparently ejected from the planet Mars, some six and one half months ago.

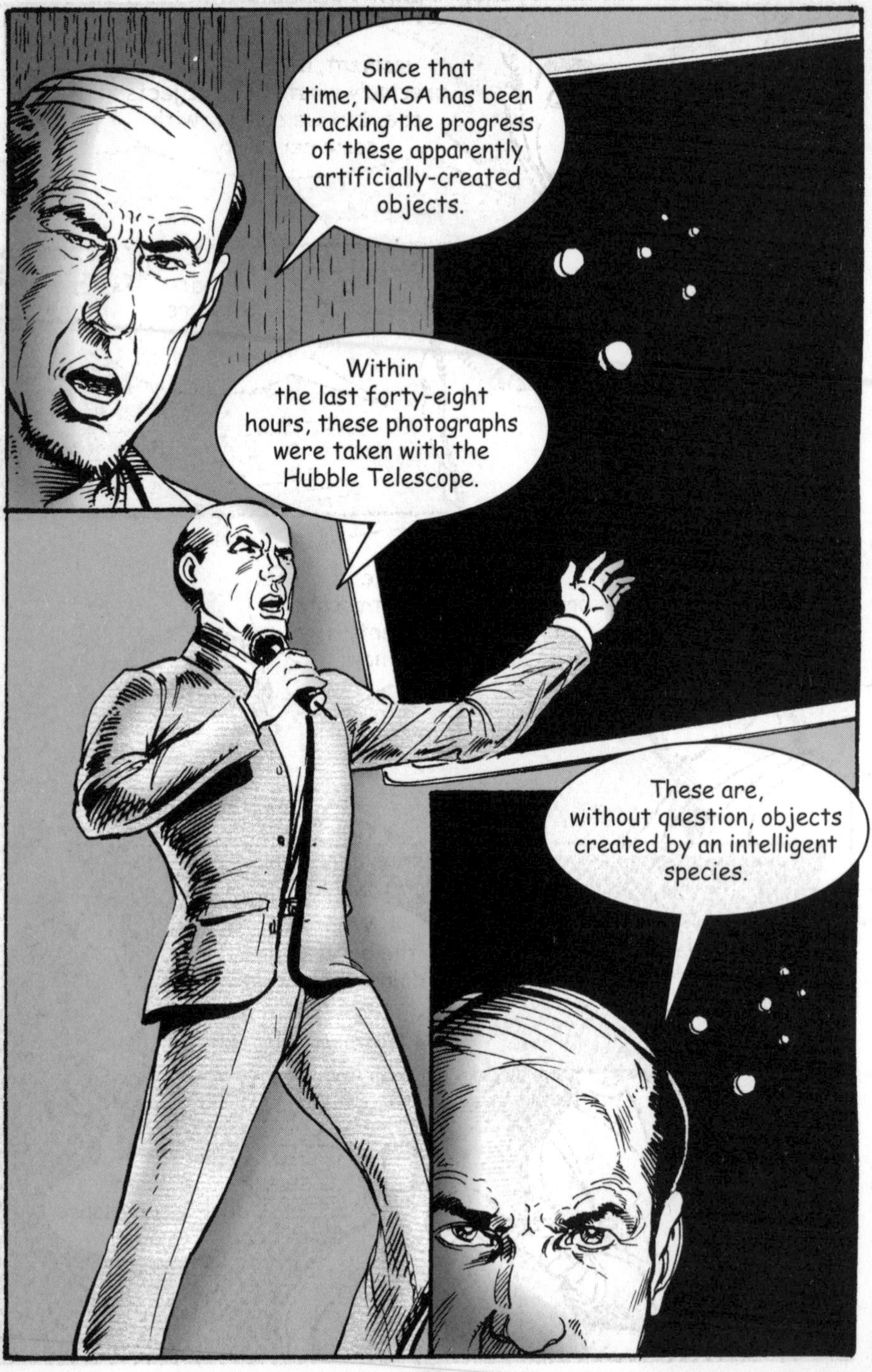
Since that time, NASA has been tracking the progress of these apparently artificially-created objects.
Within the last forty-eight hours, these photographs were taken with the Hubble Telescope.
These are, without question, objects created by an intelligent species.

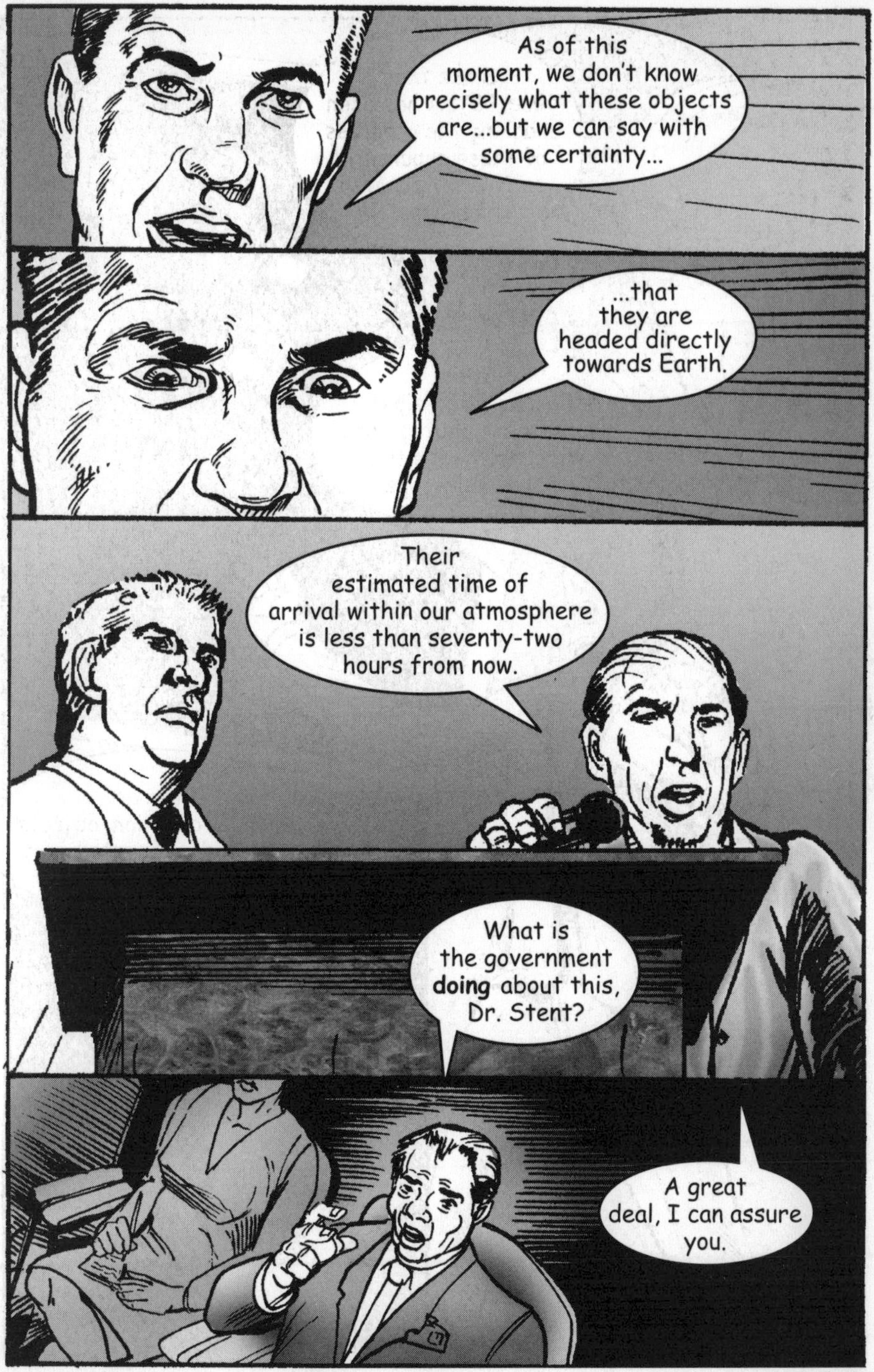
As of this moment, we don't know precisely what these objects are...but we can say with some certainty...
...that they are headed directly towards Earth.
Their estimated time of arrival within our atmosphere is less than seventy-two hours from now.
What is the government **doing** about this, Dr. Stent?
A great deal, I can assure you.

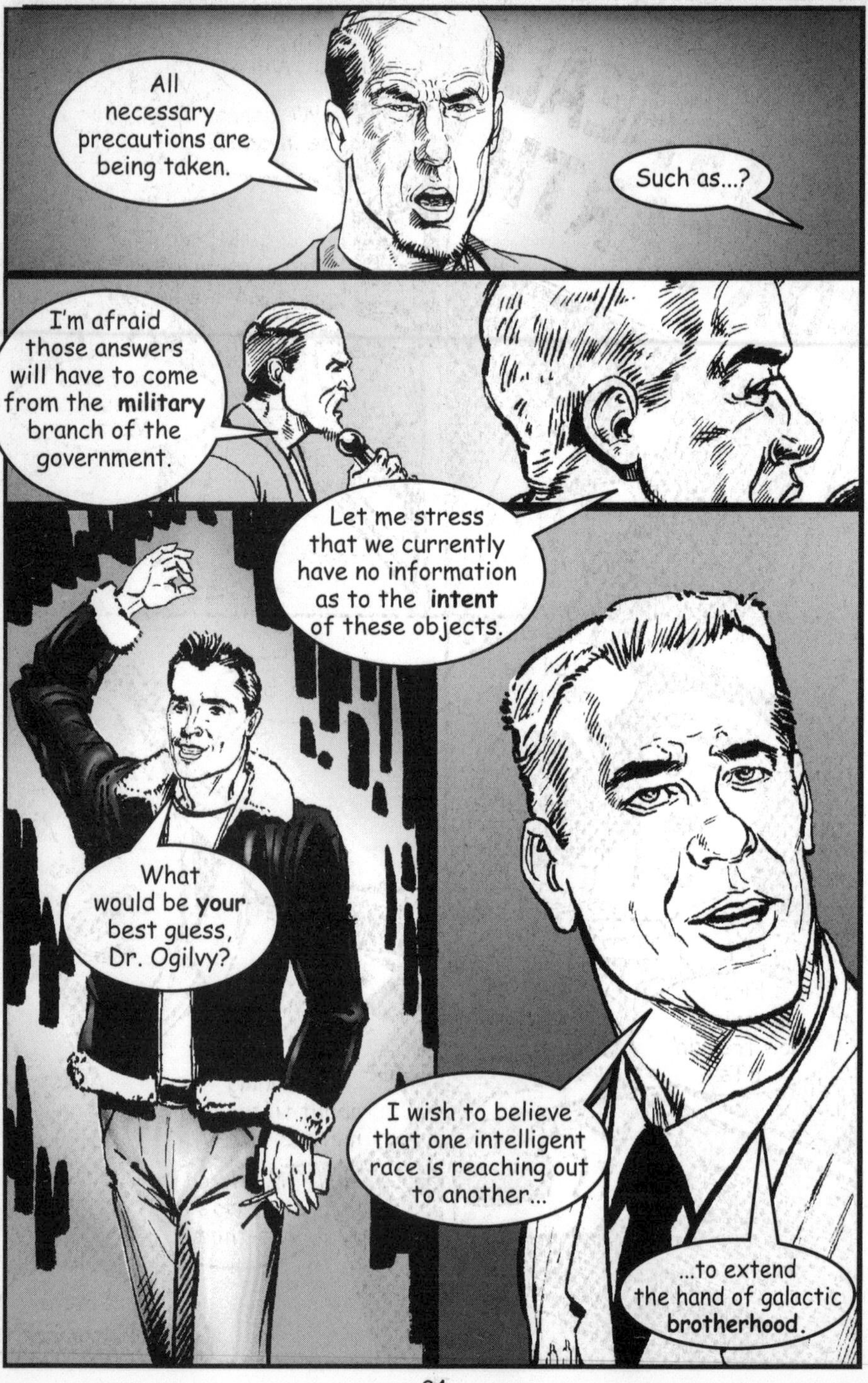
All necessary precautions are being taken.
Such as...?
I'm afraid those answers will have to come from the **military** branch of the government.
Let me stress that we currently have no information as to the **intent** of these objects.
What would be **your** best guess, Dr. Ogilvy?
I wish to believe that one intelligent race is reaching out to another...
...to extend the hand of galactic **brotherhood**.

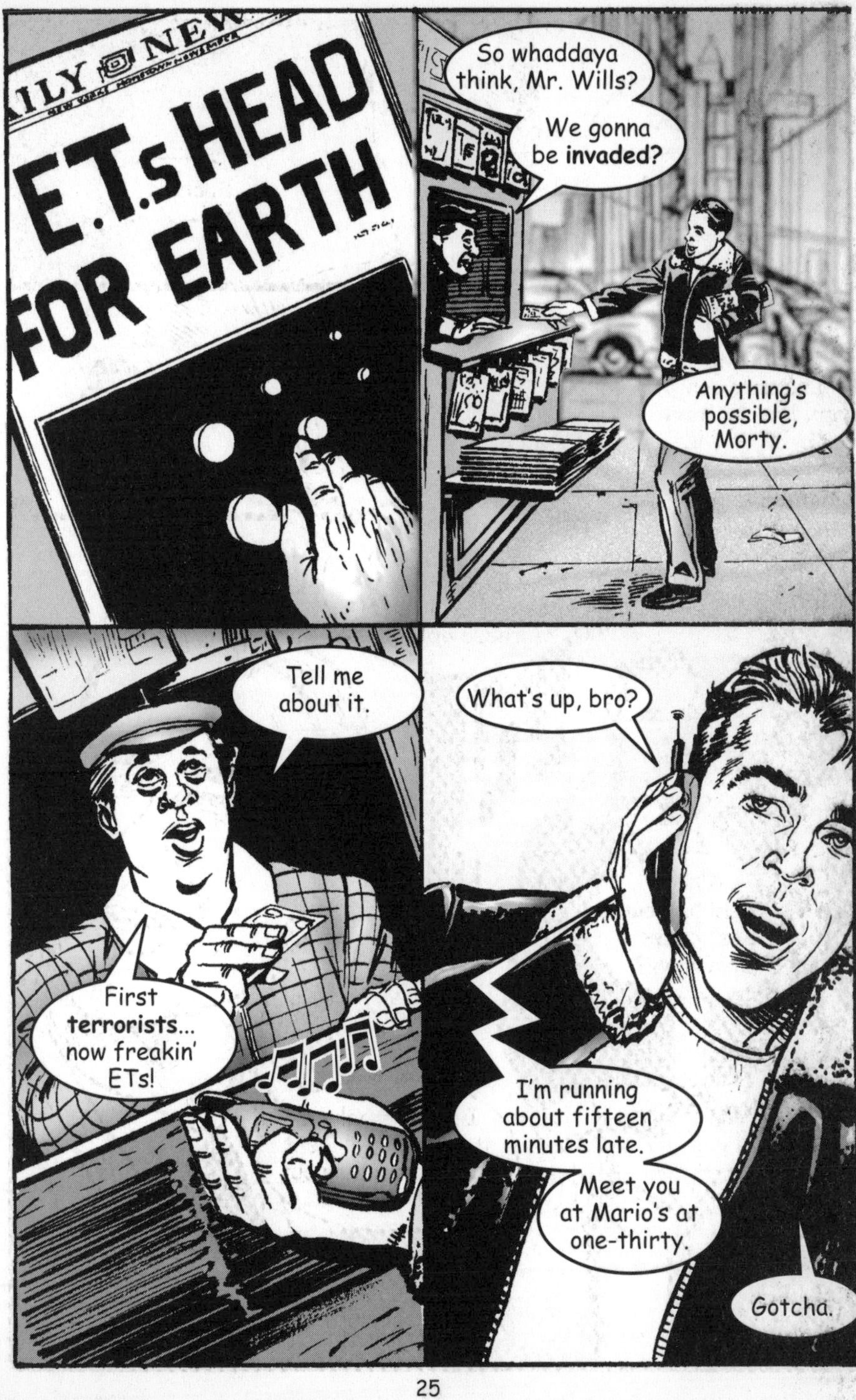
DAILY NEWS
E.T.s HEAD FOR EARTH
So whaddaya think, Mr. Wills?
We gonna be **invaded?**
Anything's possible, Morty.
Tell me about it.
First **terrorists...** now freakin' ETs!
What's up, bro?
I'm running about fifteen minutes late.
Meet you at Mario's at one-thirty.
Gotcha.

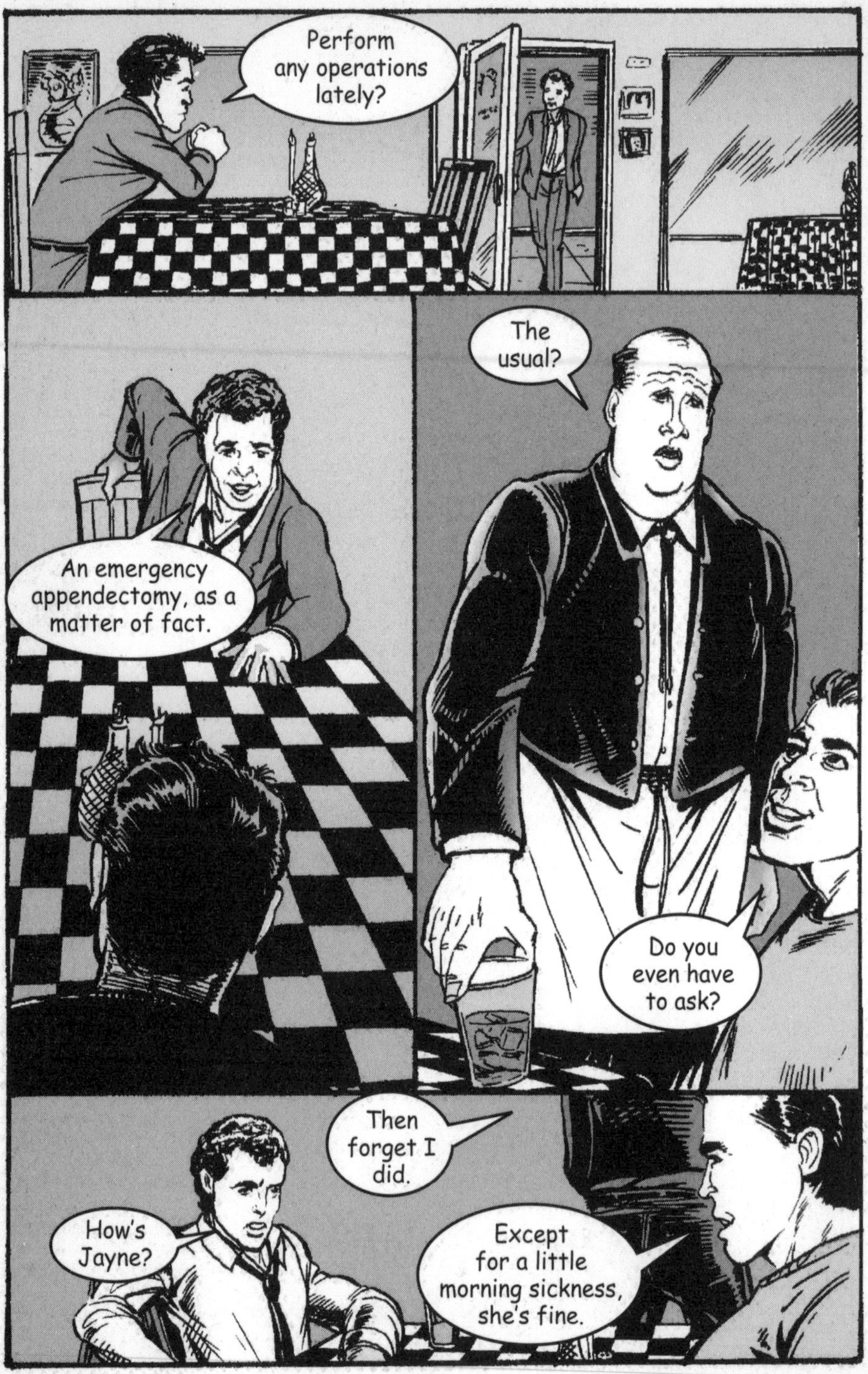
Perform any operations lately?
An emergency appendectomy, as a matter of fact.
The usual?
Do you even have to ask?
Then forget I did.
How's Jayne?
Except for a little morning sickness, she's fine.

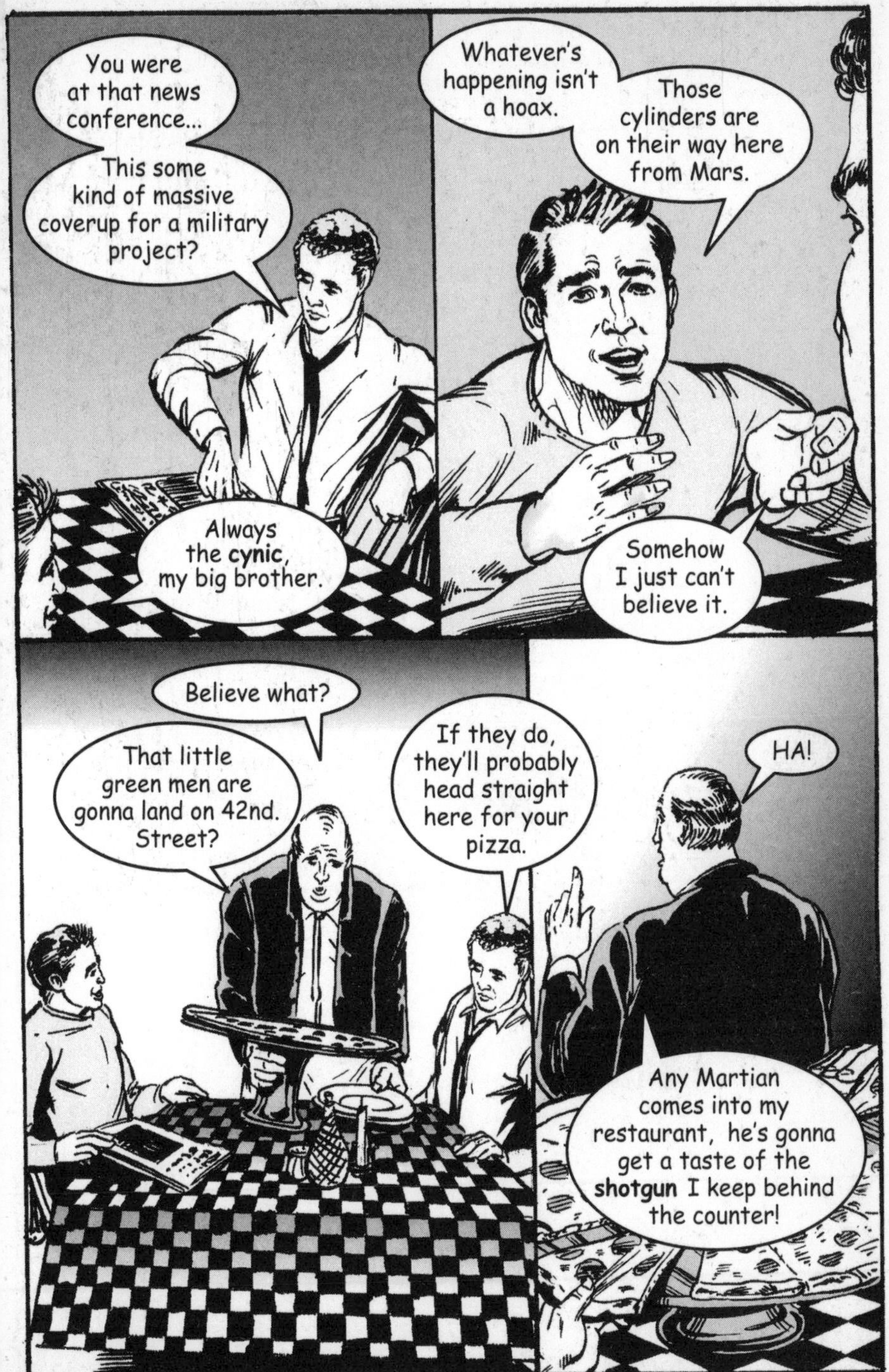
You were at that news conference...
This some kind of massive coverup for a military project?
Whatever's happening isn't a hoax.
Those cylinders are on their way here from Mars.
Always the **cynic**, my big brother.
Somehow I just can't believe it.
Believe what?
That little green men are gonna land on 42nd. Street?
If they do, they'll probably head straight here for your pizza.
HA!
Any Martian comes into my restaurant, he's gonna get a taste of the **shotgun** I keep behind the counter!

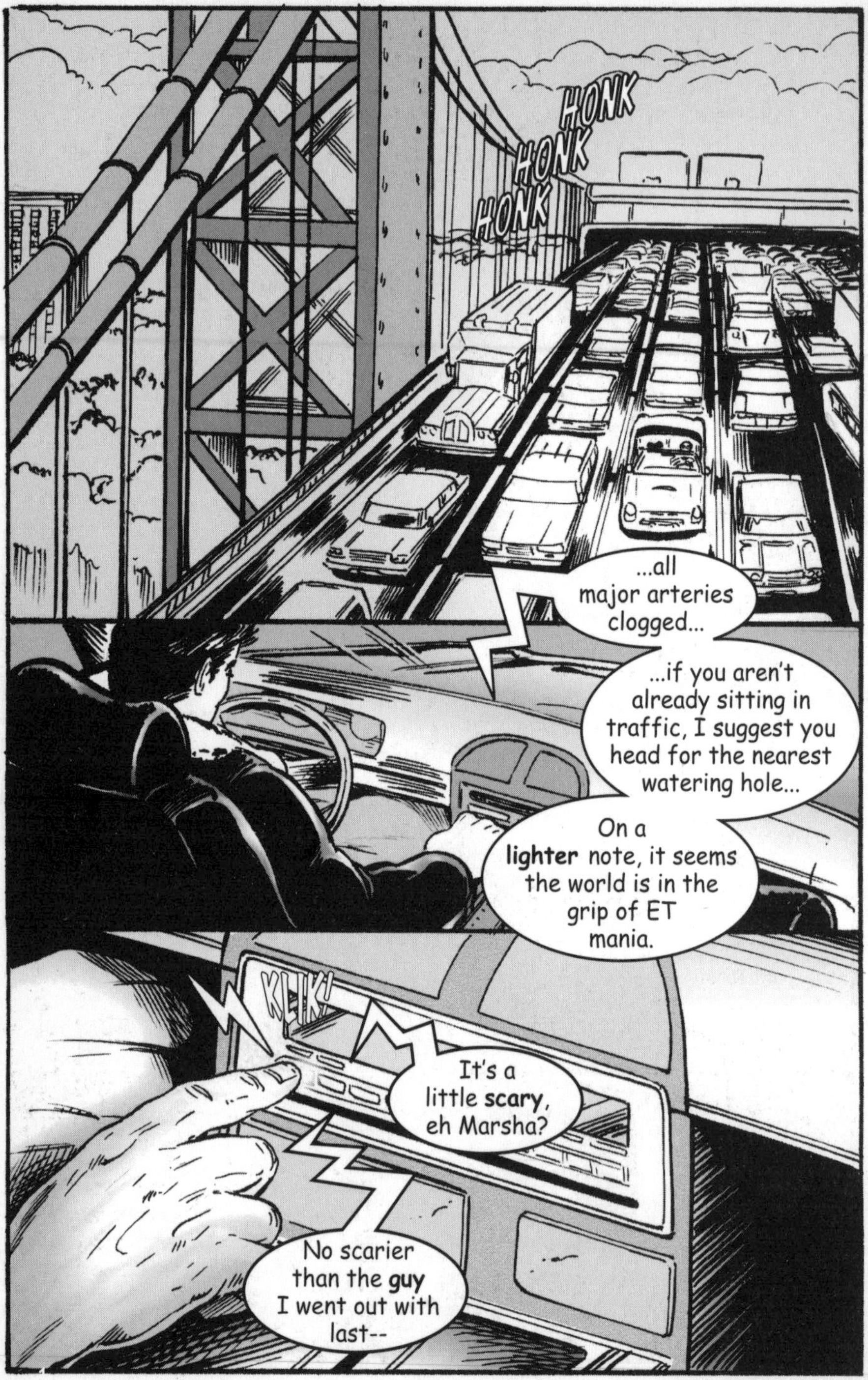
HONK
HONK
HONK
...all major arteries clogged...
...if you aren't already sitting in traffic, I suggest you head for the nearest watering hole...
On a **lighter** note, it seems the world is in the grip of ET mania.
KLIK!
It's a little **scary**, eh Marsha?
No scarier than the **guy** I went out with last--

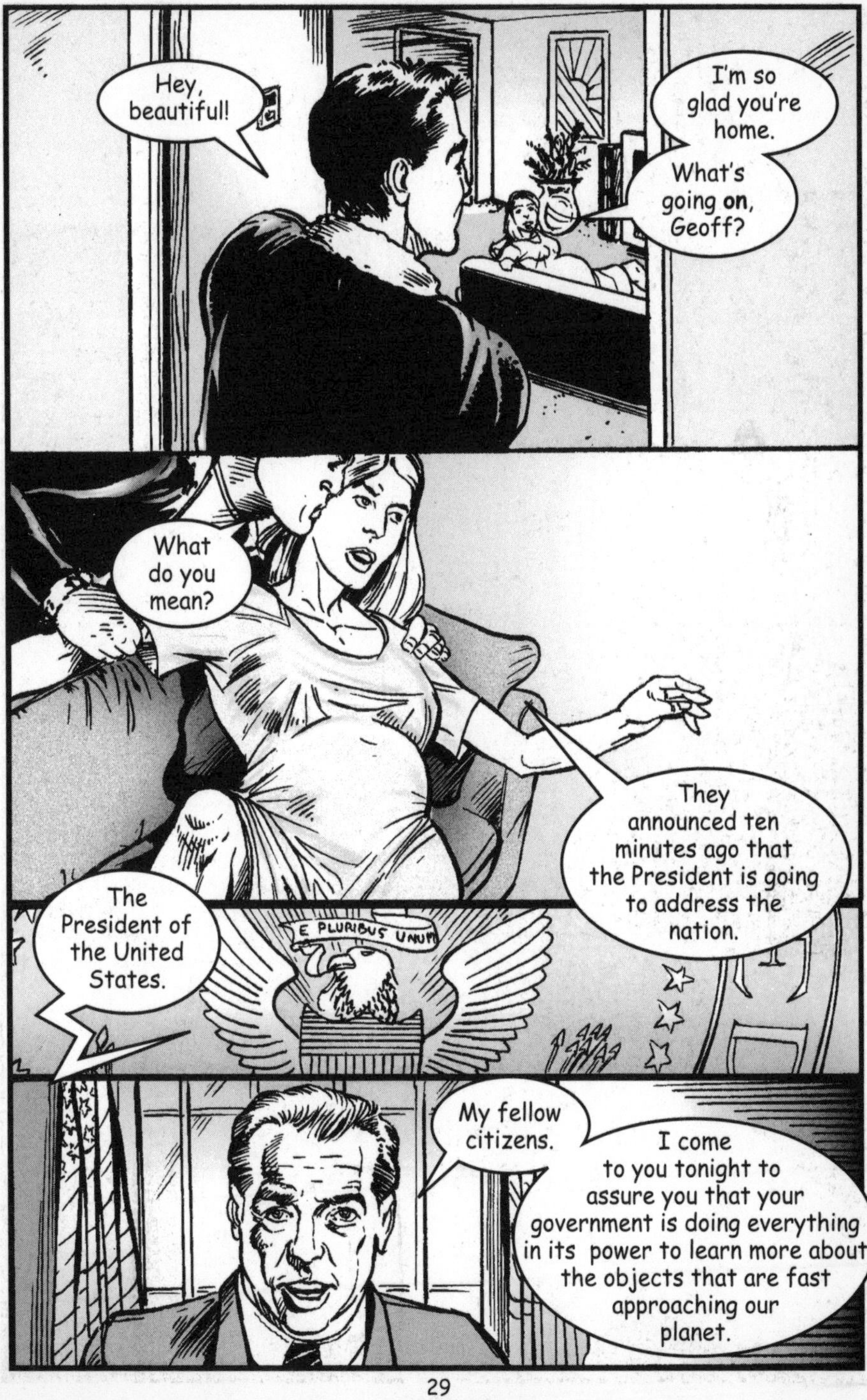
Hey, beautiful!
I'm so glad you're home.
What's going **on**, Geoff?
What do you mean?
They announced ten minutes ago that the President is going to address the nation.
The President of the United States.
E PLURIBUS UNUM
My fellow citizens.
I come to you tonight to assure you that your government is doing everything in its power to learn more about the objects that are fast approaching our planet.

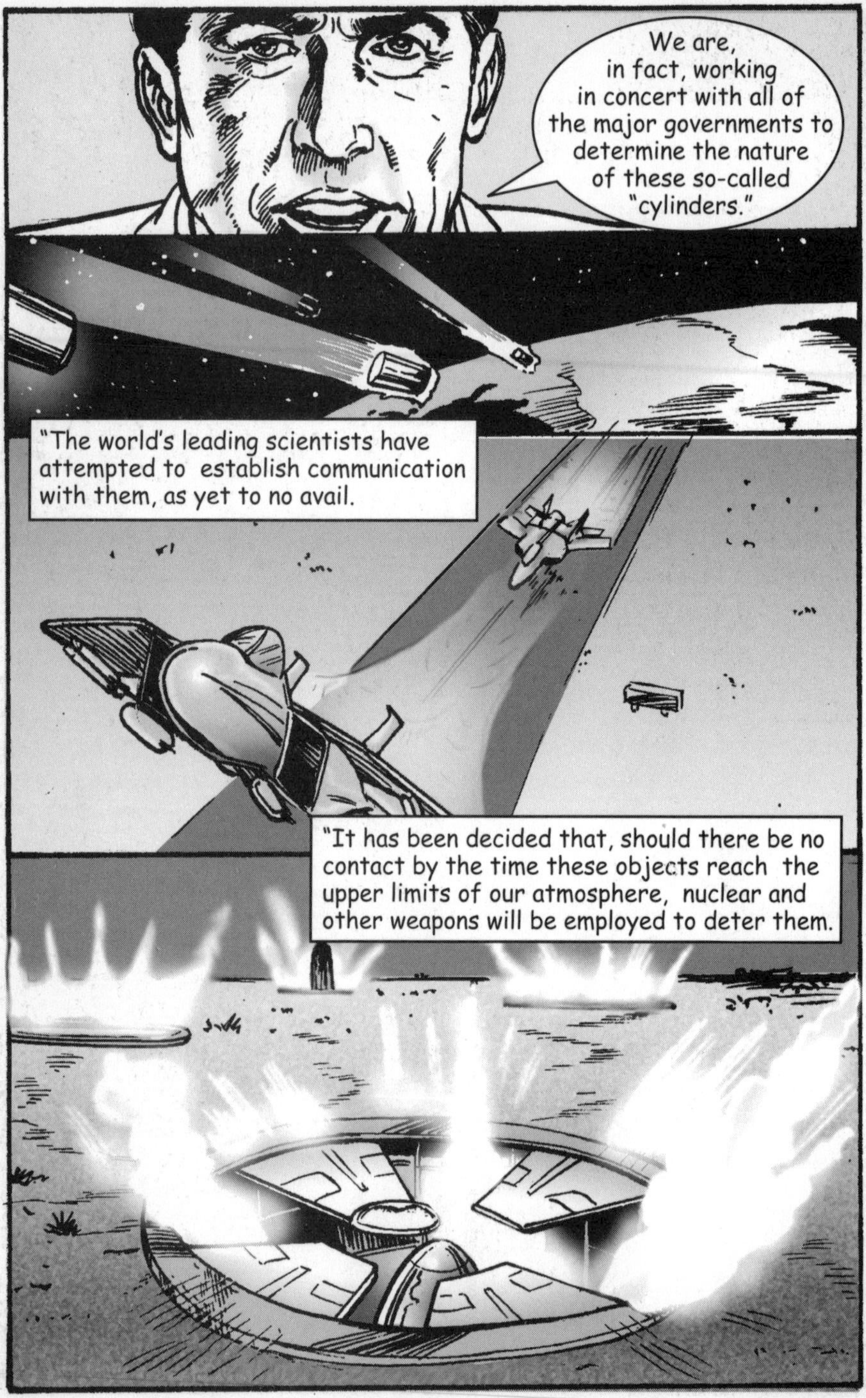
We are, in fact, working in concert with all of the major governments to determine the nature of these so-called "cylinders."
"The world's leading scientists have attempted to establish communication with them, as yet to no avail.
"It has been decided that, should there be no contact by the time these objects reach the upper limits of our atmosphere, nuclear and other weapons will be employed to deter them.

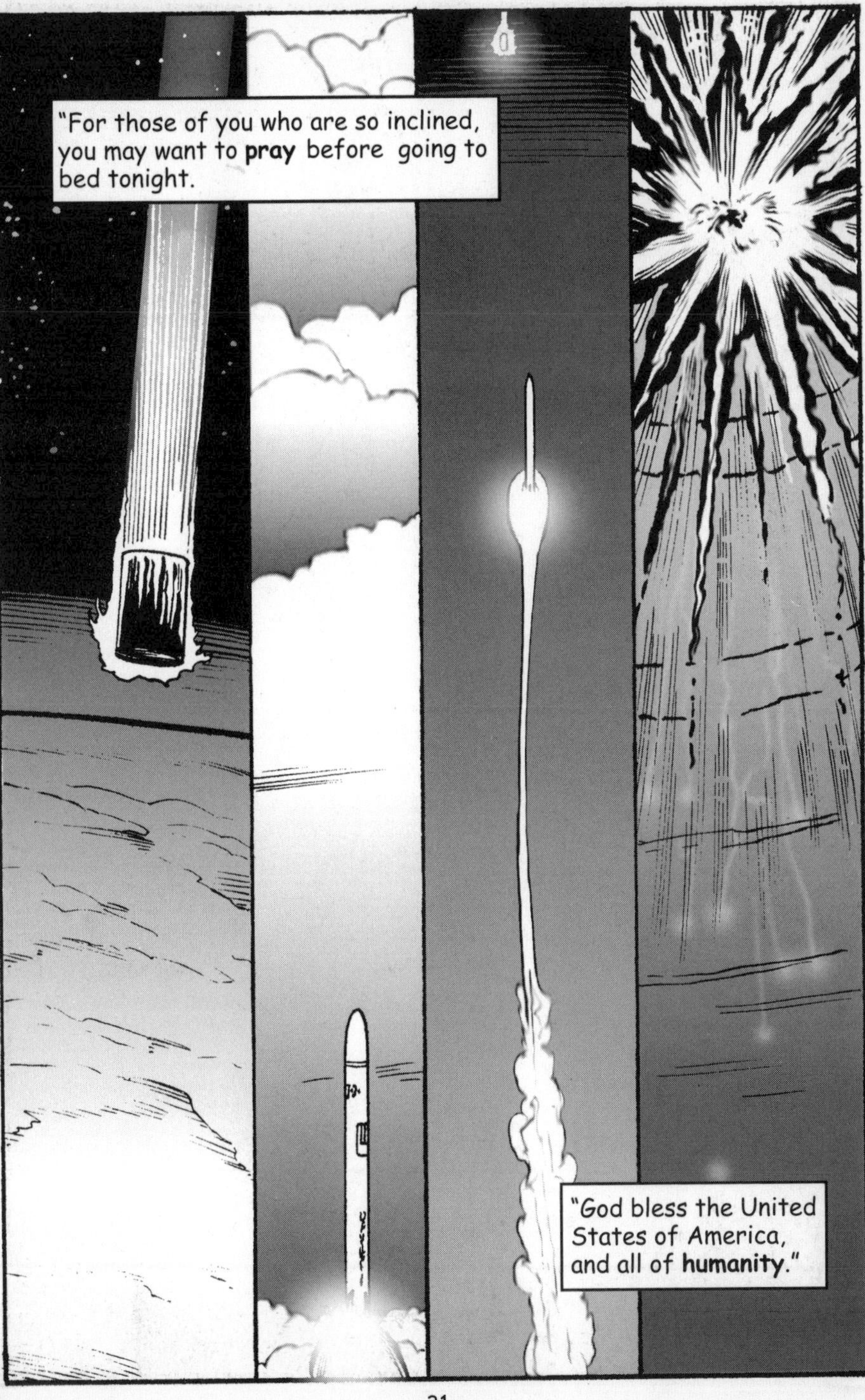
"For those of you who are so inclined, you may want to **pray** before going to bed tonight.
"God bless the United States of America, and all of **humanity**."

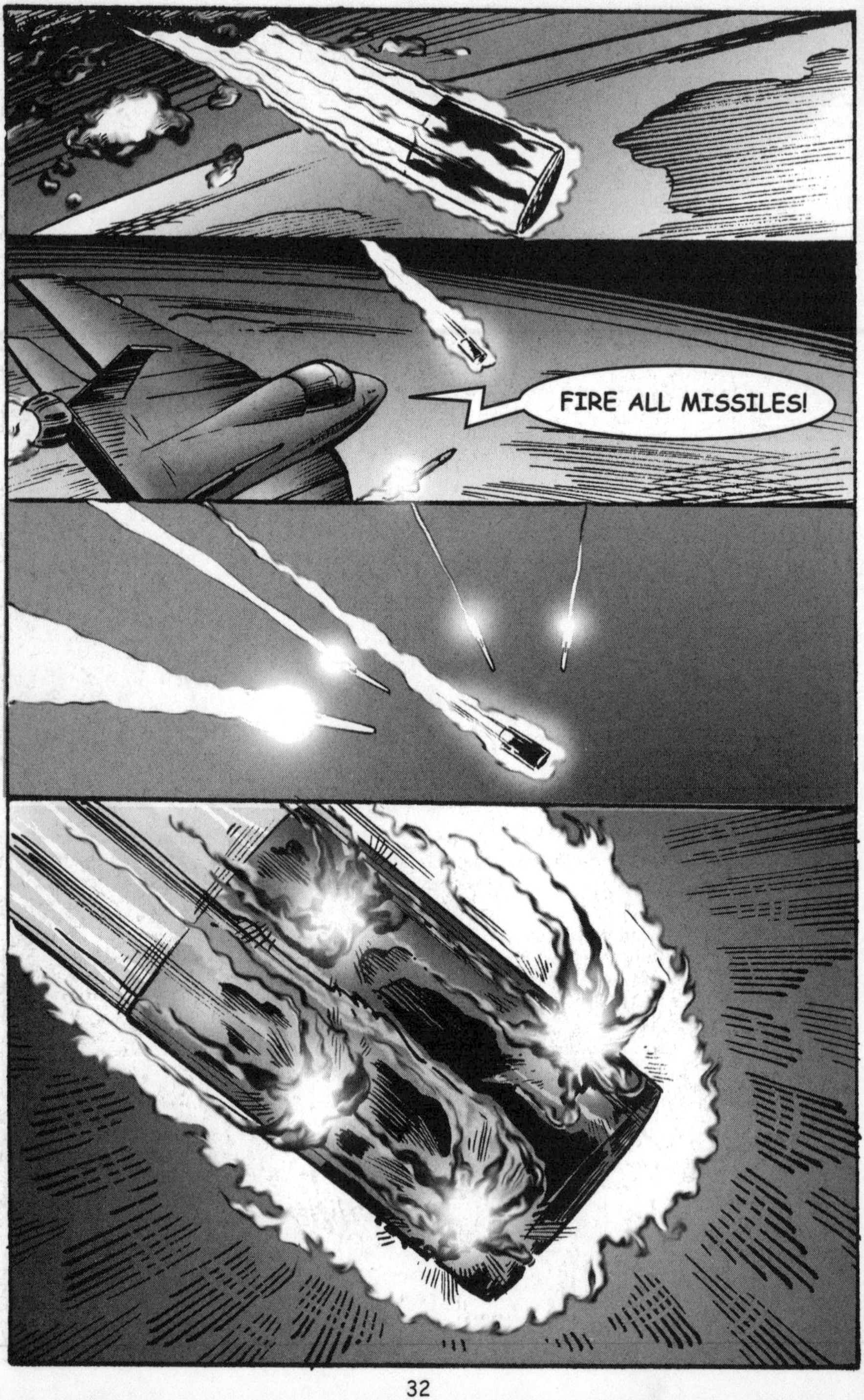
FIRE ALL MISSILES!

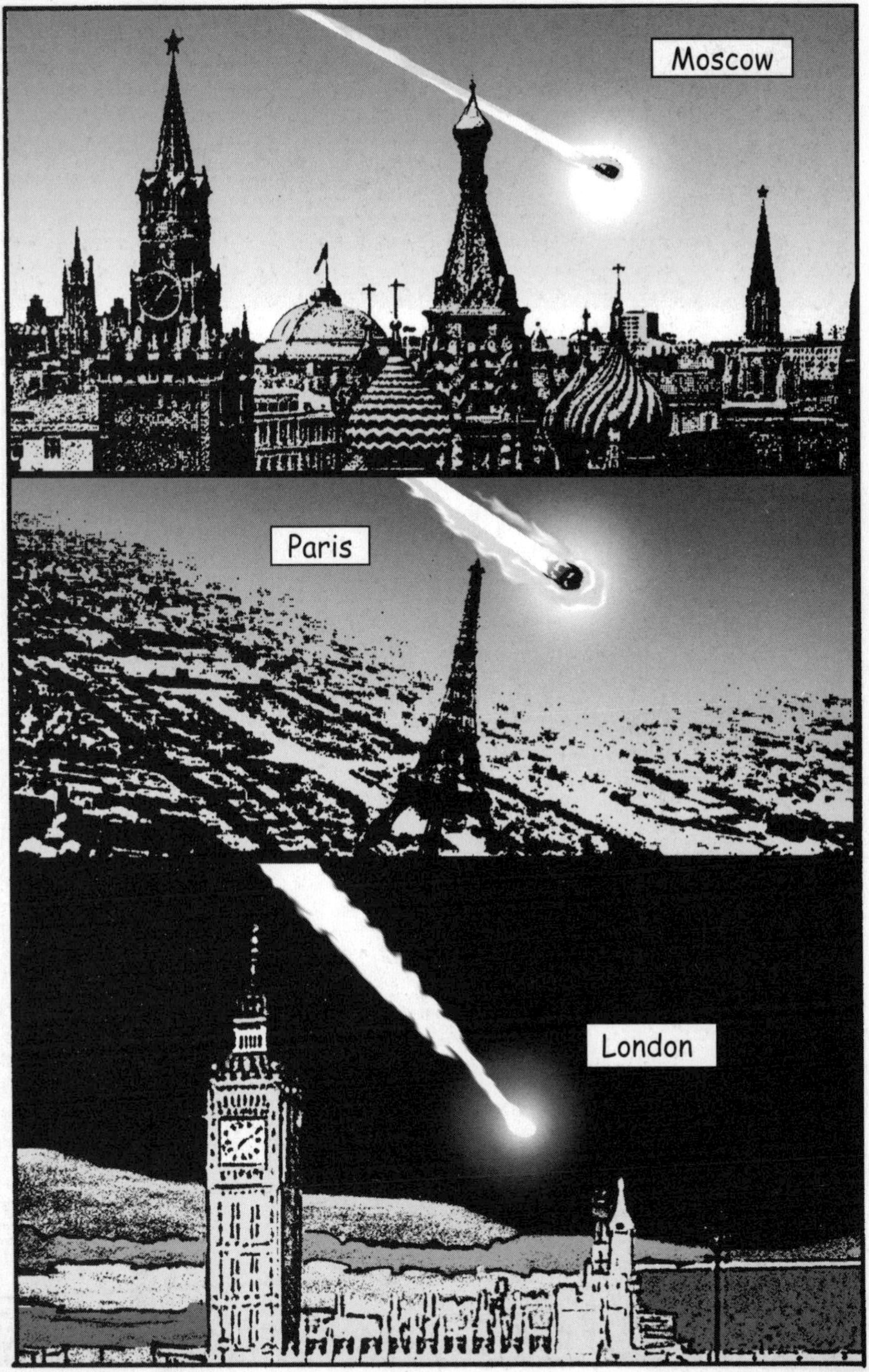
Moscow
Paris
London

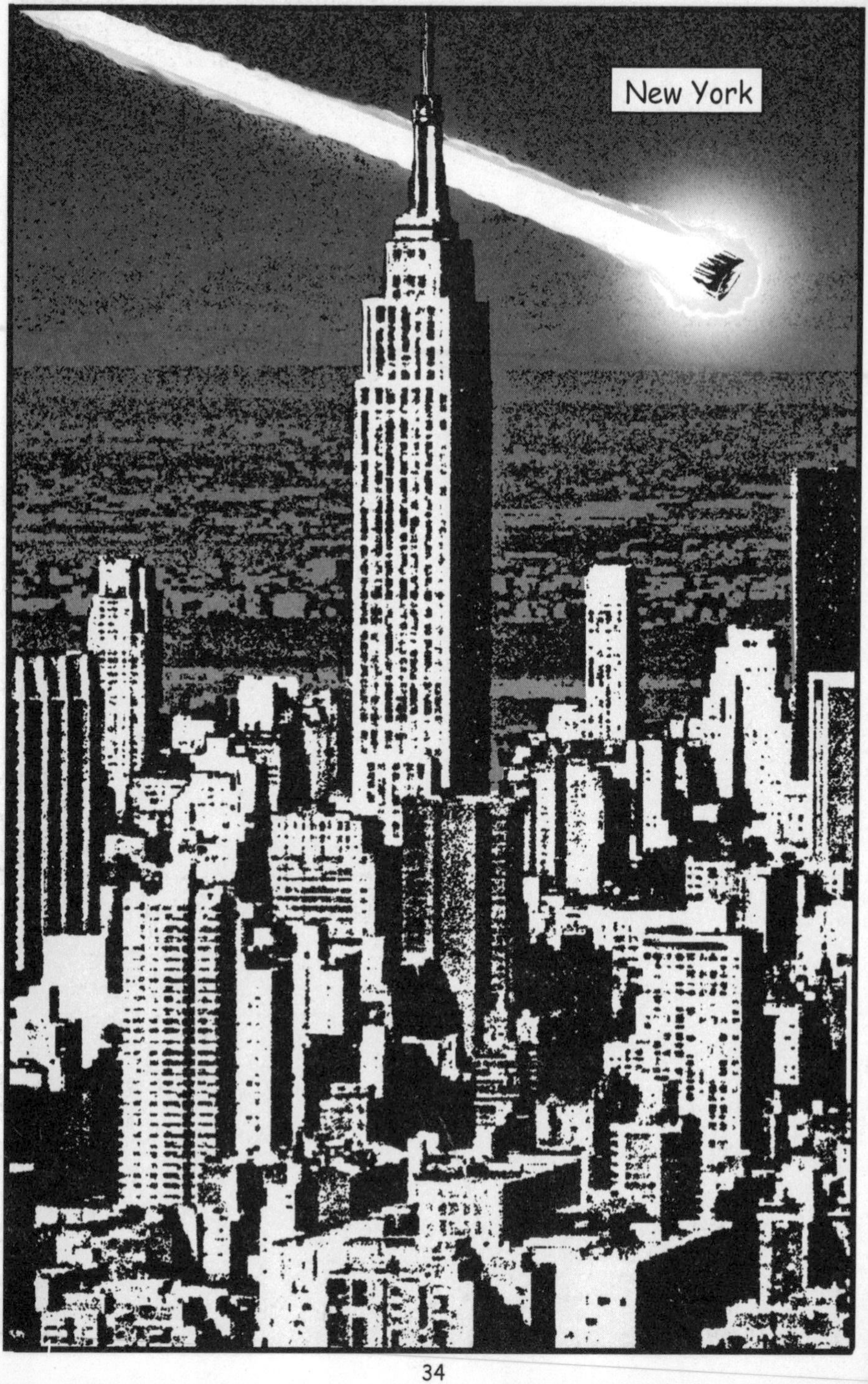
New York

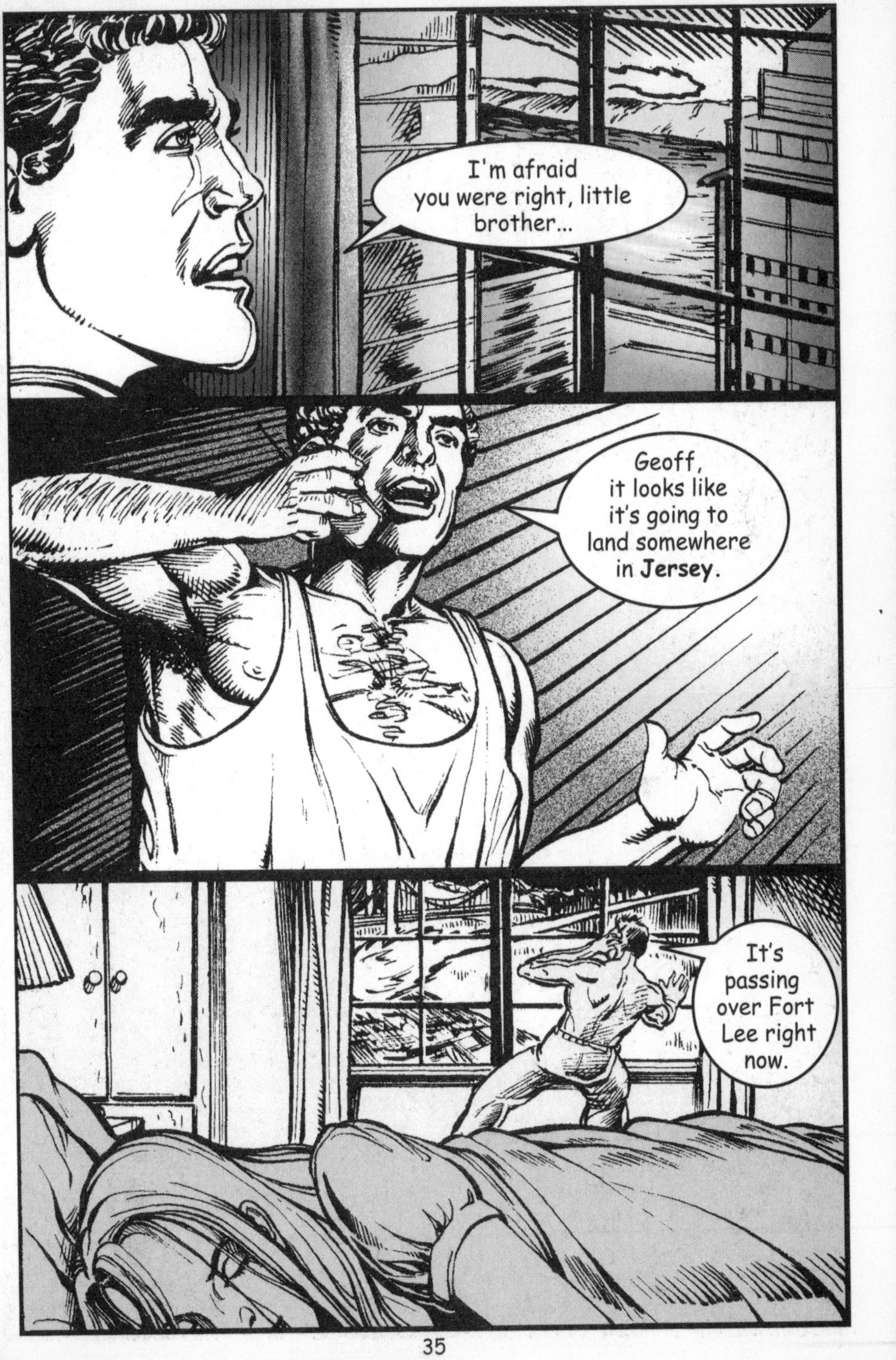
I'm afraid you were right, little brother...
Geoff, it looks like it's going to land somewhere in **Jersey**.
It's passing over Fort Lee right now.

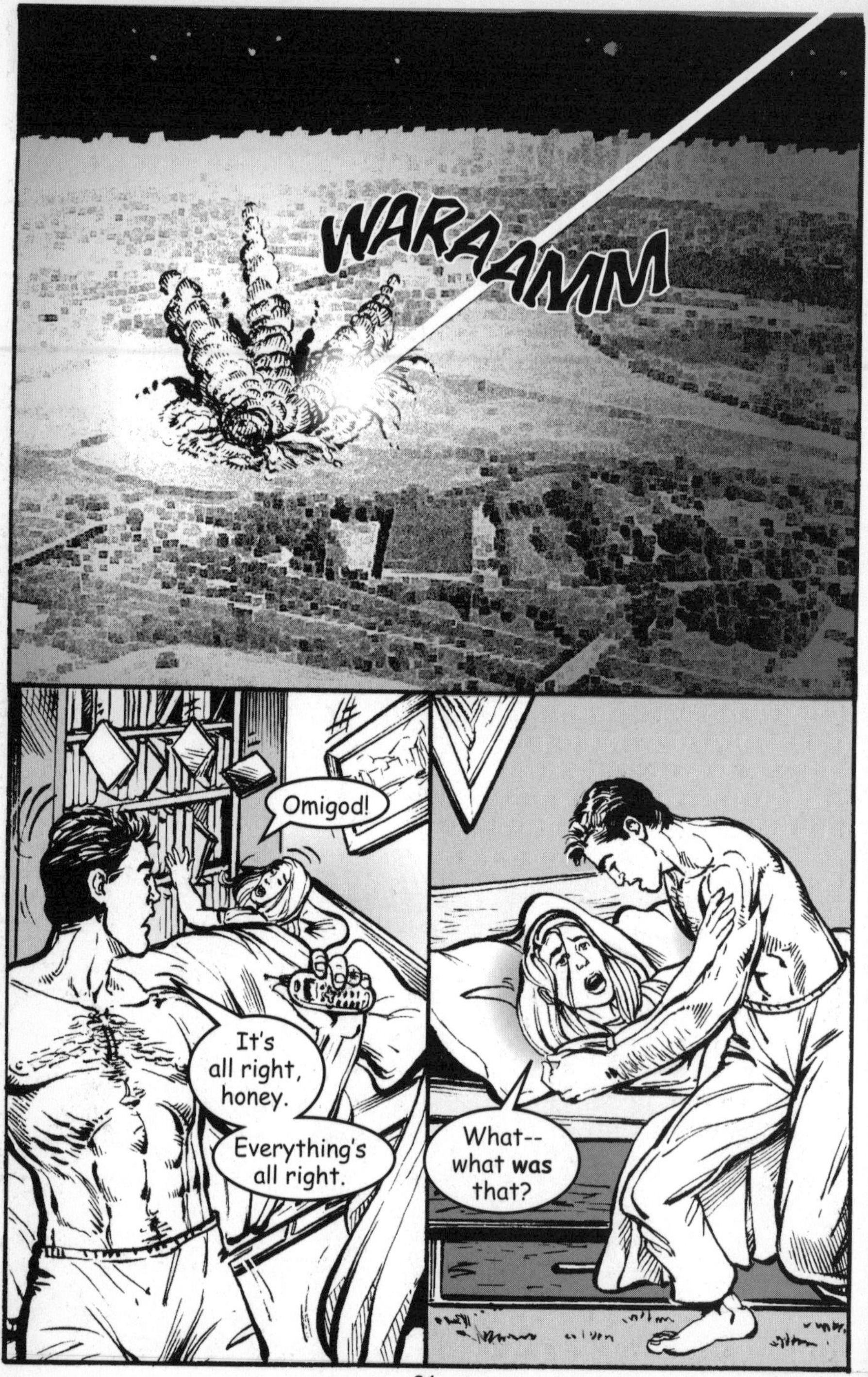
WARAAMM
Omigod!
It's all right, honey.
Everything's all right.
What-- what **was** that?

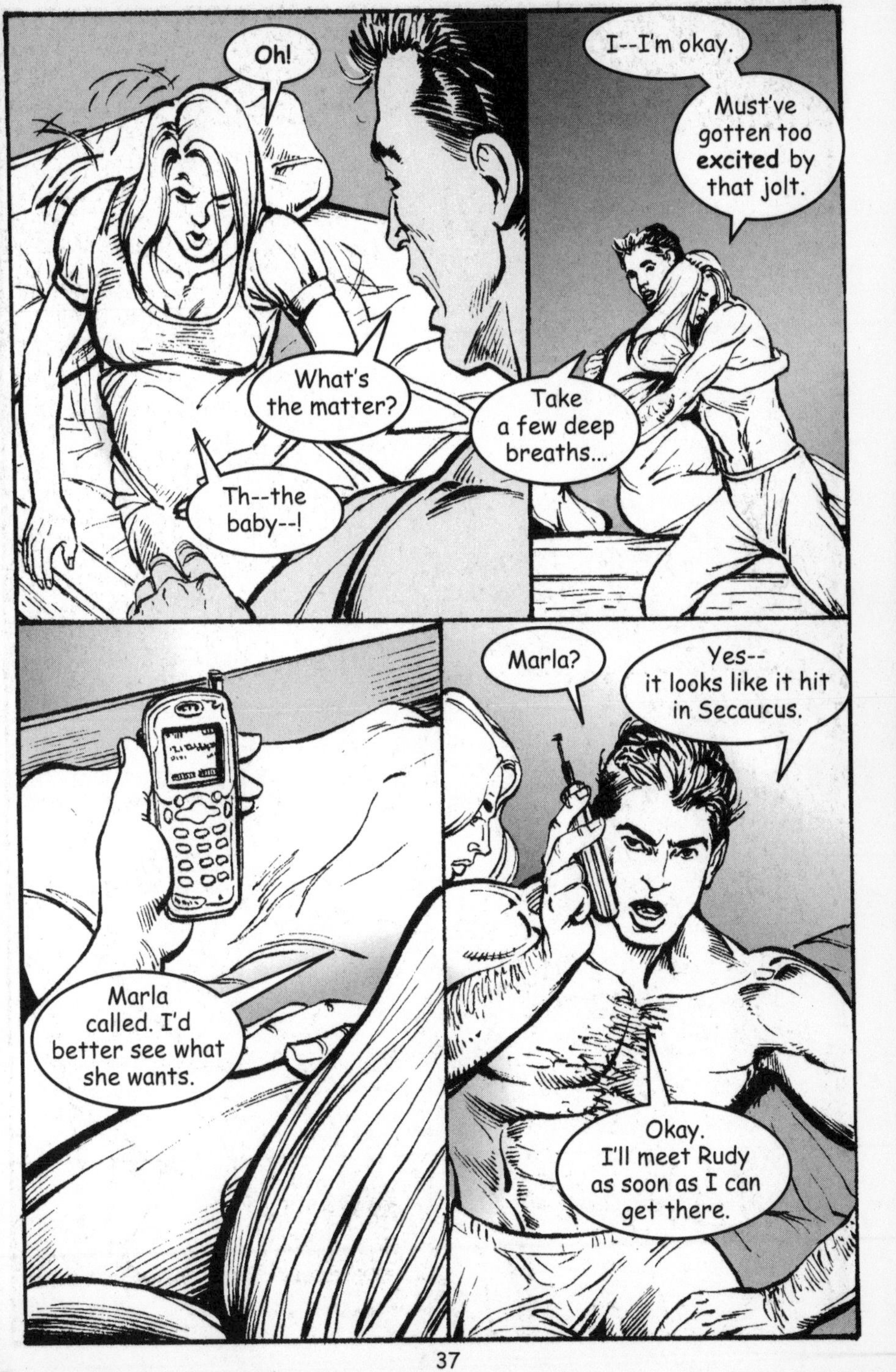
Oh!
What's the matter?
Th--the baby--!
Take a few deep breaths...
I--I'm okay.
Must've gotten too **excited** by that jolt.
Marla called. I'd better see what she wants.
Marla?
Yes-- it looks like it hit in Secaucus.
Okay. I'll meet Rudy as soon as I can get there.

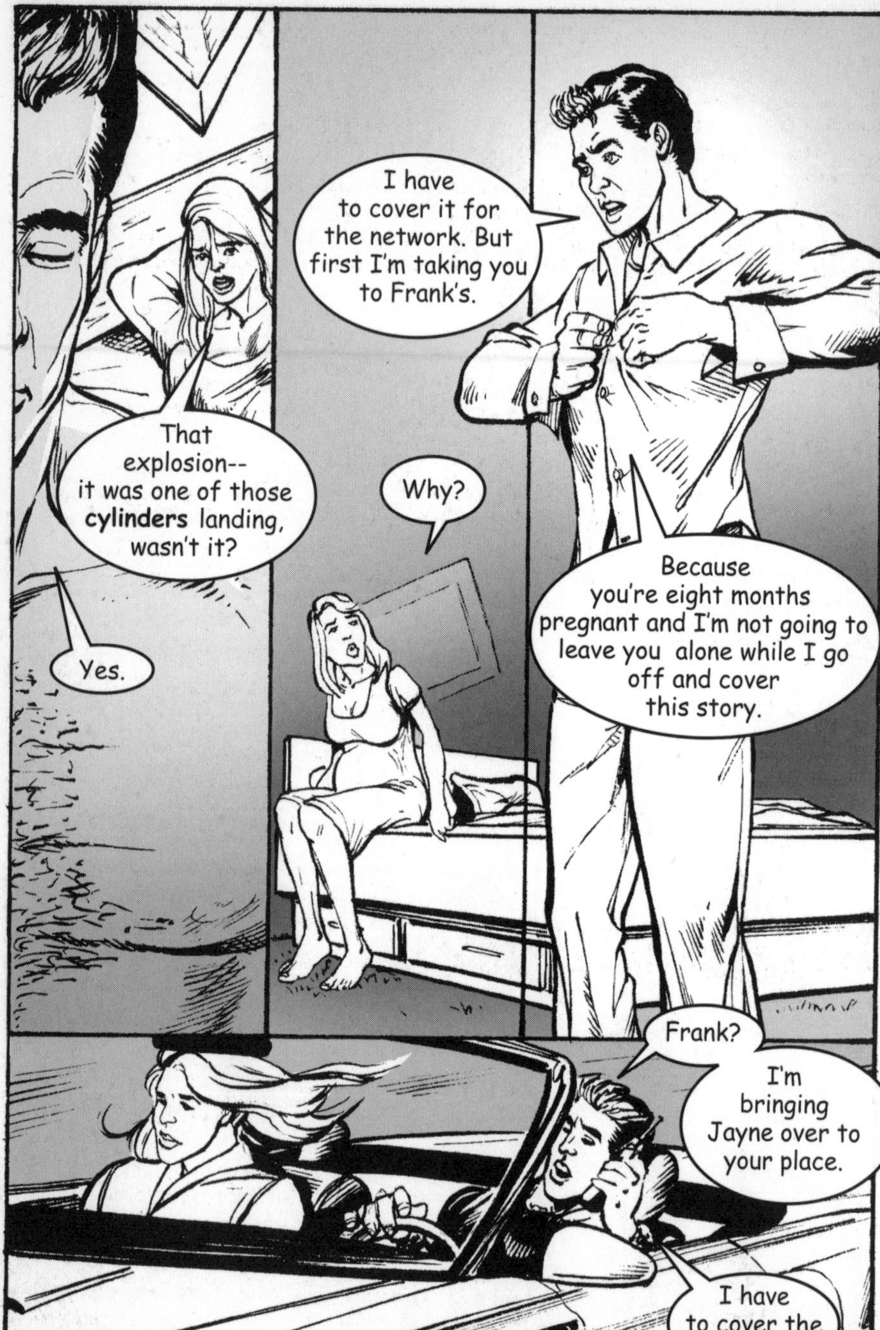
That explosion-- it was one of those **cylinders** landing, wasn't it?
Yes.
I have to cover it for the network. But first I'm taking you to Frank's.
Why?
Because you're eight months pregnant and I'm not going to leave you alone while I go off and cover this story.
Frank?
I'm bringing Jayne over to your place.
I have to cover the crash...

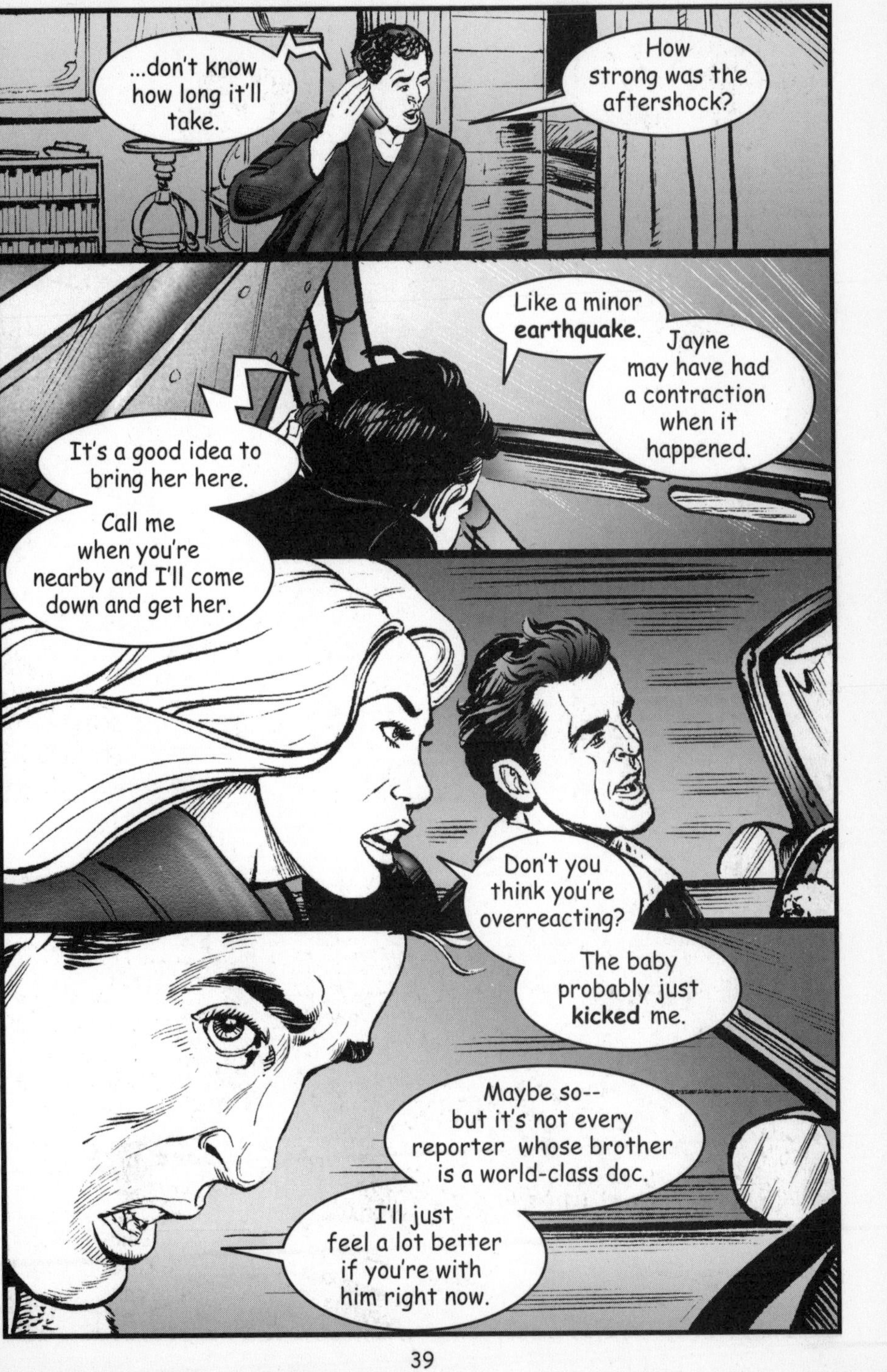
...don't know how long it'll take.
How strong was the aftershock?
Like a minor **earthquake**.
Jayne may have had a contraction when it happened.
It's a good idea to bring her here.
Call me when you're nearby and I'll come down and get her.
Don't you think you're overreacting?
The baby probably just **kicked** me.
Maybe so-- but it's not every reporter whose brother is a world-class doc.
I'll just feel a lot better if you're with him right now.

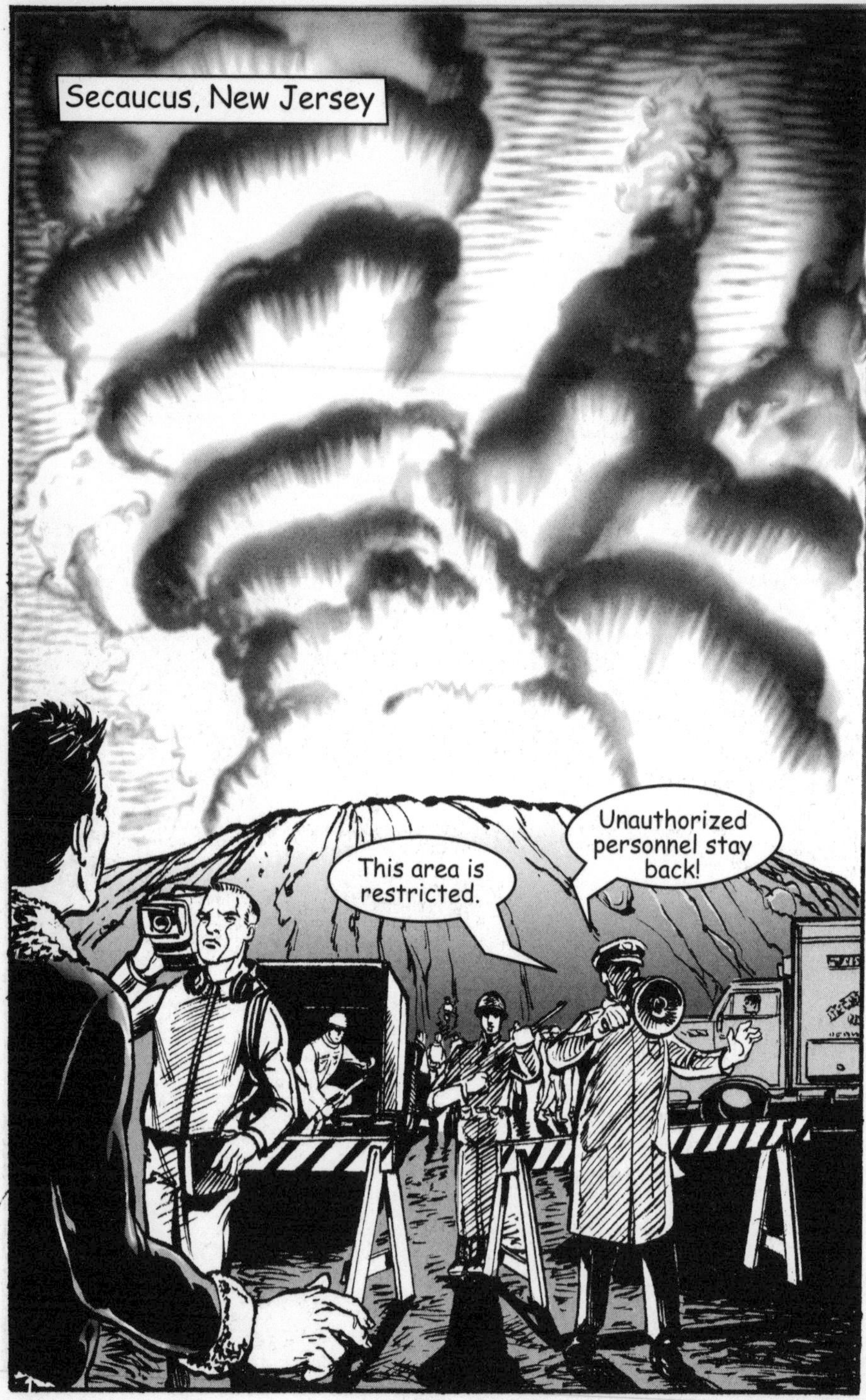
Secaucus, New Jersey
This area is restricted.
Unauthorized personnel stay back!

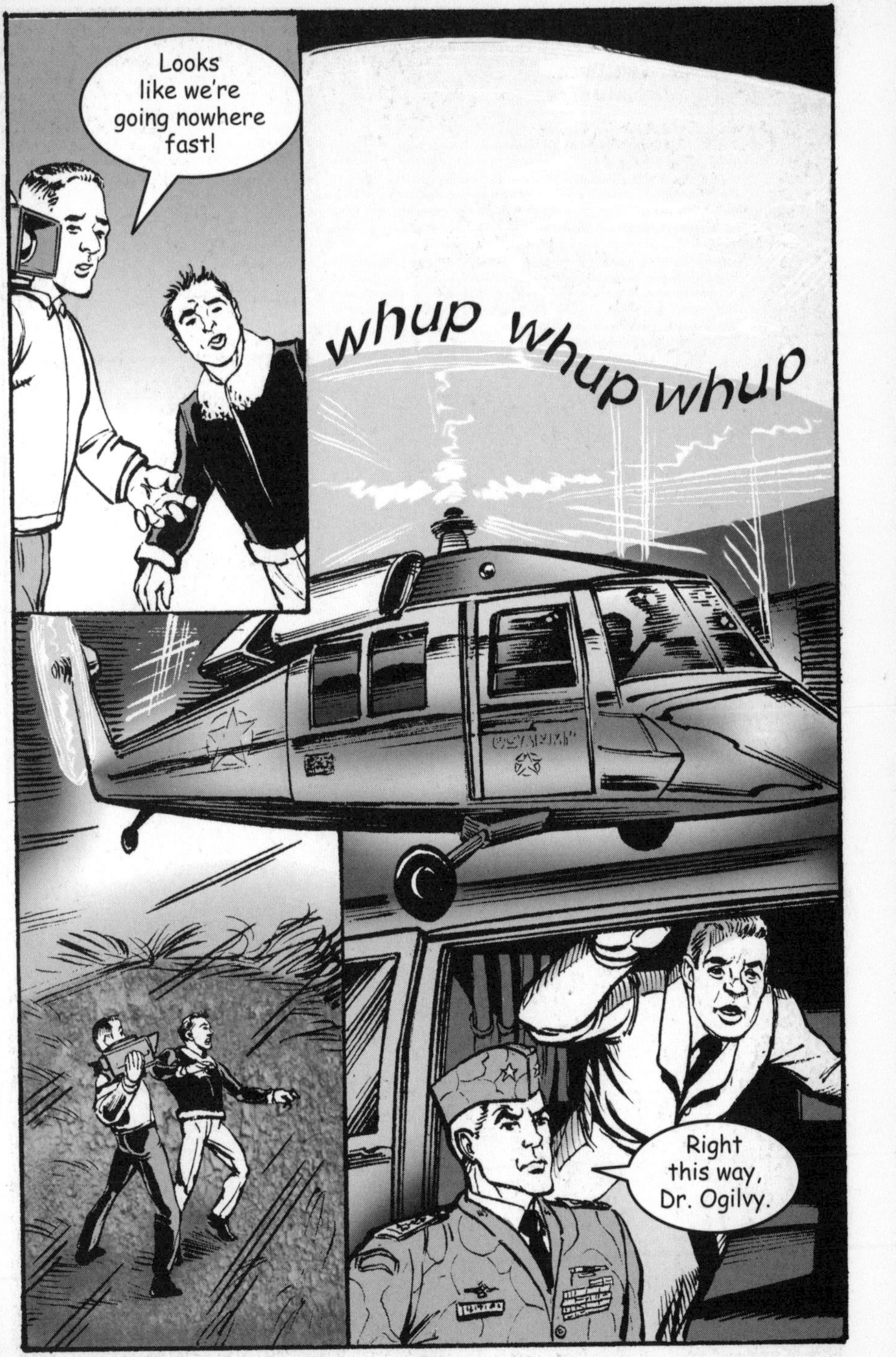
Looks like we're going nowhere fast!
whup whup whup
Right this way, Dr. Ogilvy.

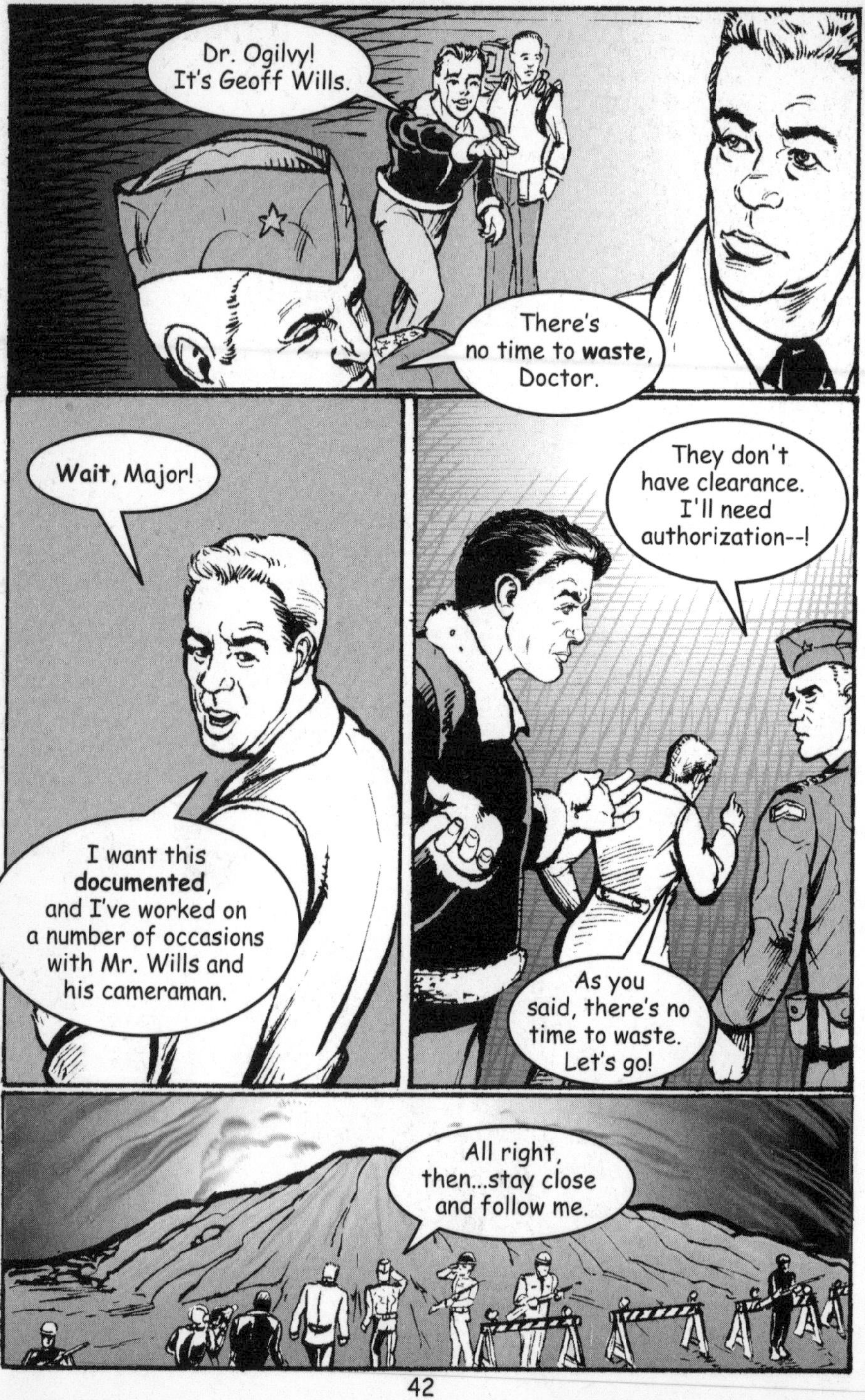
Dr. Ogilvy! It's Geoff Wills.
There's no time to **waste**, Doctor.
Wait, Major!
I want this **documented**, and I've worked on a number of occasions with Mr. Wills and his cameraman.
They don't have clearance. I'll need authorization--!
As you said, there's no time to waste. Let's go!
All right, then...stay close and follow me.

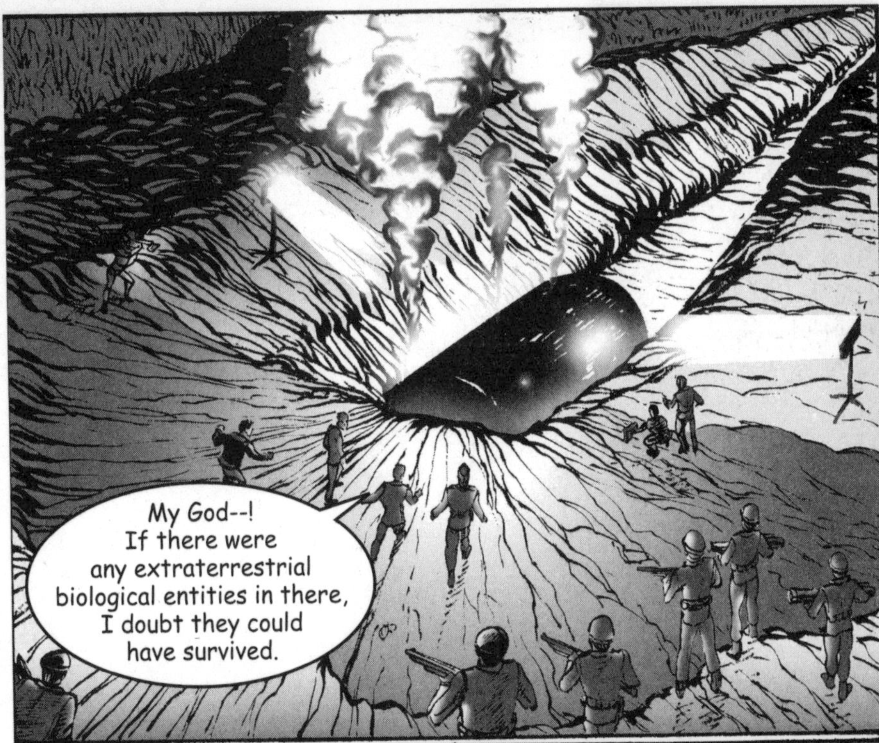
My God--! If there were any extraterrestrial biological entities in there, I doubt they could have survived.

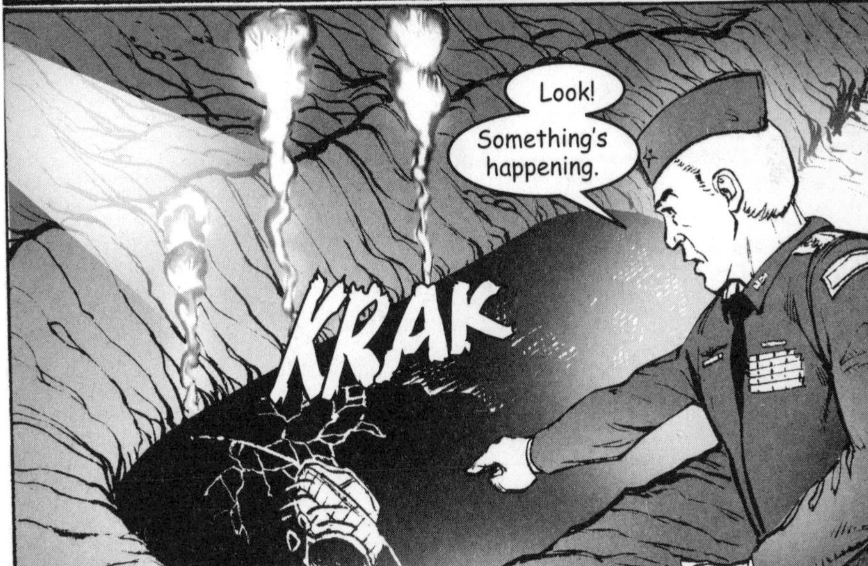
Look! Something's happening.
KRAK

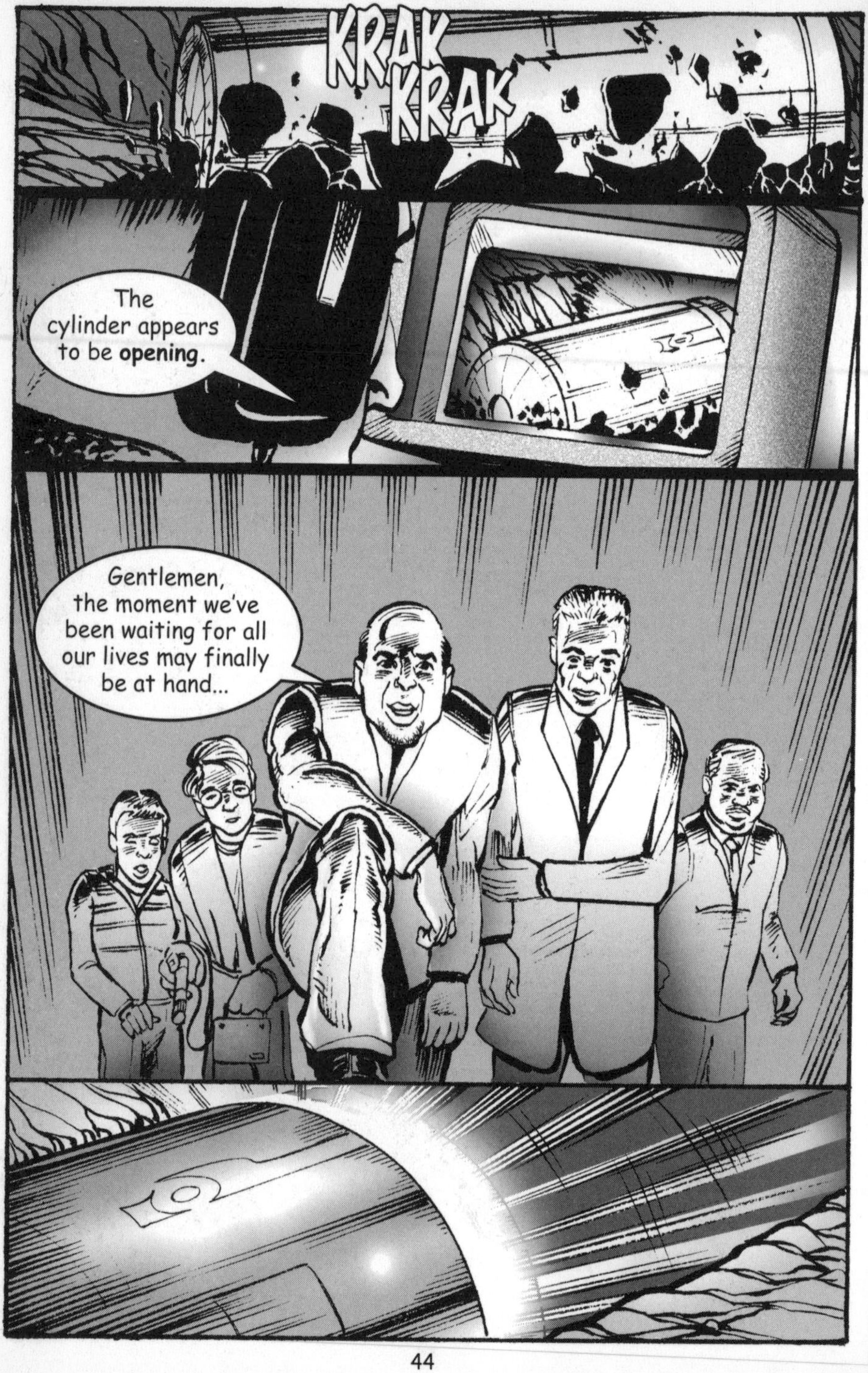
KRAK KRAK
The cylinder appears to be **opening**.
Gentlemen, the moment we've been waiting for all our lives may finally be at hand...

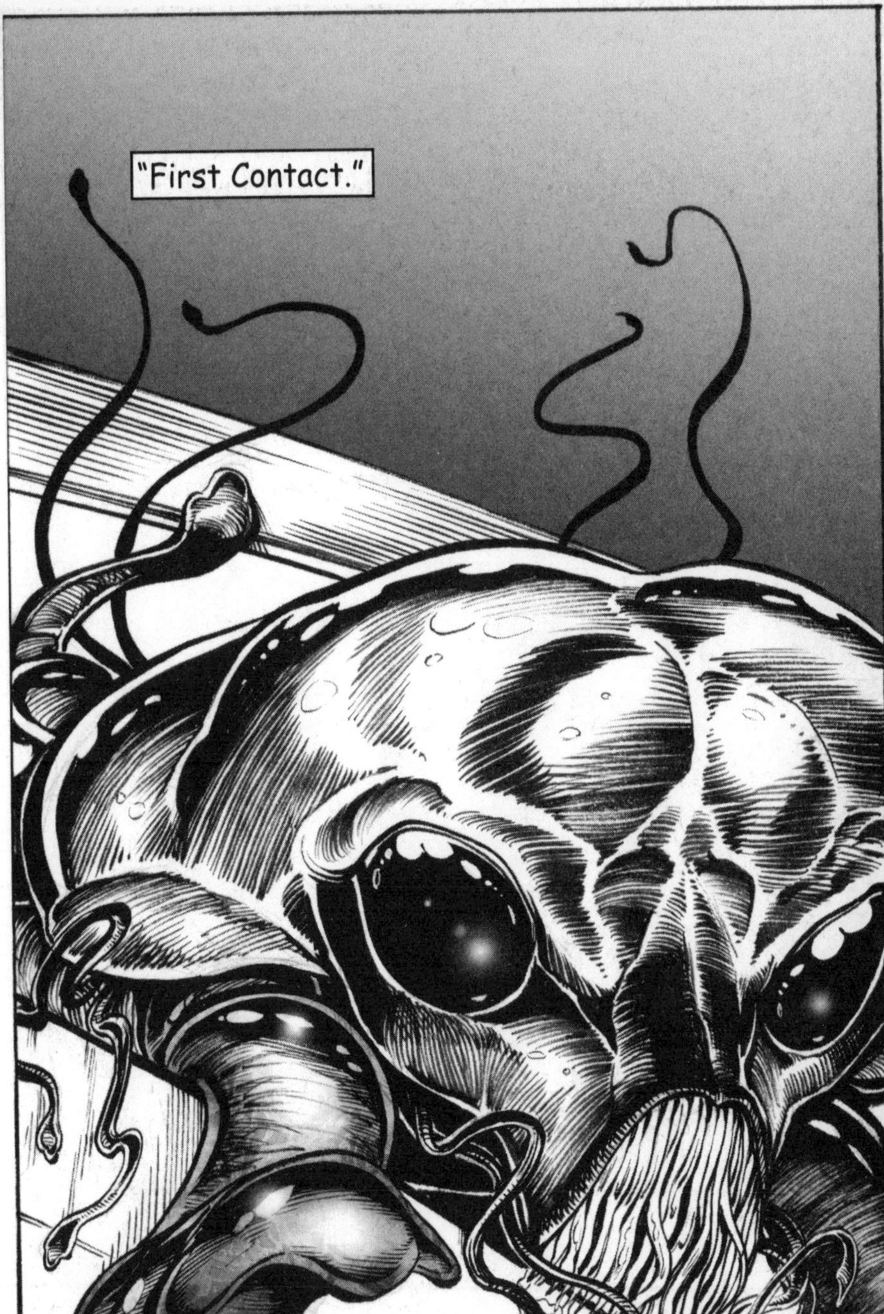
"First Contact."

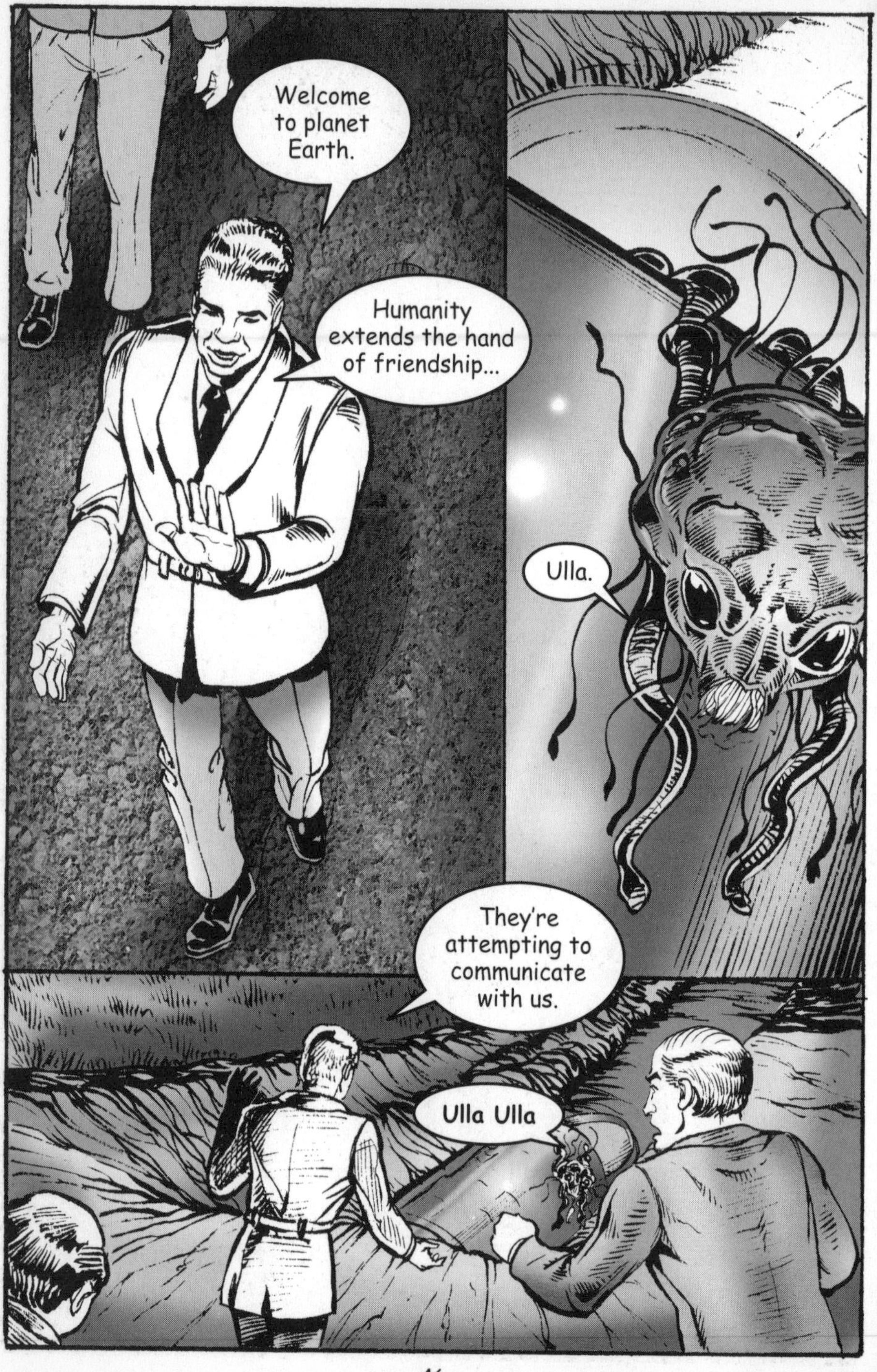
Welcome to planet Earth.
Humanity extends the hand of friendship...
Ulla.
They're attempting to communicate with us.
Ulla Ulla

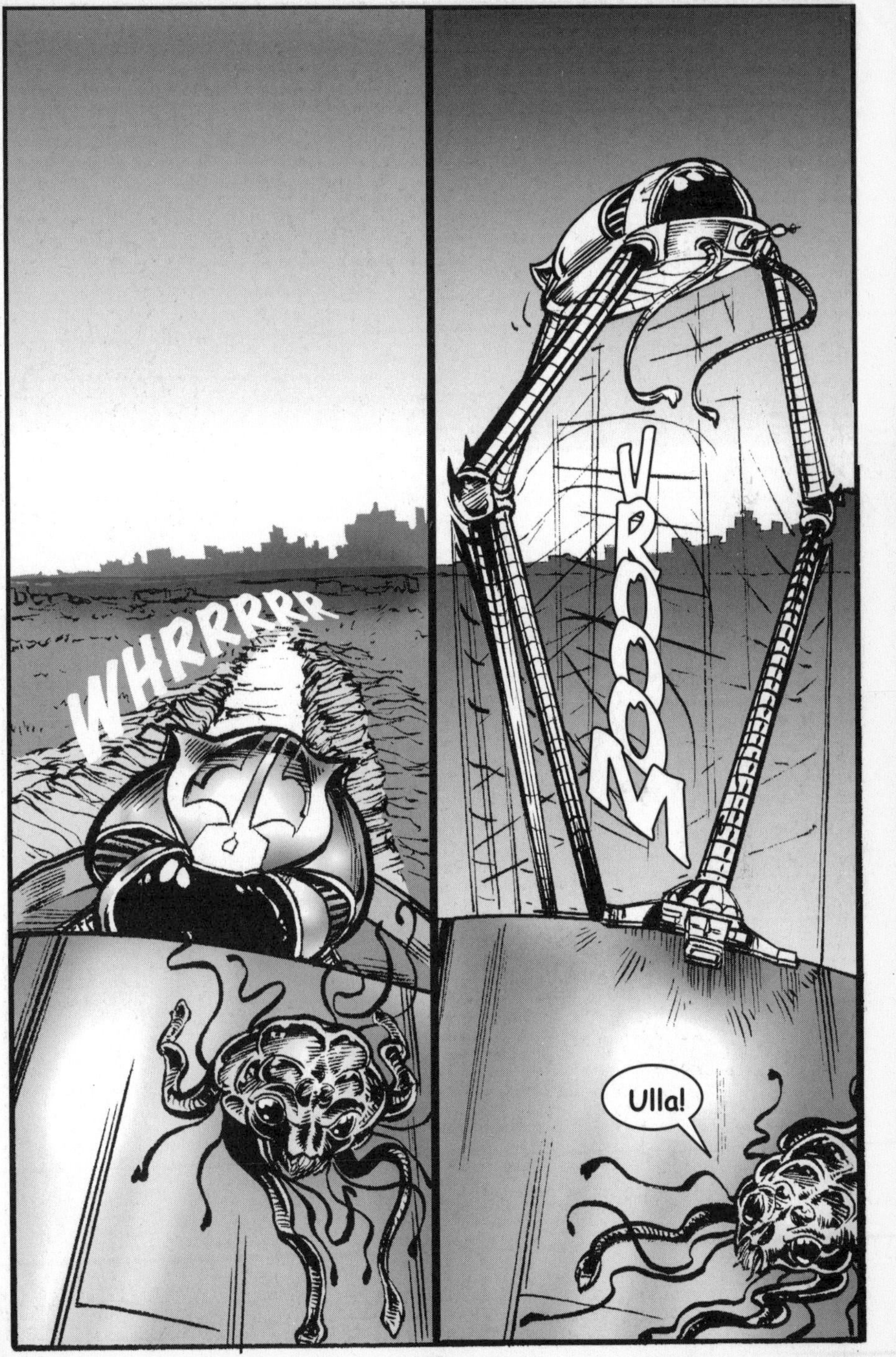
WHRRRRR
VROOOM
Ulla!

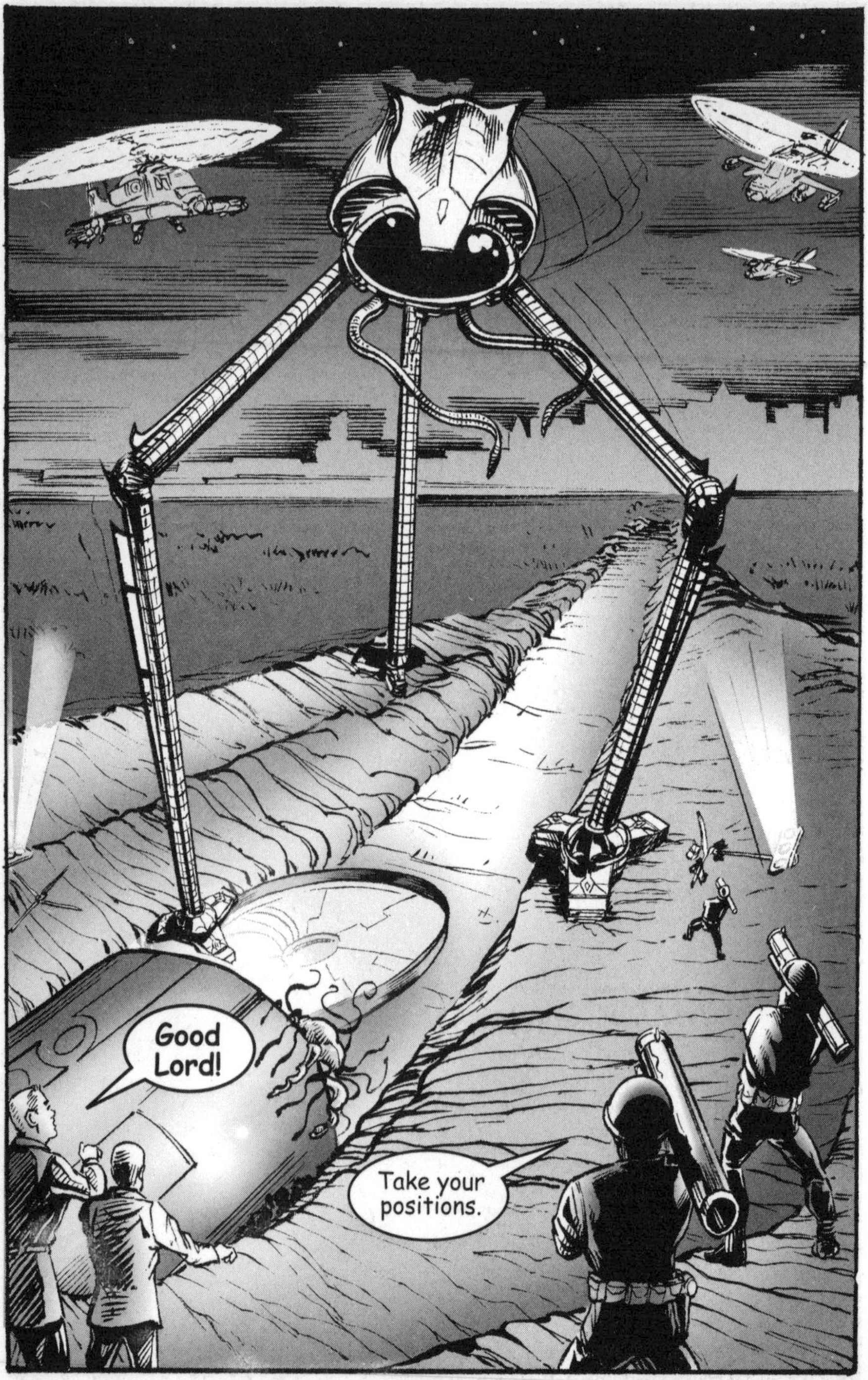
Good Lord!
Take your positions.

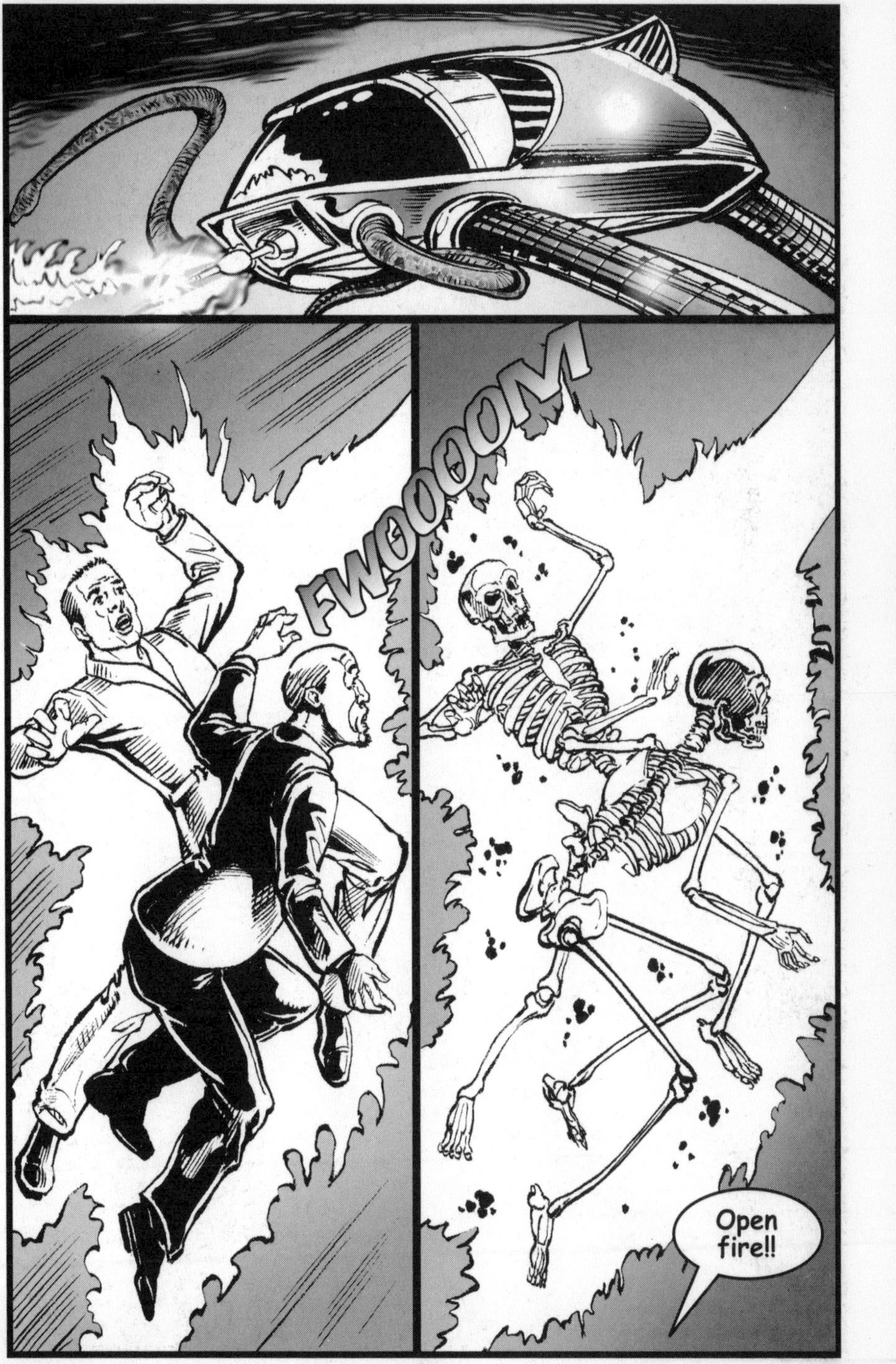
FWOOOOM!
Open fire!!

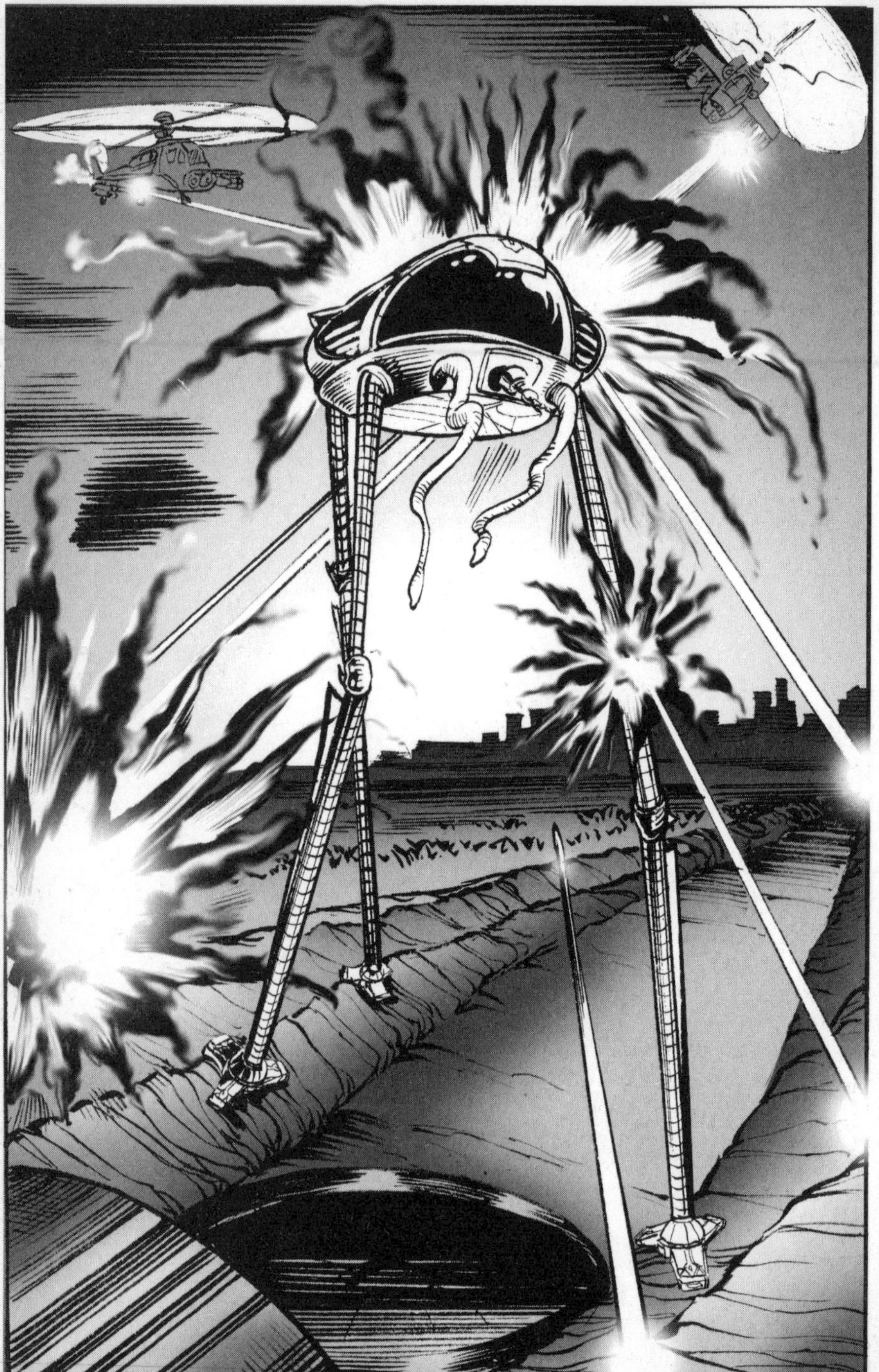

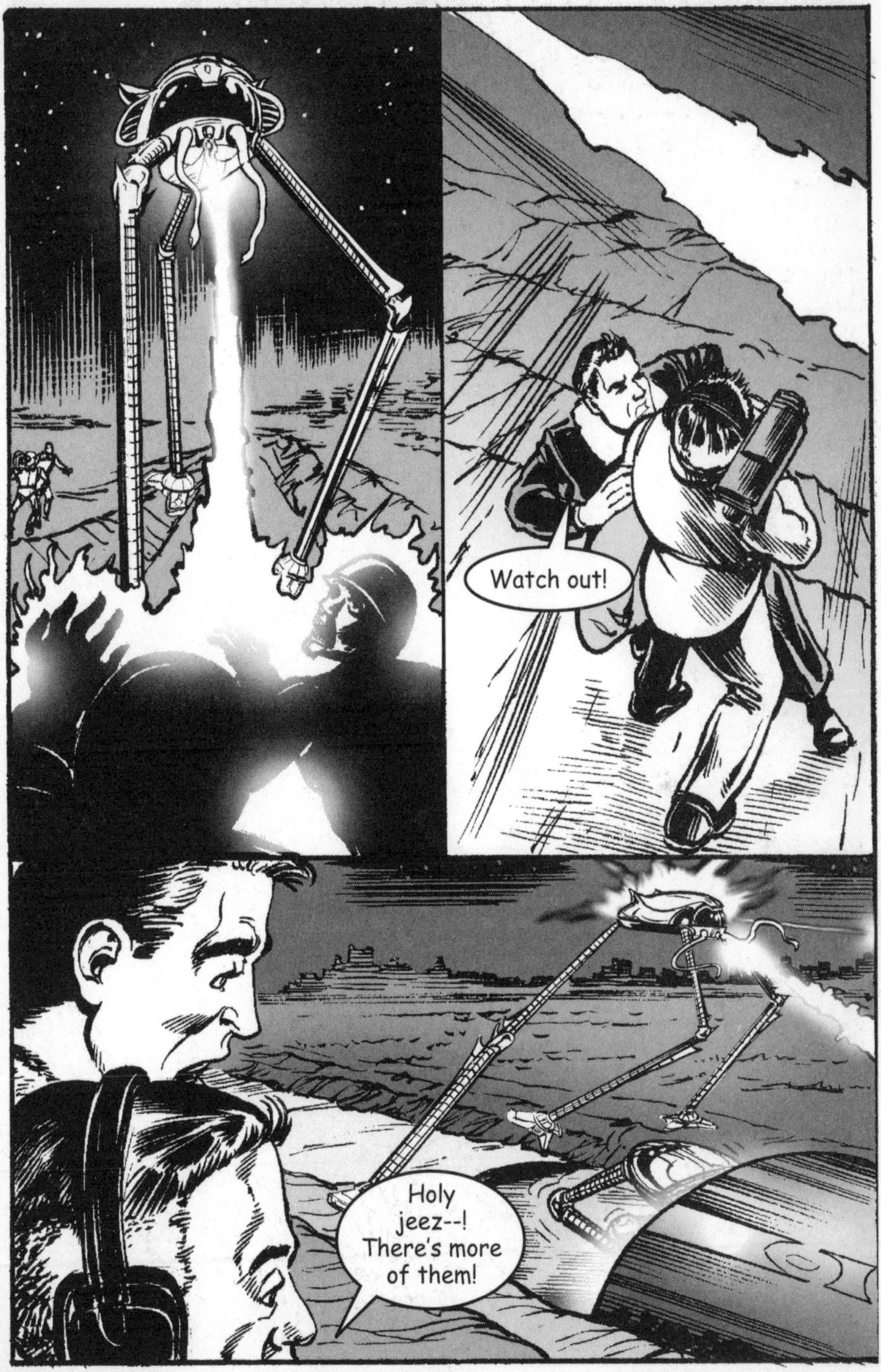
Watch out!
Holy jeez--! There's more of them!

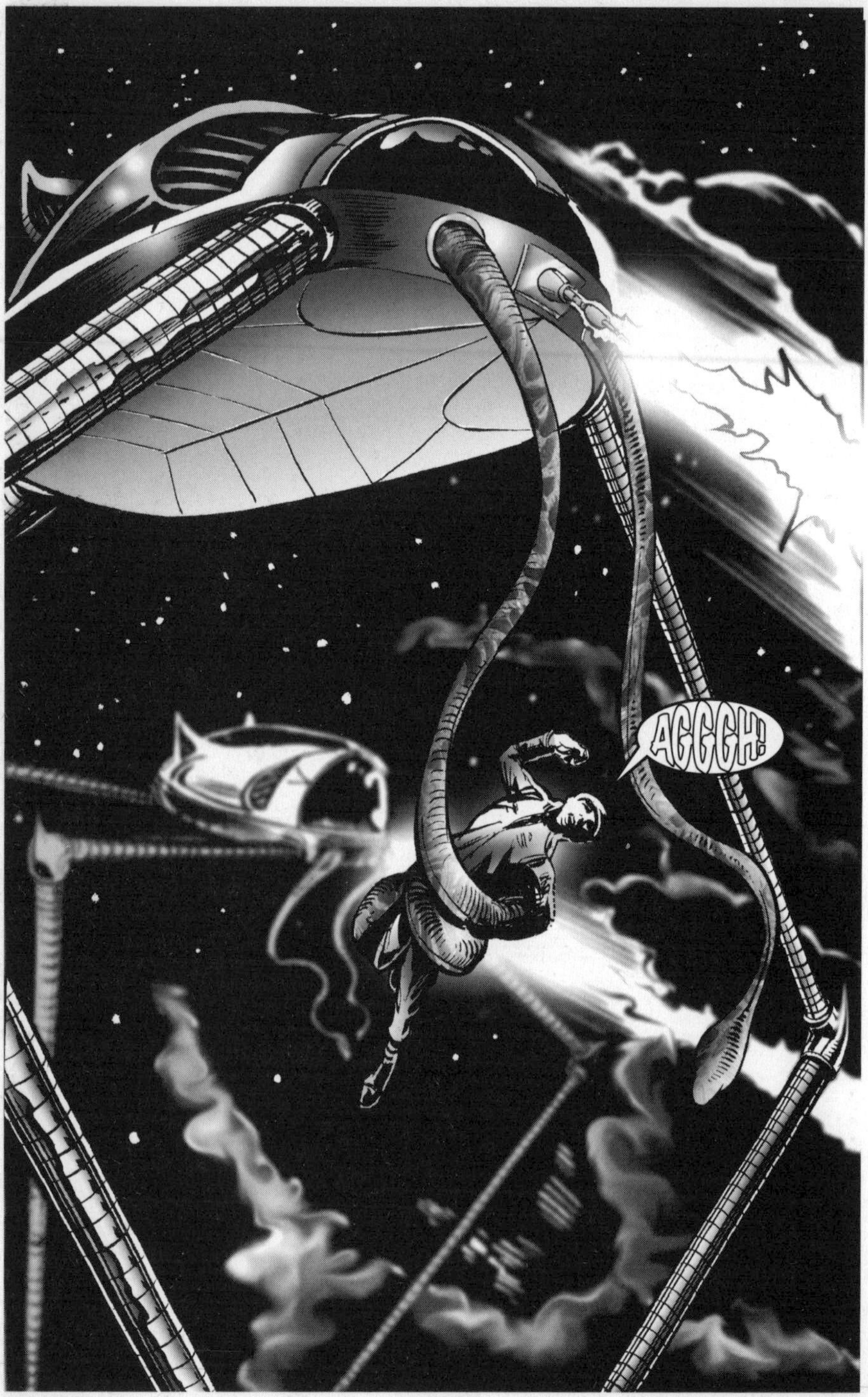
AGGGH!

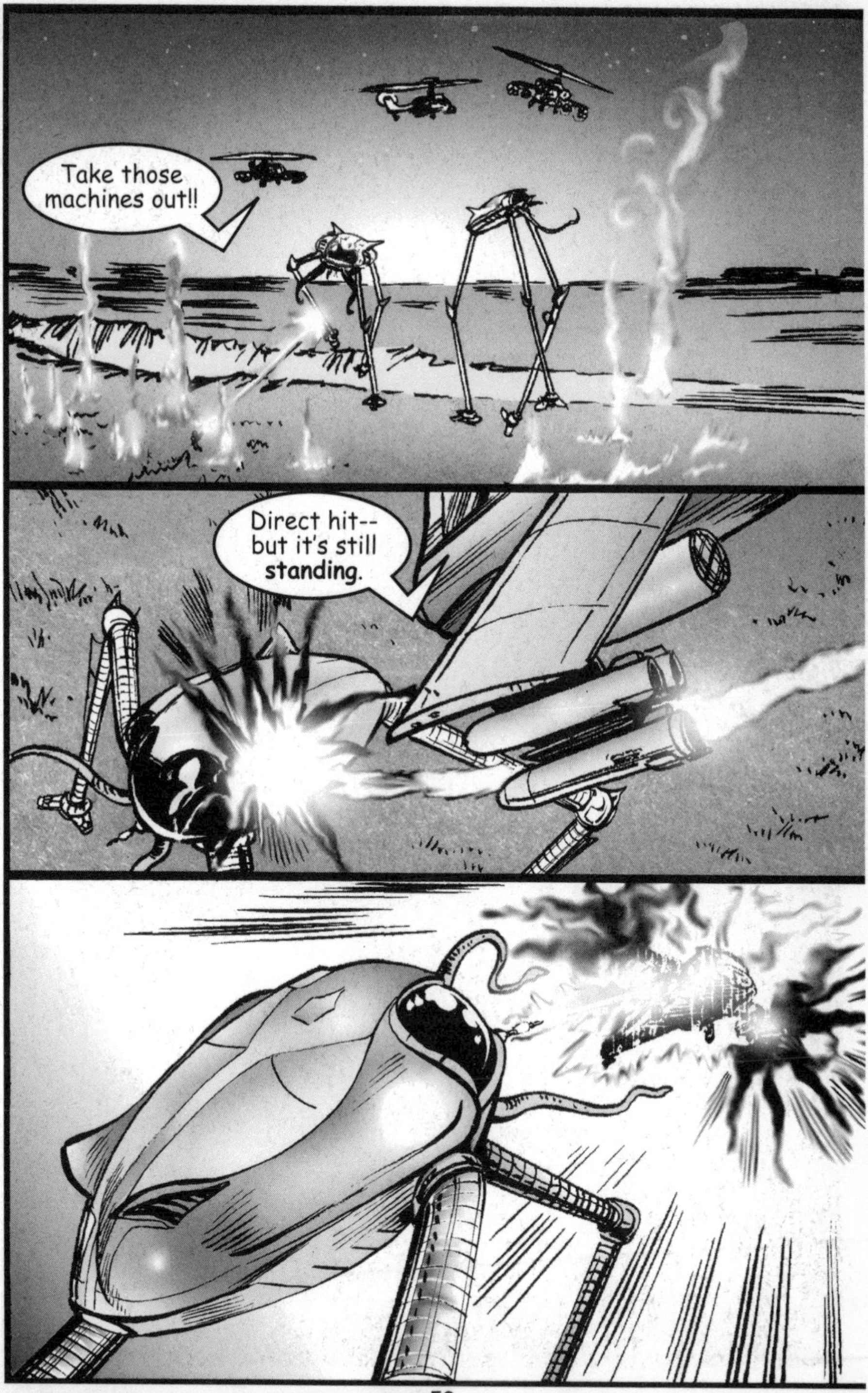
Take those machines out!!
Direct hit--but it's still **standing**.

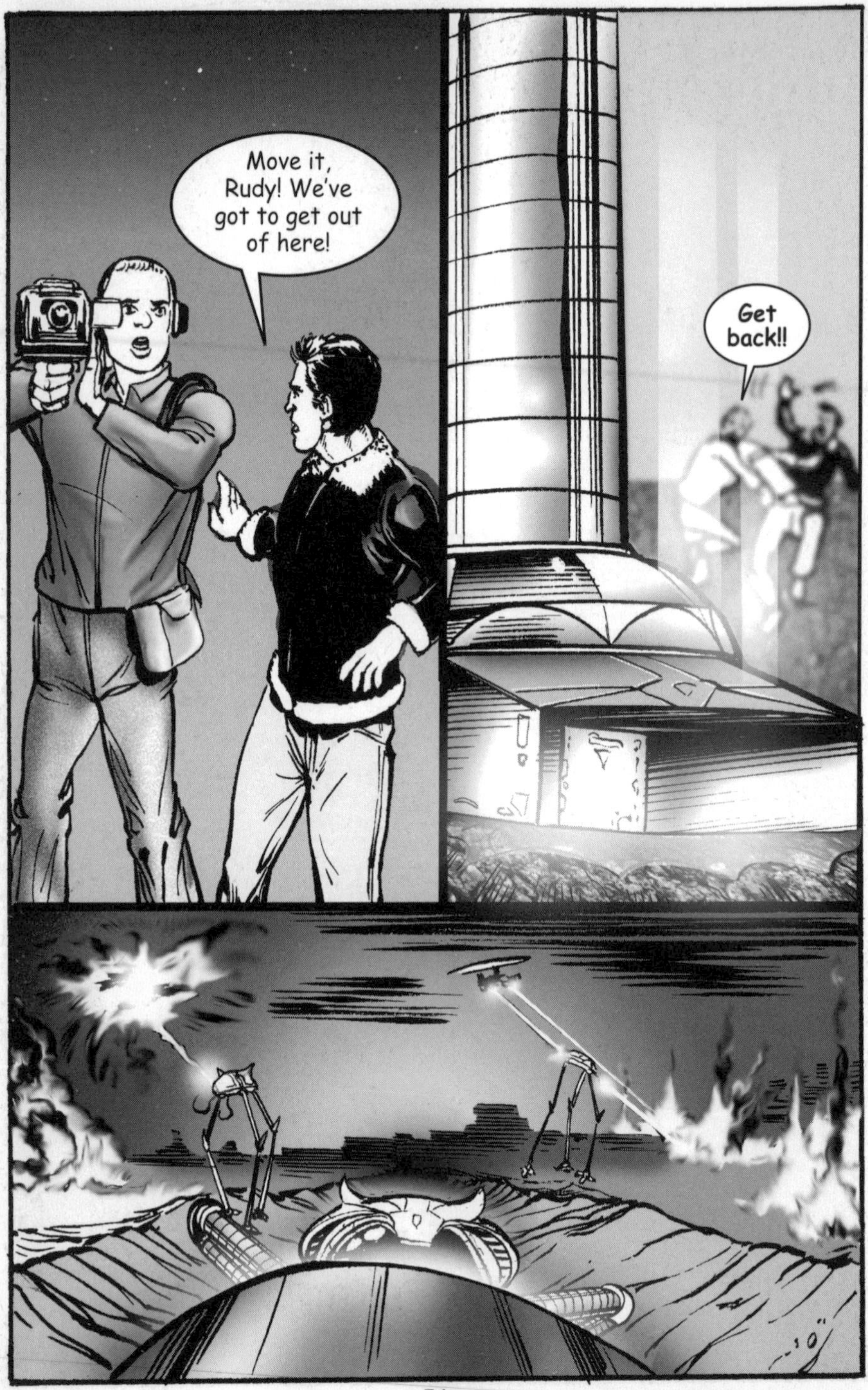
Move it, Rudy! We've got to get out of here!
Get back!!

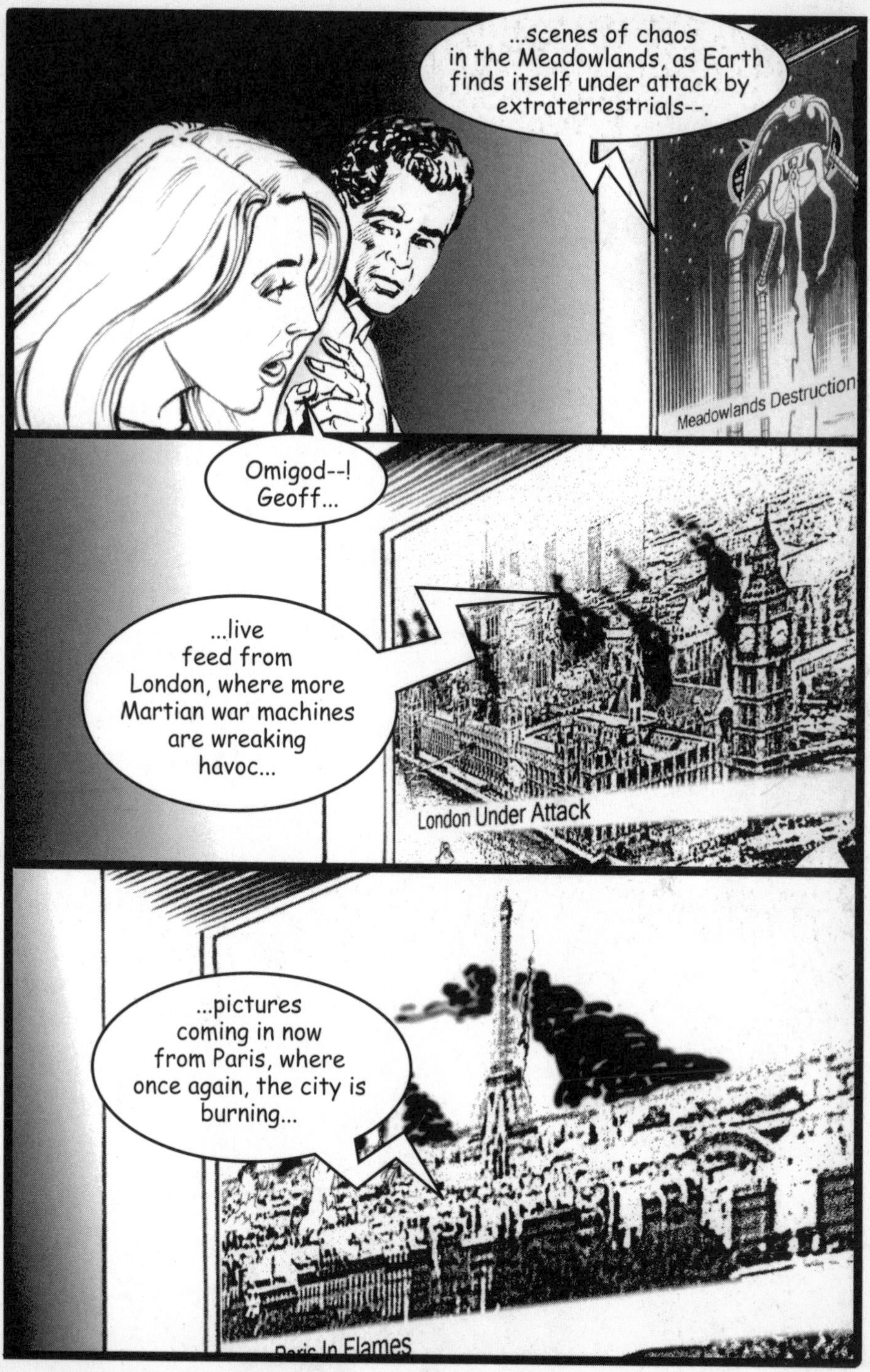
...scenes of chaos in the Meadowlands, as Earth finds itself under attack by extraterrestrials--.
Meadowlands Destruction
Omigod--! Geoff...
...live feed from London, where more Martian war machines are wreaking havoc...
London Under Attack
...pictures coming in now from Paris, where once again, the city is burning...
Paris In Flames

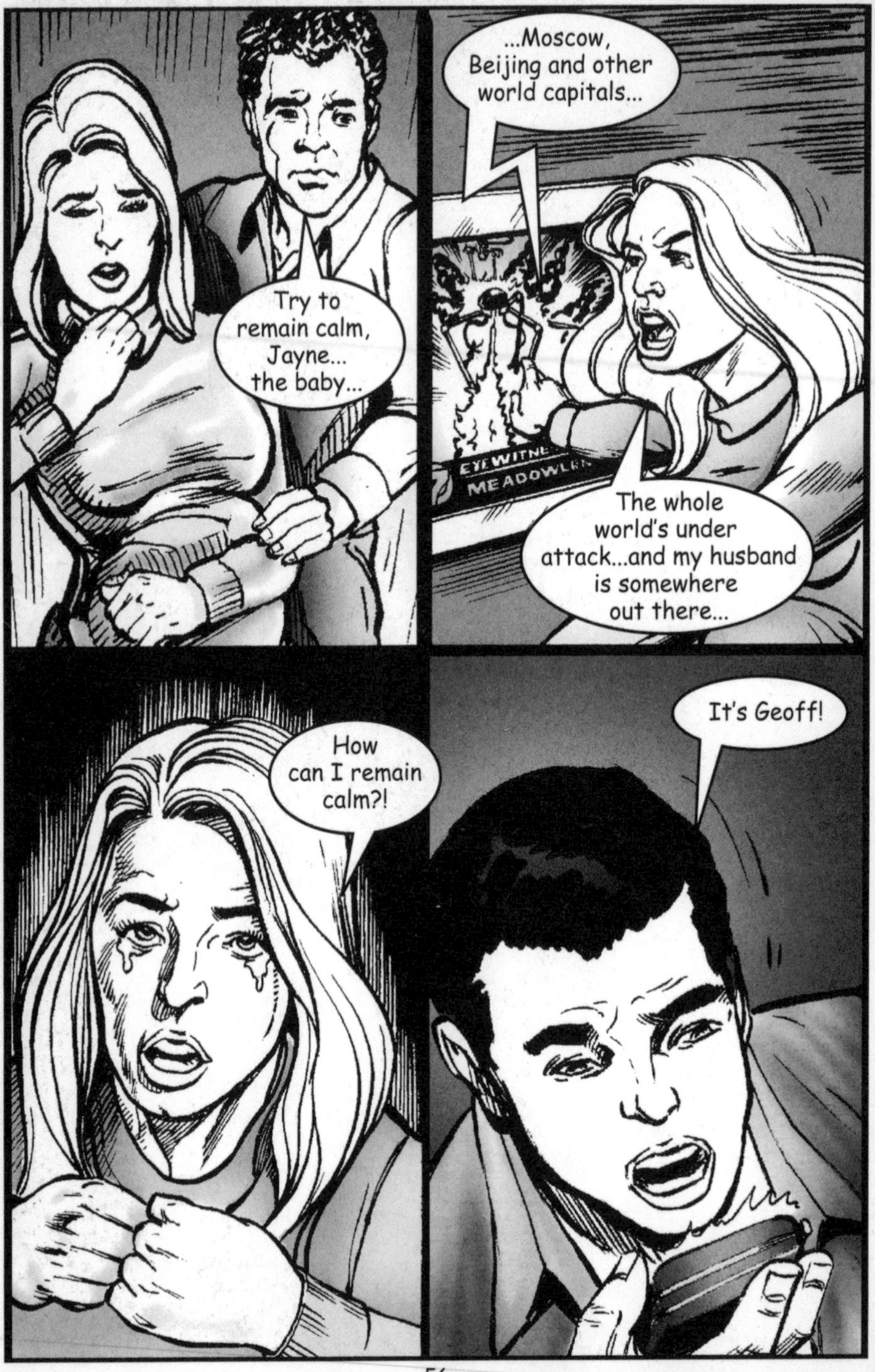
Try to remain calm, Jayne... the baby...
...Moscow, Beijing and other world capitals...
EYEWITNE
MEADOWL
The whole world's under attack...and my husband is somewhere out there...
How can I remain calm?!
It's Geoff!

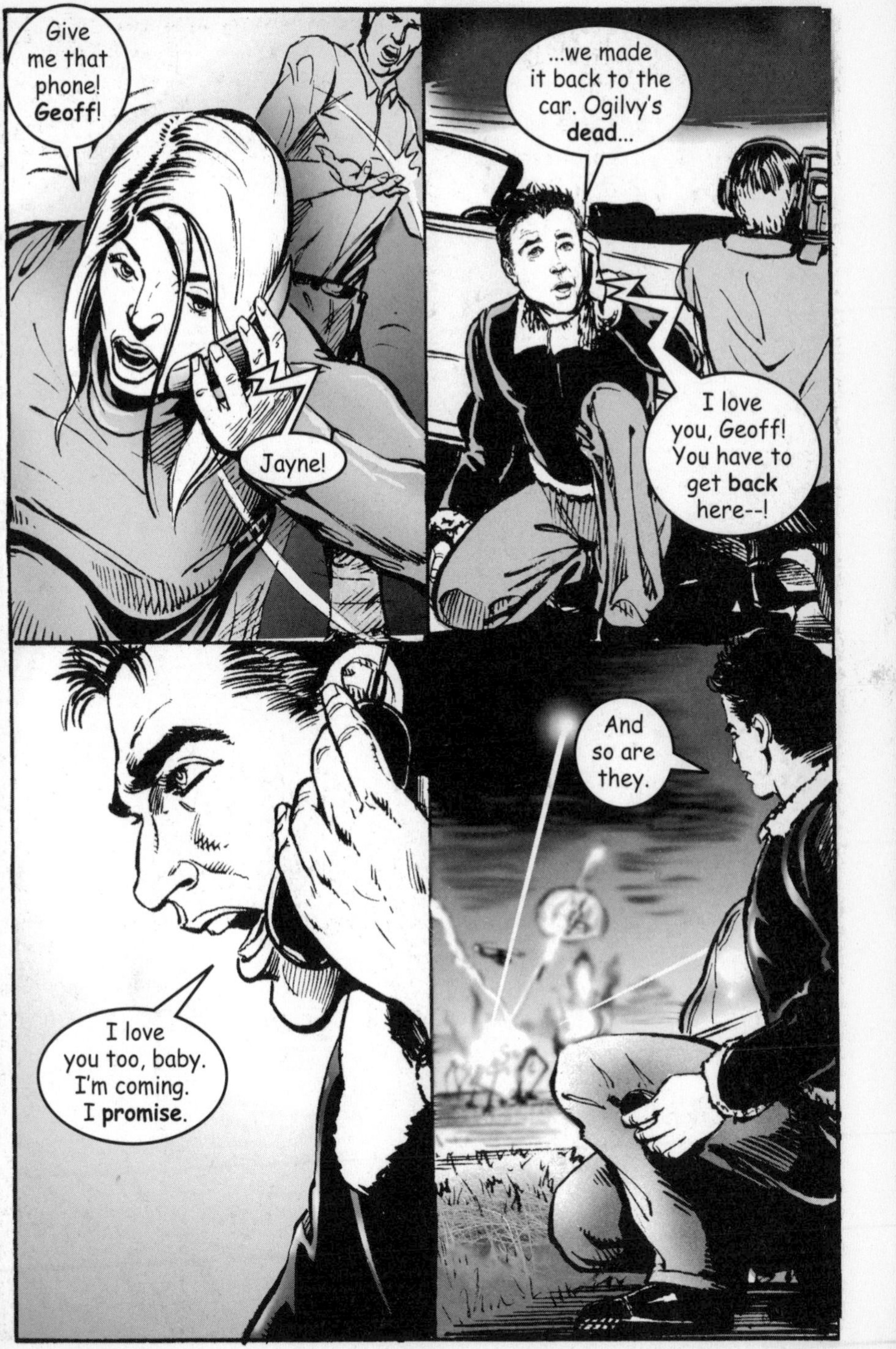
Give me that phone! Geoff!
Jayne!
...we made it back to the car. Ogilvy's dead...
I love you, Geoff! You have to get back here--!
I love you too, baby. I'm coming. I promise.
And so are they.

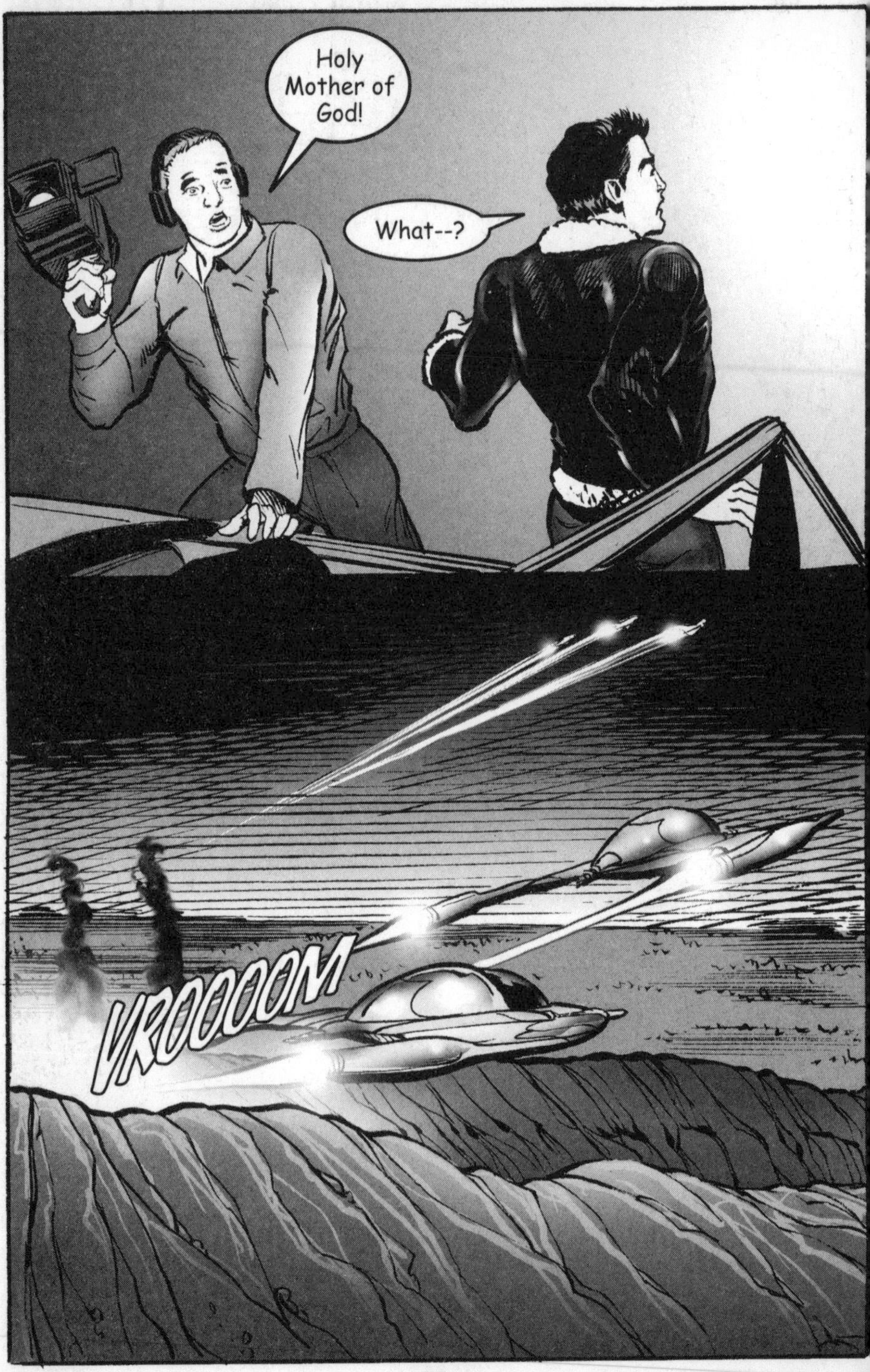
Holy Mother of God!
What--?
VROOOOOM

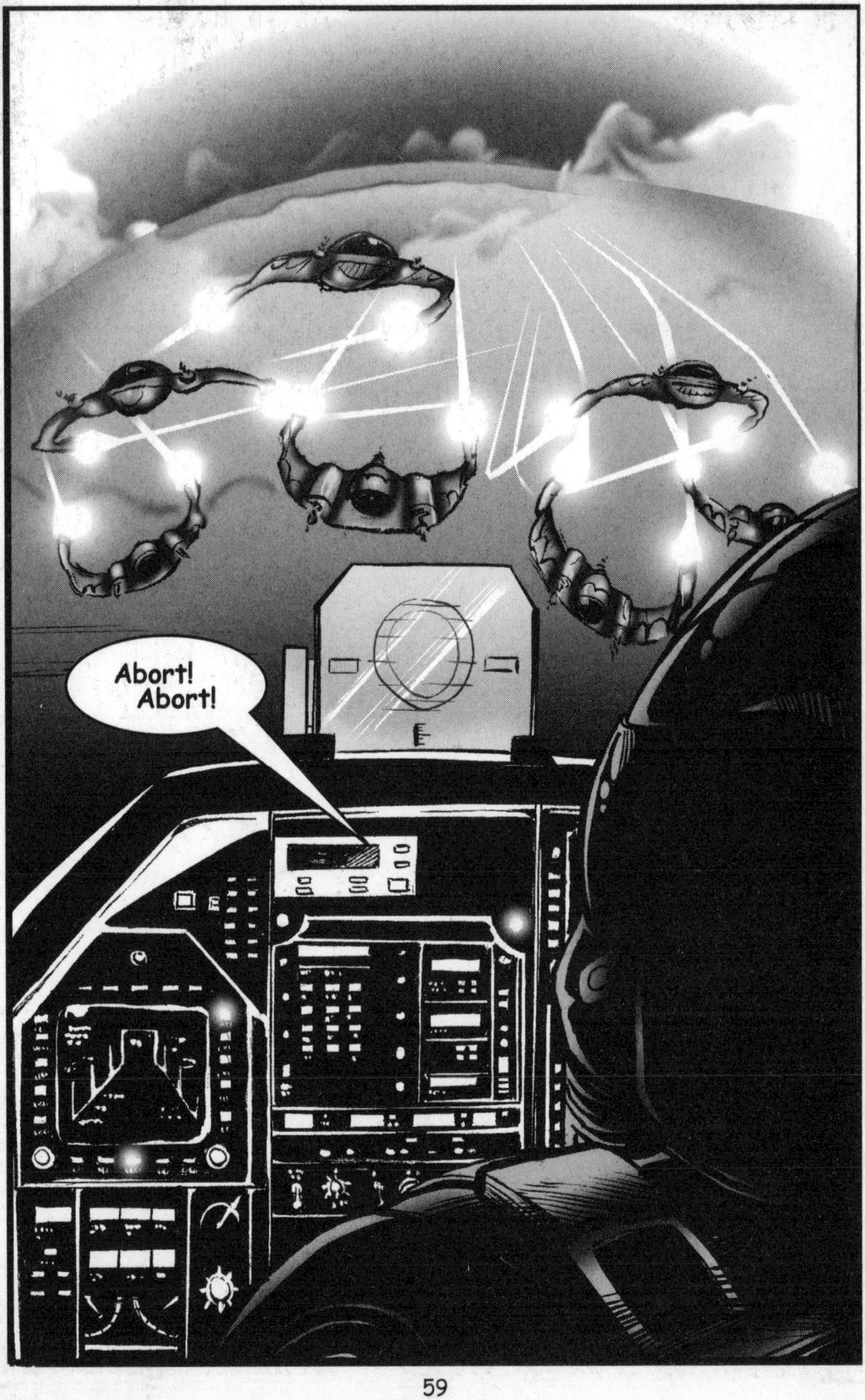
Abort! Abort!

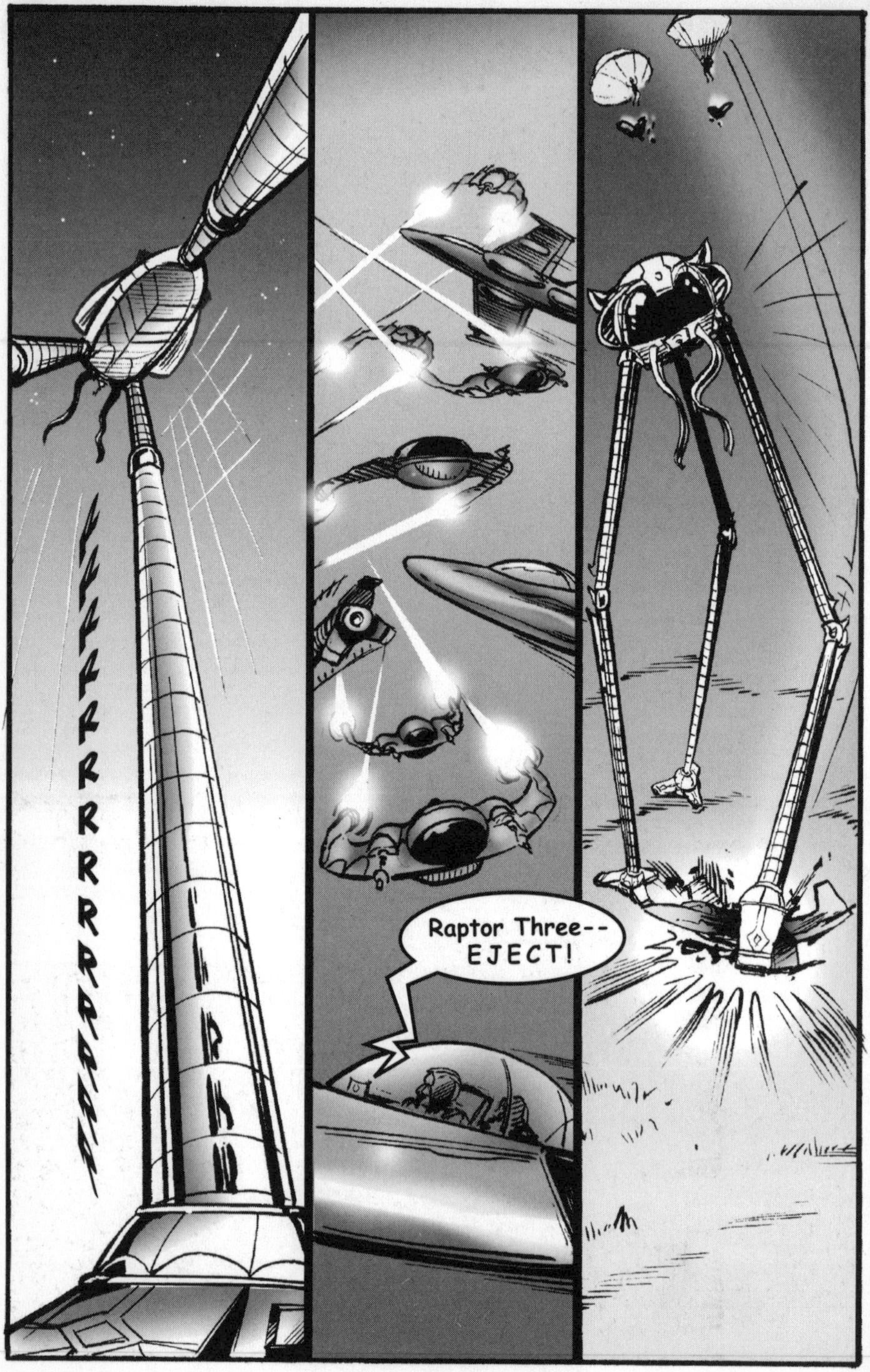
Raptor Three--
EJECT!

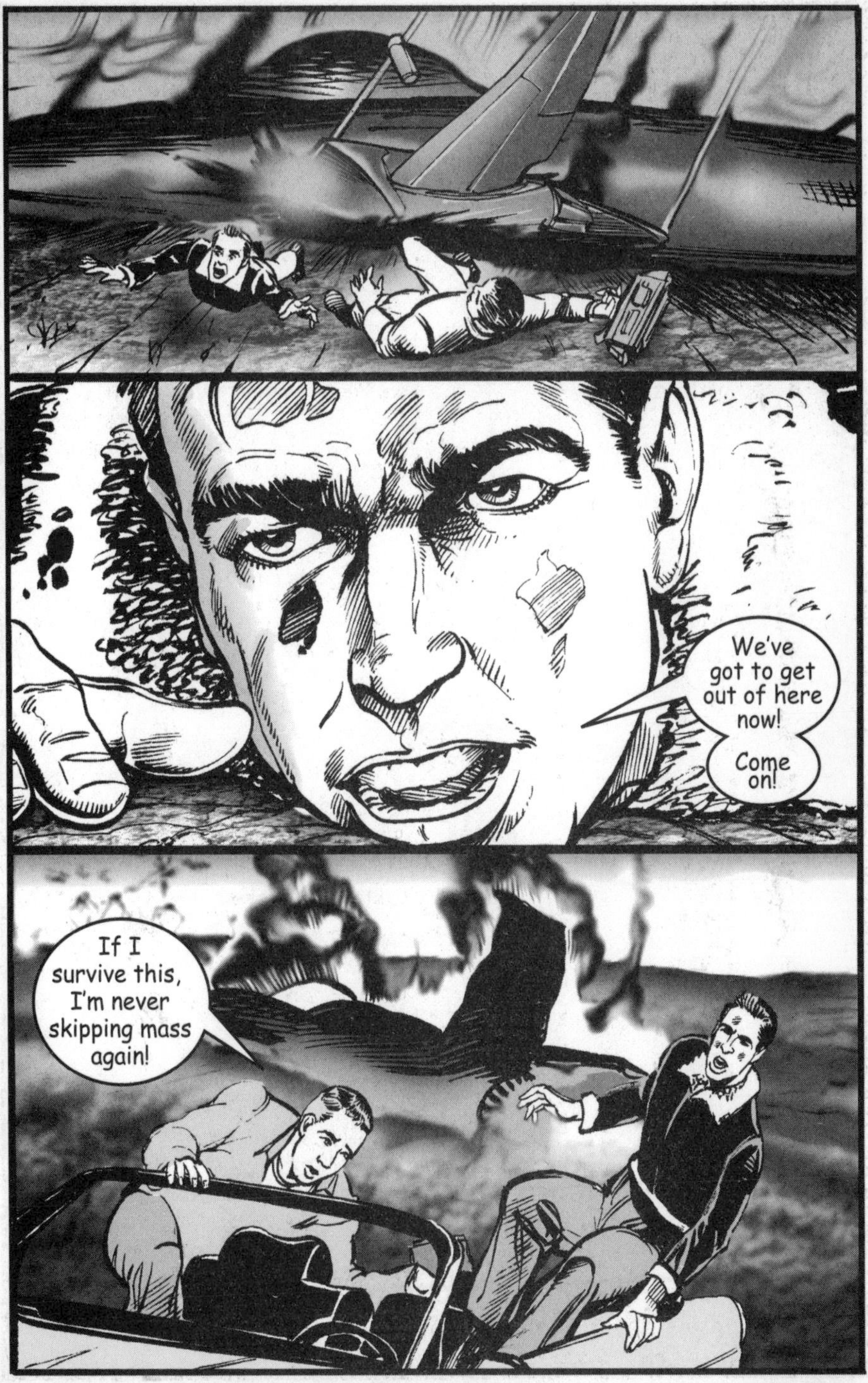
We've got to get out of here now!
Come on!
If I survive this, I'm never skipping mass again!

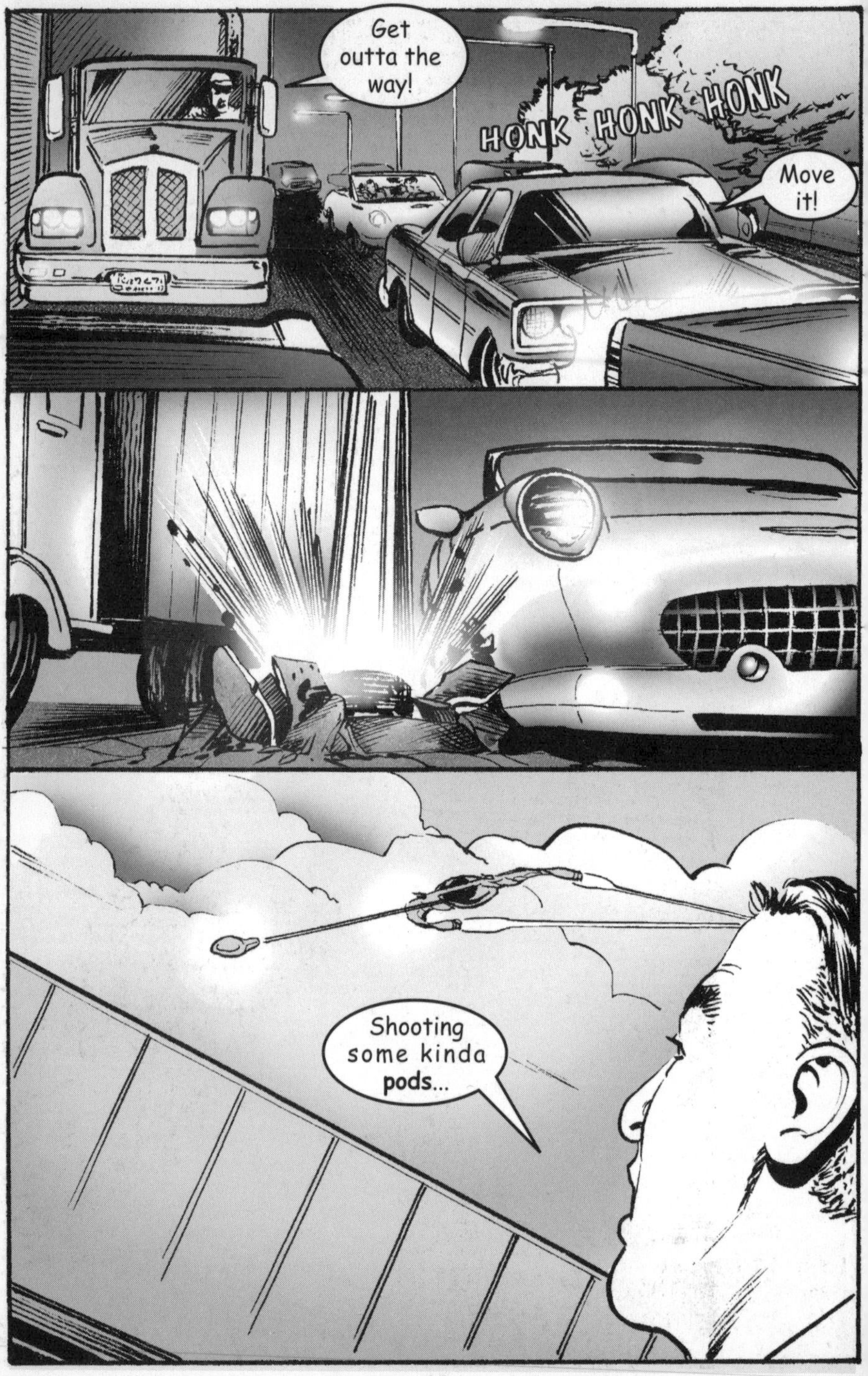
Get outta the way!
HONK HONK HONK
Move it!
Shooting some kinda **pods**...

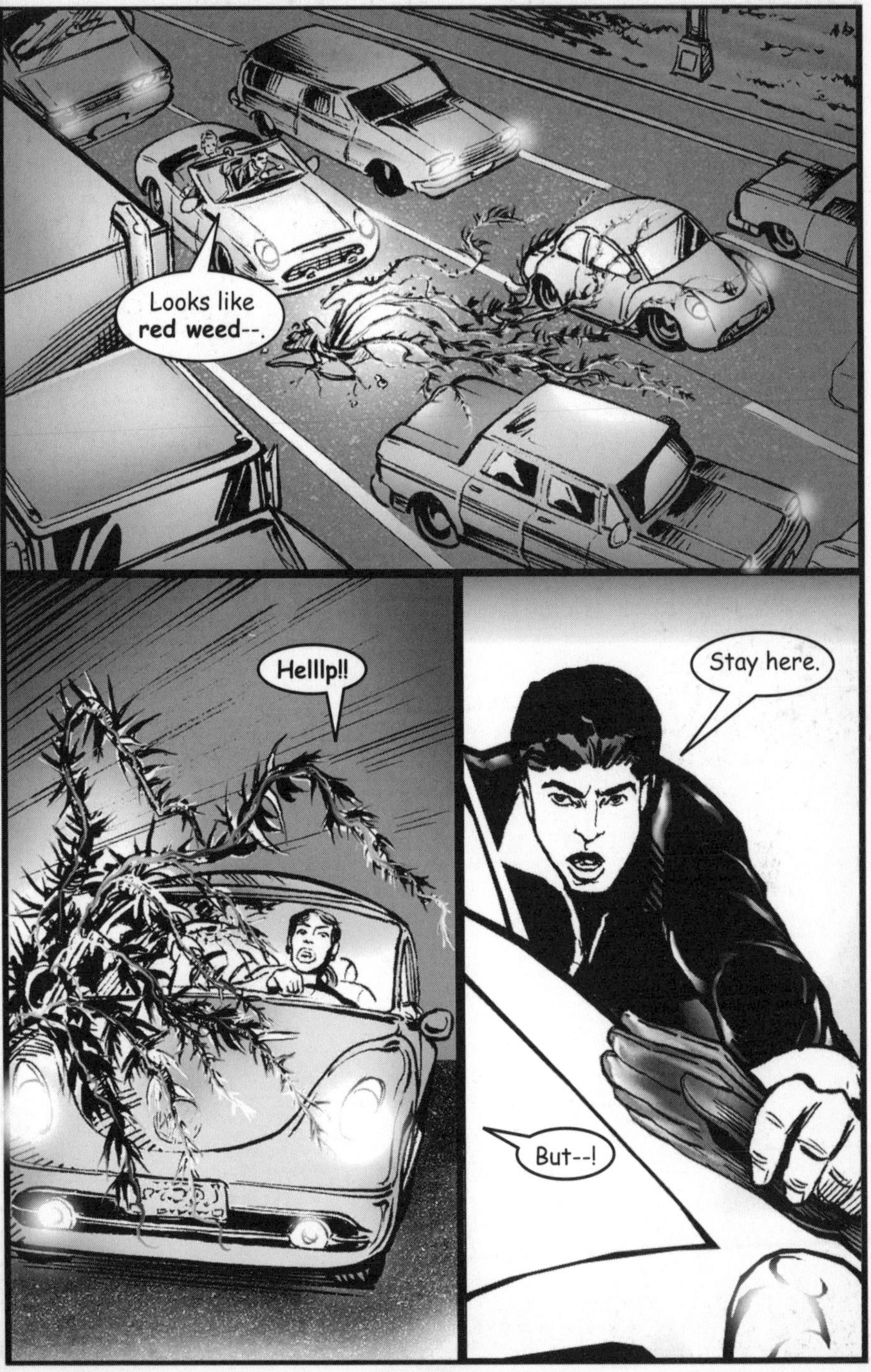
Looks like red weed--.
Helllp!!
Stay here.
But--!

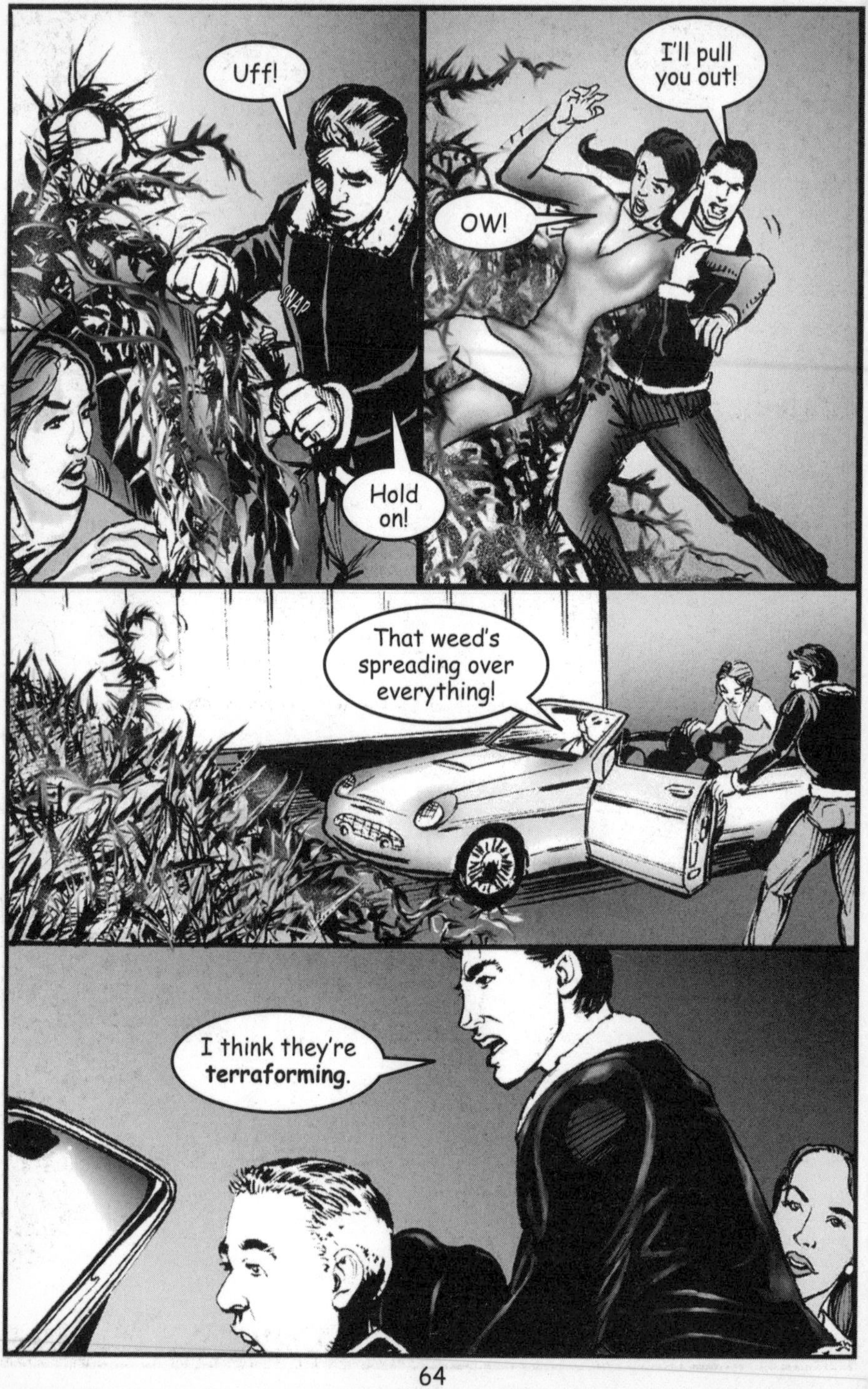
Uff!
SNAP
Hold on!
I'll pull you out!
OW!
That weed's spreading over everything!
I think they're **terraforming**.

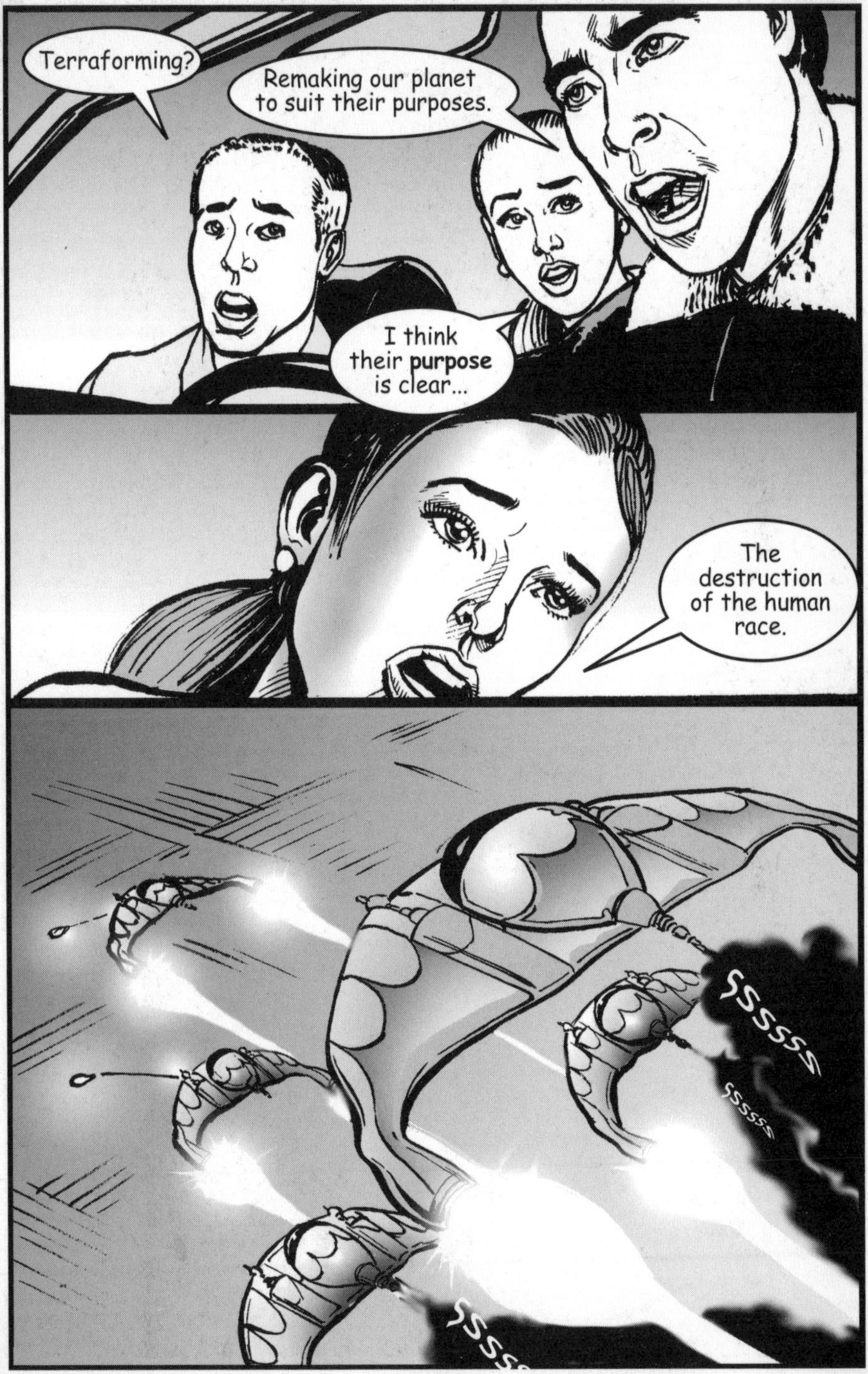
Terraforming?
Remaking our planet to suit their purposes.
I think their **purpose** is clear...
The destruction of the human race.
SSSSSS
SSSSSS

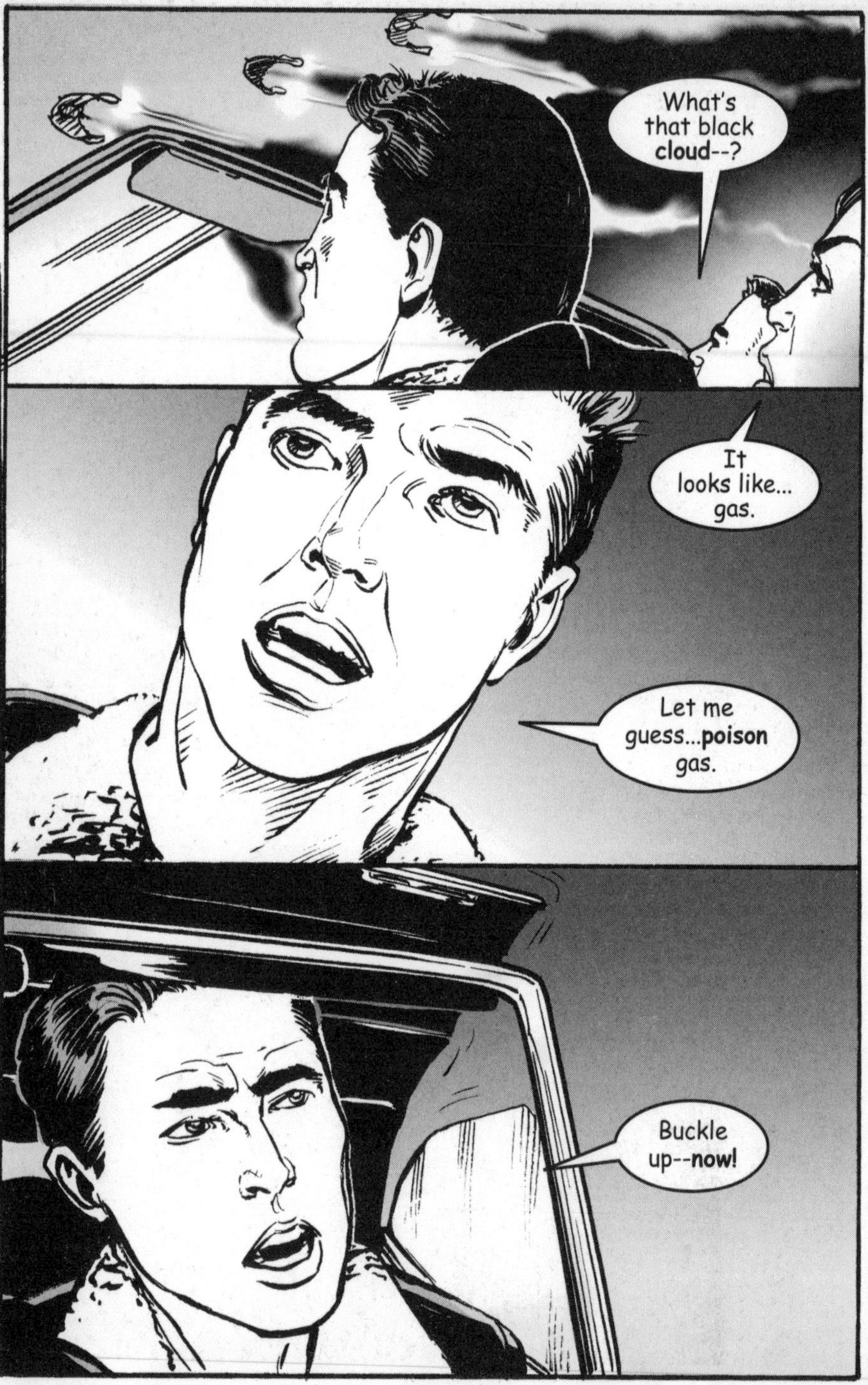
What's that black cloud--?
It looks like... gas.
Let me guess...poison gas.
Buckle up--now!

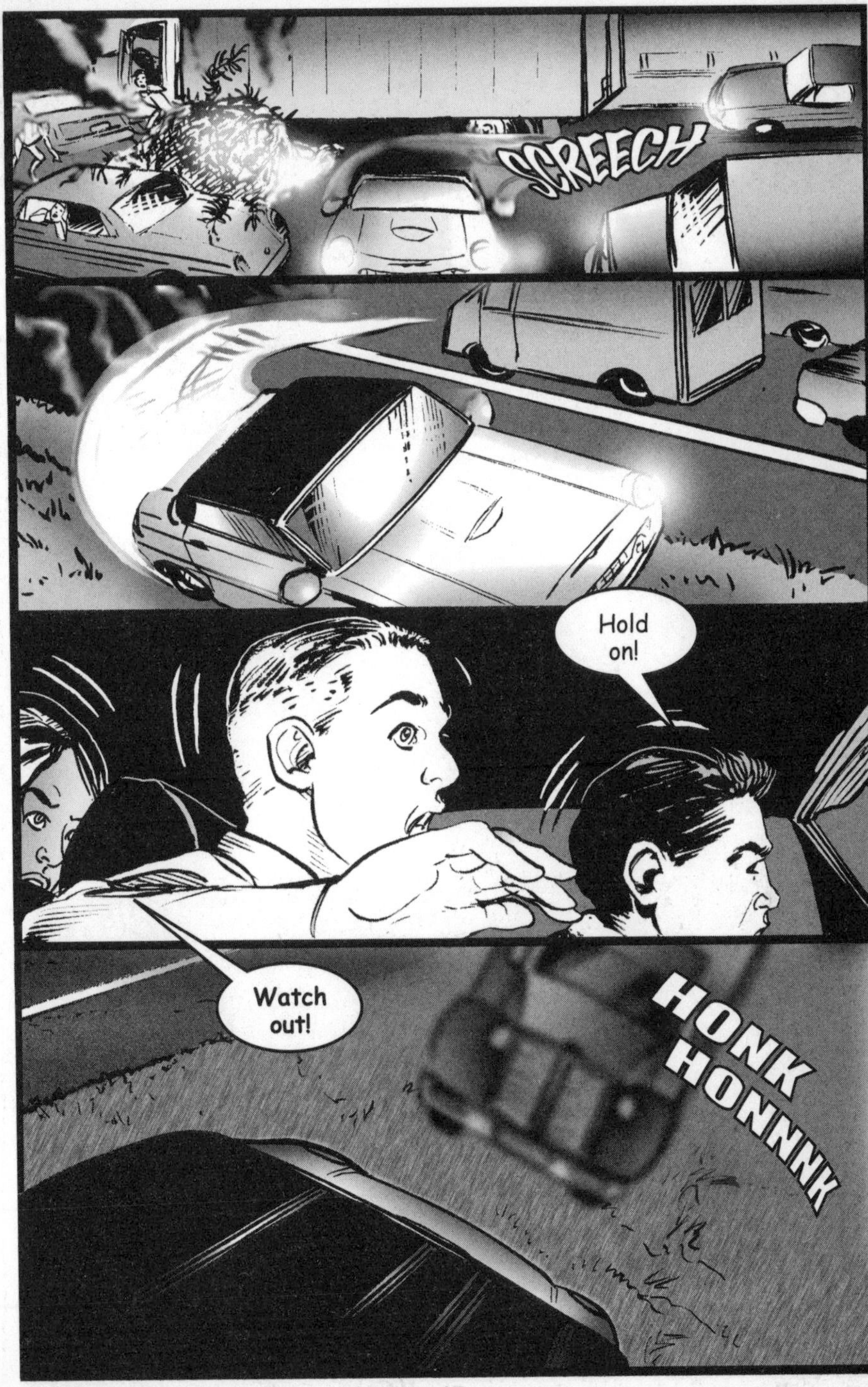
SCREECH
Hold on!
Watch out!
HONK HONNNNK

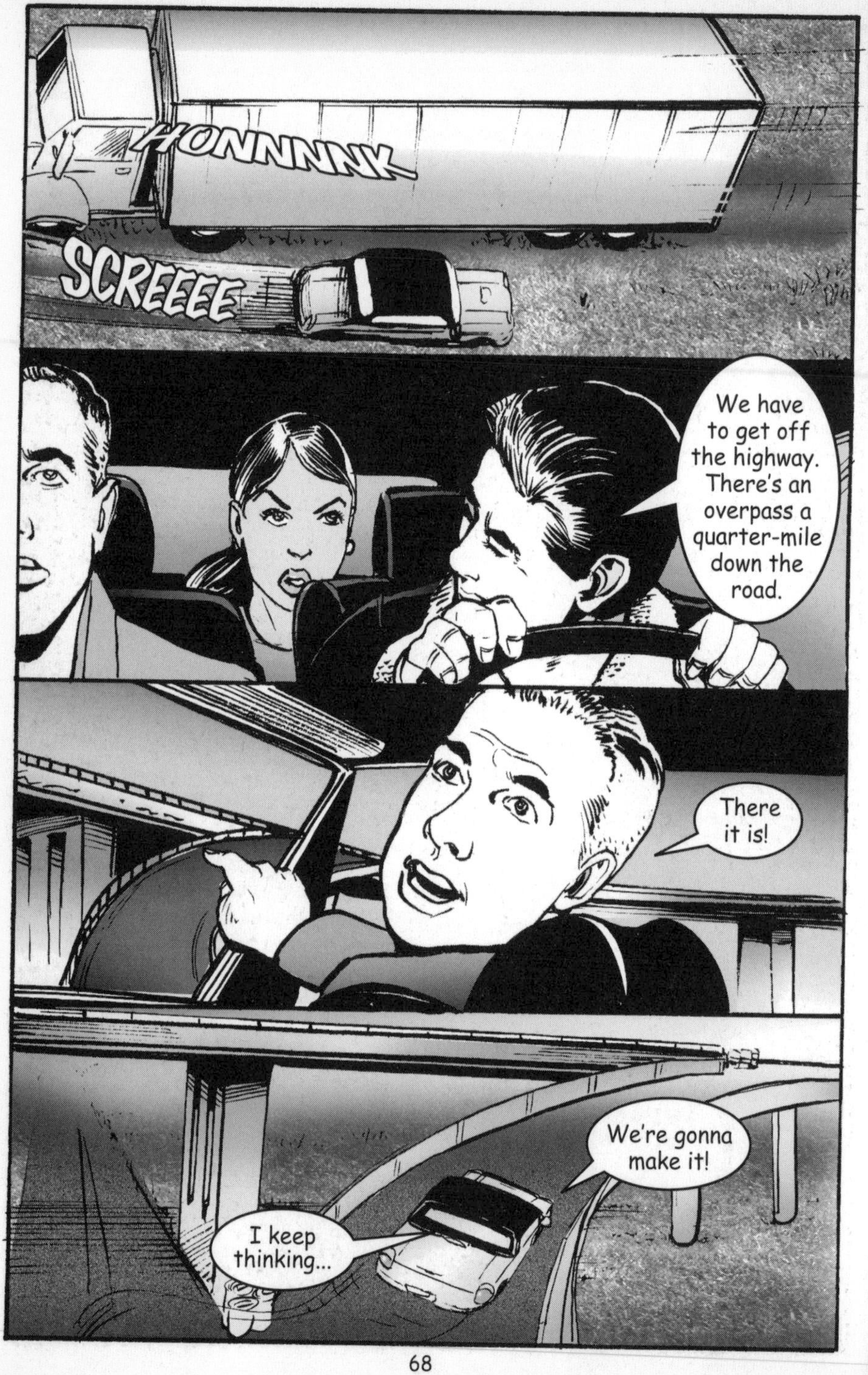
HONNNNNK
SCREEEEE
We have to get off the highway. There's an overpass a quarter-mile down the road.
There it is!
We're gonna make it!
I keep thinking...

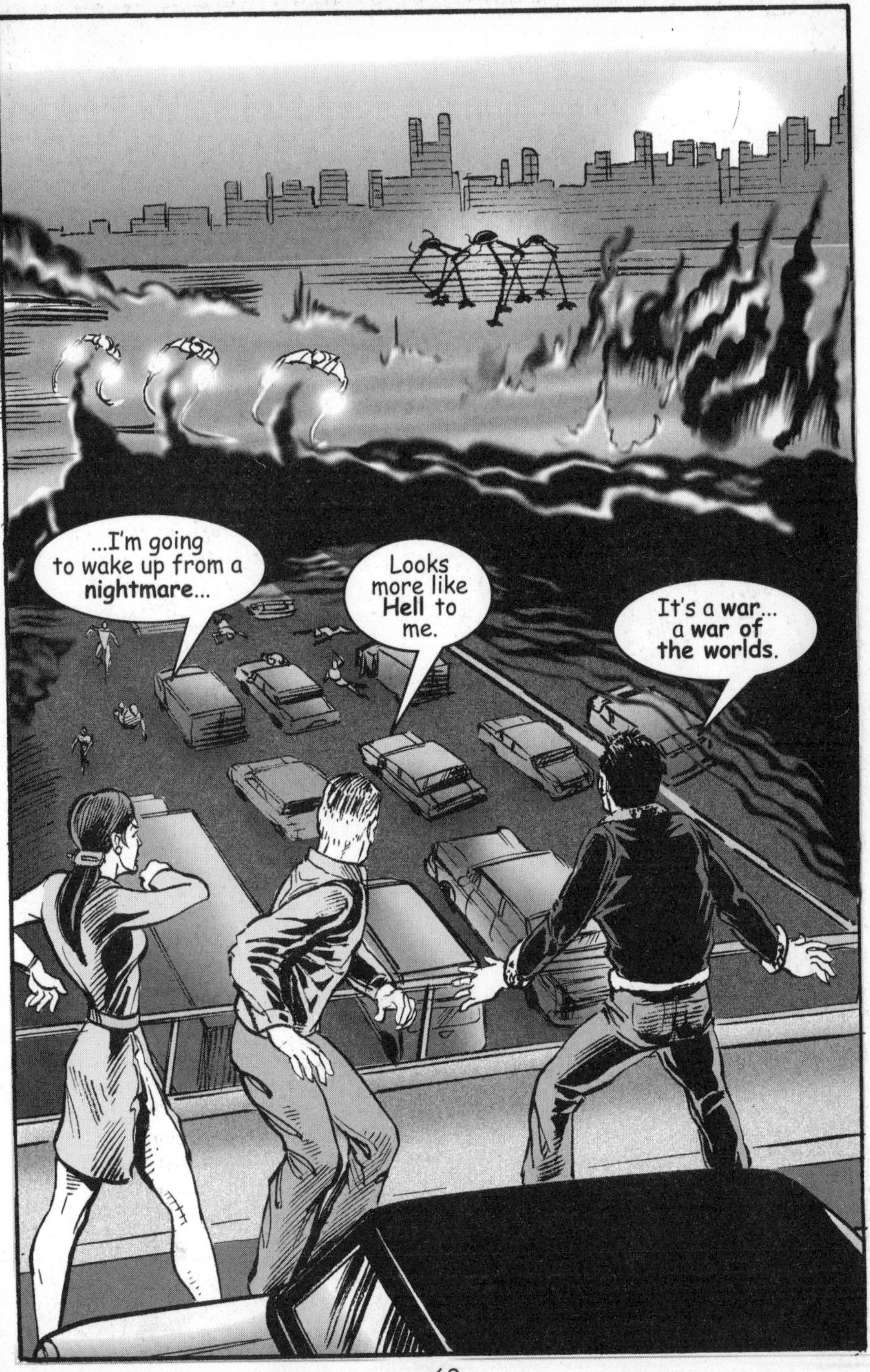
...I'm going to wake up from a nightmare...
Looks more like Hell to me.
It's a war... a war of the worlds.

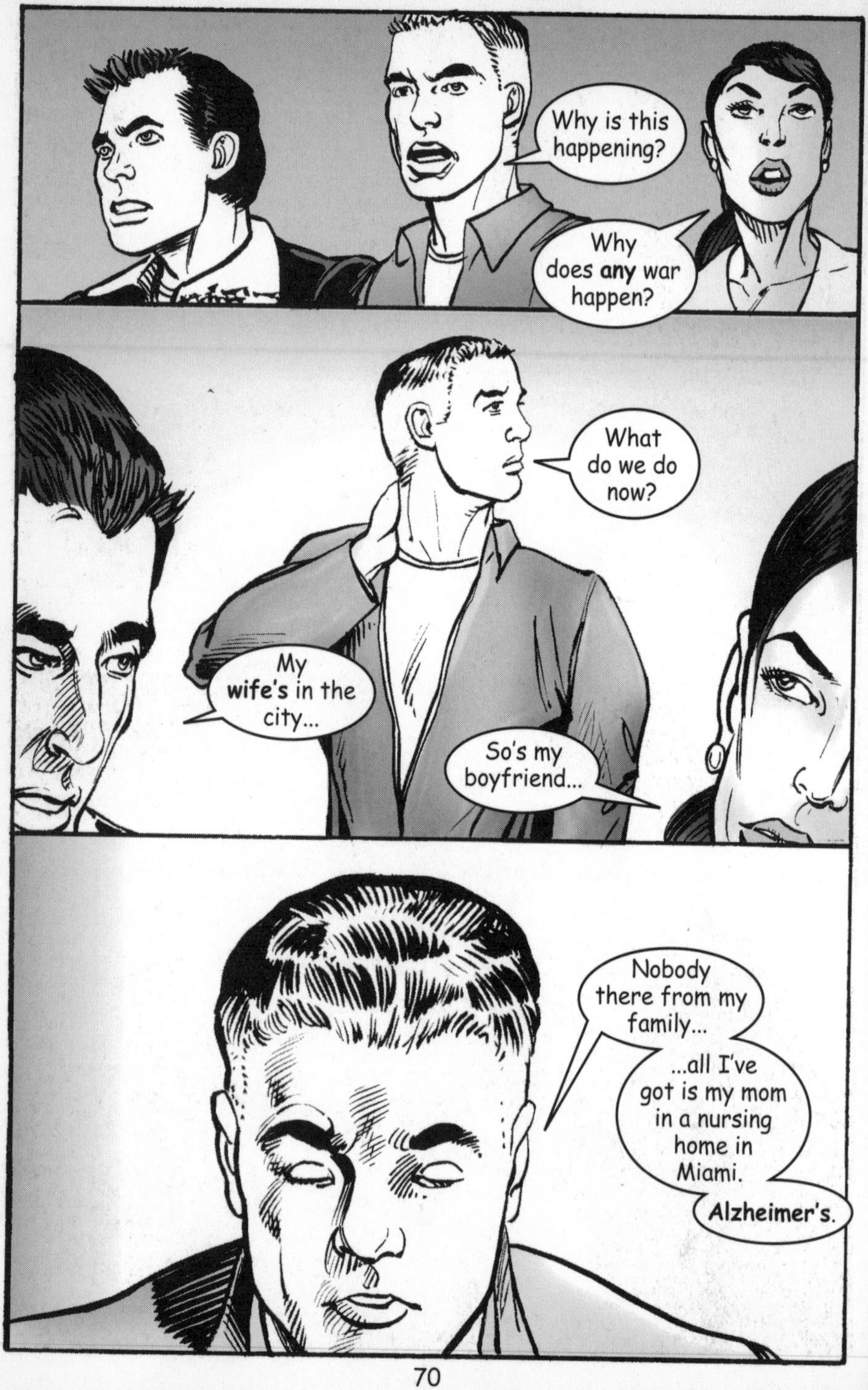
Why is this happening?
Why does **any** war happen?
What do we do now?
My **wife's** in the city...
So's my boyfriend...
Nobody there from my family...
...all I've got is my mom in a nursing home in Miami.
Alzheimer's.

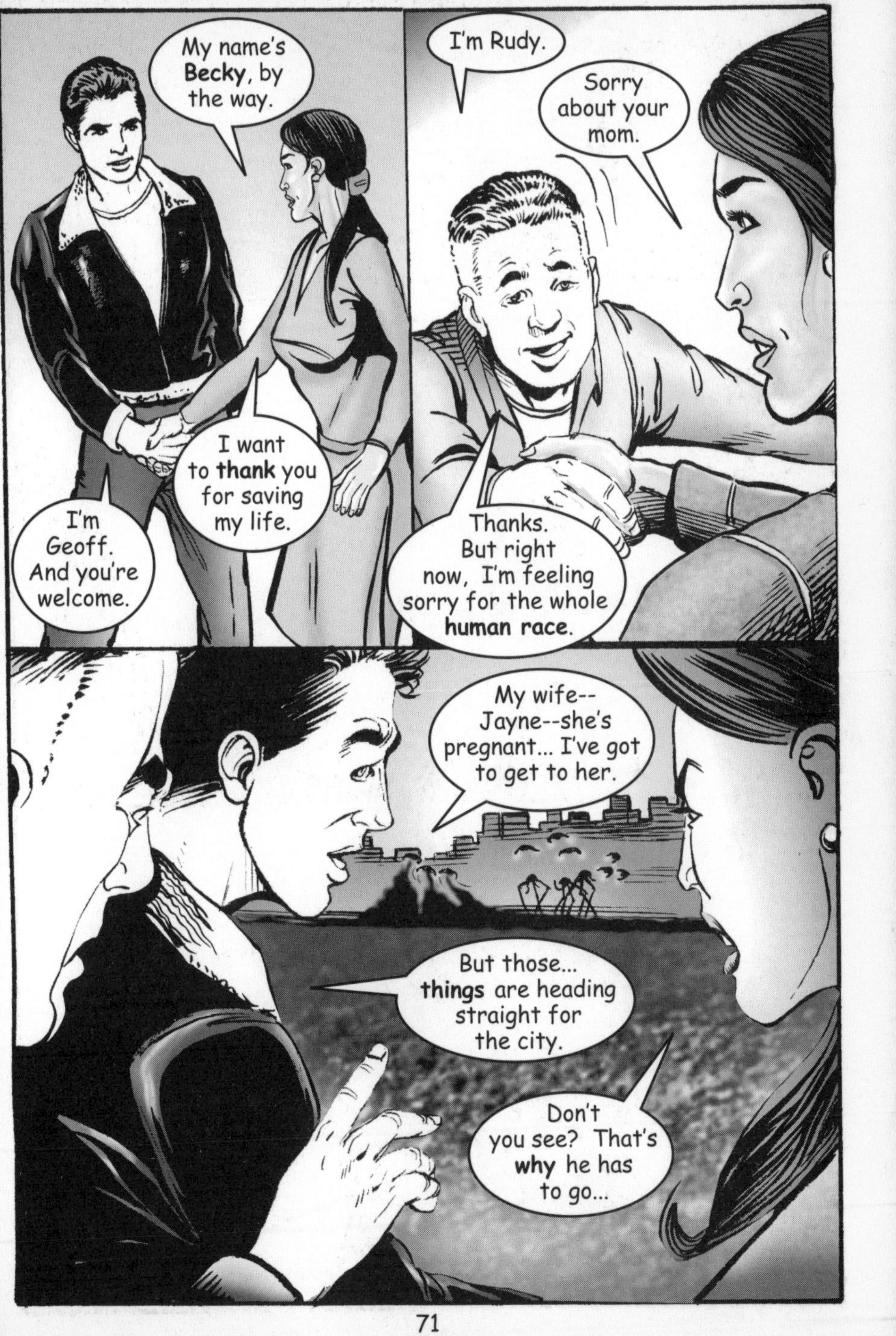
My name's **Becky**, by the way.
I want to **thank** you for saving my life.
I'm Geoff. And you're welcome.
I'm Rudy.
Sorry about your mom.
Thanks. But right now, I'm feeling sorry for the whole **human race**.
My wife-- Jayne--she's pregnant... I've got to get to her.
But those... **things** are heading straight for the city.
Don't you see? That's **why** he has to go...

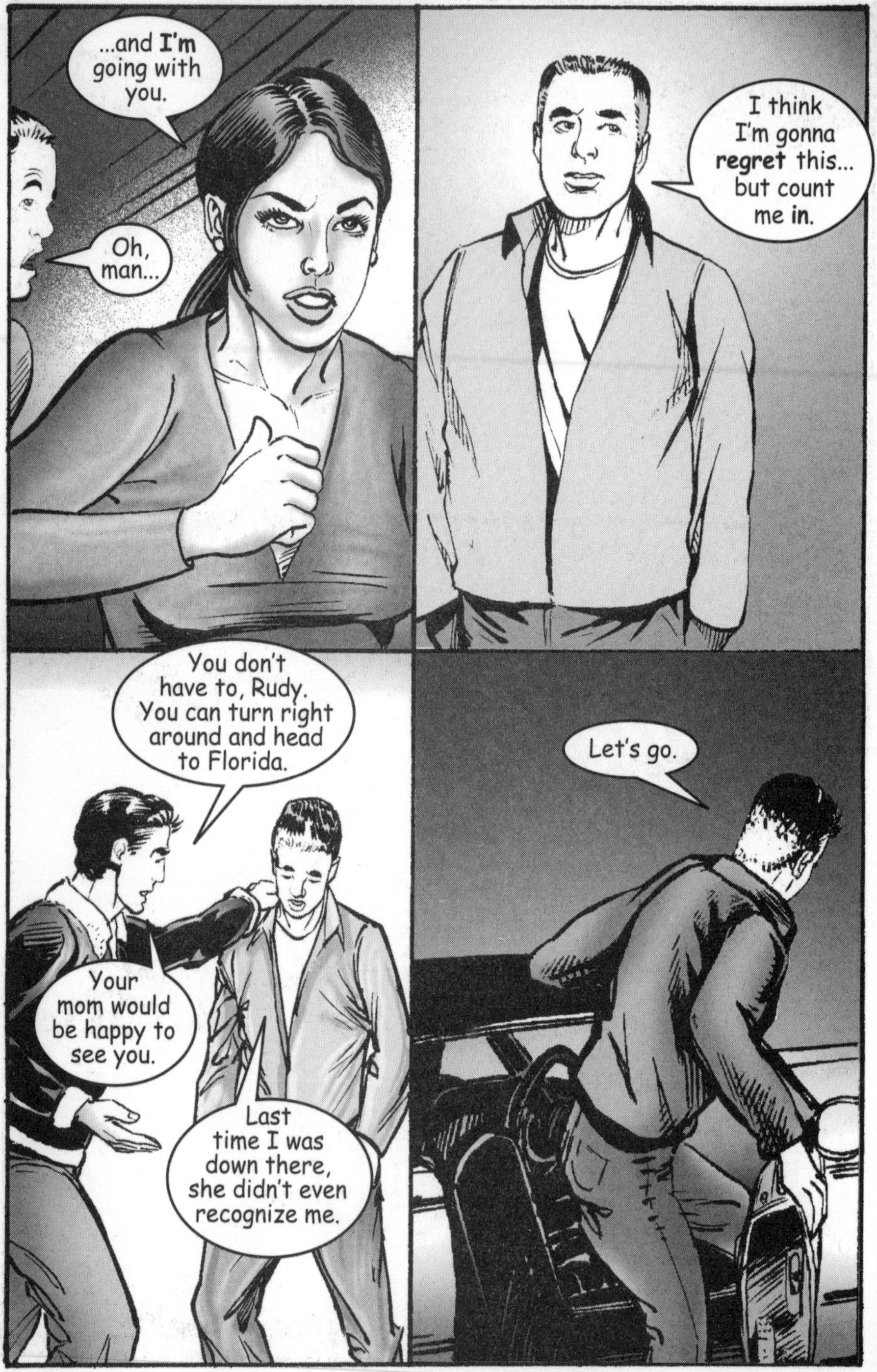
...and **I'm** going with you.
Oh, man...
I think I'm gonna **regret** this... but count me **in**.
You don't have to, Rudy. You can turn right around and head to Florida.
Your mom would be happy to see you.
Last time I was down there, she didn't even recognize me.
Let's go.

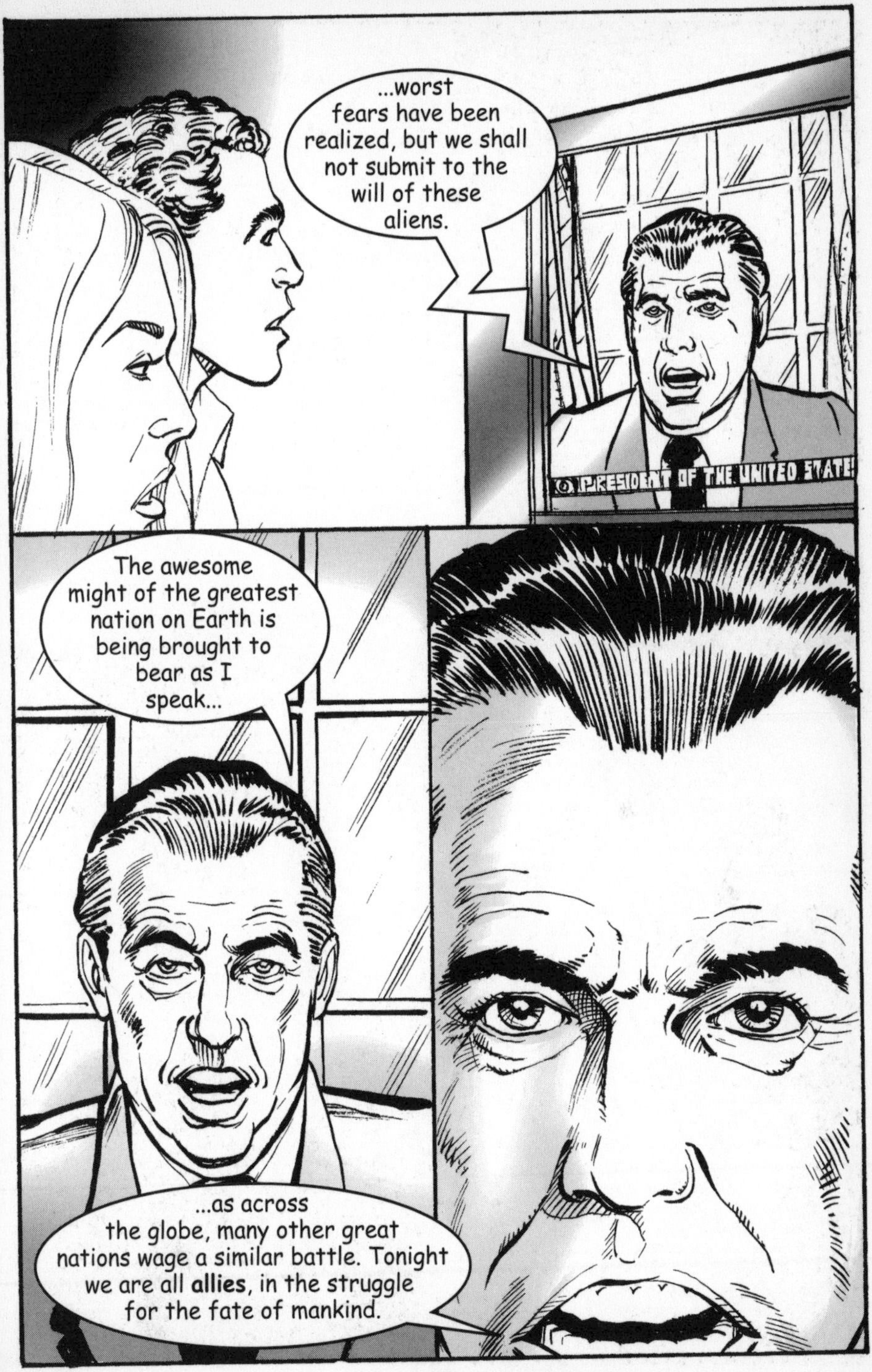
...worst fears have been realized, but we shall not submit to the will of these aliens.
PRESIDENT OF THE UNITED STATE
The awesome might of the greatest nation on Earth is being brought to bear as I speak...
...as across the globe, many other great nations wage a similar battle. Tonight we are all **allies**, in the struggle for the fate of mankind.

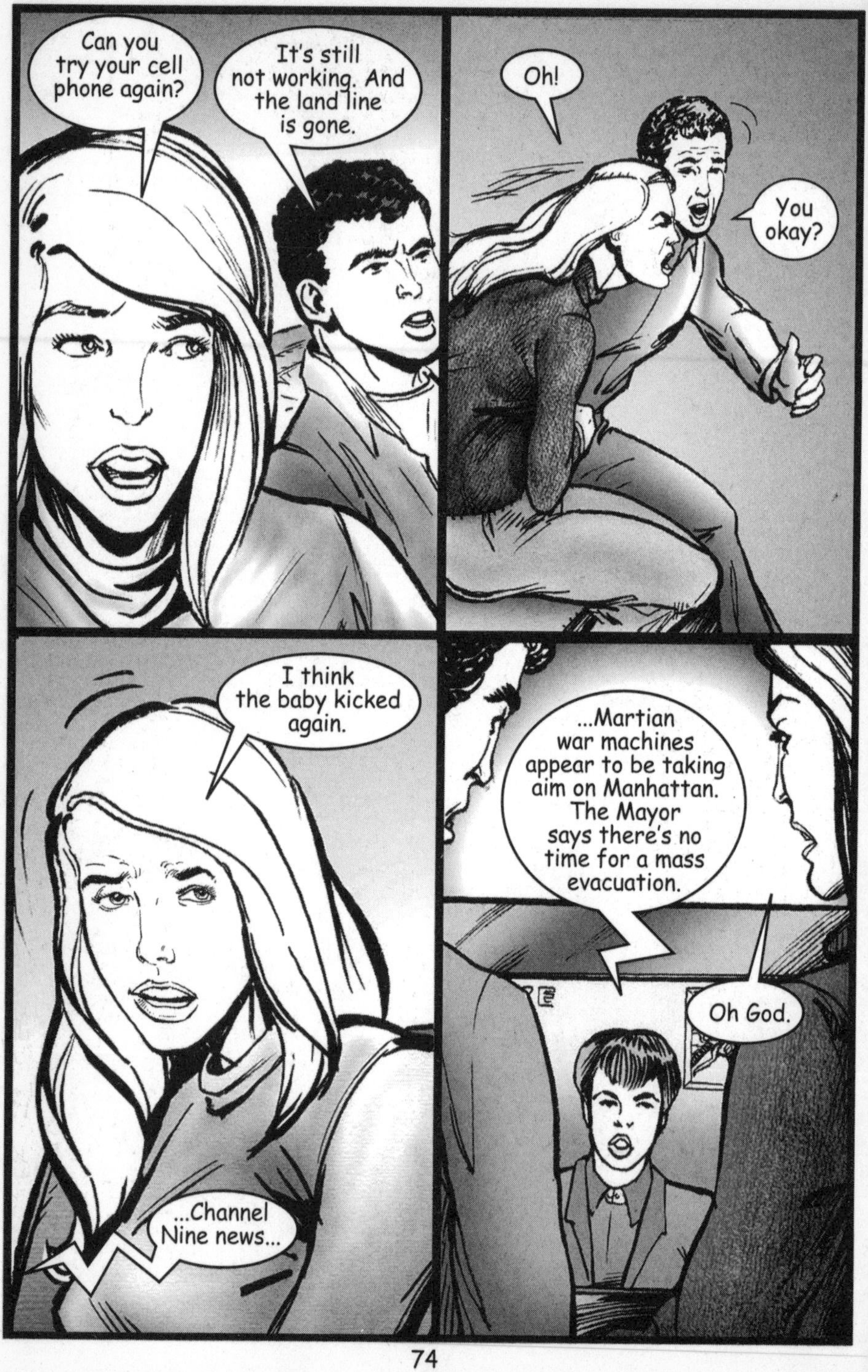
Can you try your cell phone again?
It's still not working. And the land line is gone.
Oh!
You okay?
I think the baby kicked again.
...Channel Nine news...
...Martian war machines appear to be taking aim on Manhattan. The Mayor says there's no time for a mass evacuation.
Oh God.

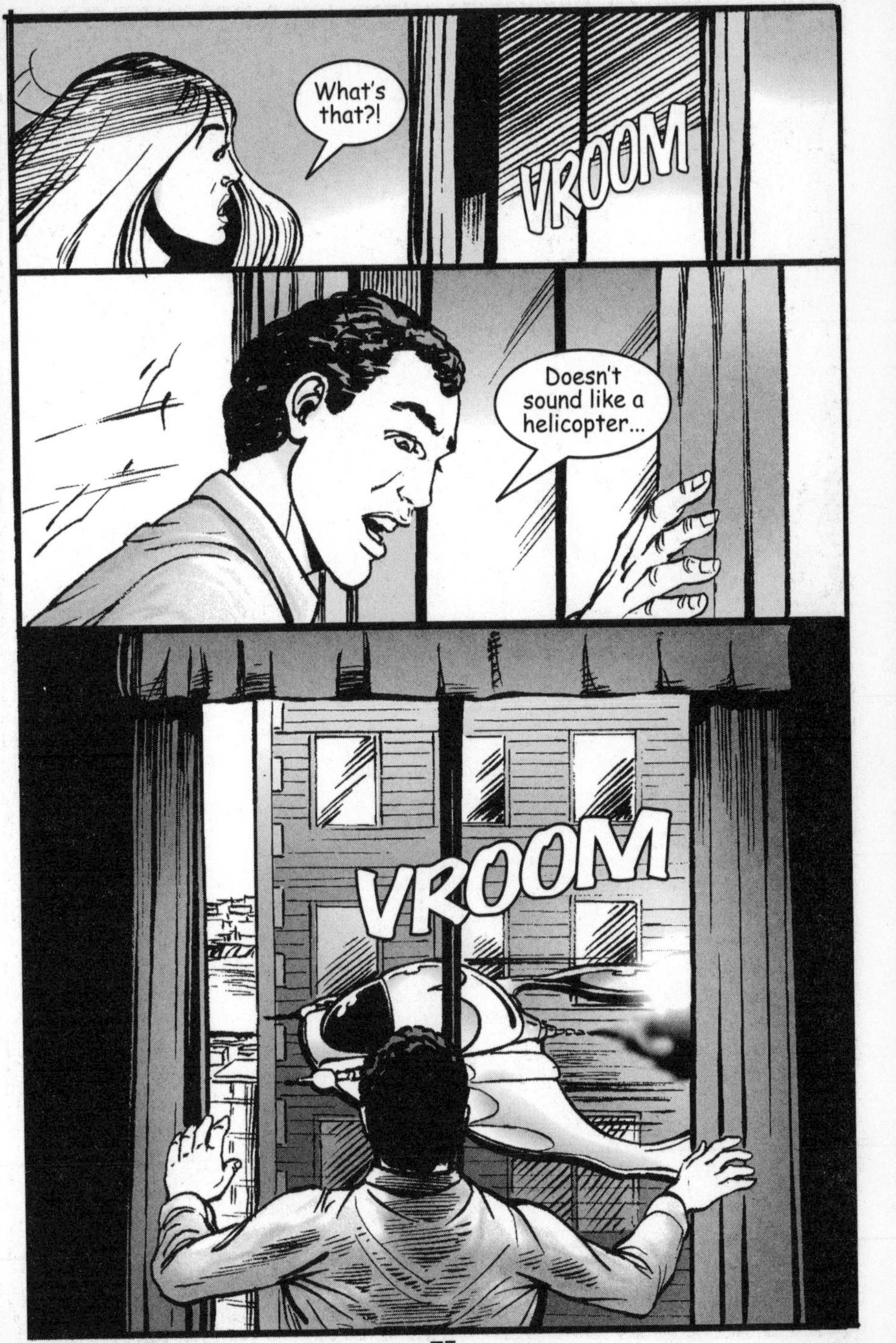
What's that?!
VROOM
Doesn't sound like a helicopter...
VROOM

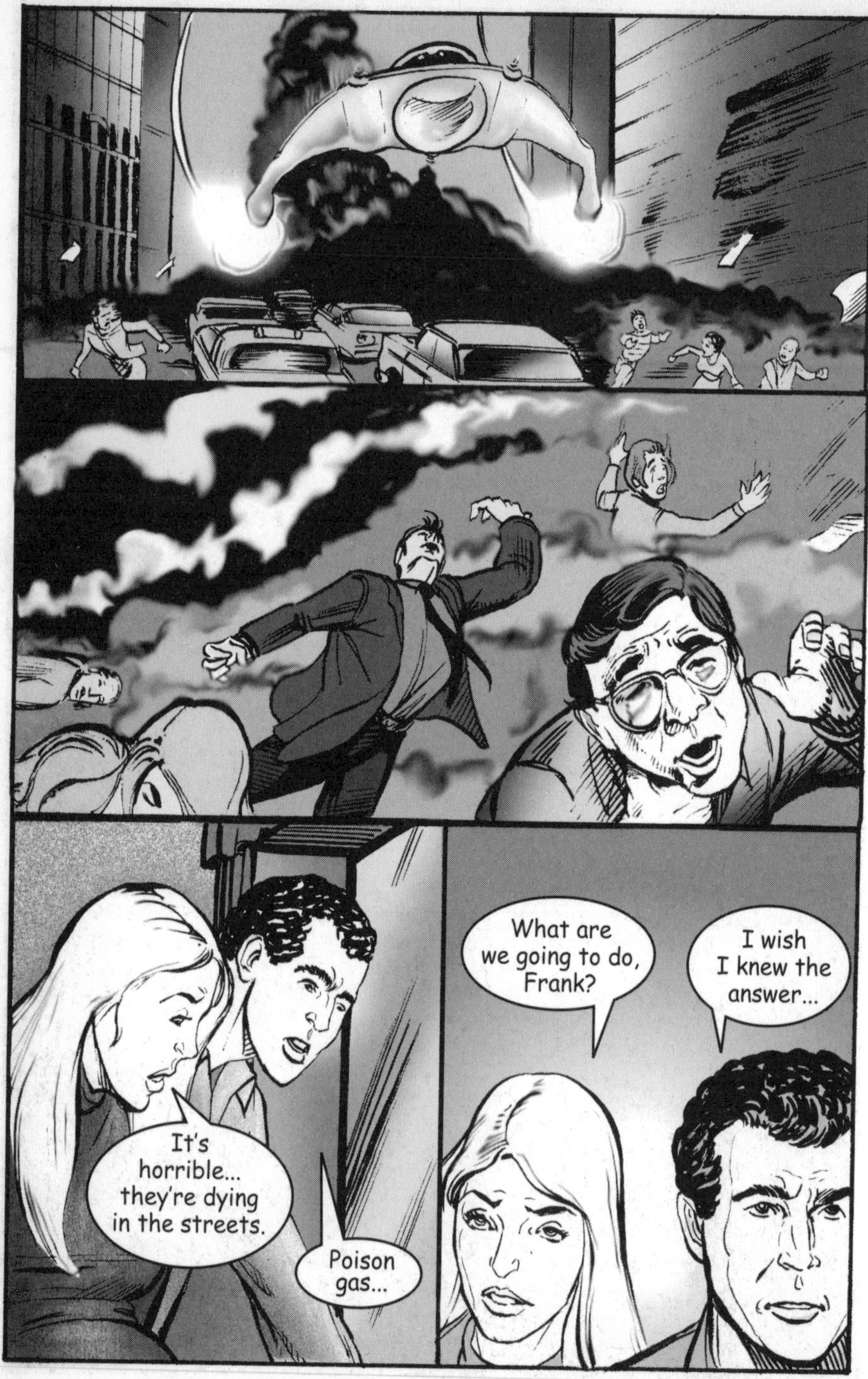
It's horrible... they're dying in the streets.
Poison gas...
What are we going to do, Frank?
I wish I knew the answer...

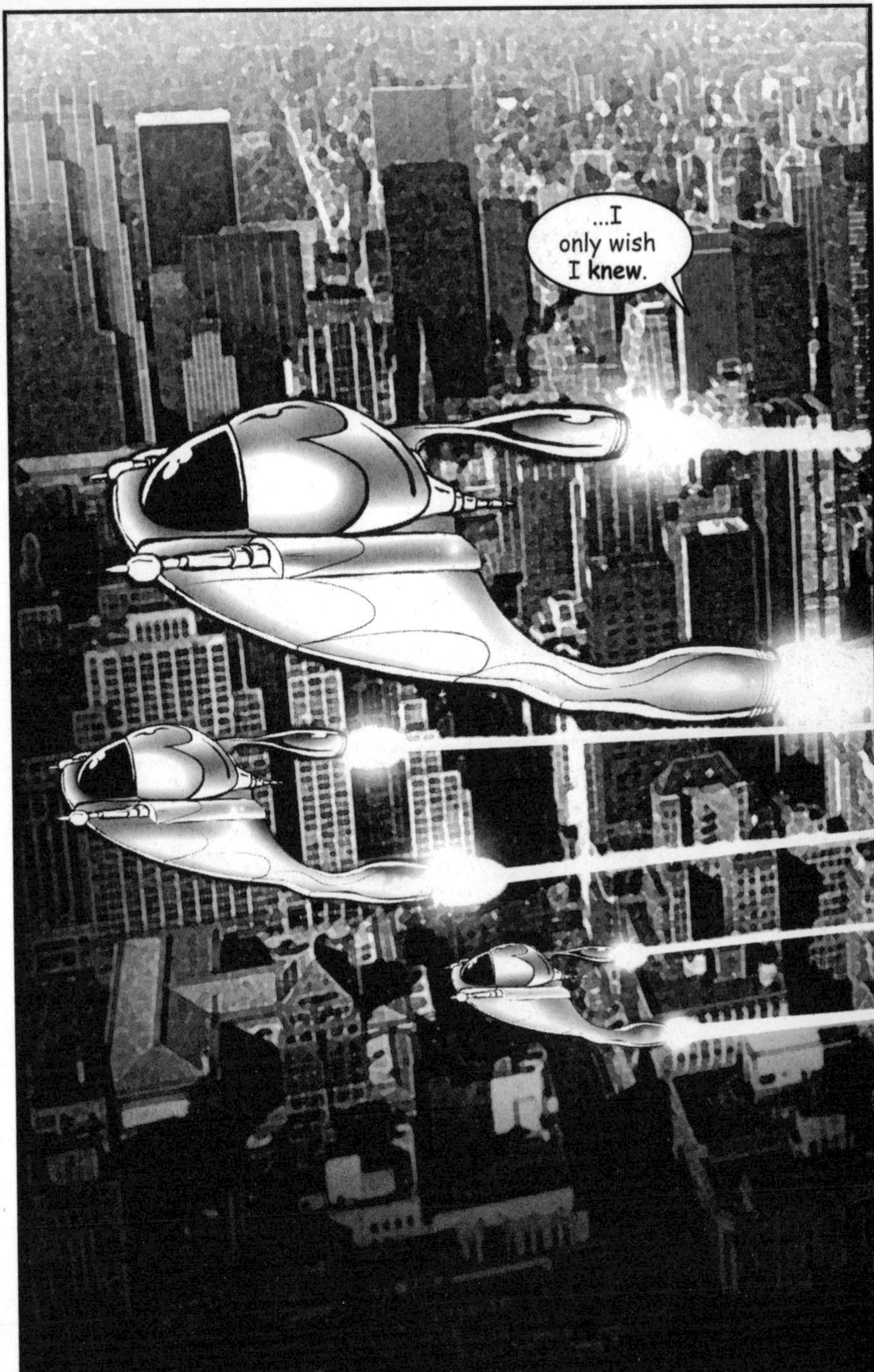
...I only wish I knew.

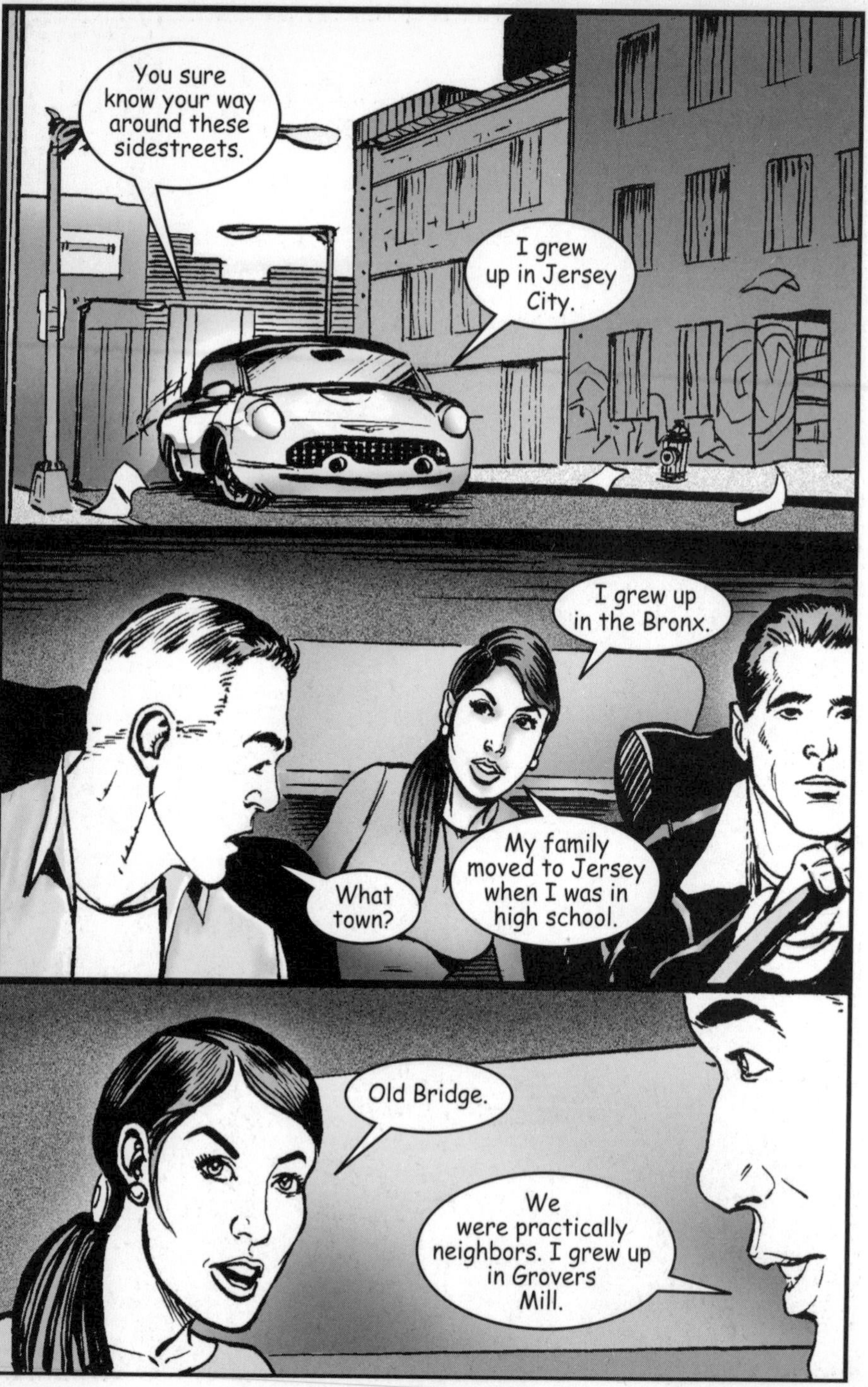
You sure know your way around these sidestreets.
I grew up in Jersey City.
I grew up in the Bronx.
My family moved to Jersey when I was in high school.
What town?
Old Bridge.
We were practically neighbors. I grew up in Grovers Mill.

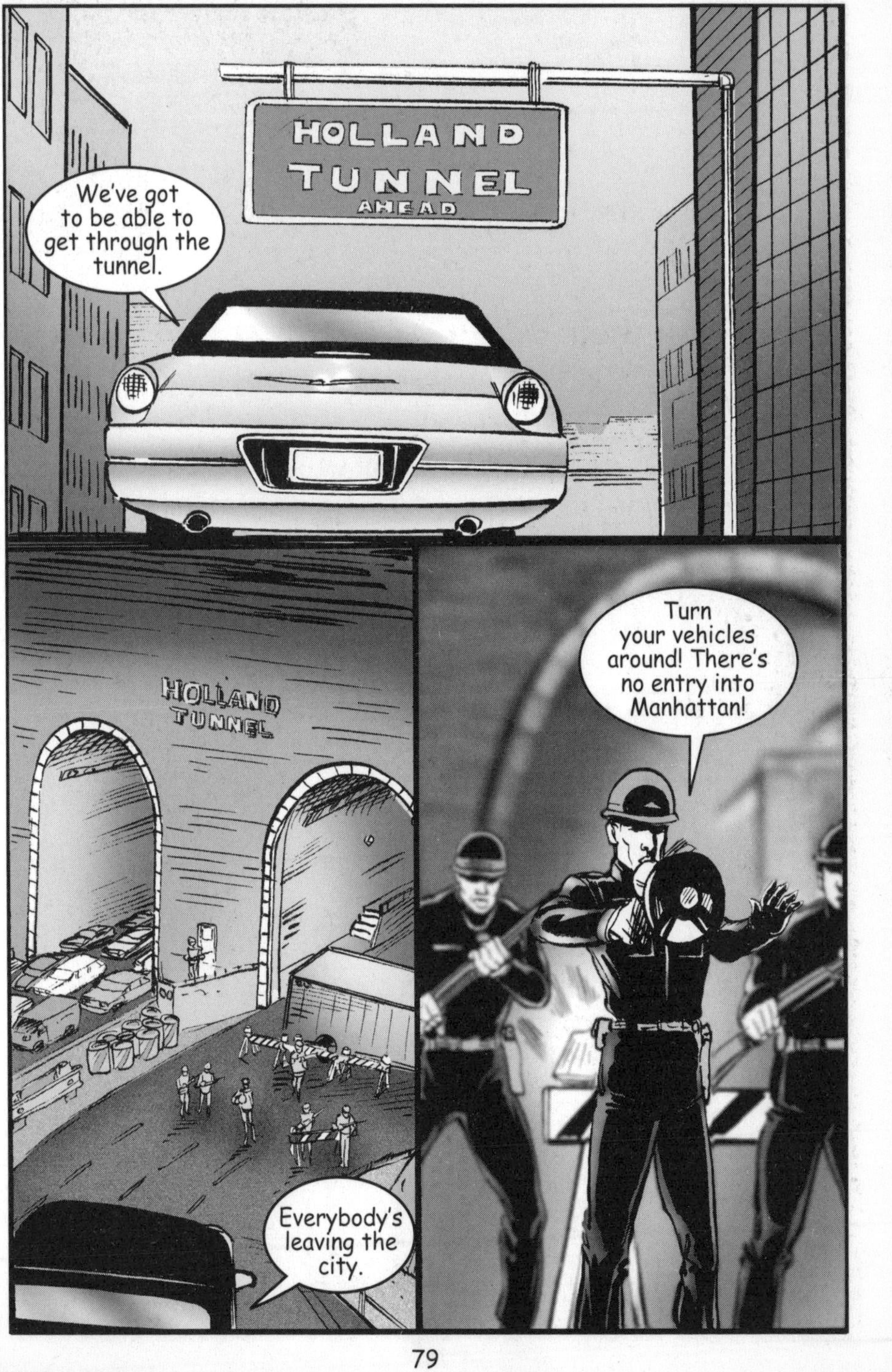
HOLLAND TUNNEL AHEAD
We've got to be able to get through the tunnel.
HOLLAND TUNNEL
Everybody's leaving the city.
Turn your vehicles around! There's no entry into Manhattan!

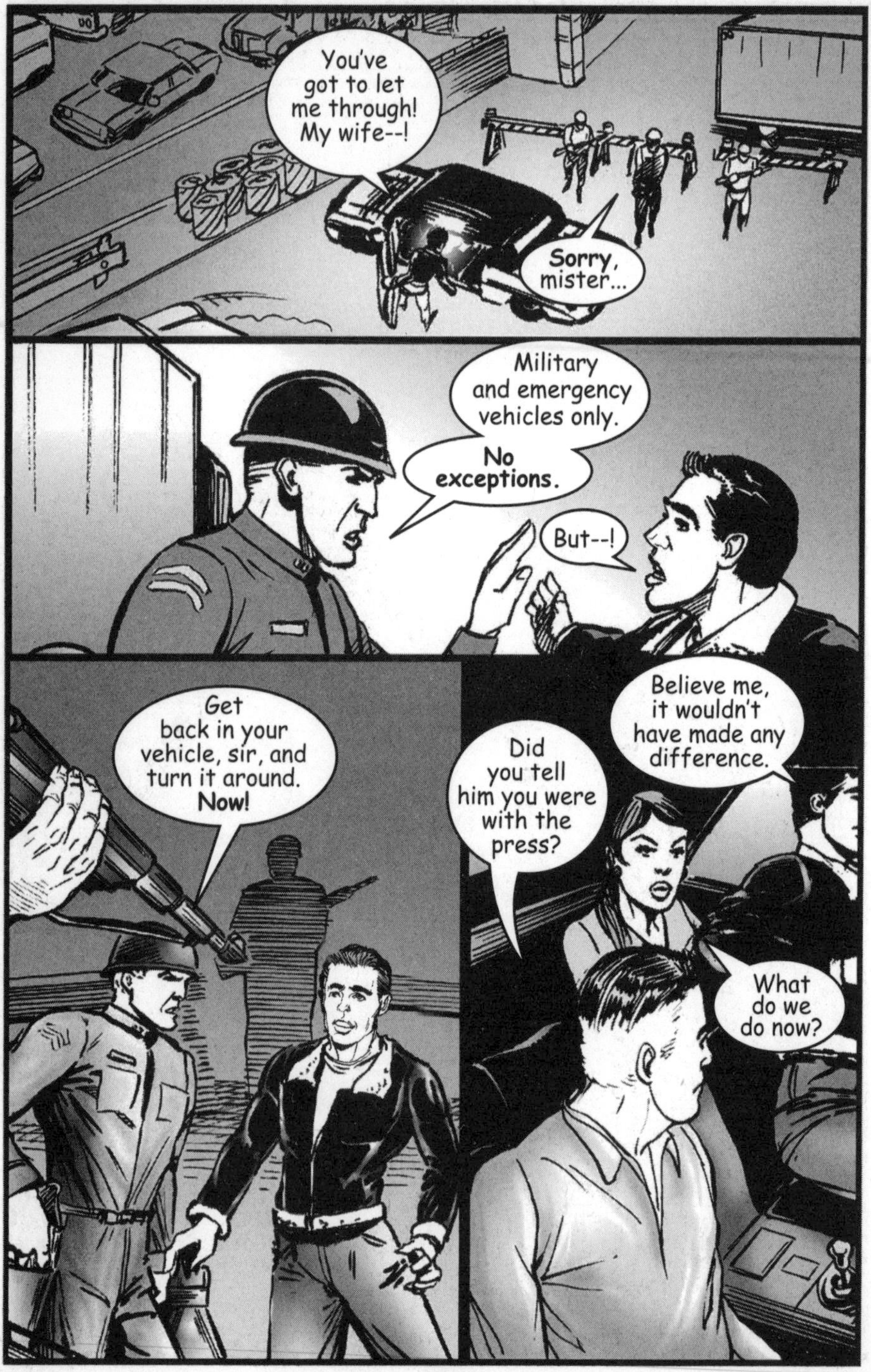
You've got to let me through! My wife--!
Sorry, mister...
Military and emergency vehicles only.
No exceptions.
But--!
Get back in your vehicle, sir, and turn it around. Now!
Believe me, it wouldn't have made any difference.
Did you tell him you were with the press?
What do we do now?

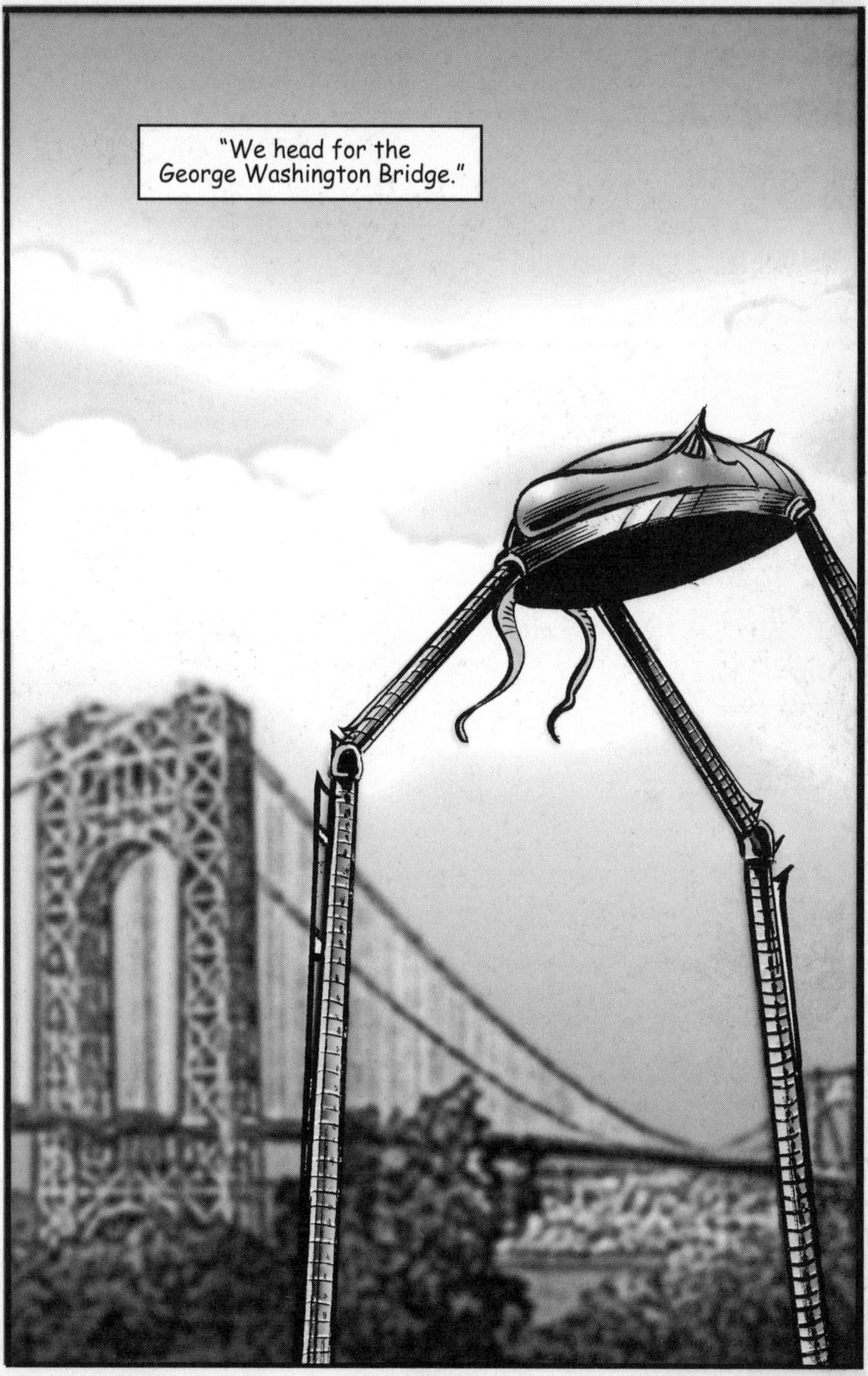
"We head for the George Washington Bridge."

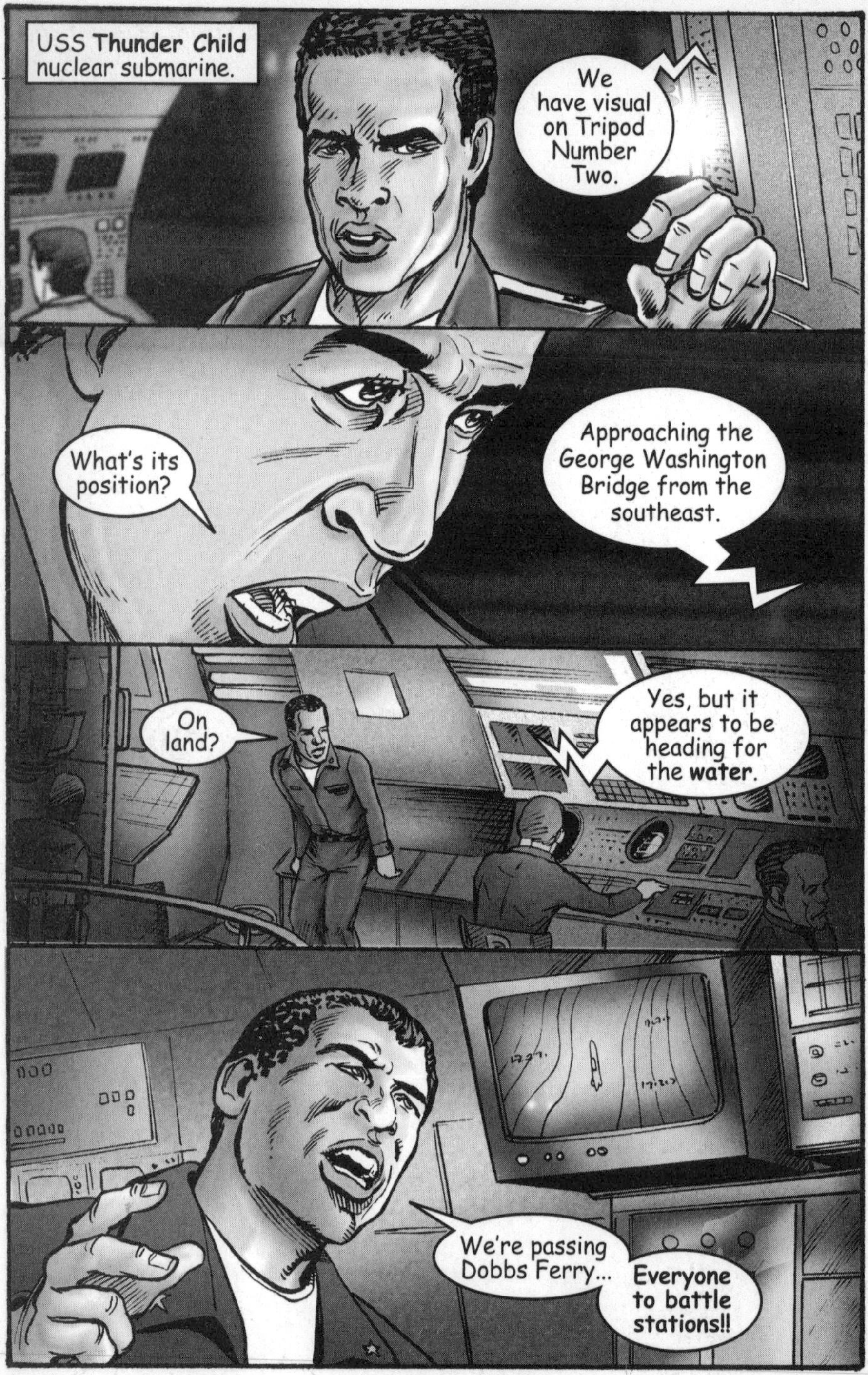
USS **Thunder Child** nuclear submarine.
We have visual on Tripod Number Two.
What's its position?
Approaching the George Washington Bridge from the southeast.
On land?
Yes, but it appears to be heading for the **water**.
We're passing Dobbs Ferry...
Everyone to battle stations!!

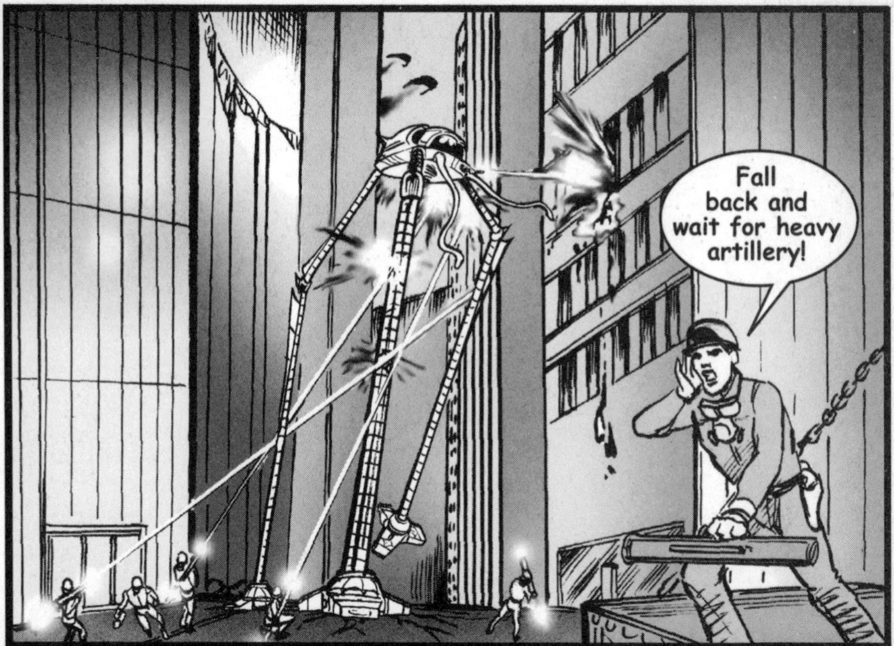
Fall back and wait for heavy artillery!

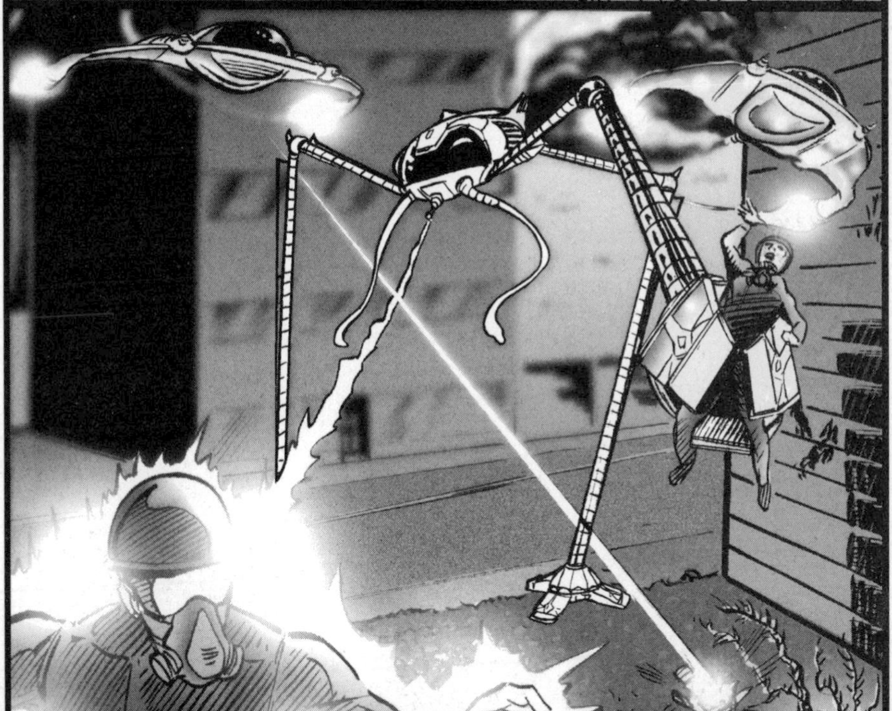

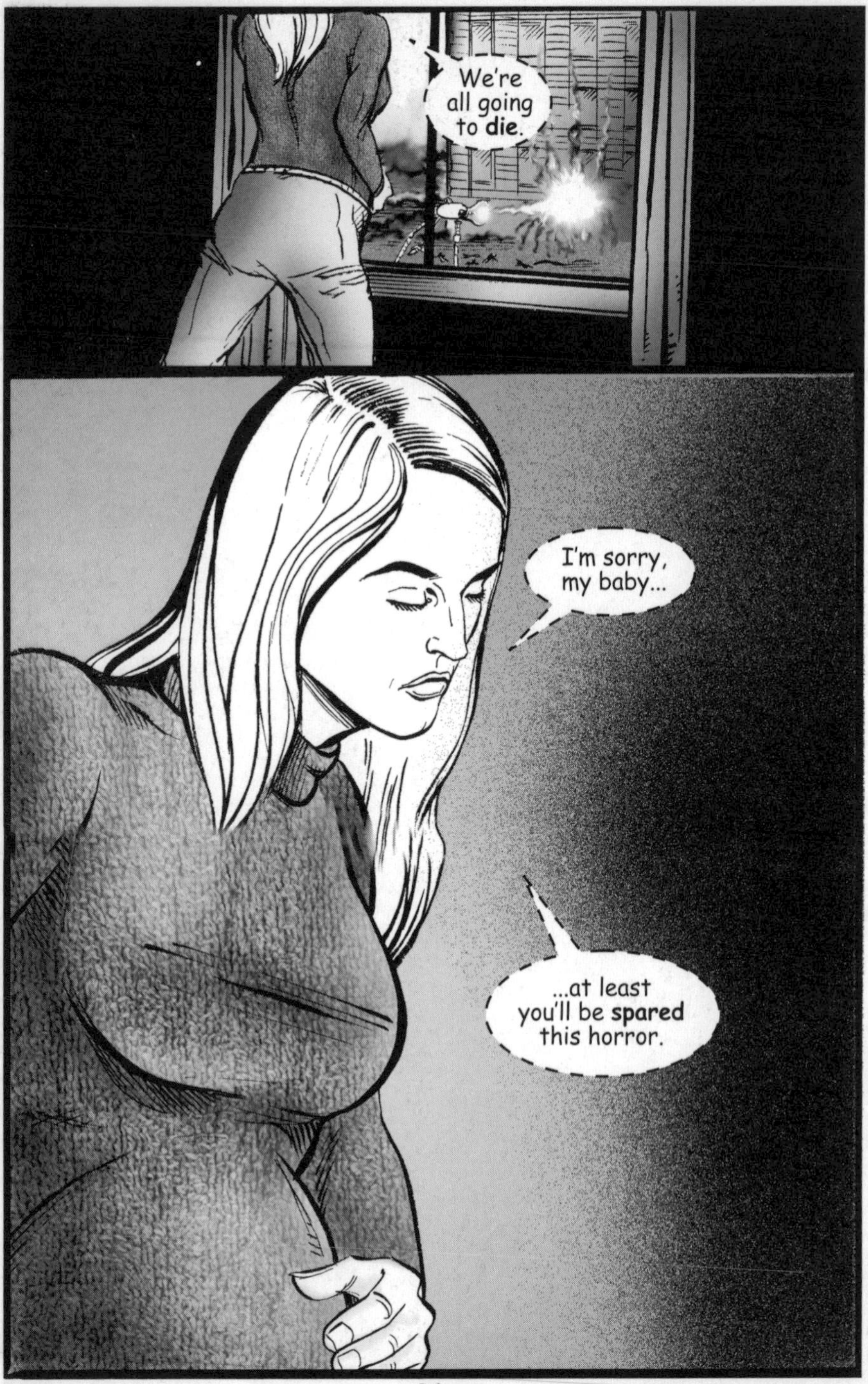
We're all going to die.
I'm sorry, my baby...
...at least you'll be spared this horror.

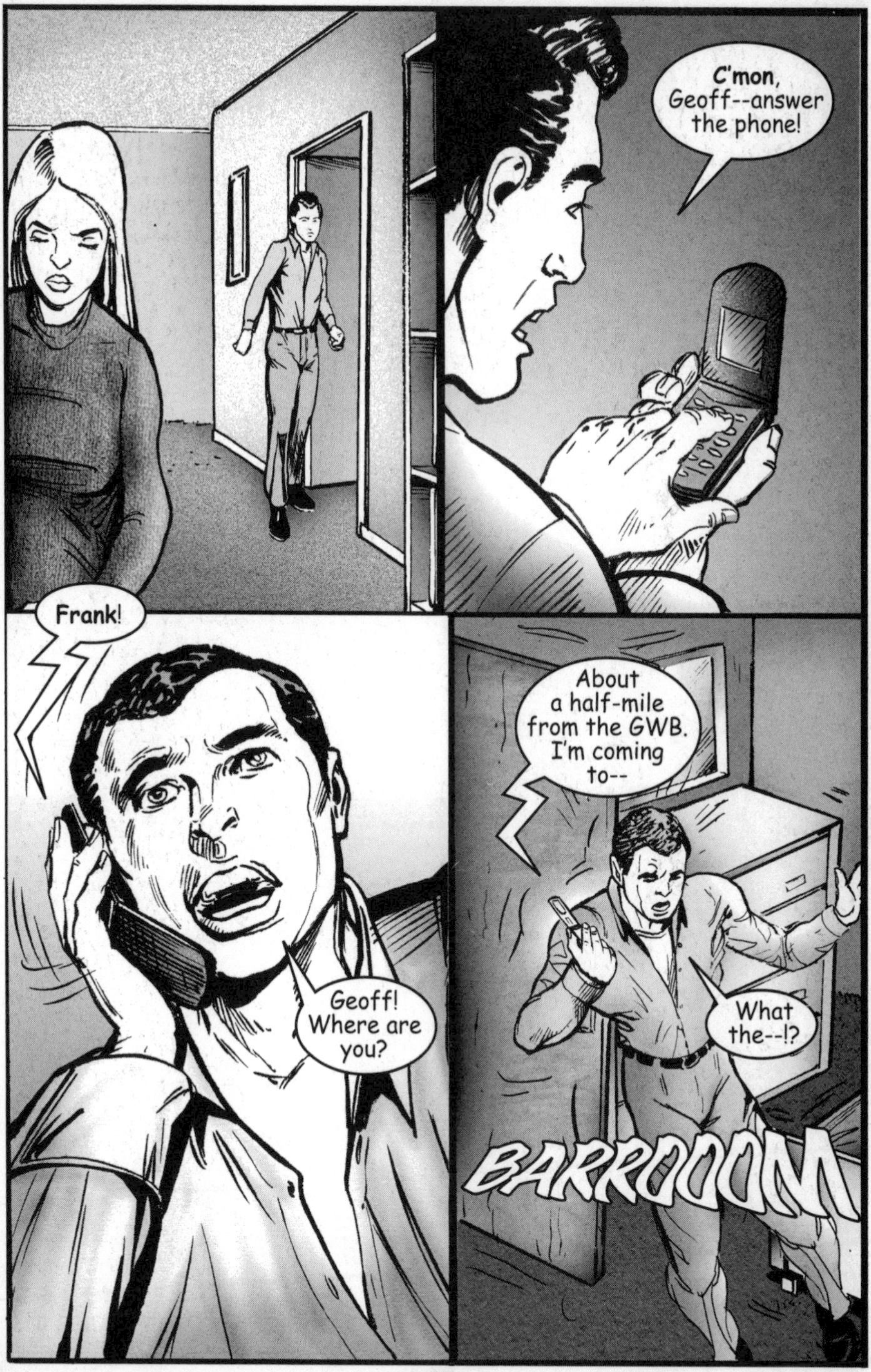
C'mon, Geoff--answer the phone!
Frank!
Geoff! Where are you?
About a half-mile from the GWB. I'm coming to--
What the--!?
BARROOOM

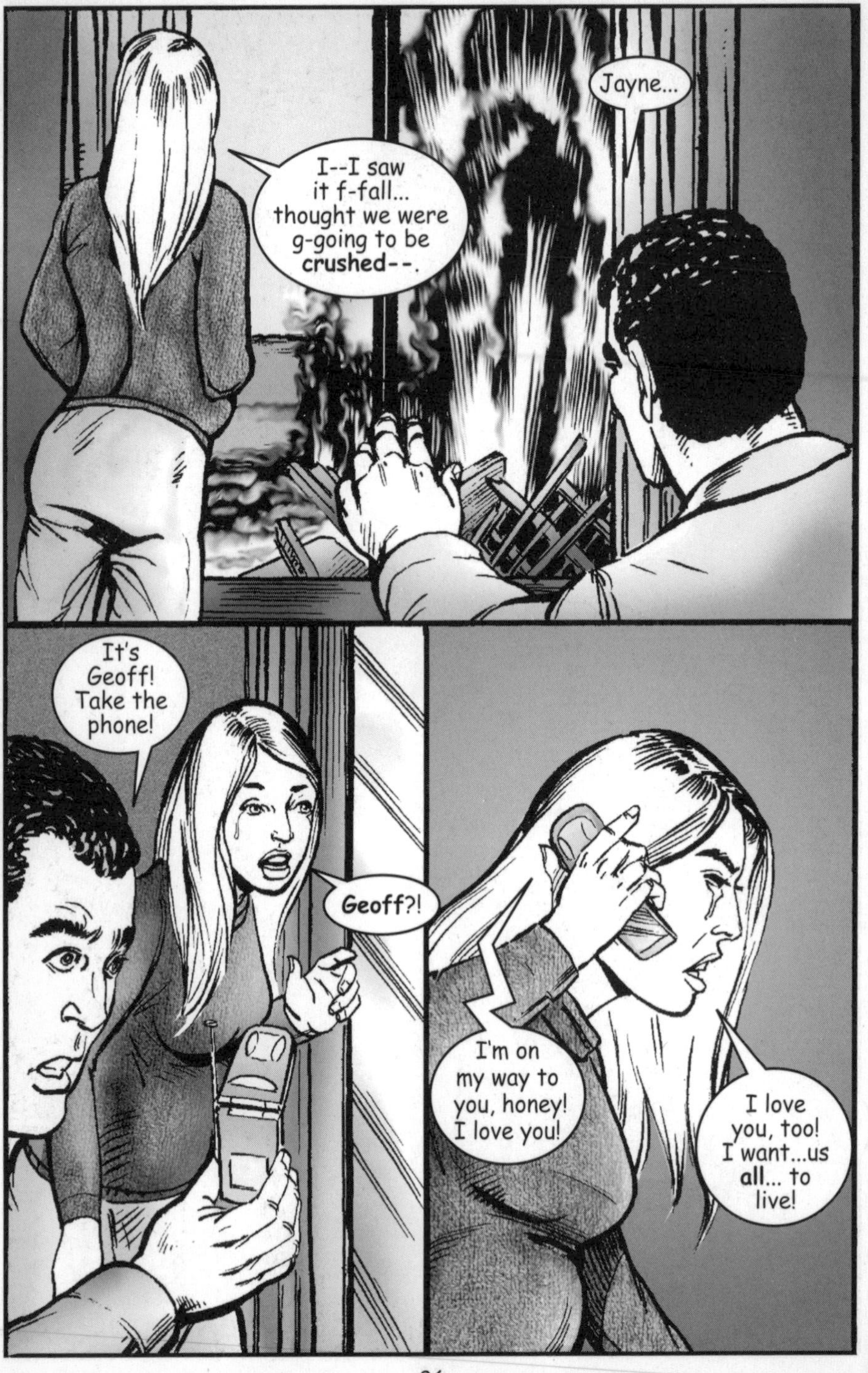
I--I saw it f-fall... thought we were g-going to be **crushed**--.
Jayne...
It's Geoff! Take the phone!
Geoff?!
I'm on my way to you, honey! I love you!
I love you, too! I want...us **all**... to live!

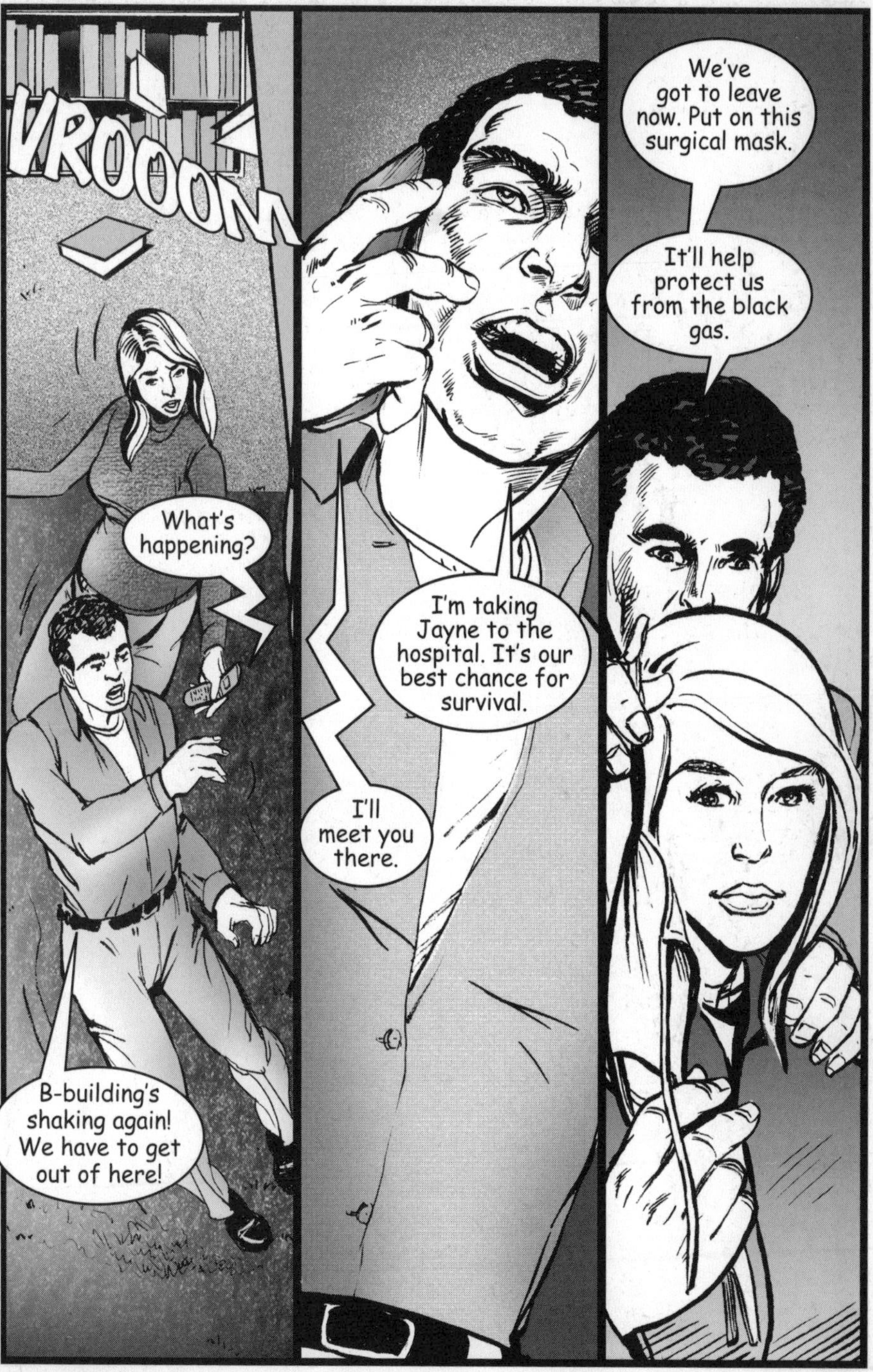
VROOOM
What's happening?
B-building's shaking again! We have to get out of here!
I'm taking Jayne to the hospital. It's our best chance for survival.
I'll meet you there.
We've got to leave now. Put on this surgical mask.
It'll help protect us from the black gas.

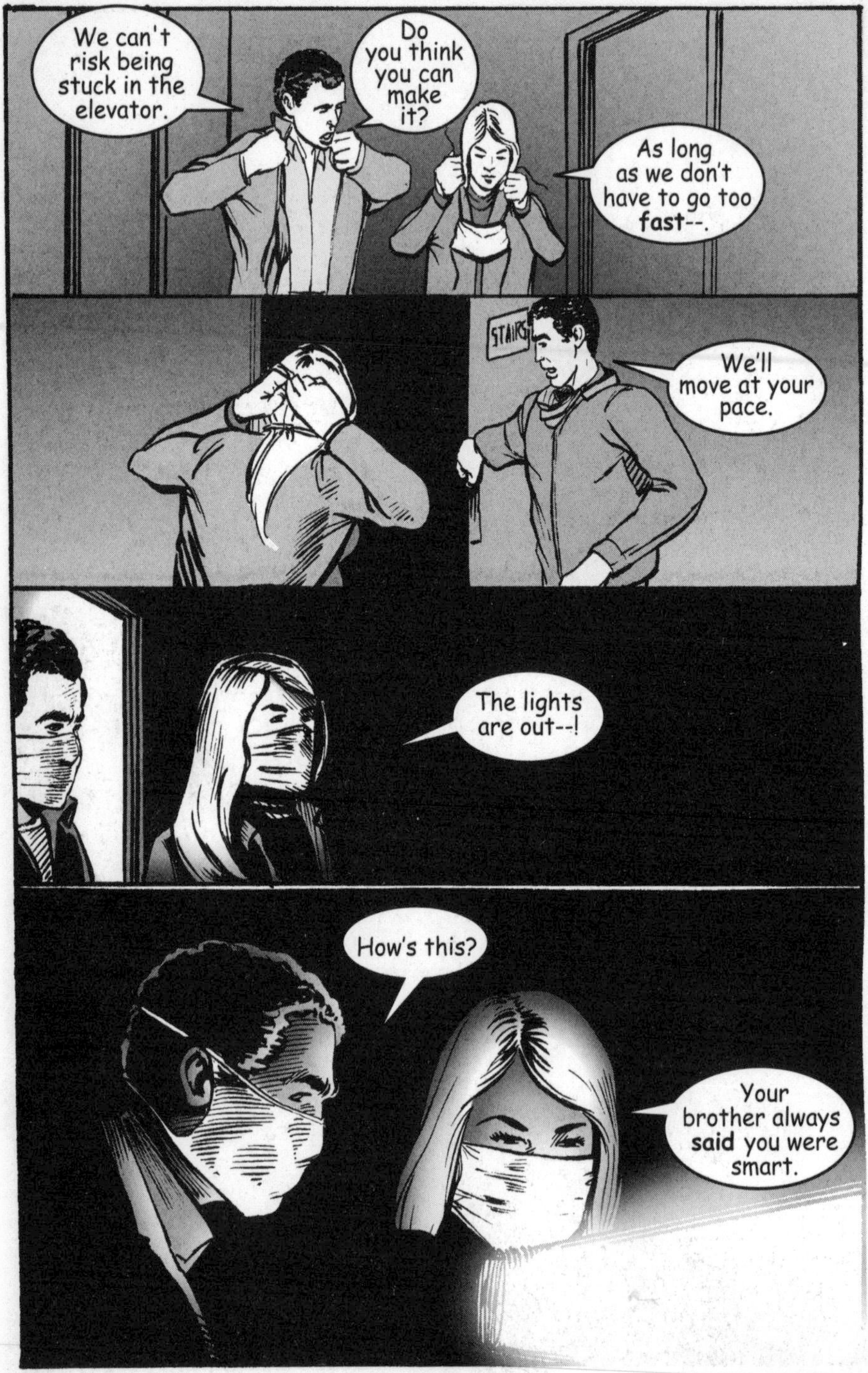
We can't risk being stuck in the elevator.
Do you think you can make it?
As long as we don't have to go too **fast**--.
We'll move at your pace.
The lights are out--!
How's this?
Your brother always **said** you were smart.

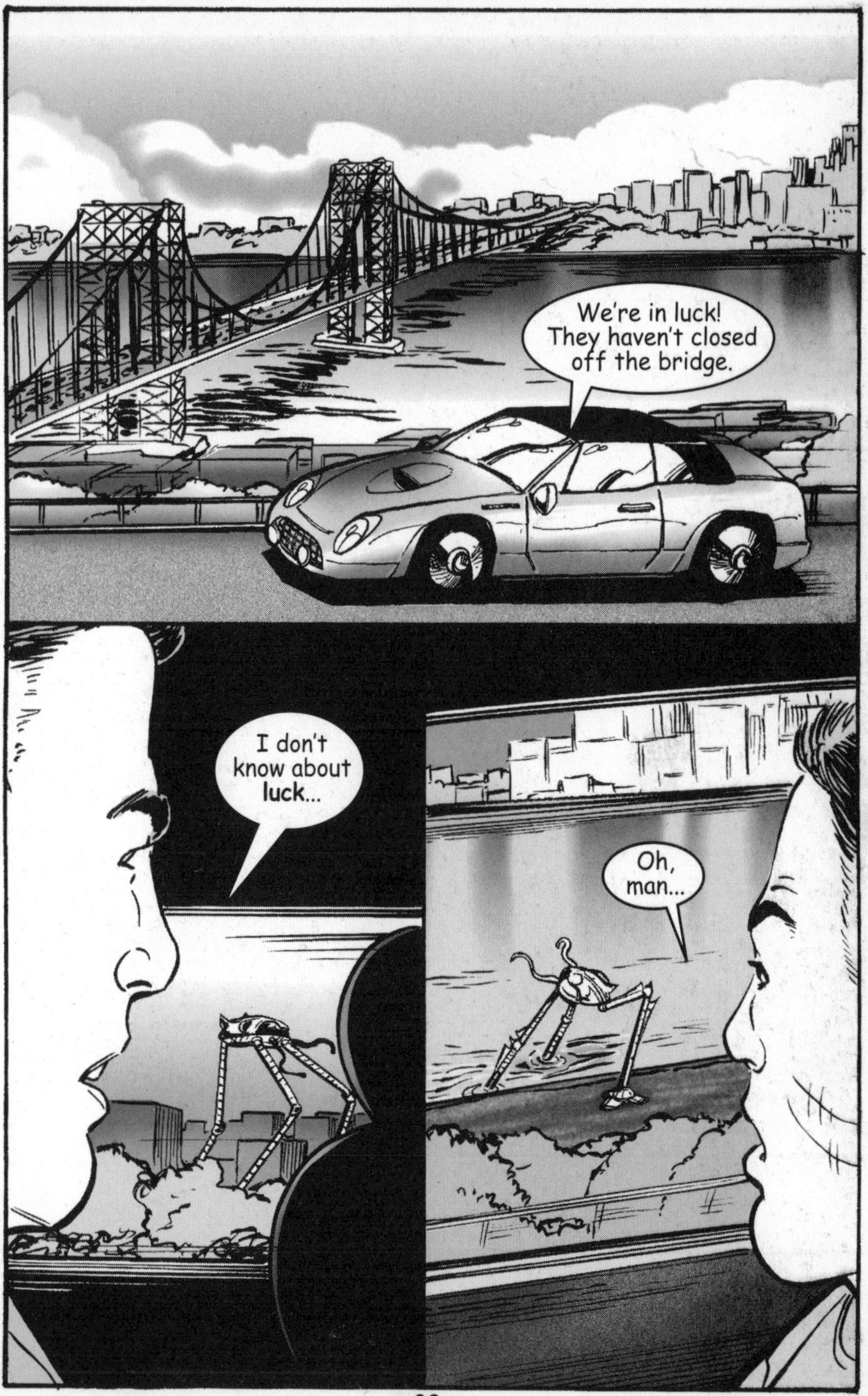
We're in luck! They haven't closed off the bridge.
I don't know about luck...
Oh, man...

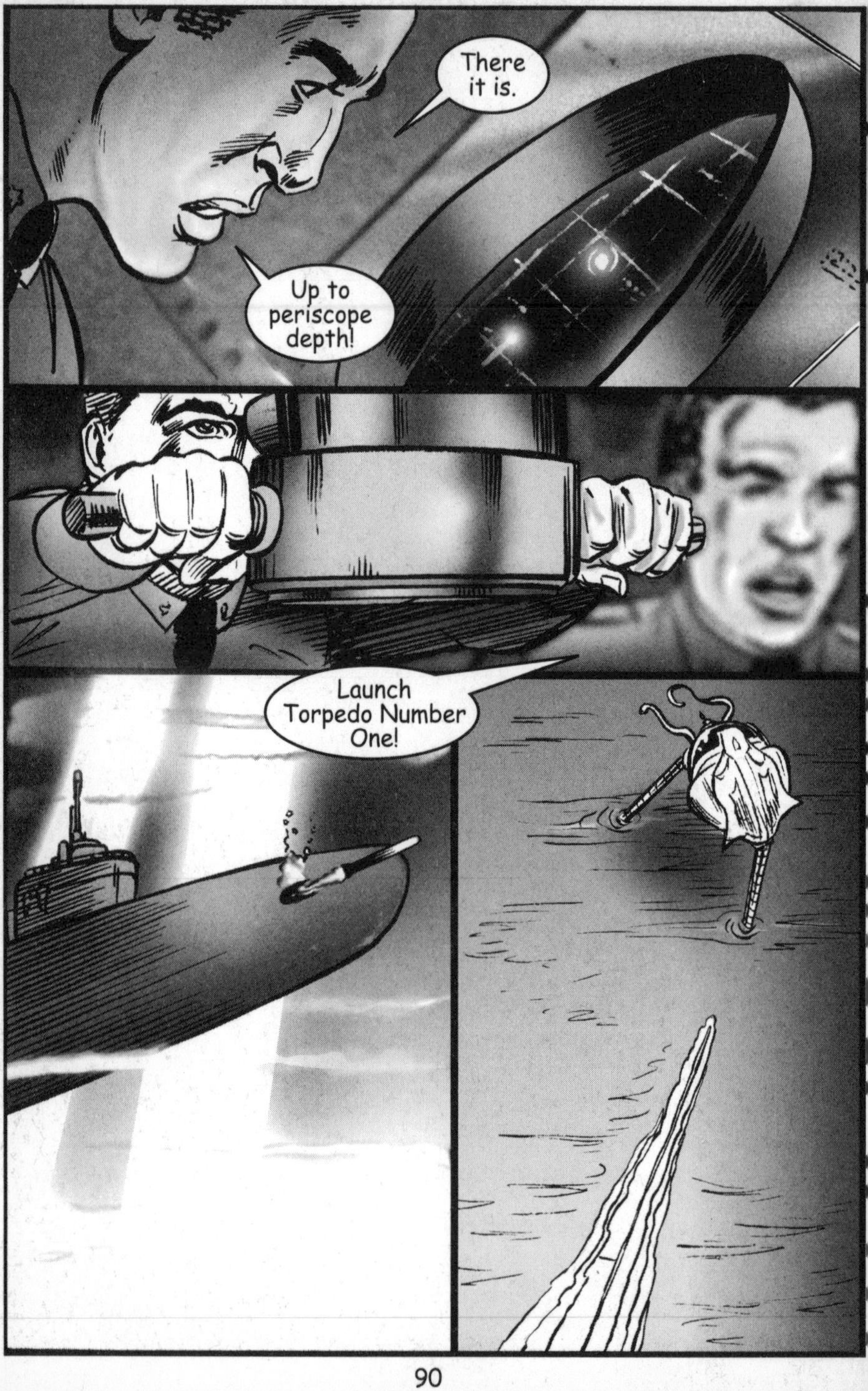
There it is.
Up to periscope depth!
Launch Torpedo Number One!

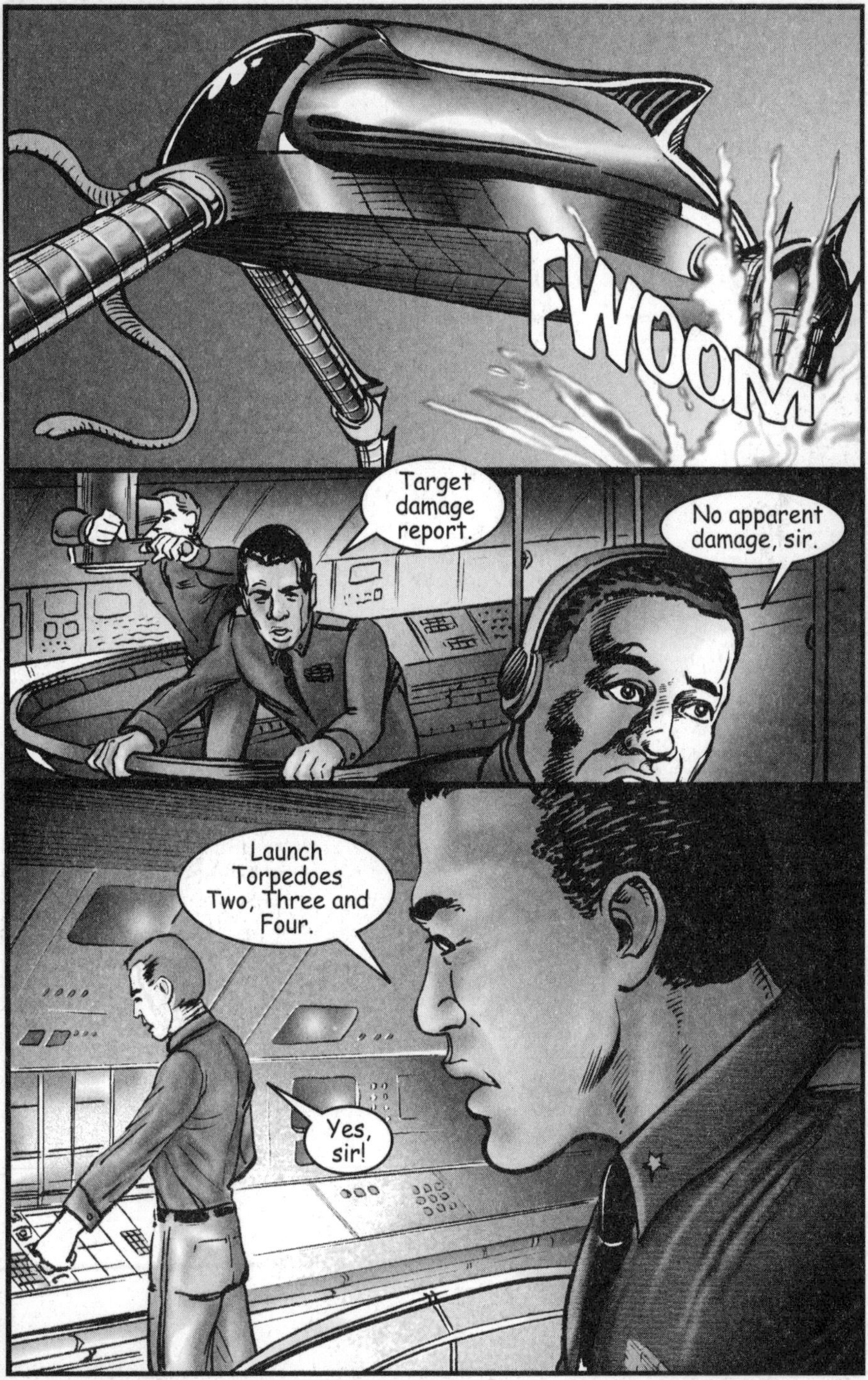
FWOOM
Target damage report.
No apparent damage, sir.
Launch Torpedoes Two, Three and Four.
Yes, sir!

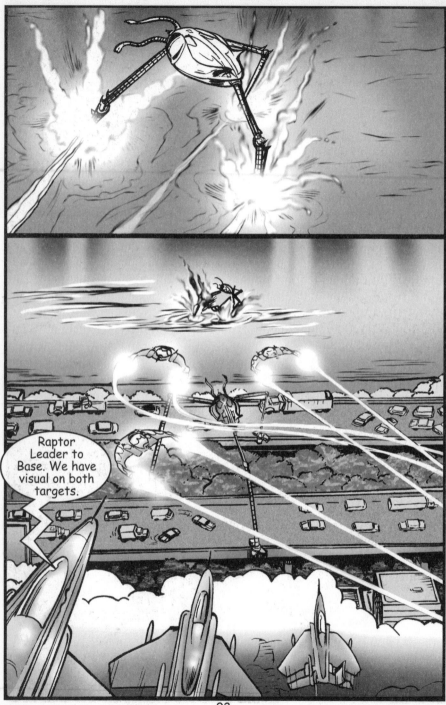

Raptor Leader to Base. We have visual on both targets.

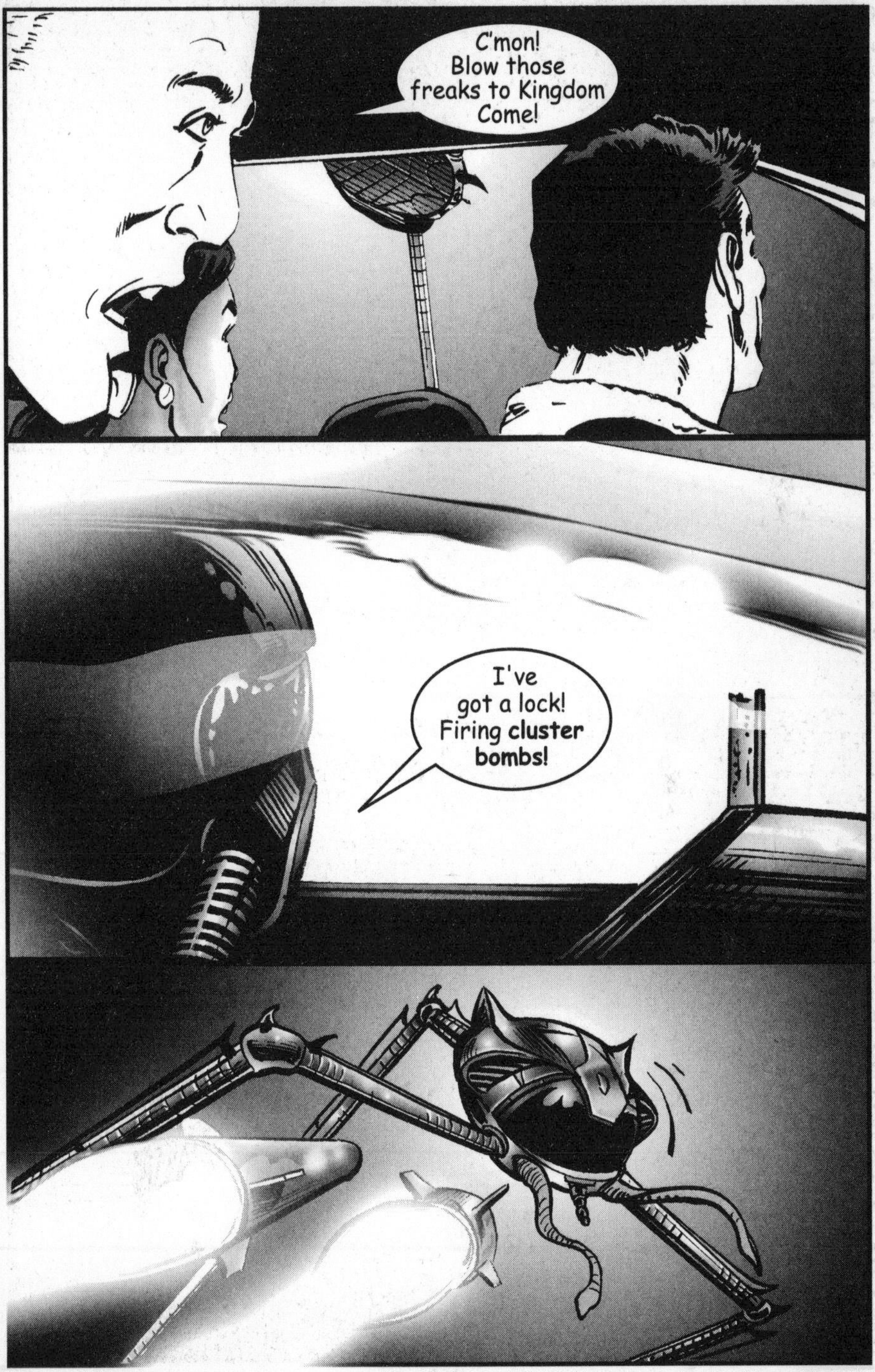
C'mon! Blow those freaks to Kingdom Come!
I've got a lock! Firing **cluster bombs!**

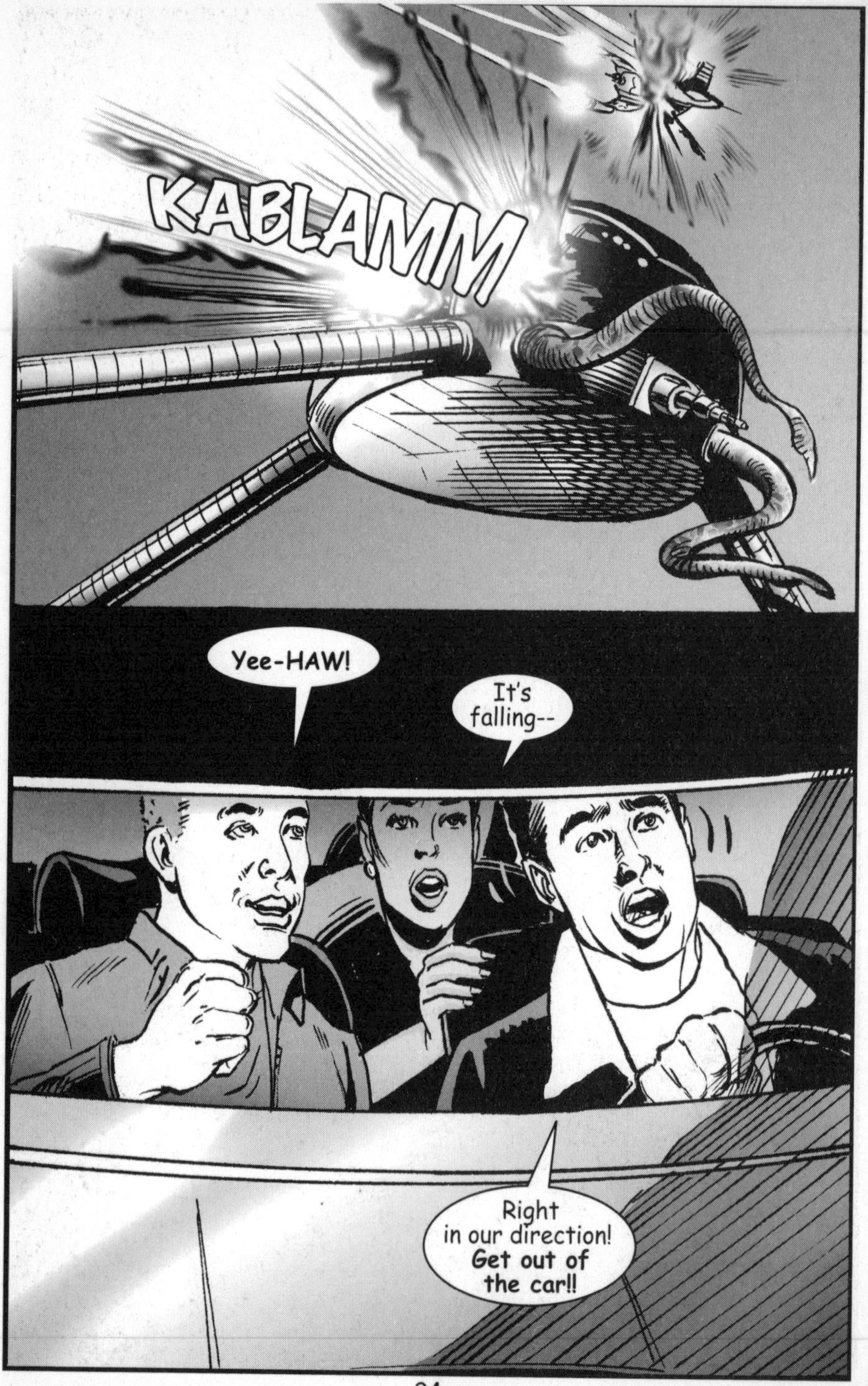
KABLAMM
Yee-HAW!
It's falling--
Right in our direction! **Get out of the car!!**

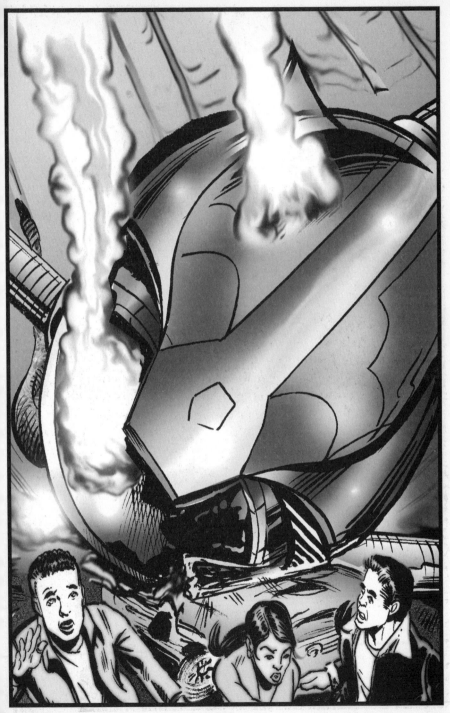

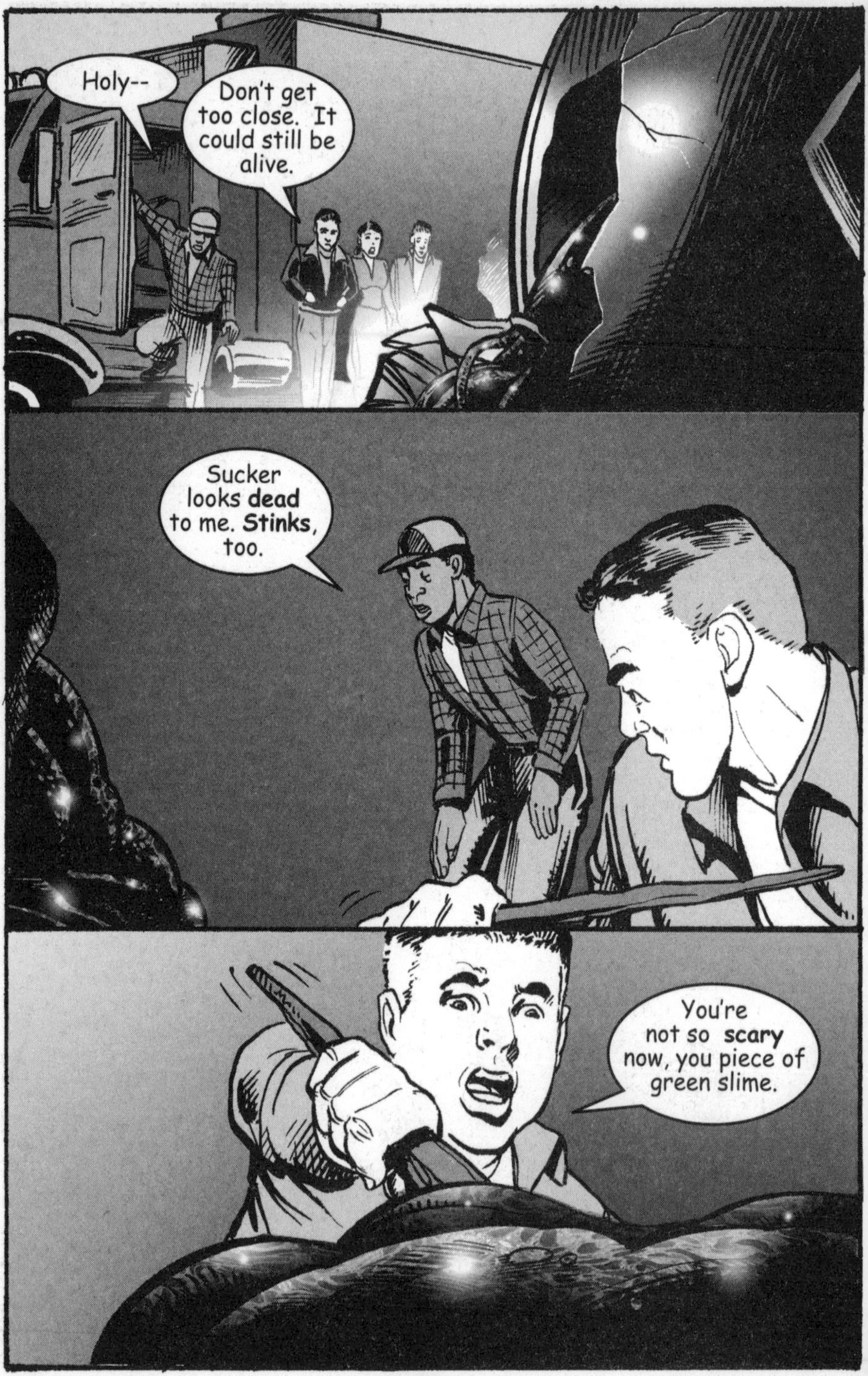
Holy--
Don't get too close. It could still be alive.
Sucker looks **dead** to me. **Stinks**, too.
You're not so **scary** now, you piece of green slime.

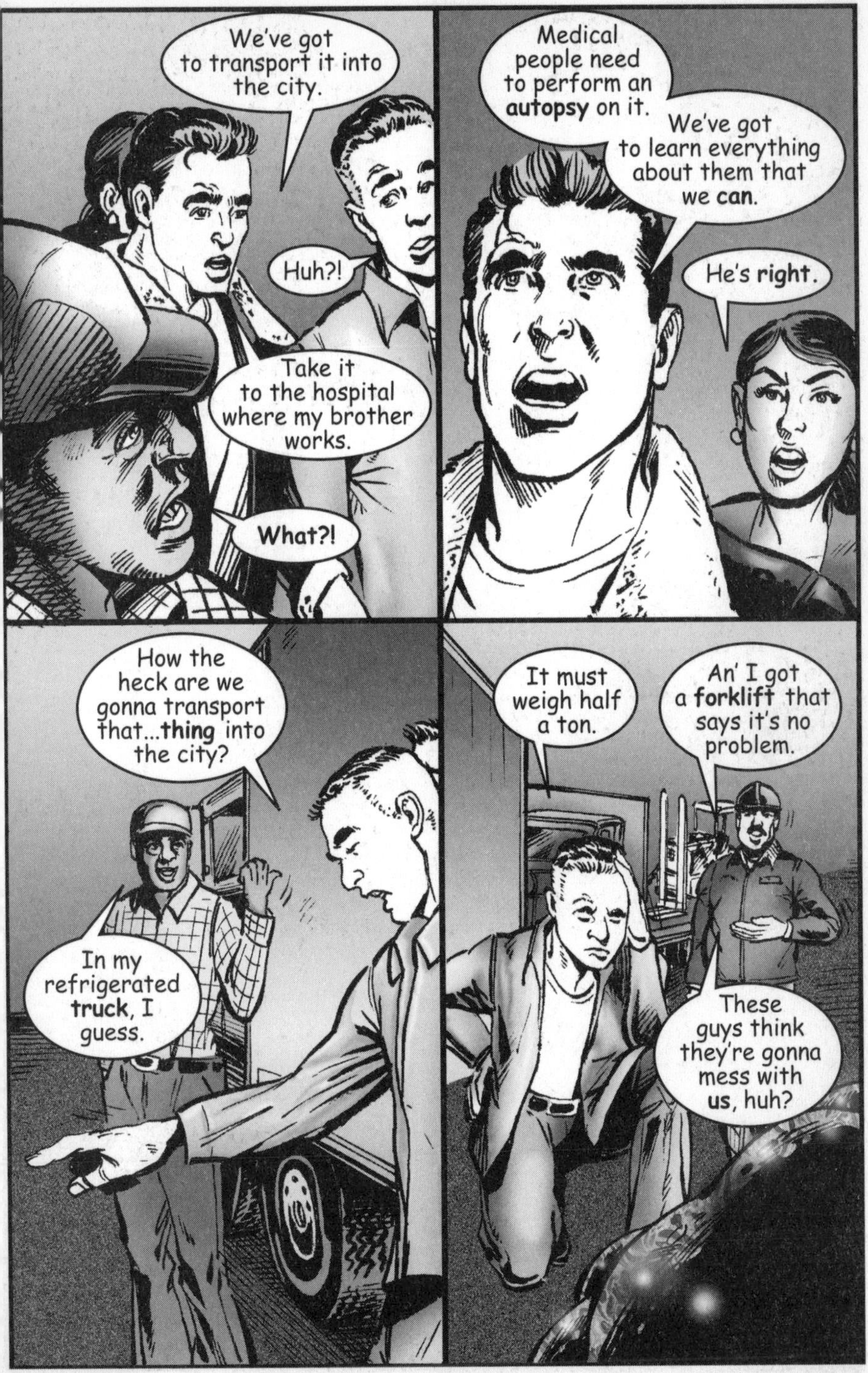
We've got to transport it into the city.
Huh?!
Take it to the hospital where my brother works.
What?!
Medical people need to perform an **autopsy** on it.
We've got to learn everything about them that we **can**.
He's **right**.
How the heck are we gonna transport that...**thing** into the city?
In my refrigerated **truck**, I guess.
It must weigh half a ton.
An' I got a **forklift** that says it's no problem.
These guys think they're gonna mess with **us**, huh?

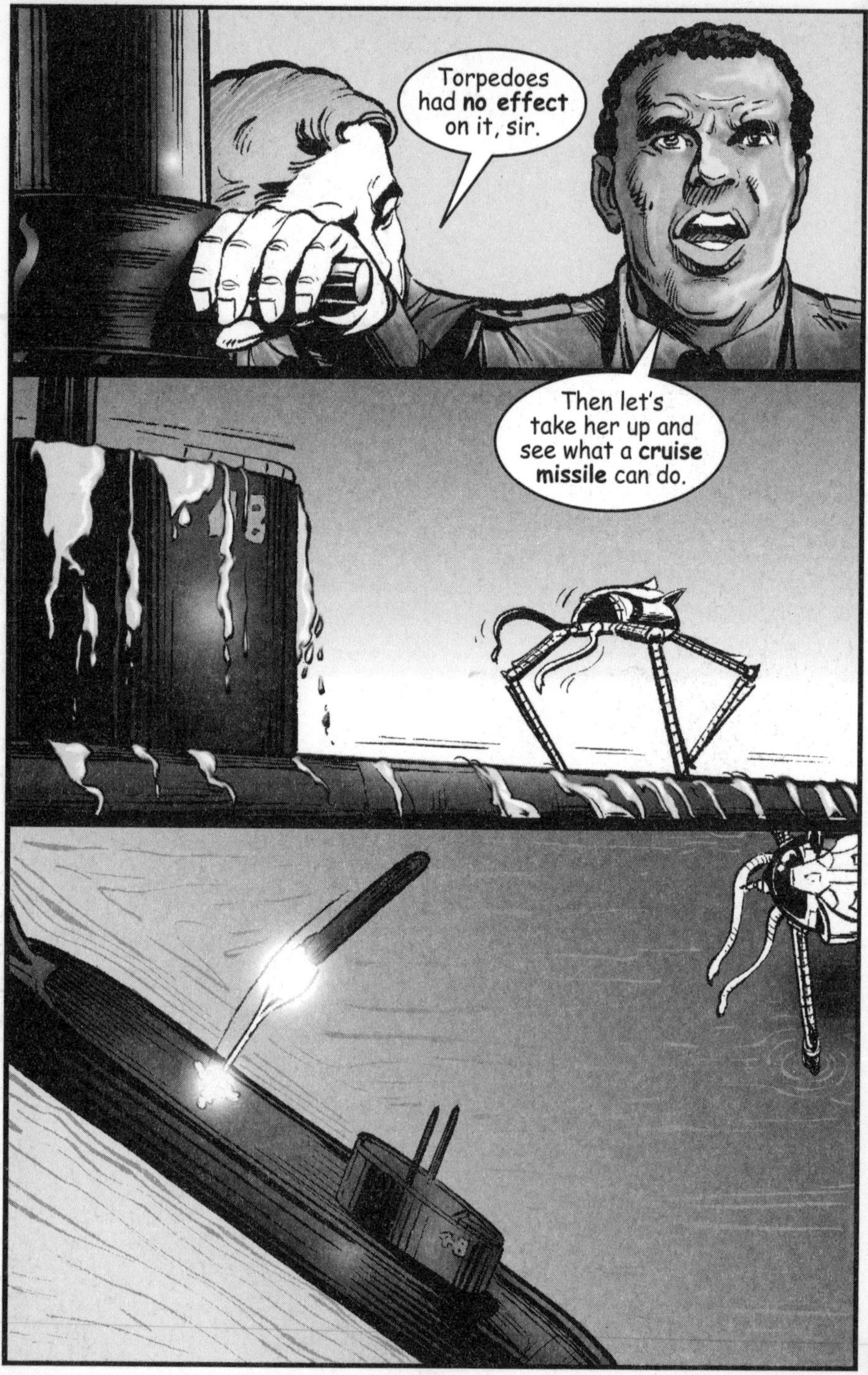
Torpedoes had **no effect** on it, sir.
Then let's take her up and see what a **cruise missile** can do.

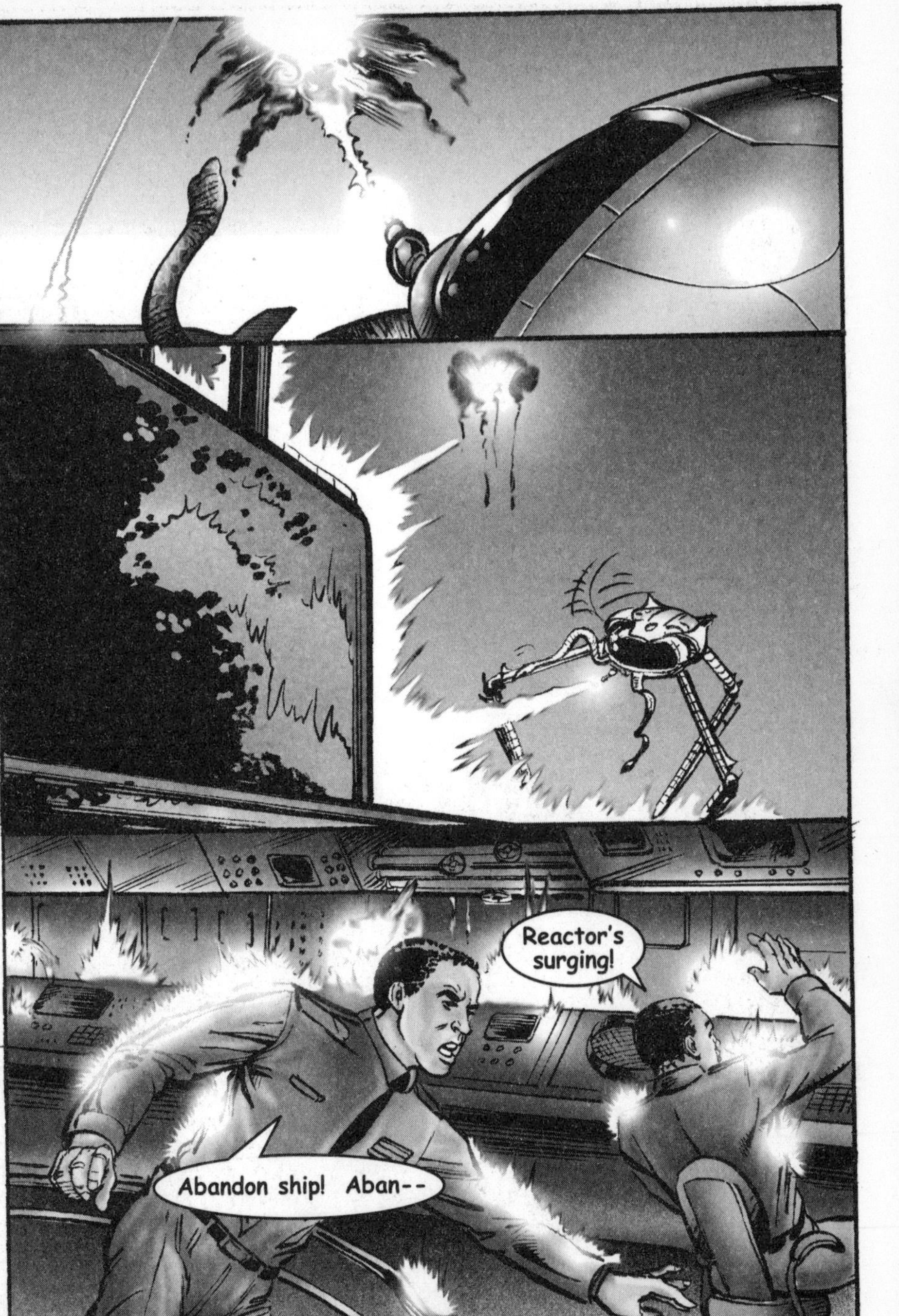
Reactor's surging!
Abandon ship! Aban--

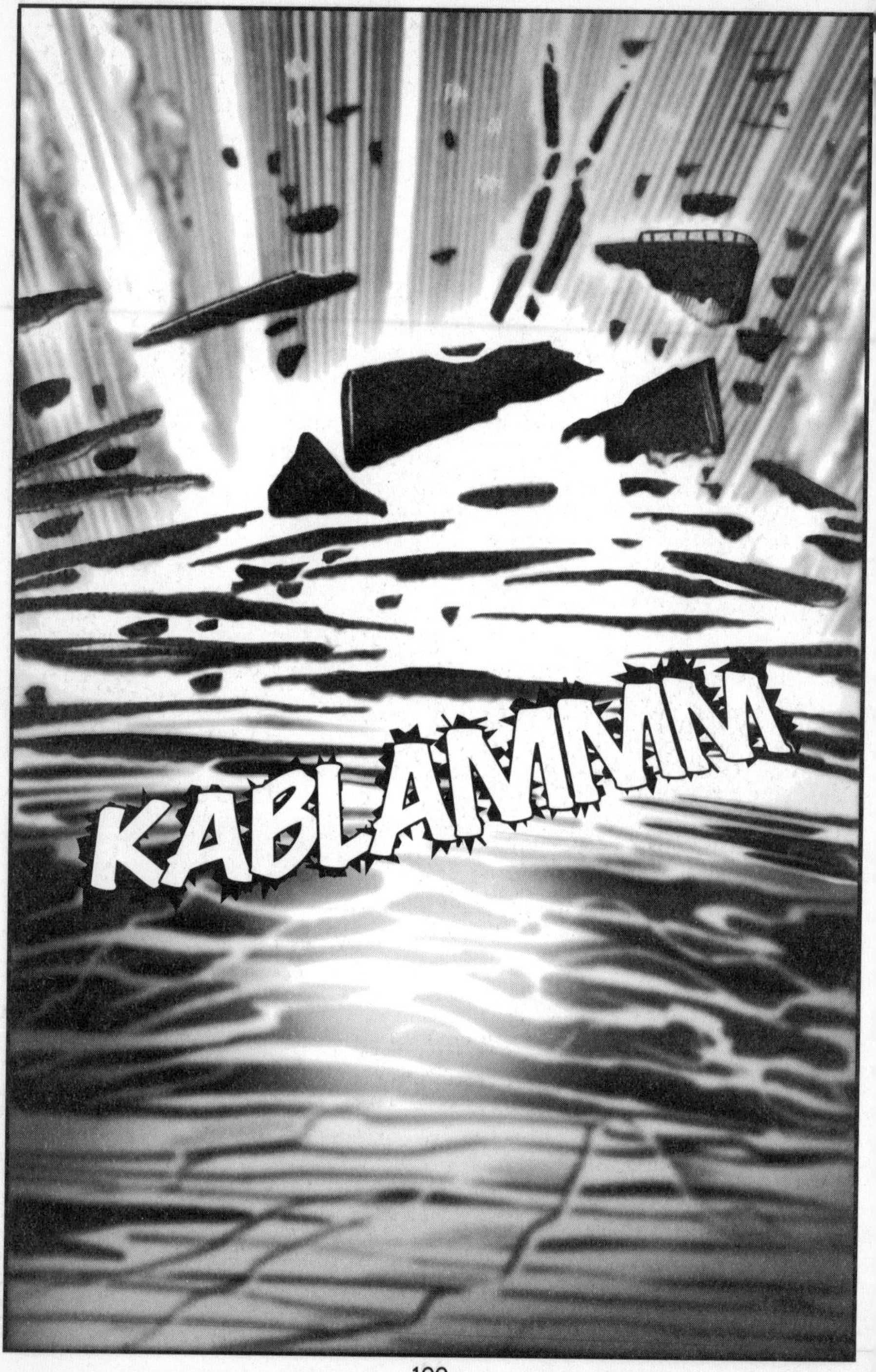
KABLAMMM

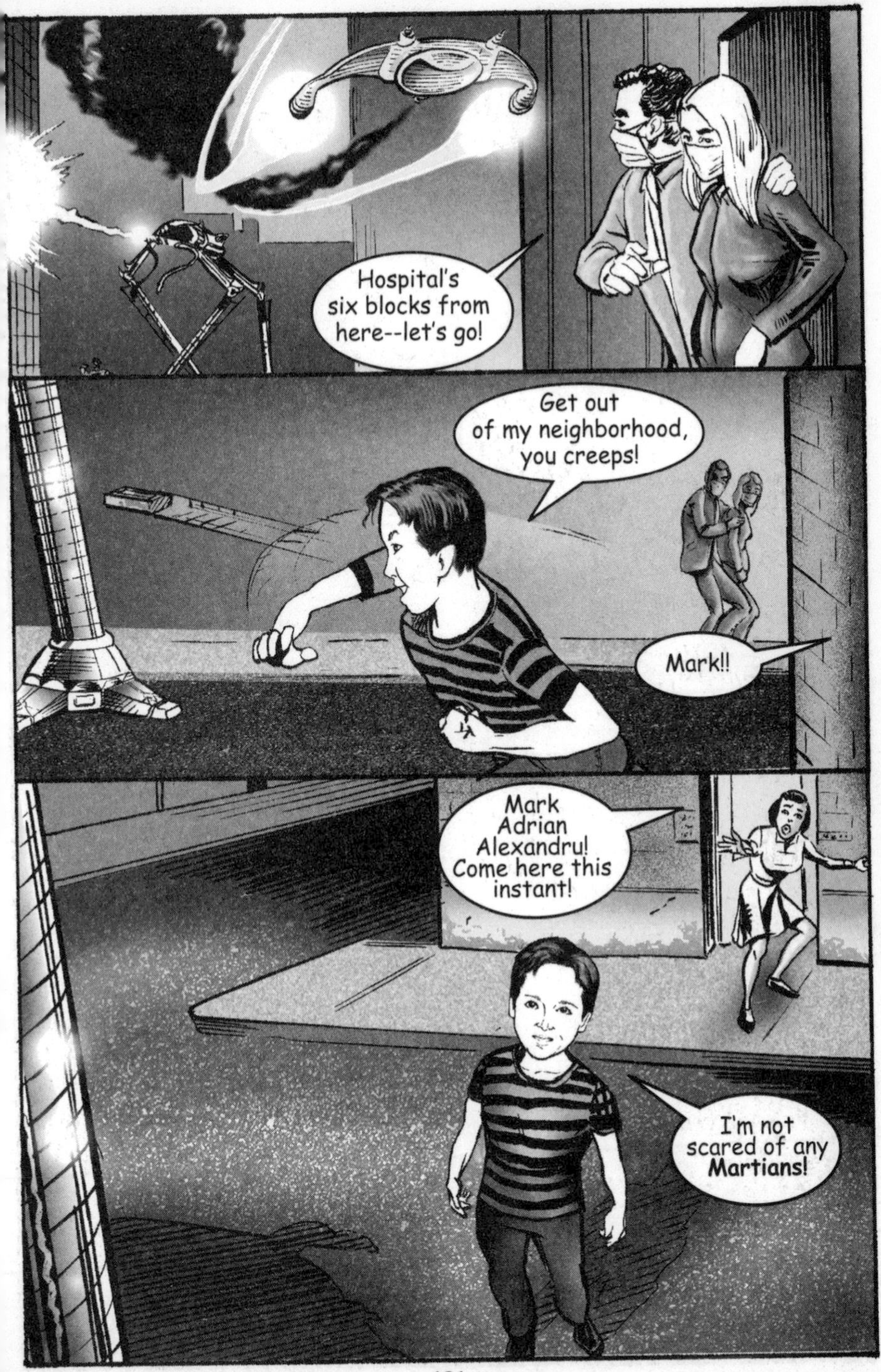
Hospital's six blocks from here--let's go!
Get out of my neighborhood, you creeps!
Mark!!
Mark Adrian Alexandru! Come here this instant!
I'm not scared of any **Martians!**

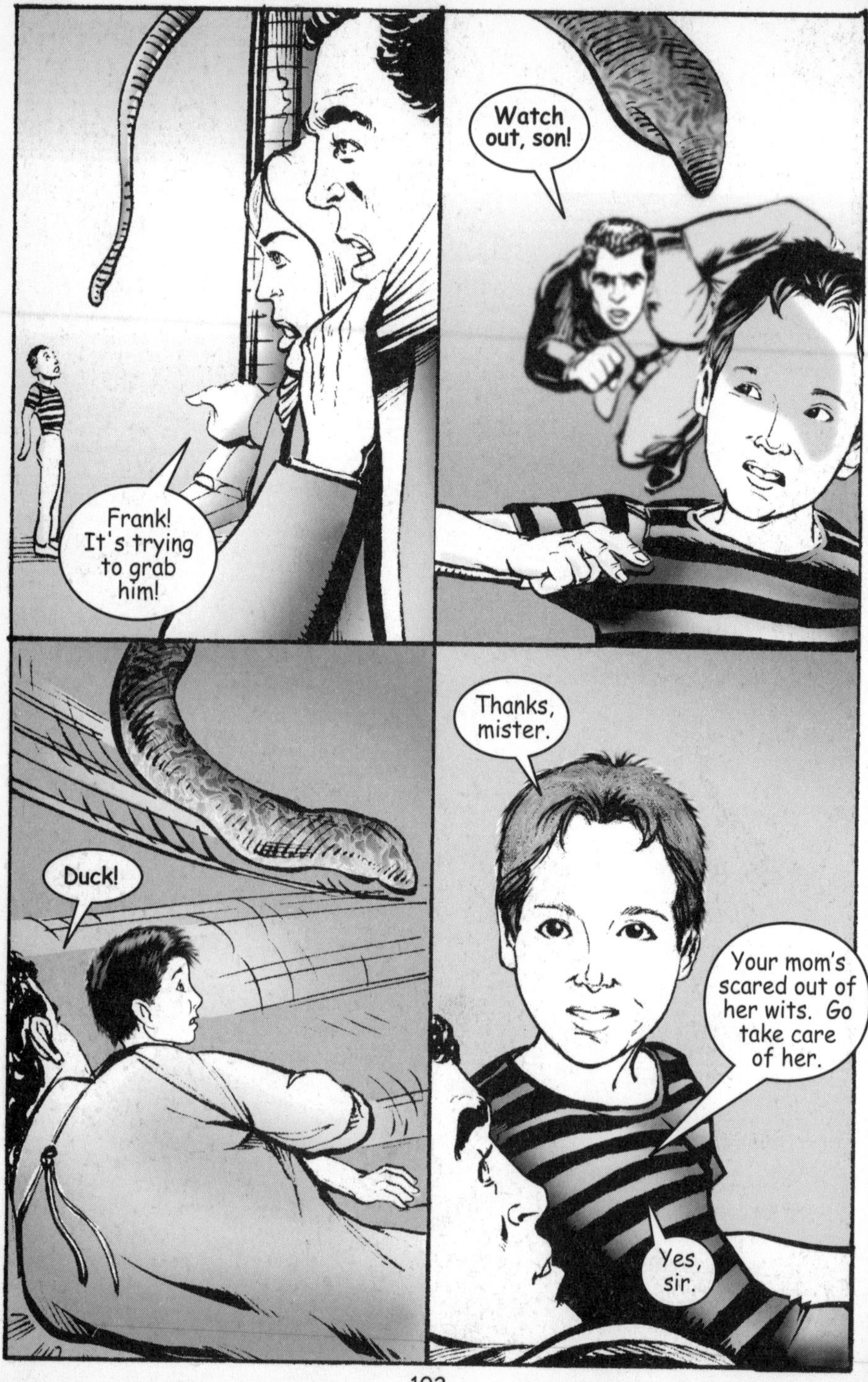
Frank! It's trying to grab him!
Watch out, son!
Duck!
Thanks, mister.
Your mom's scared out of her wits. Go take care of her.
Yes, sir.

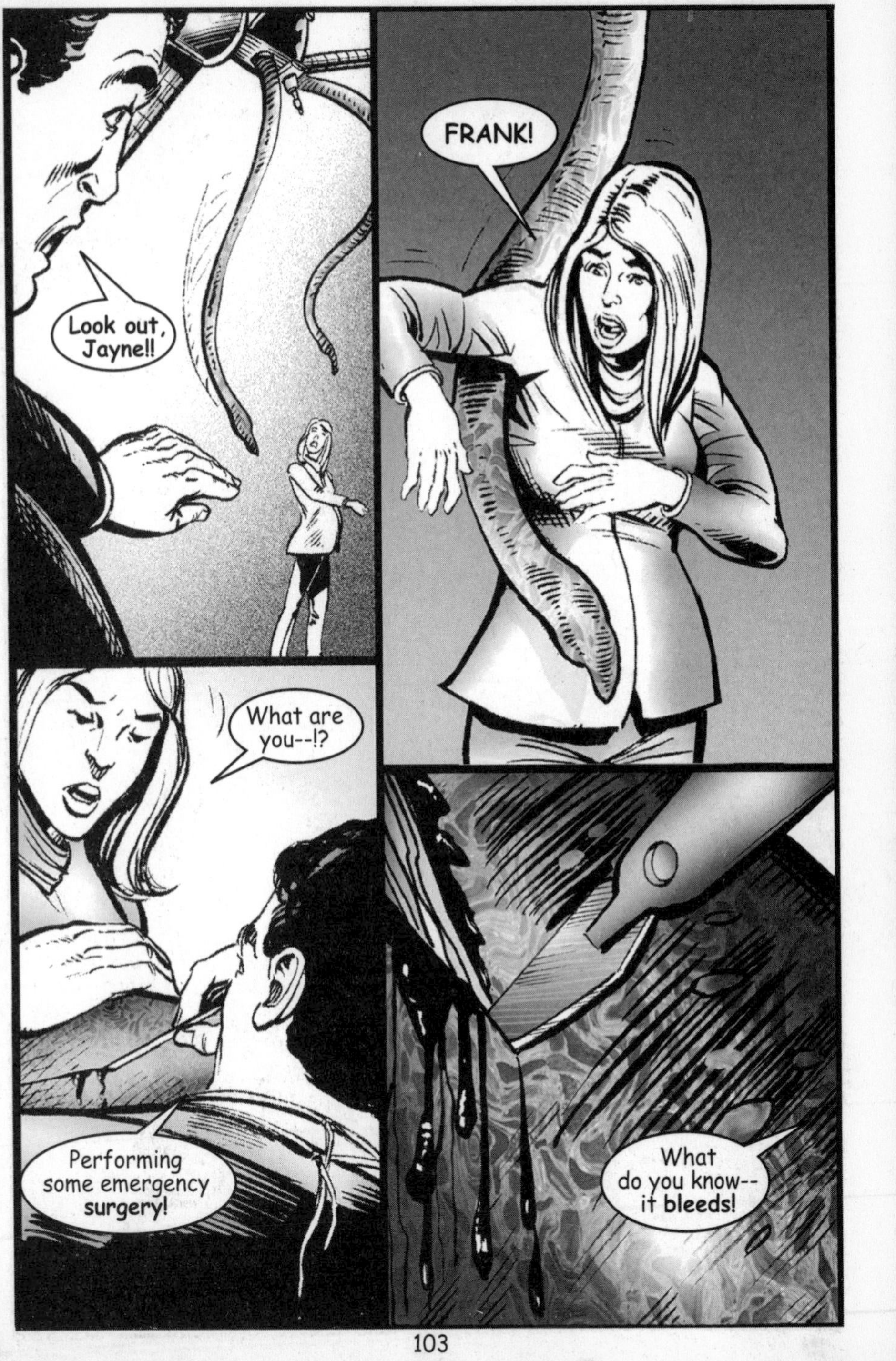
Look out, Jayne!!
FRANK!
What are you--!?
Performing some emergency surgery!
What do you know-- it bleeds!

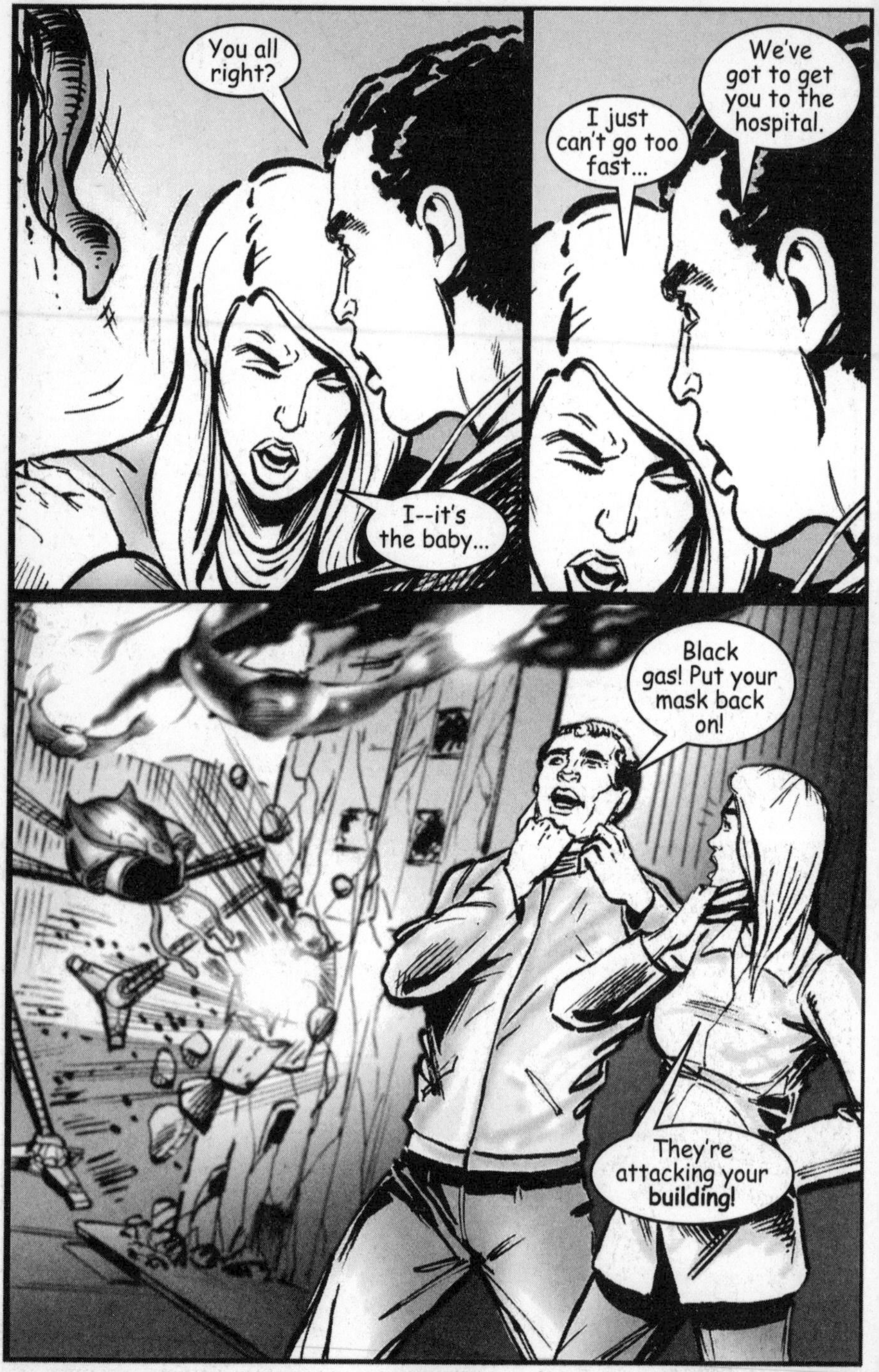
You all right?
I--it's the baby...
I just can't go too fast...
We've got to get you to the hospital.
Black gas! Put your mask back on!
They're attacking your **building!**

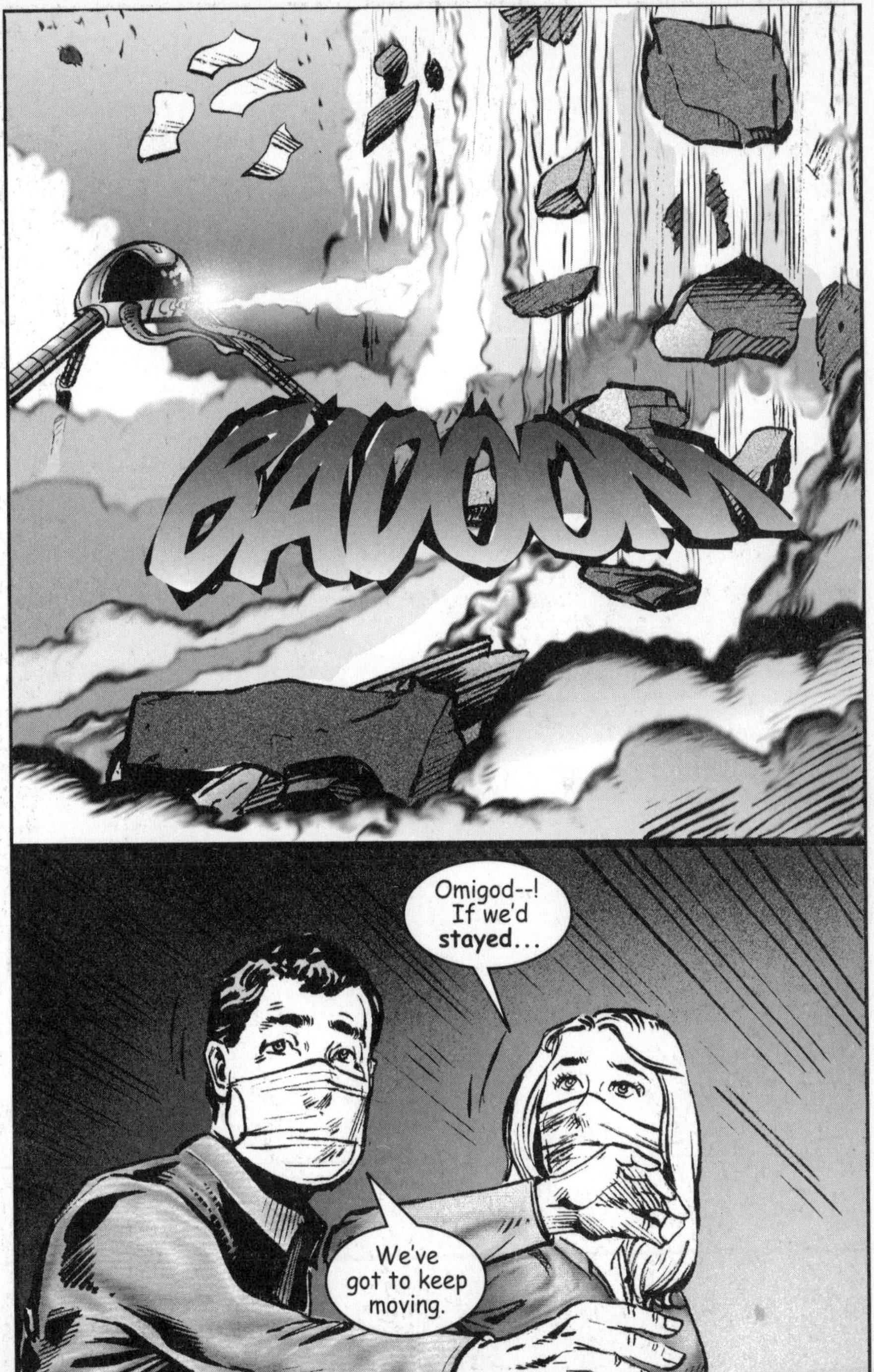
BADOOM
Omigod--! If we'd stayed...
We've got to keep moving.

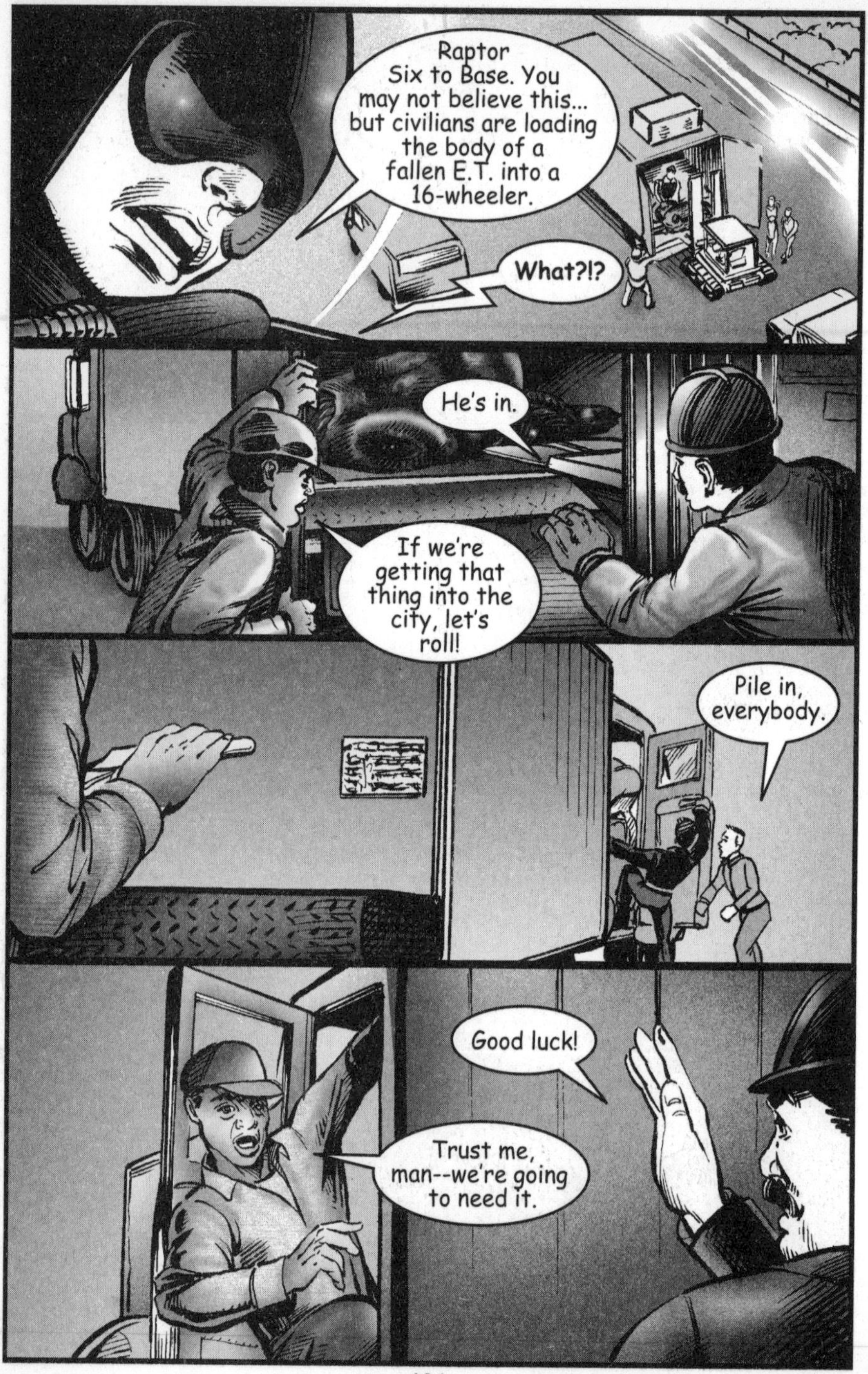
Raptor Six to Base. You may not believe this... but civilians are loading the body of a fallen E.T. into a 16-wheeler.
What?!?
He's in.
If we're getting that thing into the city, let's roll!
Pile in, everybody.
Good luck!
Trust me, man--we're going to need it.

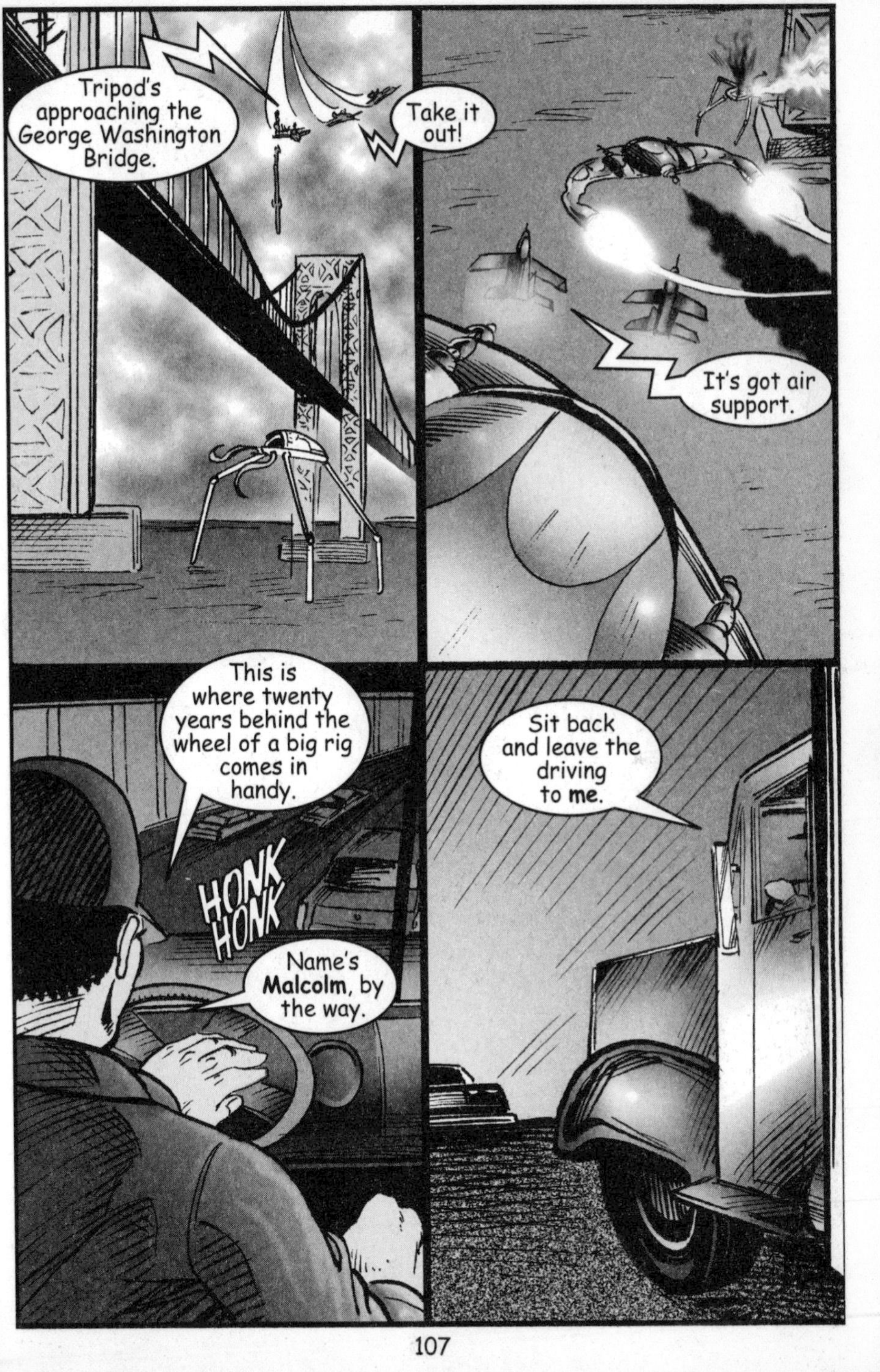
Tripod's approaching the George Washington Bridge.
Take it out!
It's got air support.
This is where twenty years behind the wheel of a big rig comes in handy.
HONK HONK
Name's **Malcolm**, by the way.
Sit back and leave the driving to **me**.

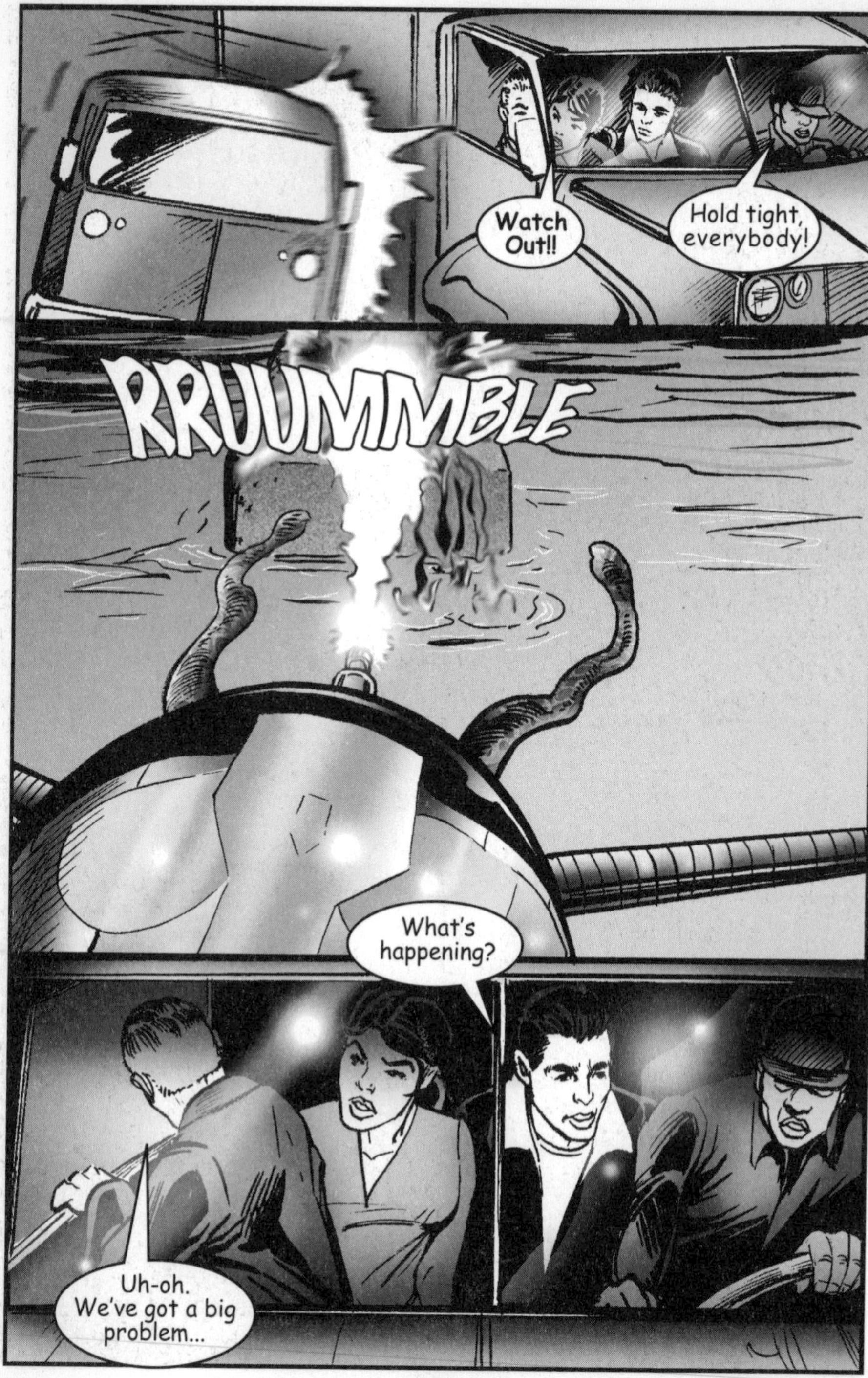
Watch Out!!
Hold tight, everybody!
RRUUMMBLE
What's happening?
Uh-oh. We've got a big problem...

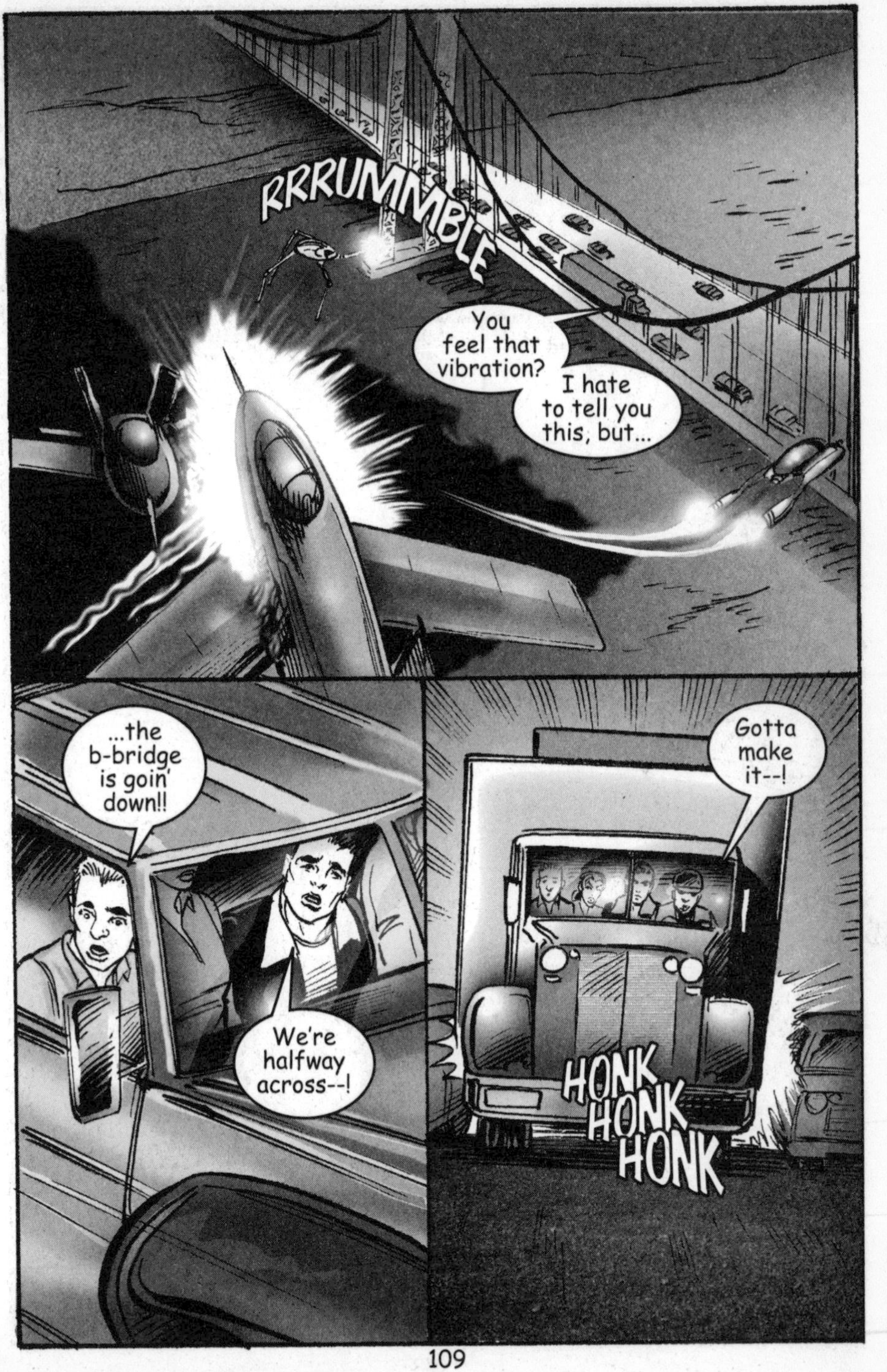
RRRUMMBLE
You feel that vibration?
I hate to tell you this, but...
...the b-bridge is goin' down!!
We're halfway across--!
Gotta make it--!
HONK HONK HONK

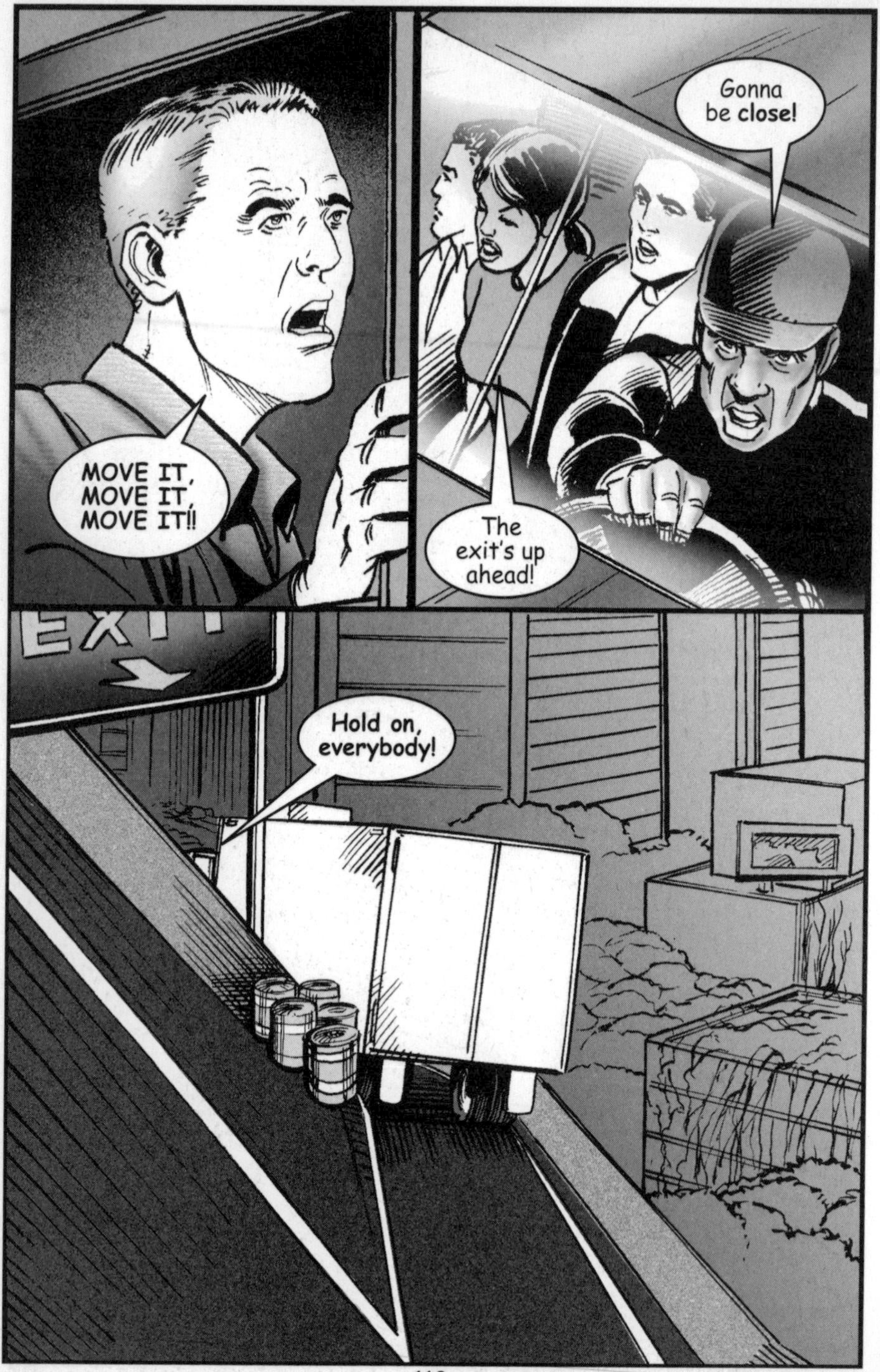
MOVE IT, MOVE IT, MOVE IT!!
Gonna be **close!**
The exit's up ahead!
EXIT
Hold on, everybody!

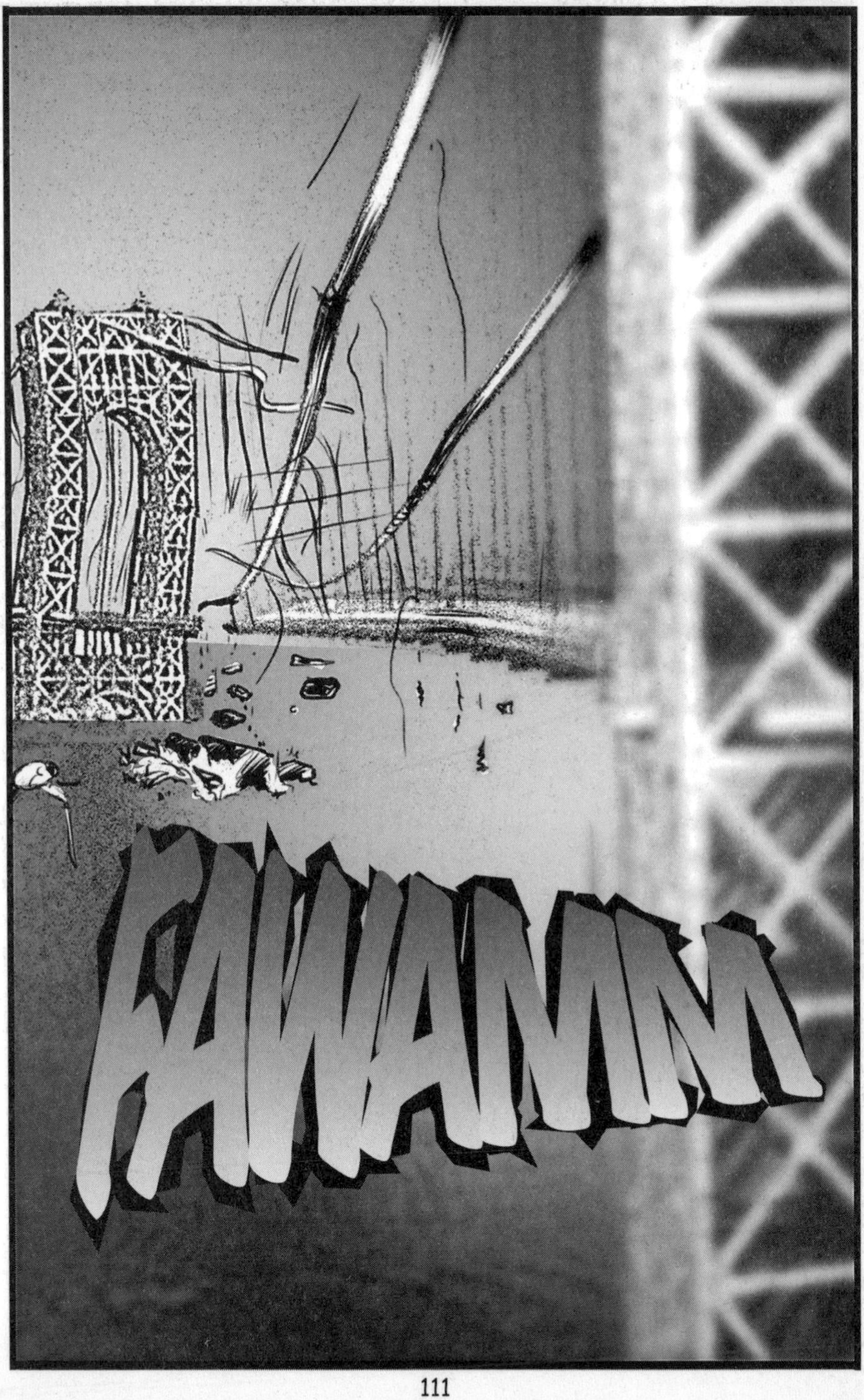
FAWAMM

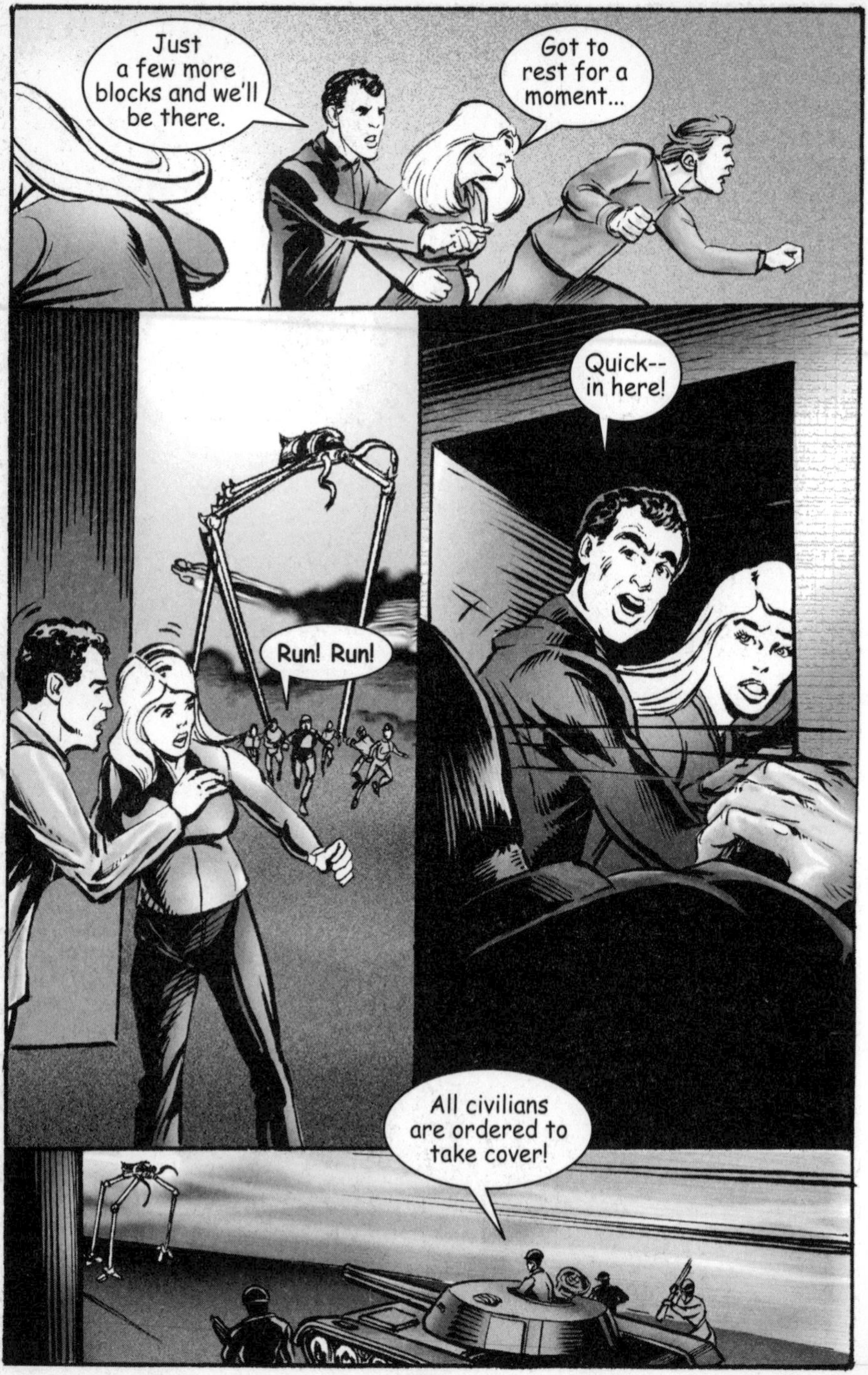
Just a few more blocks and we'll be there.
Got to rest for a moment...
Run! Run!
Quick-- in here!
All civilians are ordered to take cover!

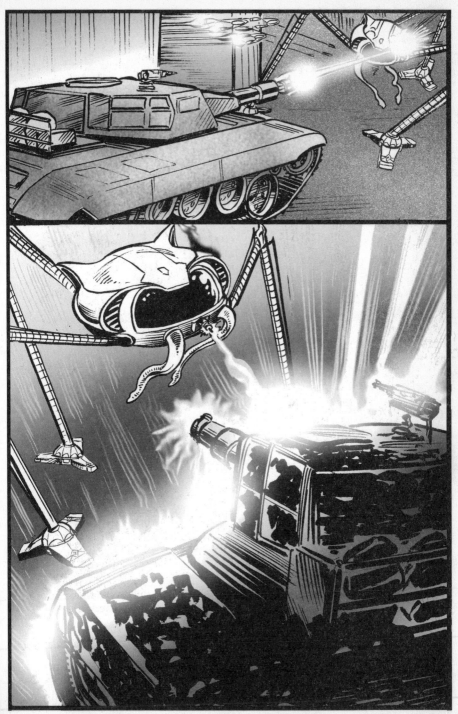

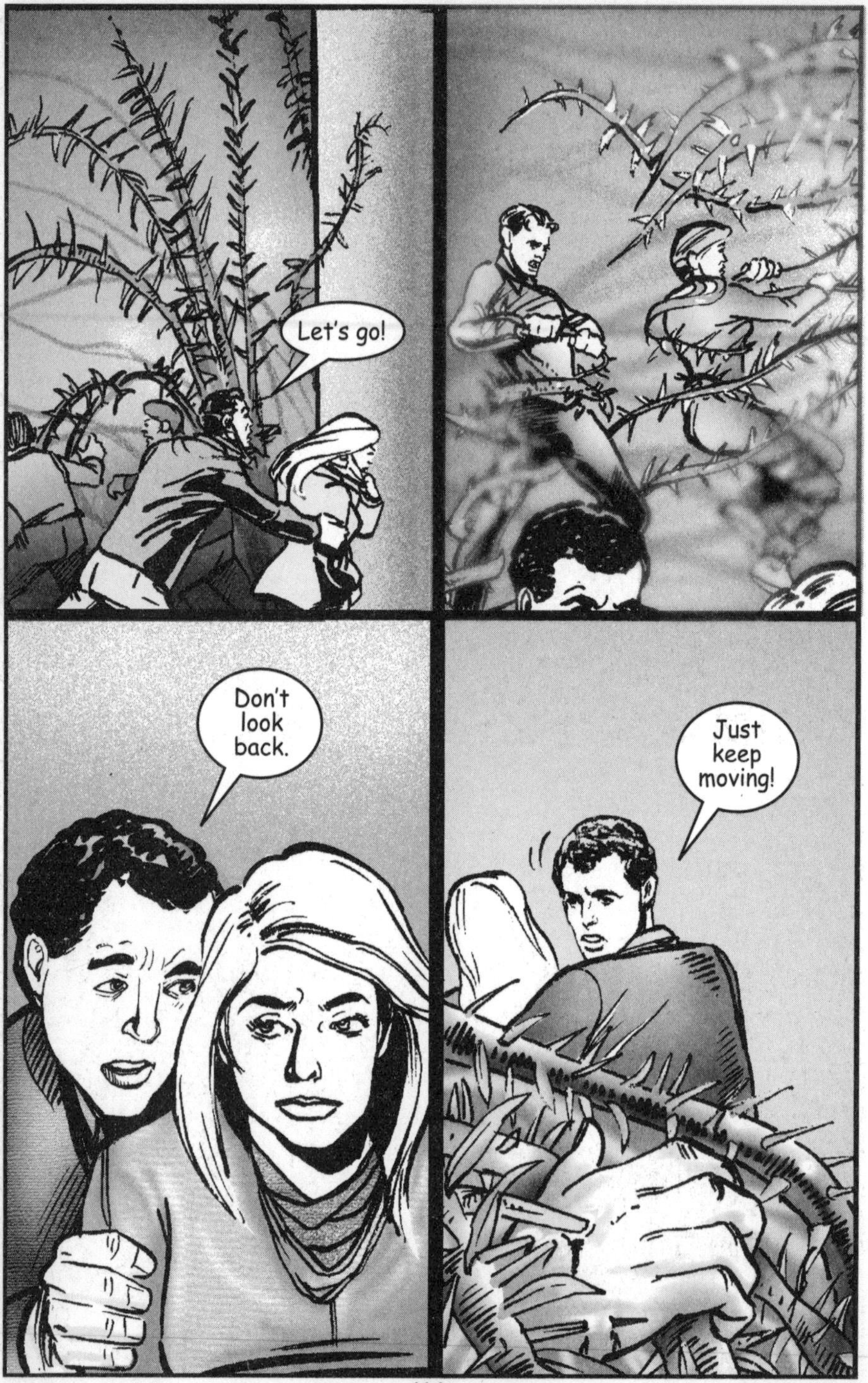
Let's go!
Don't look back.
Just keep moving!

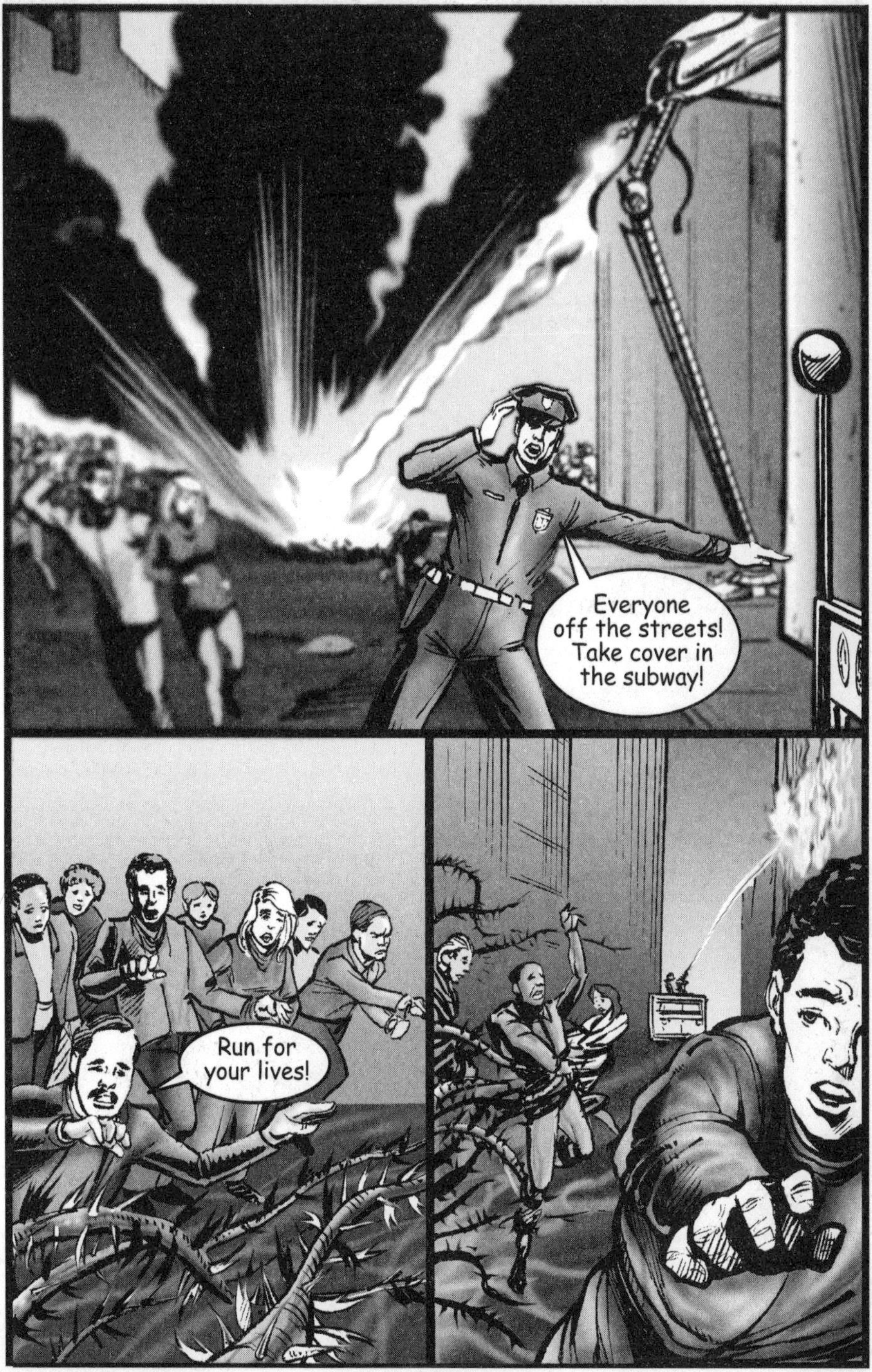
Everyone off the streets! Take cover in the subway!
Run for your lives!

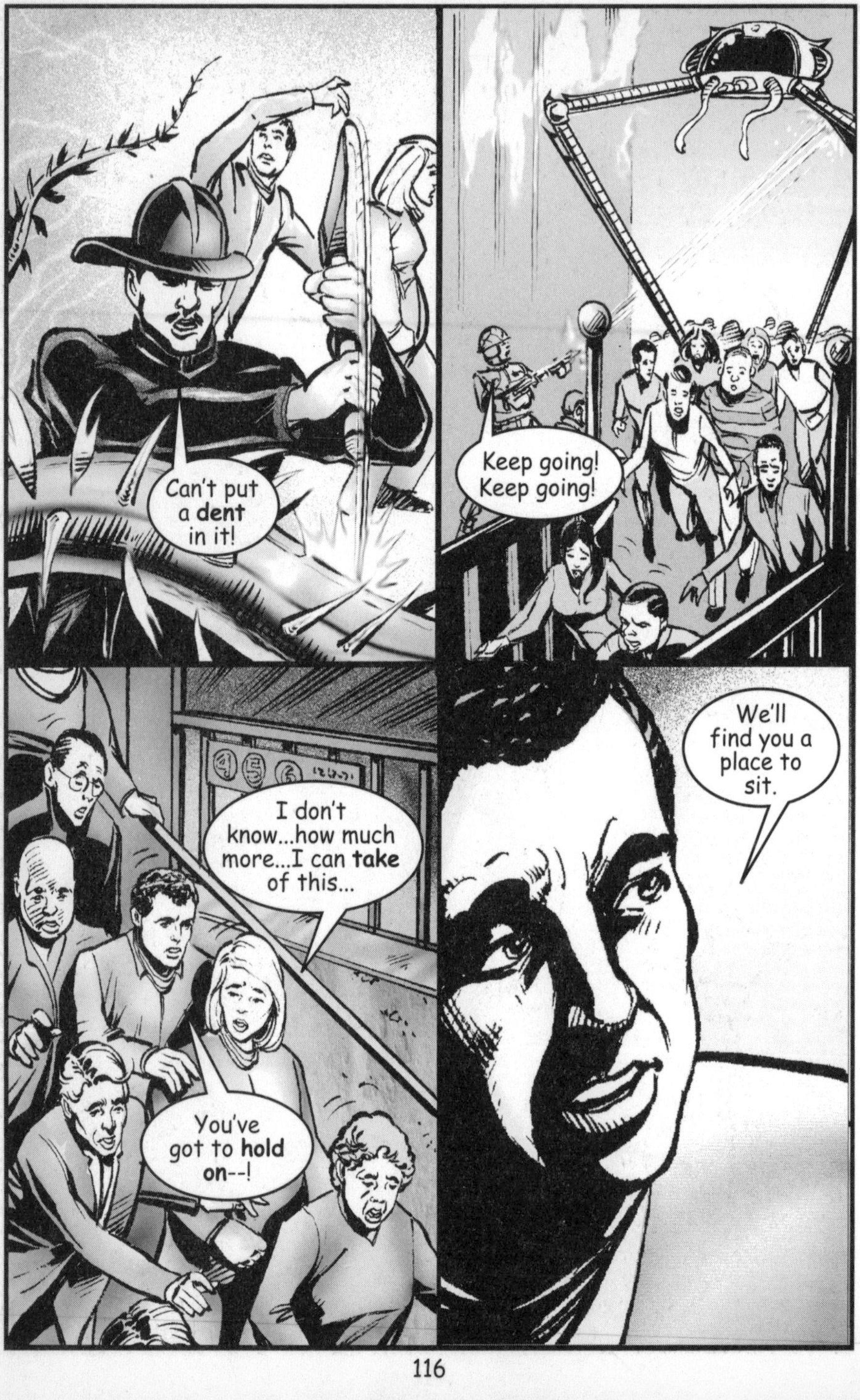
Can't put a **dent** in it!
Keep going! Keep going!
I don't know...how much more...I can **take** of this...
You've got to **hold on**--!
We'll find you a place to sit.

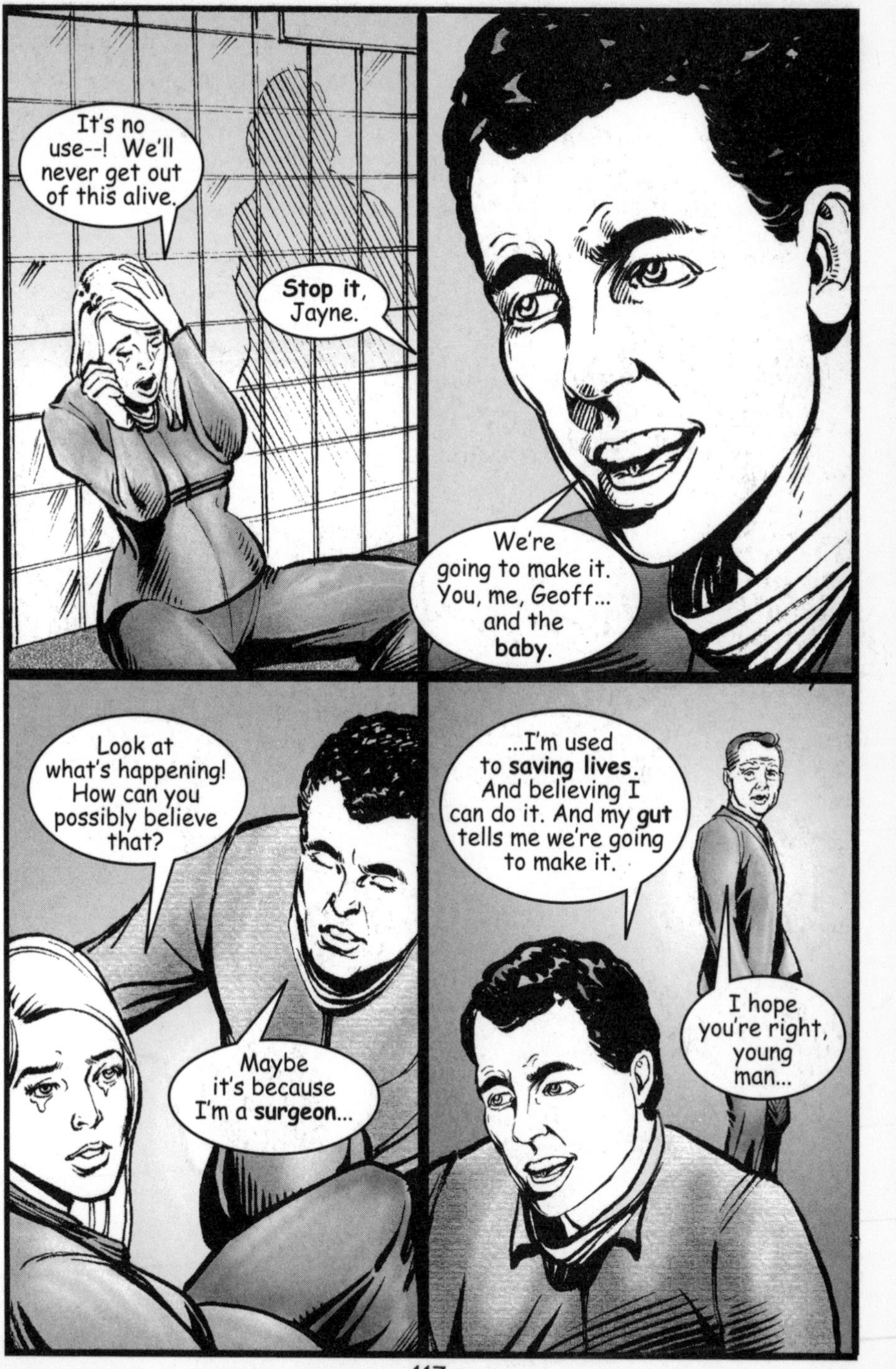
It's no use--! We'll never get out of this alive.
Stop it, Jayne.
We're going to make it. You, me, Geoff... and the **baby**.
Look at what's happening! How can you possibly believe that?
Maybe it's because I'm a **surgeon**...
...I'm used to **saving lives**. And believing I can do it. And my **gut** tells me we're going to make it.
I hope you're right, young man...

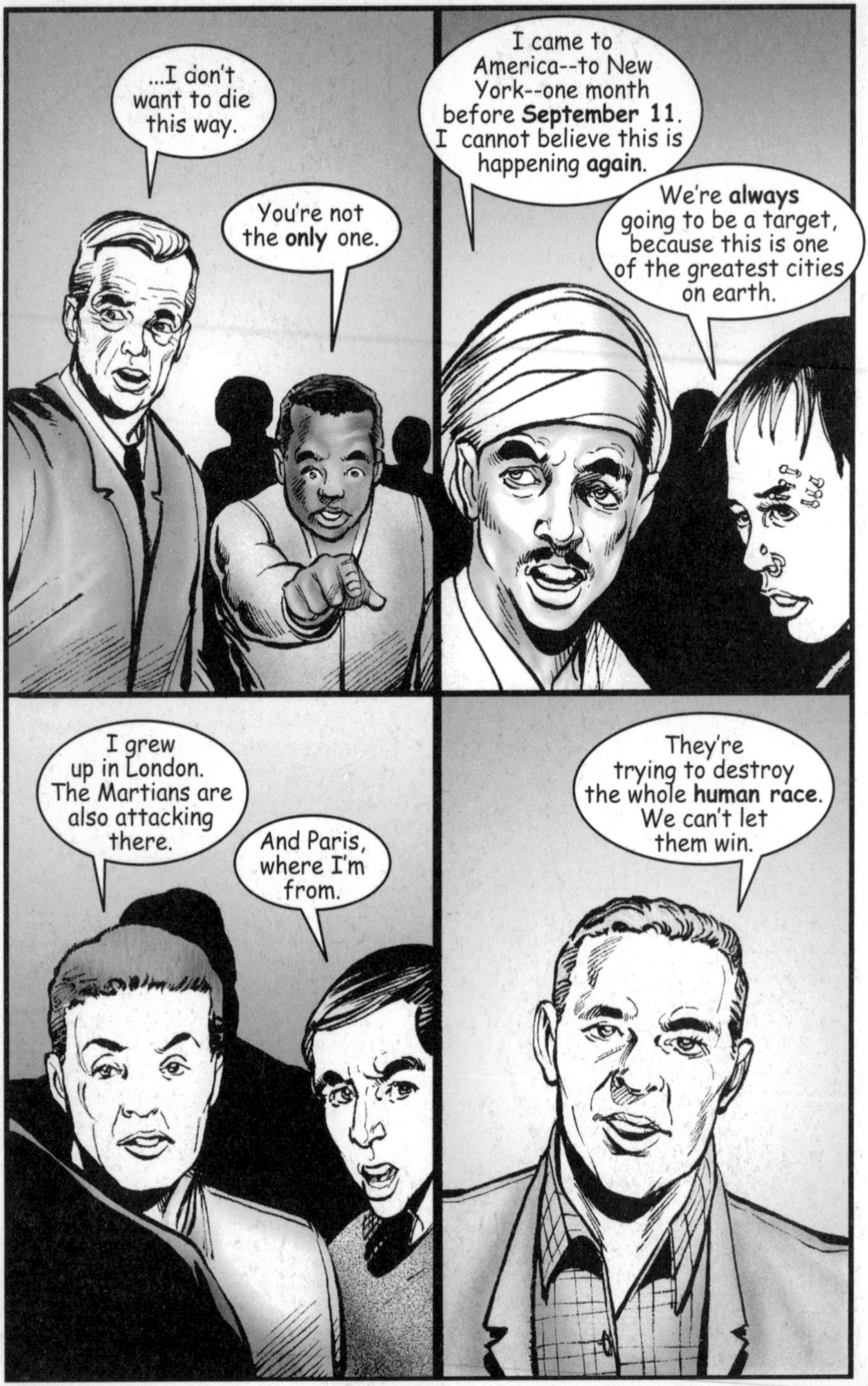
...I don't want to die this way.
You're not the **only** one.
I came to America--to New York--one month before **September 11**. I cannot believe this is happening **again**.
We're **always** going to be a target, because this is one of the greatest cities on earth.
I grew up in London. The Martians are also attacking there.
And Paris, where I'm from.
They're trying to destroy the whole **human race**. We can't let them win.

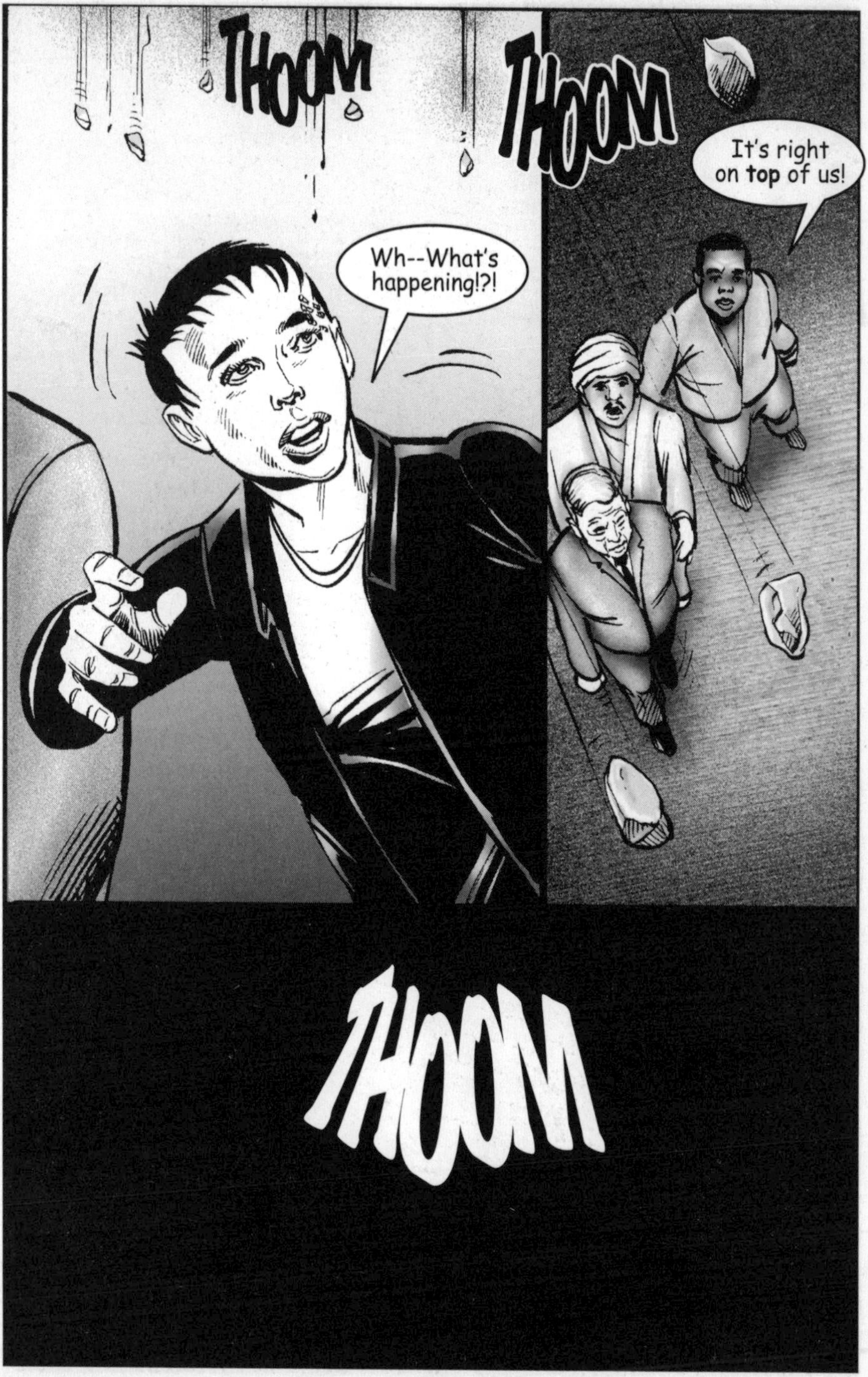
THOOM
THOOM
It's right on **top** of us!
Wh--What's happening!?!
THOOM

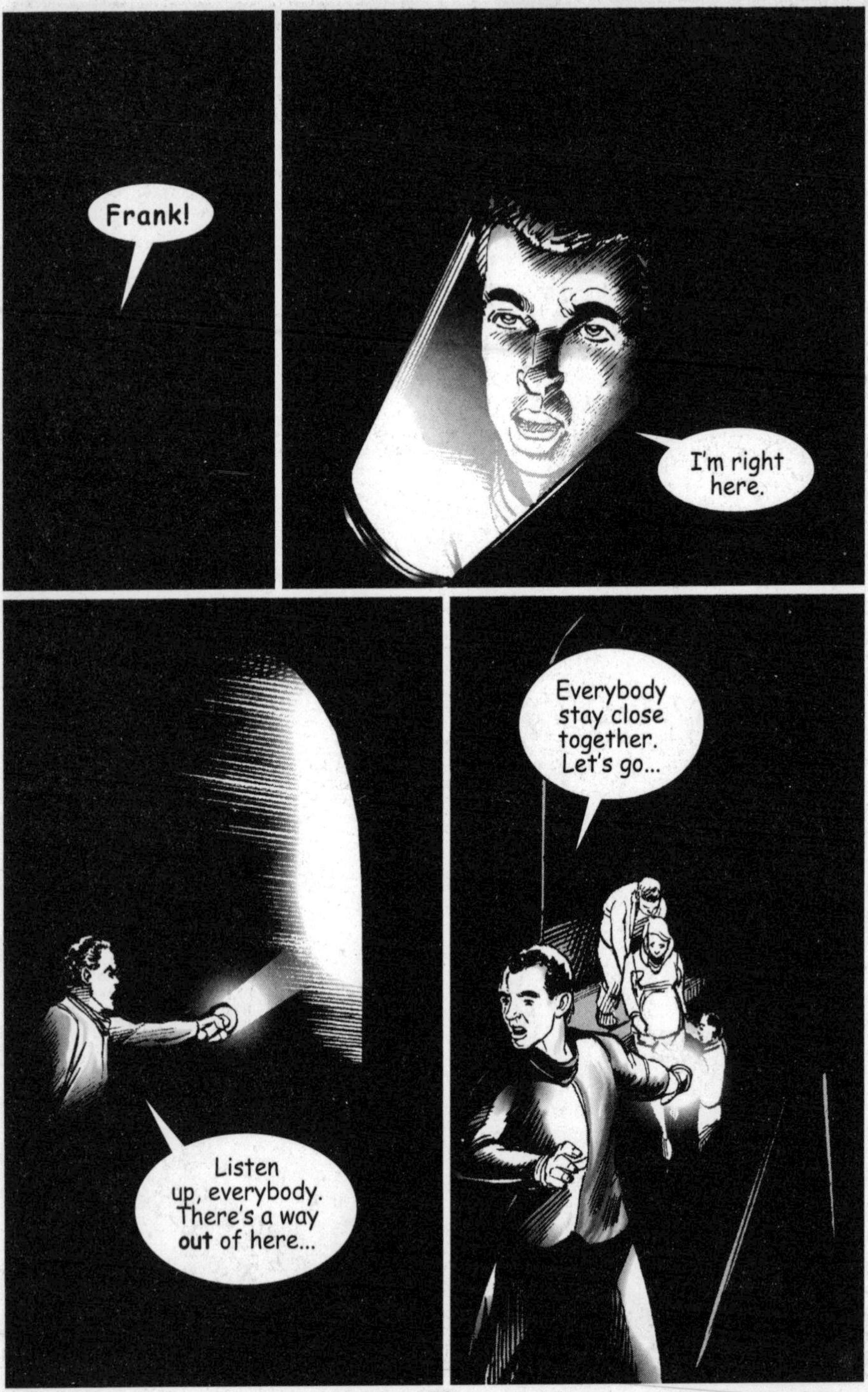
Frank!
I'm right here.
Listen up, everybody. There's a way out of here...
Everybody stay close together. Let's go...

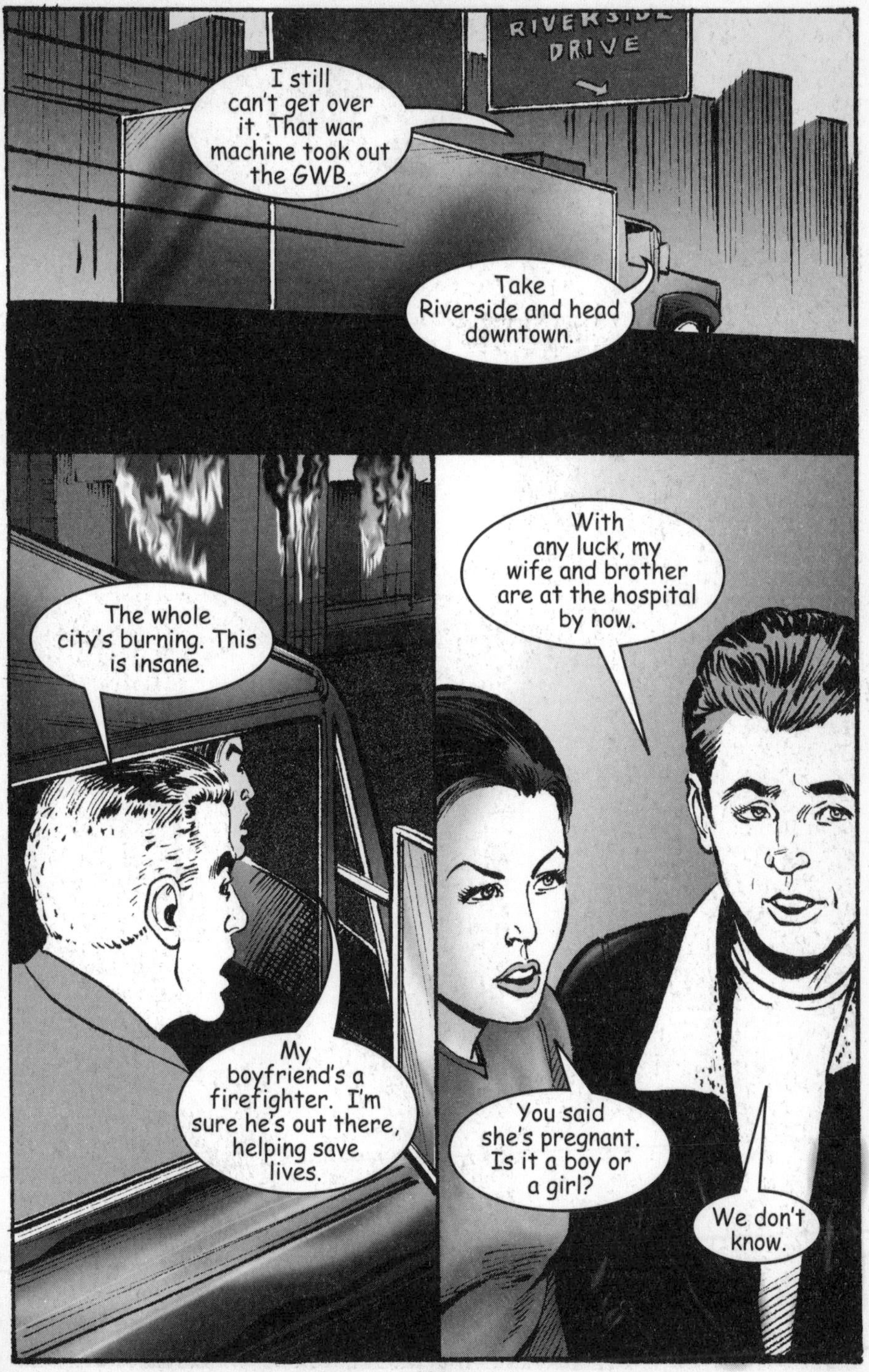
RIVERSIDE DRIVE
I still can't get over it. That war machine took out the GWB.
Take Riverside and head downtown.
The whole city's burning. This is insane.
My boyfriend's a firefighter. I'm sure he's out there, helping save lives.
With any luck, my wife and brother are at the hospital by now.
You said she's pregnant. Is it a boy or a girl?
We don't know.

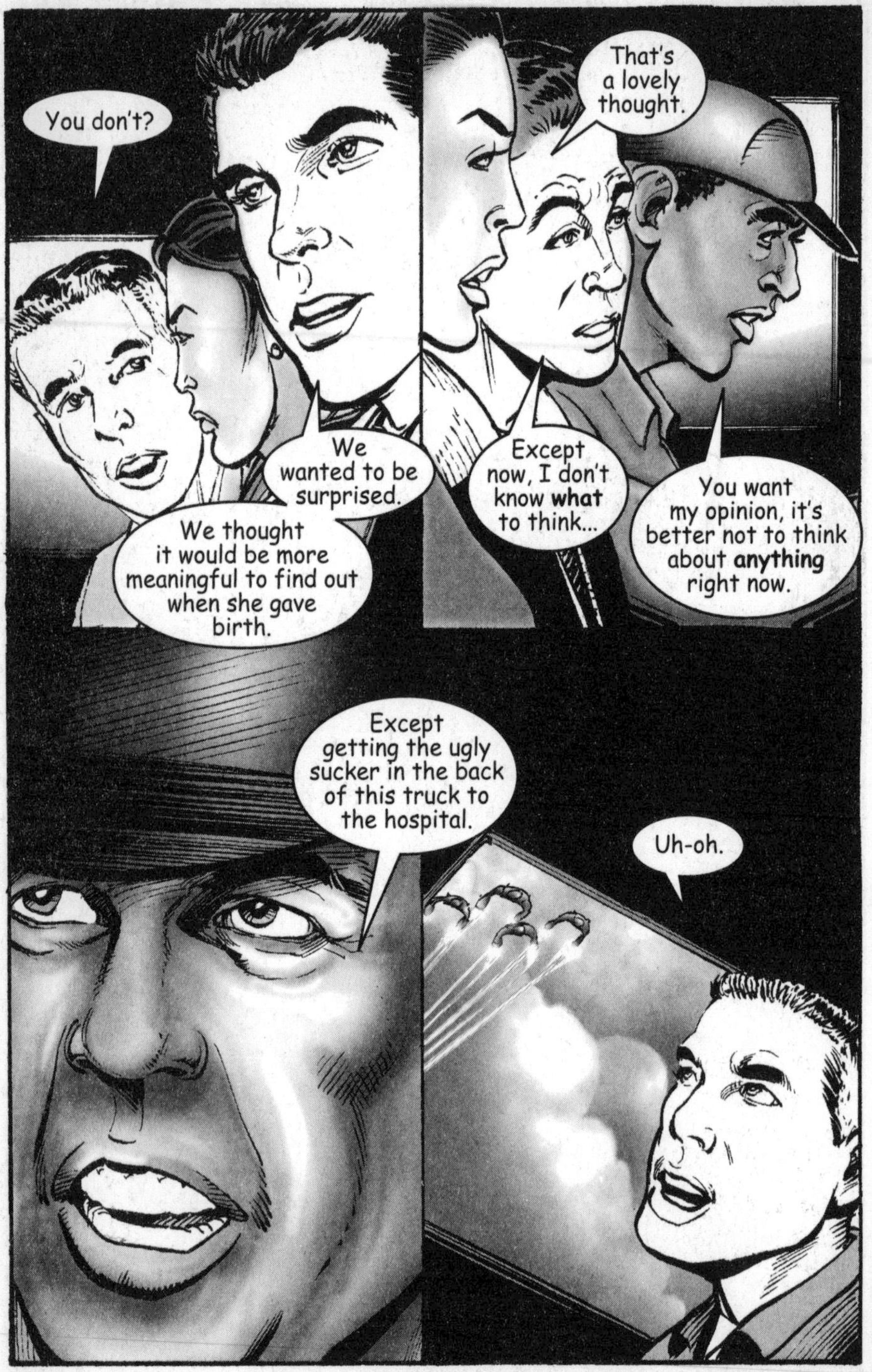
You don't?
We wanted to be surprised.
We thought it would be more meaningful to find out when she gave birth.
That's a lovely thought.
Except now, I don't know **what** to think...
You want my opinion, it's better not to think about **anything** right now.
Except getting the ugly sucker in the back of this truck to the hospital.
Uh-oh.

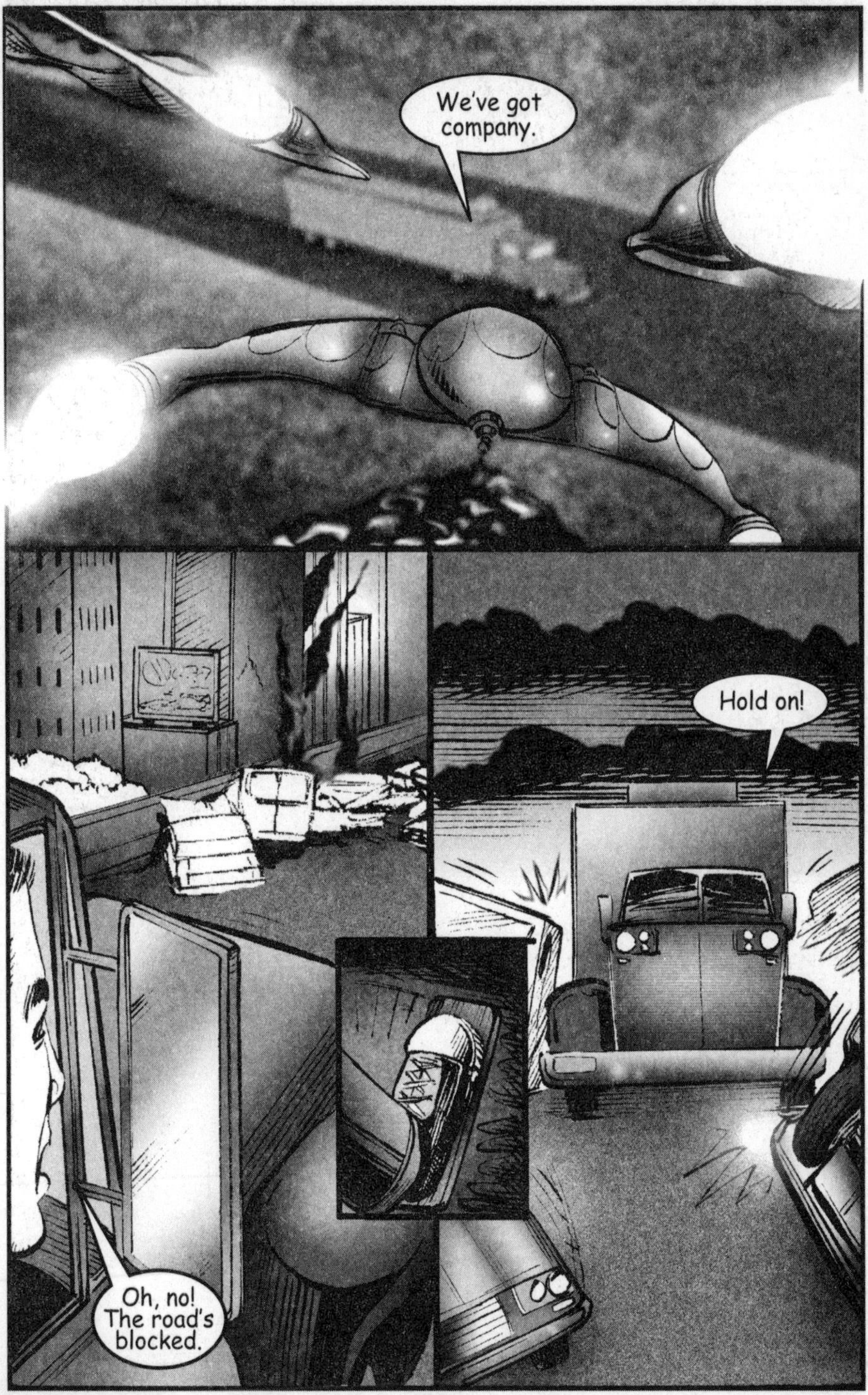
We've got company.
Oh, no! The road's blocked.
Hold on!

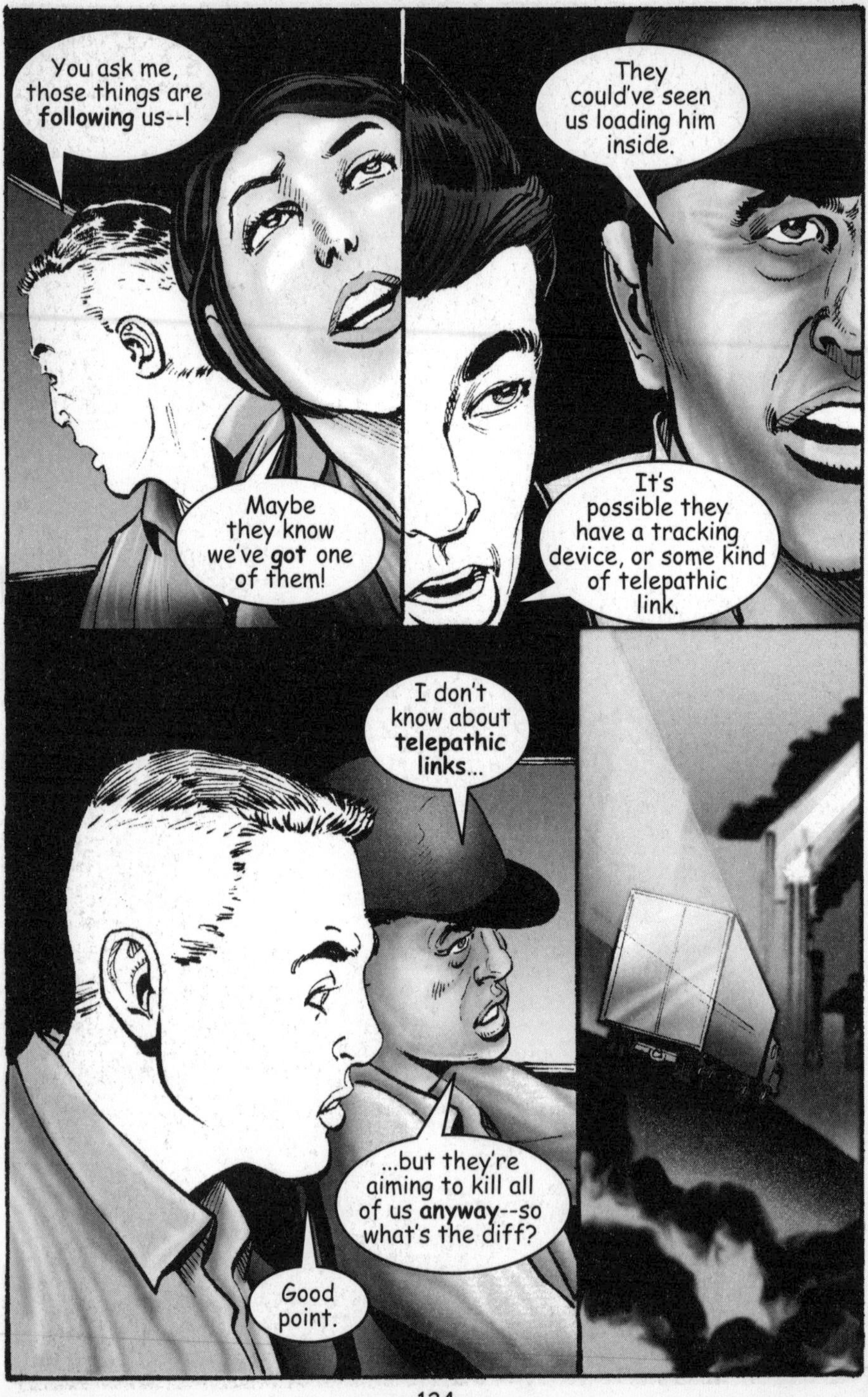
You ask me, those things are **following** us--!
They could've seen us loading him inside.
Maybe they know we've **got** one of them!
It's possible they have a tracking device, or some kind of telepathic link.
I don't know about **telepathic links**...
...but they're aiming to kill all of us **anyway**--so what's the diff?
Good point.

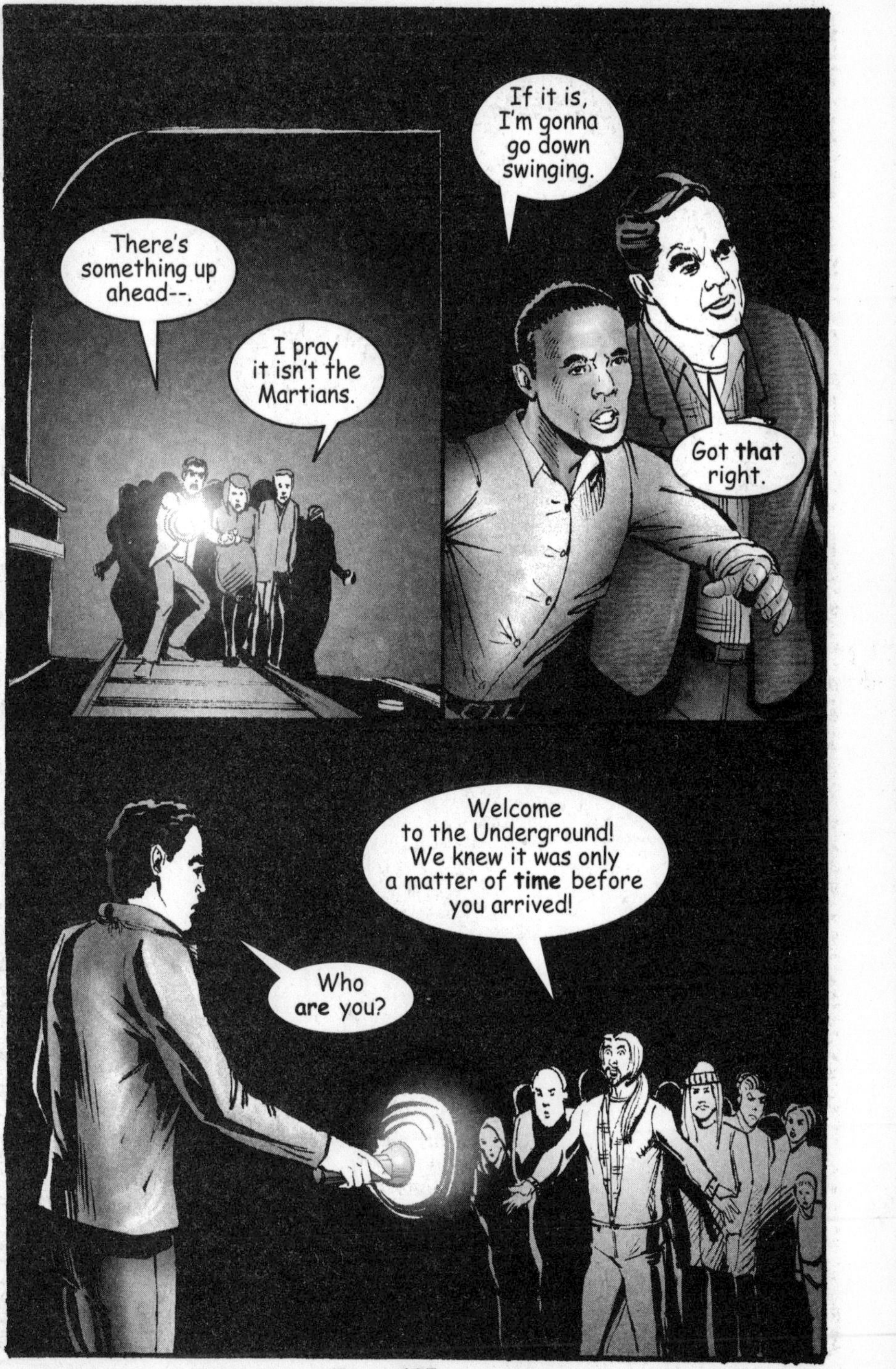
There's something up ahead--.
I pray it isn't the Martians.
If it is, I'm gonna go down swinging.
Got that right.
Welcome to the Underground! We knew it was only a matter of **time** before you arrived!
Who **are** you?

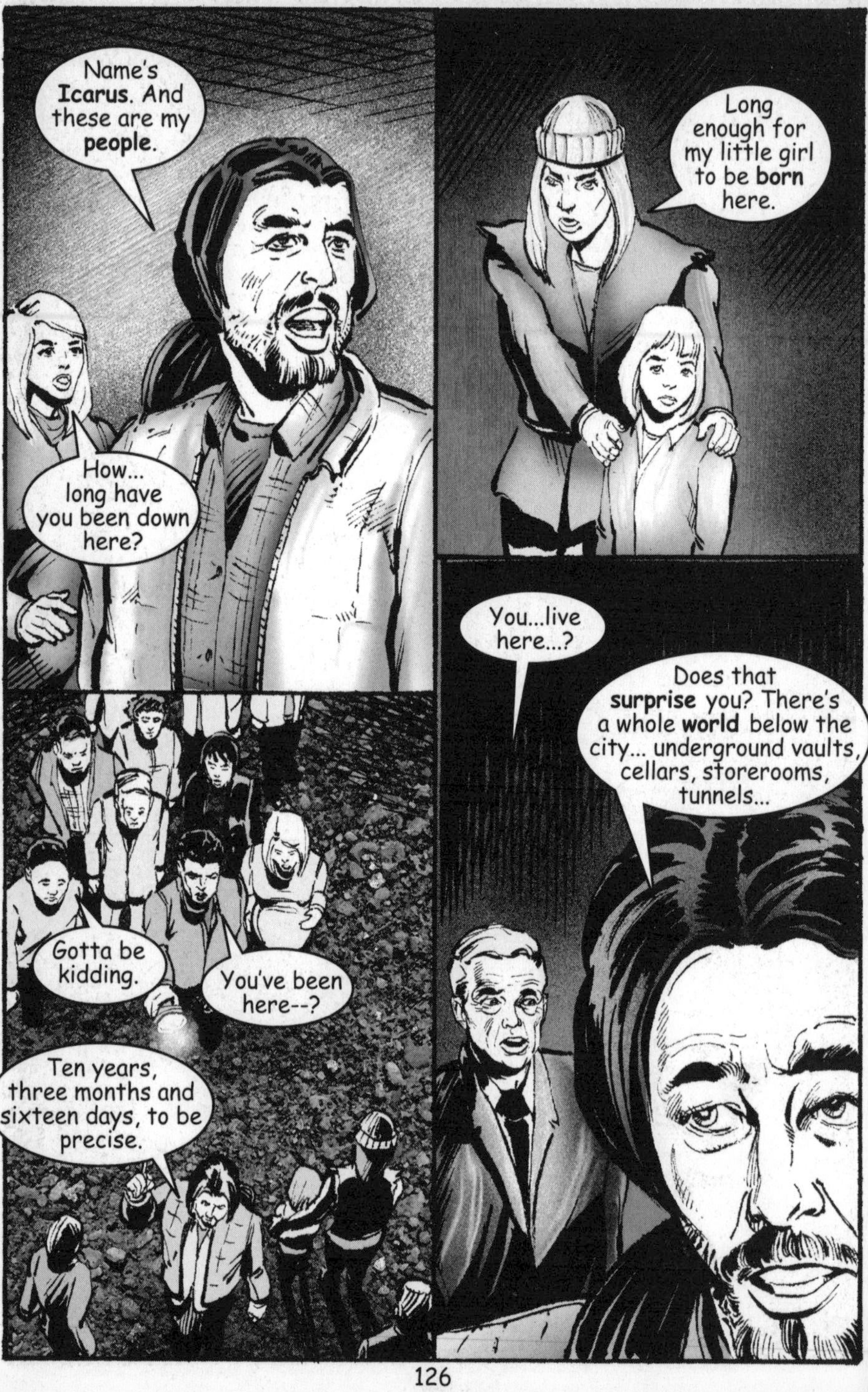

Name's **Icarus**. And these are my **people**.
How... long have you been down here?
Long enough for my little girl to be **born** here.
Gotta be kidding.
You've been here--?
Ten years, three months and sixteen days, to be precise.
You...live here...?
Does that **surprise** you? There's a whole **world** below the city... underground vaults, cellars, storerooms, tunnels...

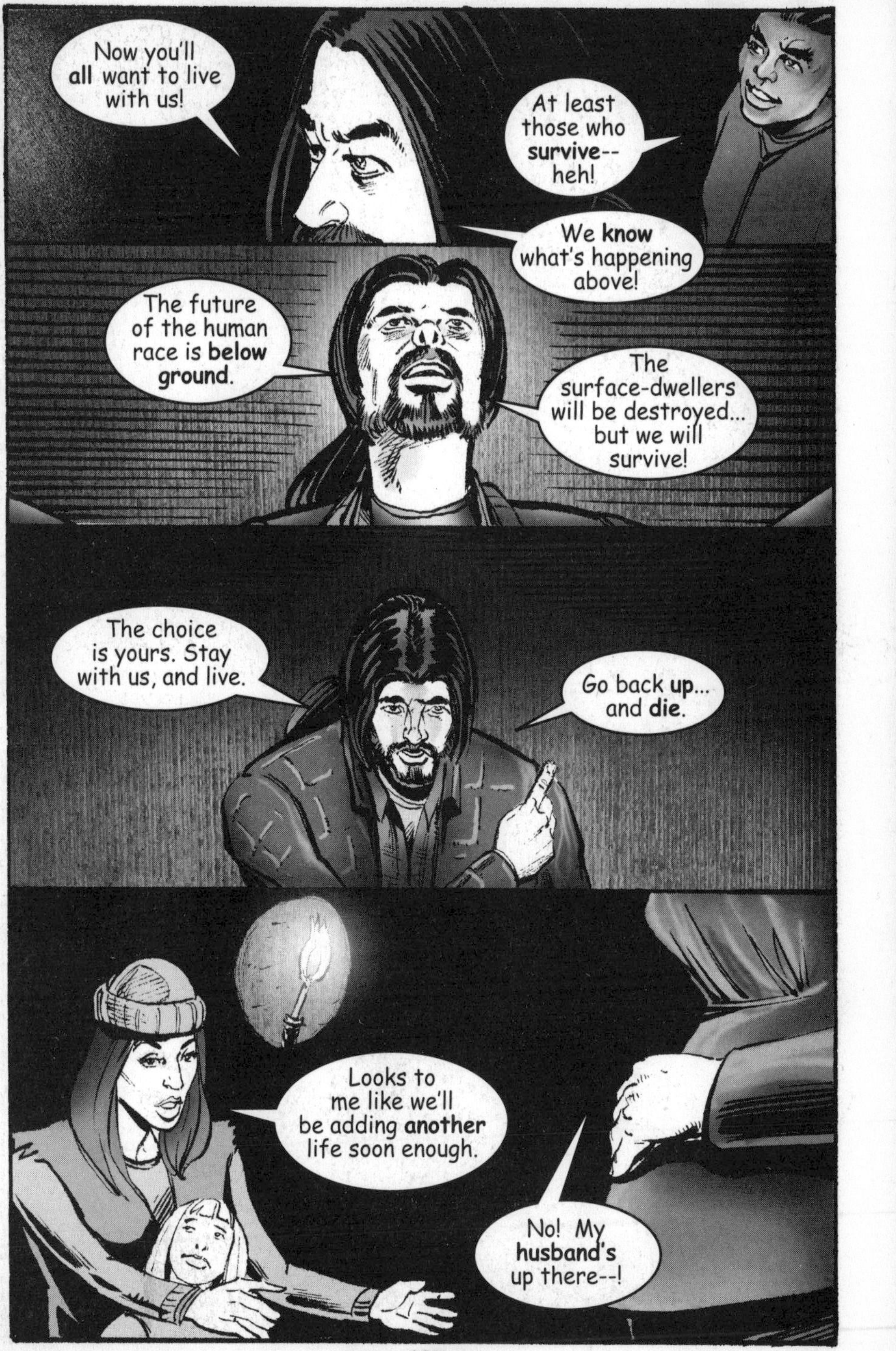
Now you'll **all** want to live with us!
At least those who **survive**-- heh!
We **know** what's happening above!
The future of the human race is **below ground**.
The surface-dwellers will be destroyed... but we will survive!
The choice is yours. Stay with us, and live.
Go back **up**... and **die**.
Looks to me like we'll be adding **another** life soon enough.
No! My **husband's** up there--!

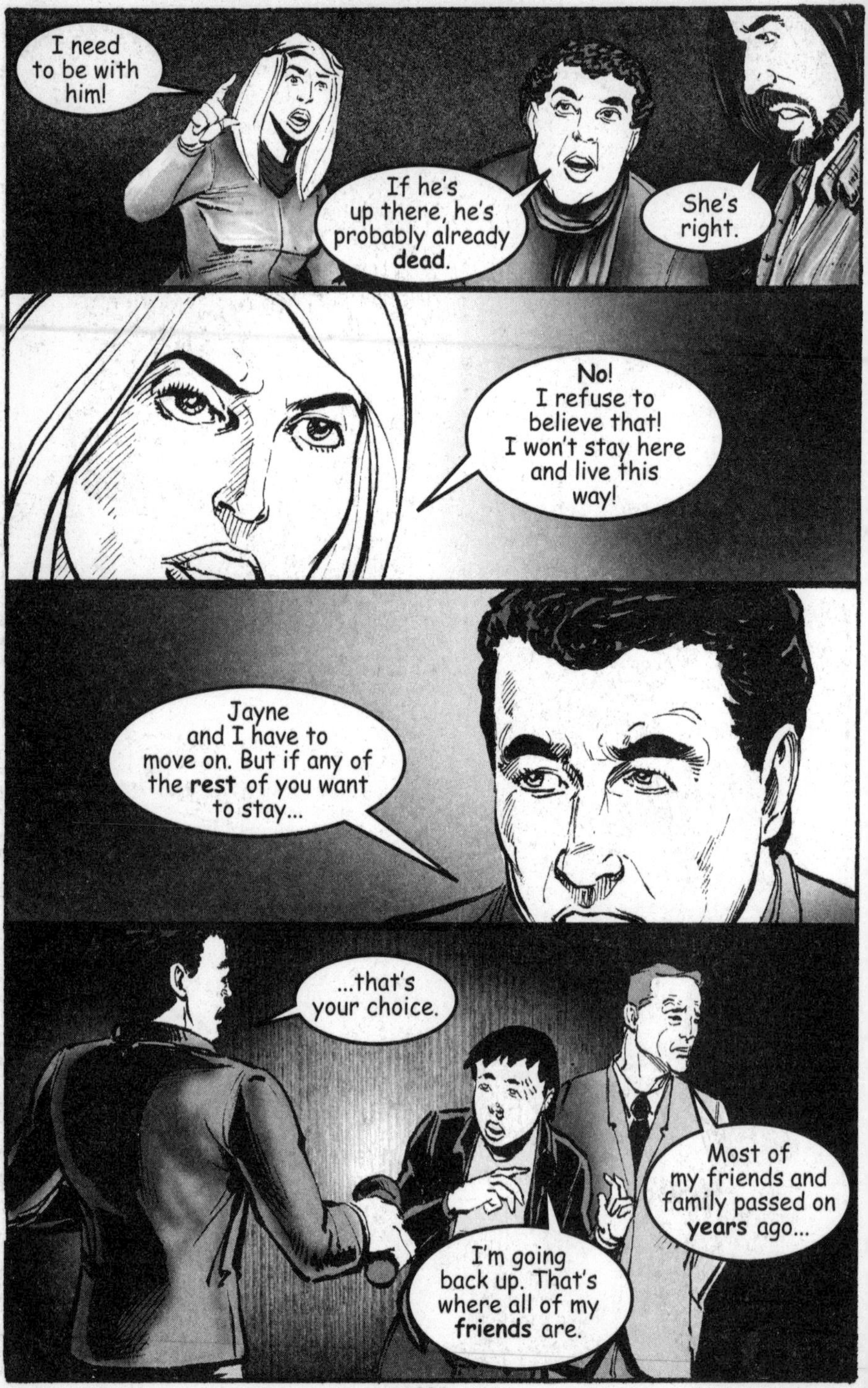
I need to be with him!
If he's up there, he's probably already **dead**.
She's right.
No! I refuse to believe that! I won't stay here and live this way!
Jayne and I have to move on. But if any of the **rest** of you want to stay...
...that's your choice.
Most of my friends and family passed on **years** ago...
I'm going back up. That's where all of my **friends** are.

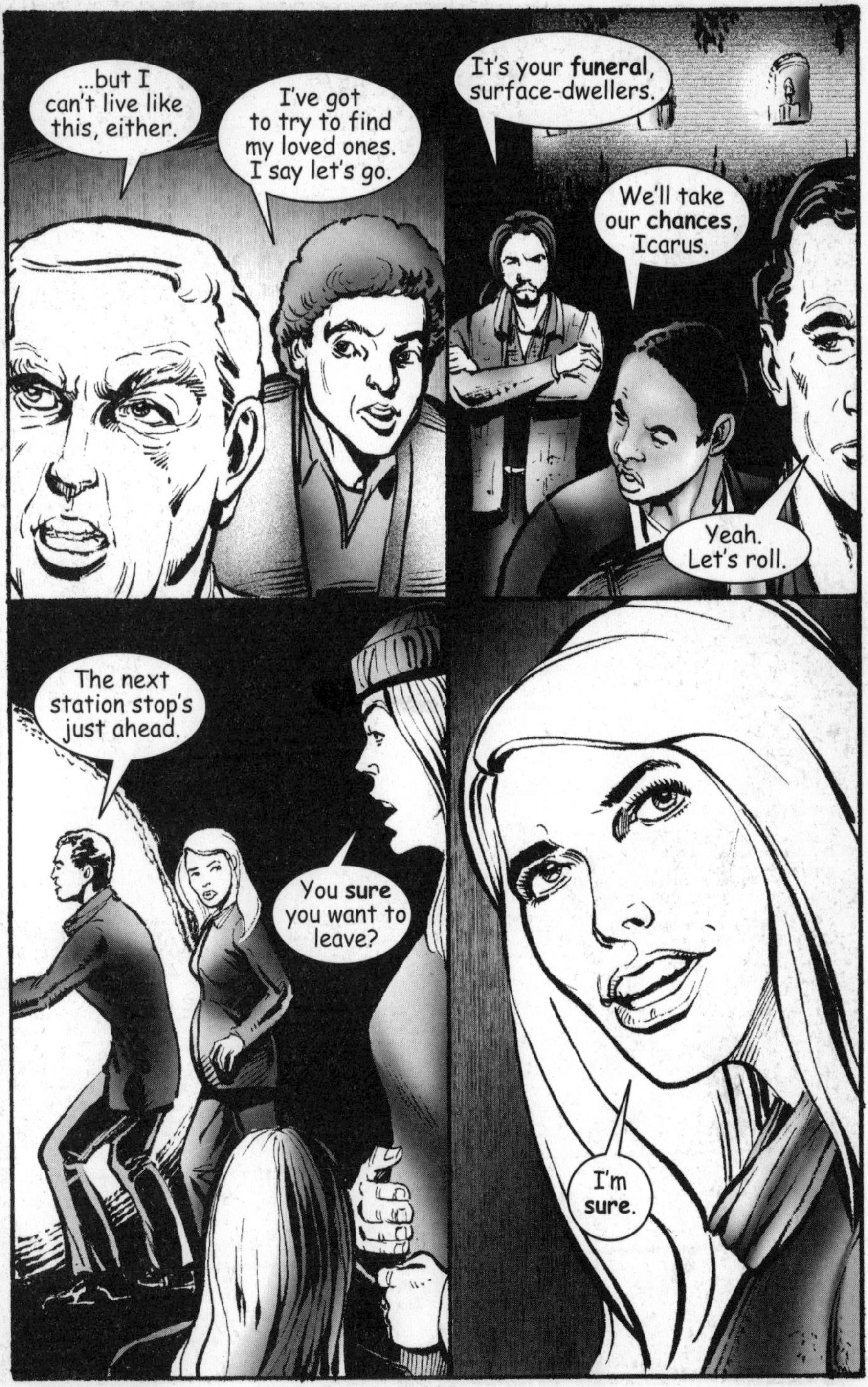
...but I can't live like this, either.
I've got to try to find my loved ones. I say let's go.
It's your **funeral**, surface-dwellers.
We'll take our **chances**, Icarus.
Yeah. Let's roll.
The next station stop's just ahead.
You **sure** you want to leave?
I'm **sure**.

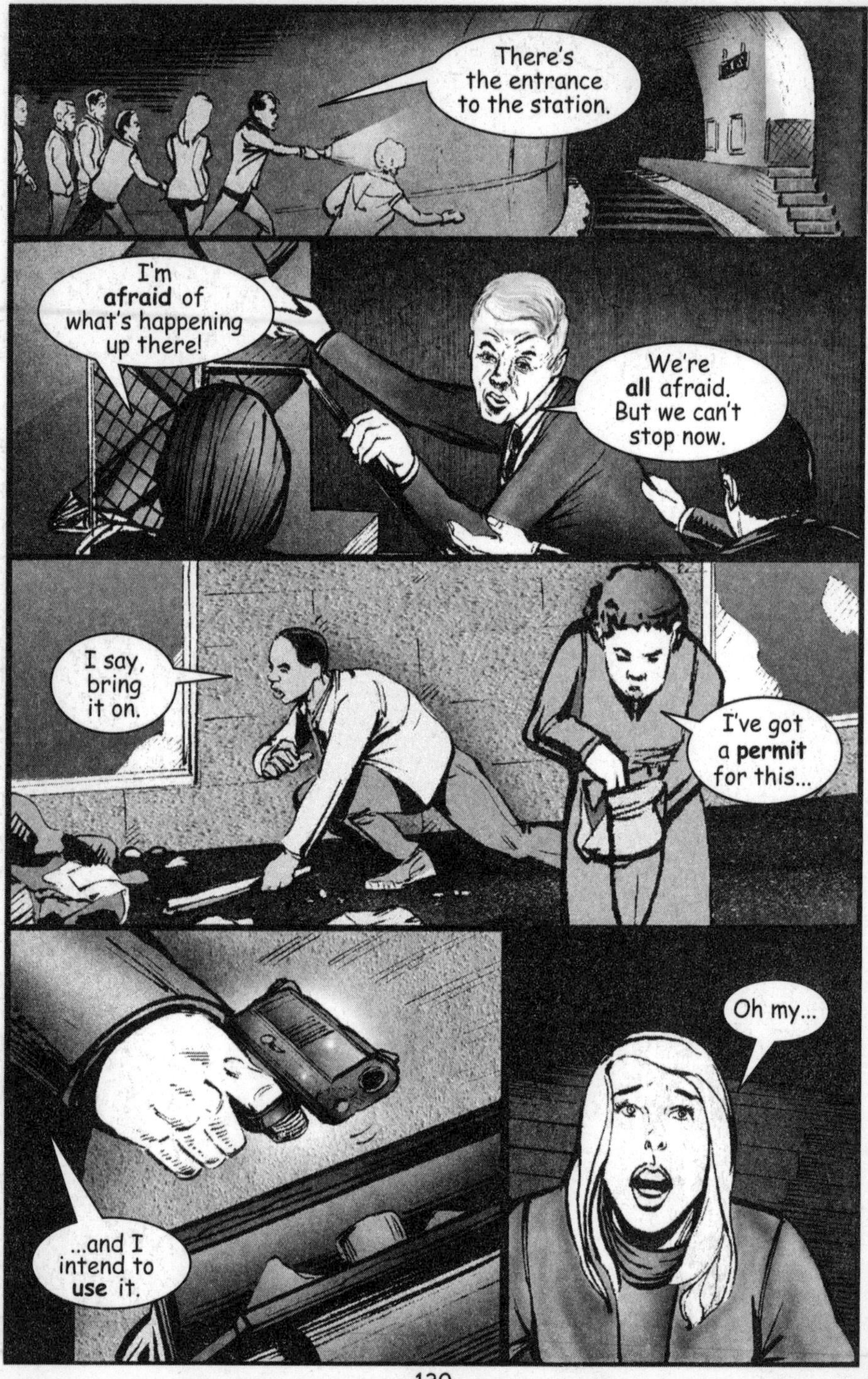
There's the entrance to the station.
I'm **afraid** of what's happening up there!
We're **all** afraid. But we can't stop now.
I say, bring it on.
I've got a **permit** for this...
...and I intend to **use** it.
Oh my...

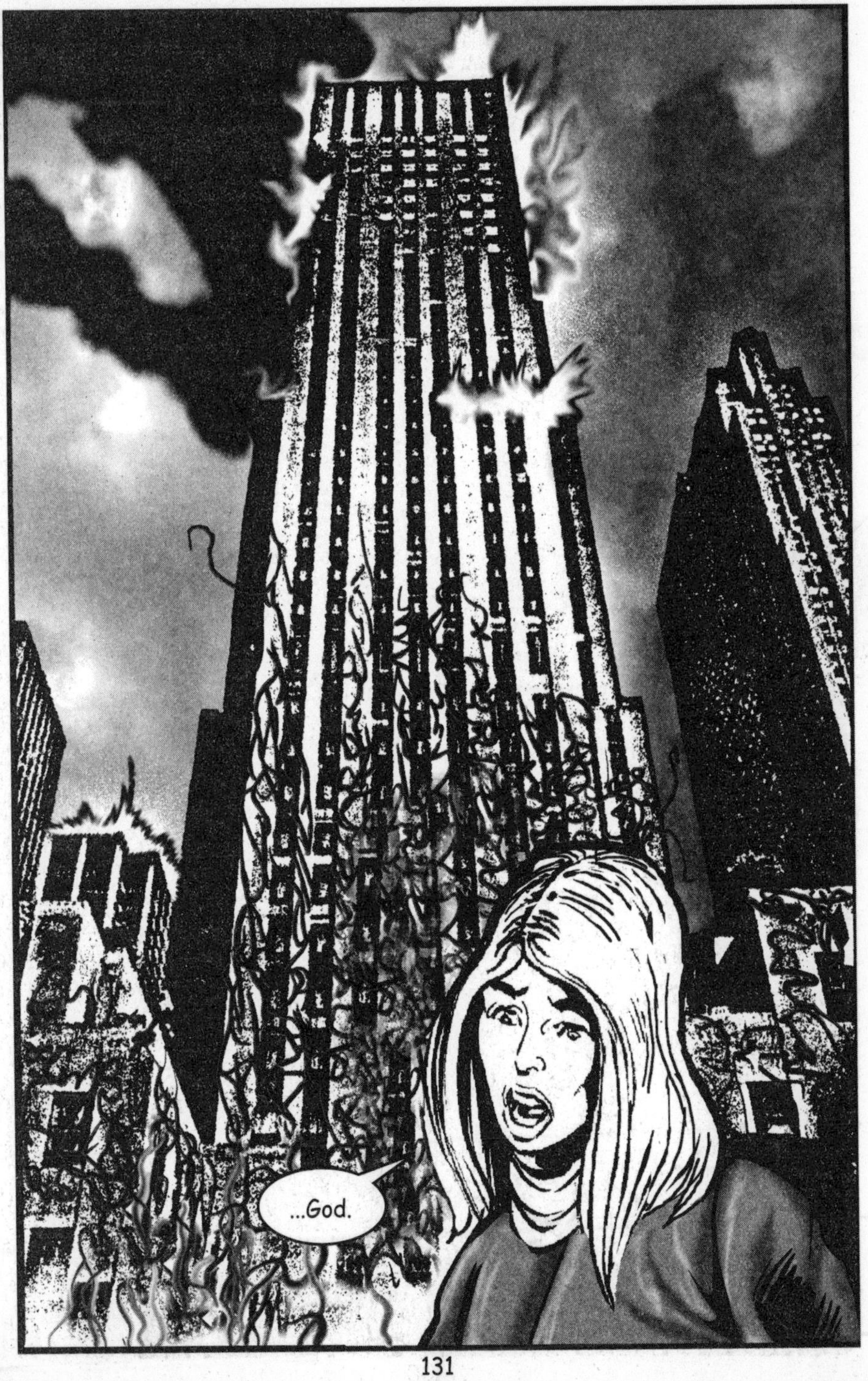
...God.

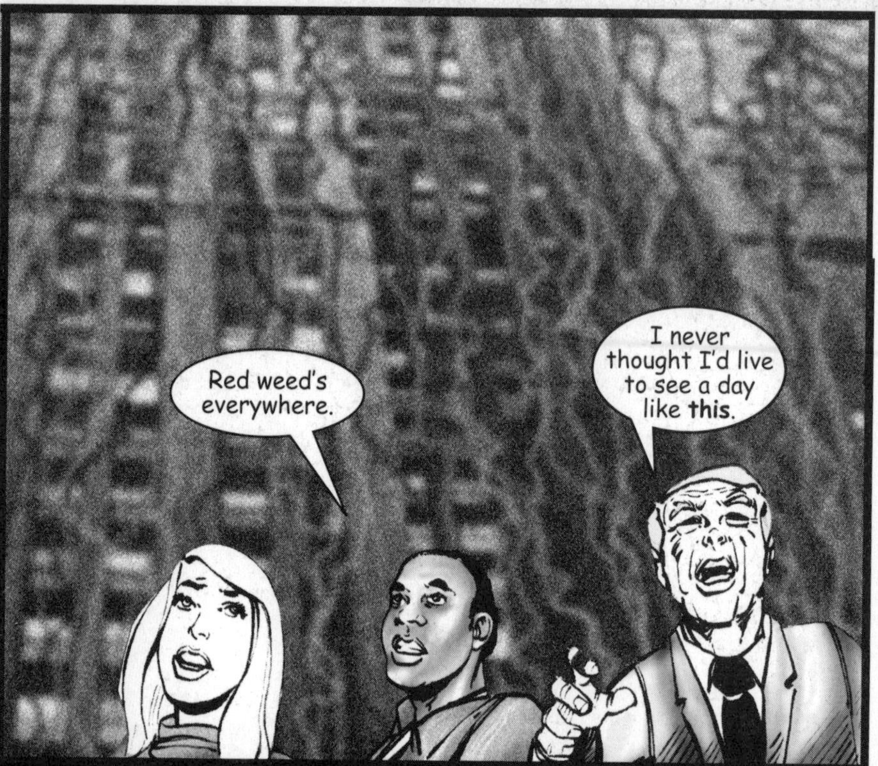
Red weed's everywhere.
I never thought I'd live to see a day like **this**.

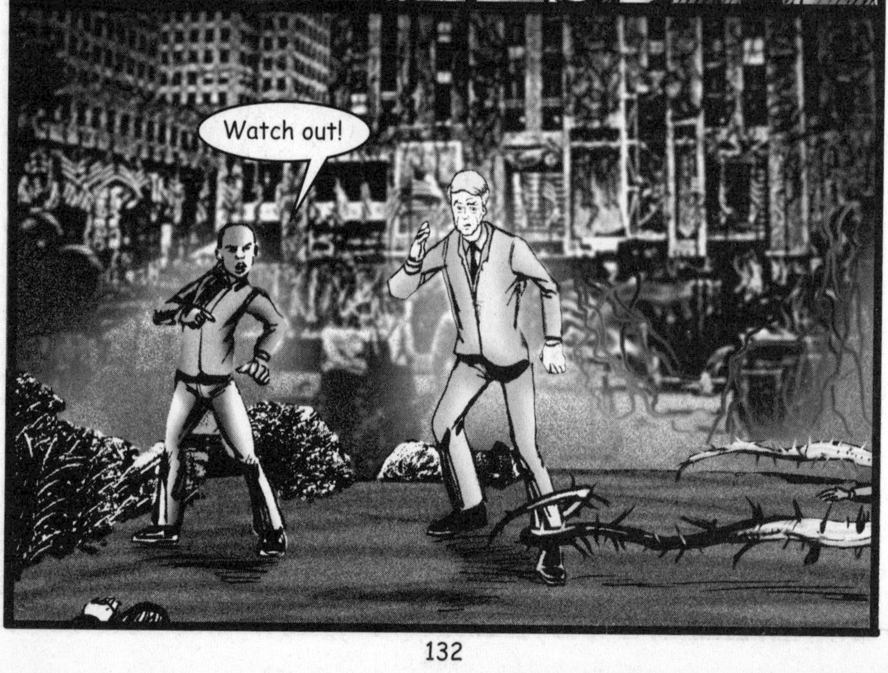
Watch out!

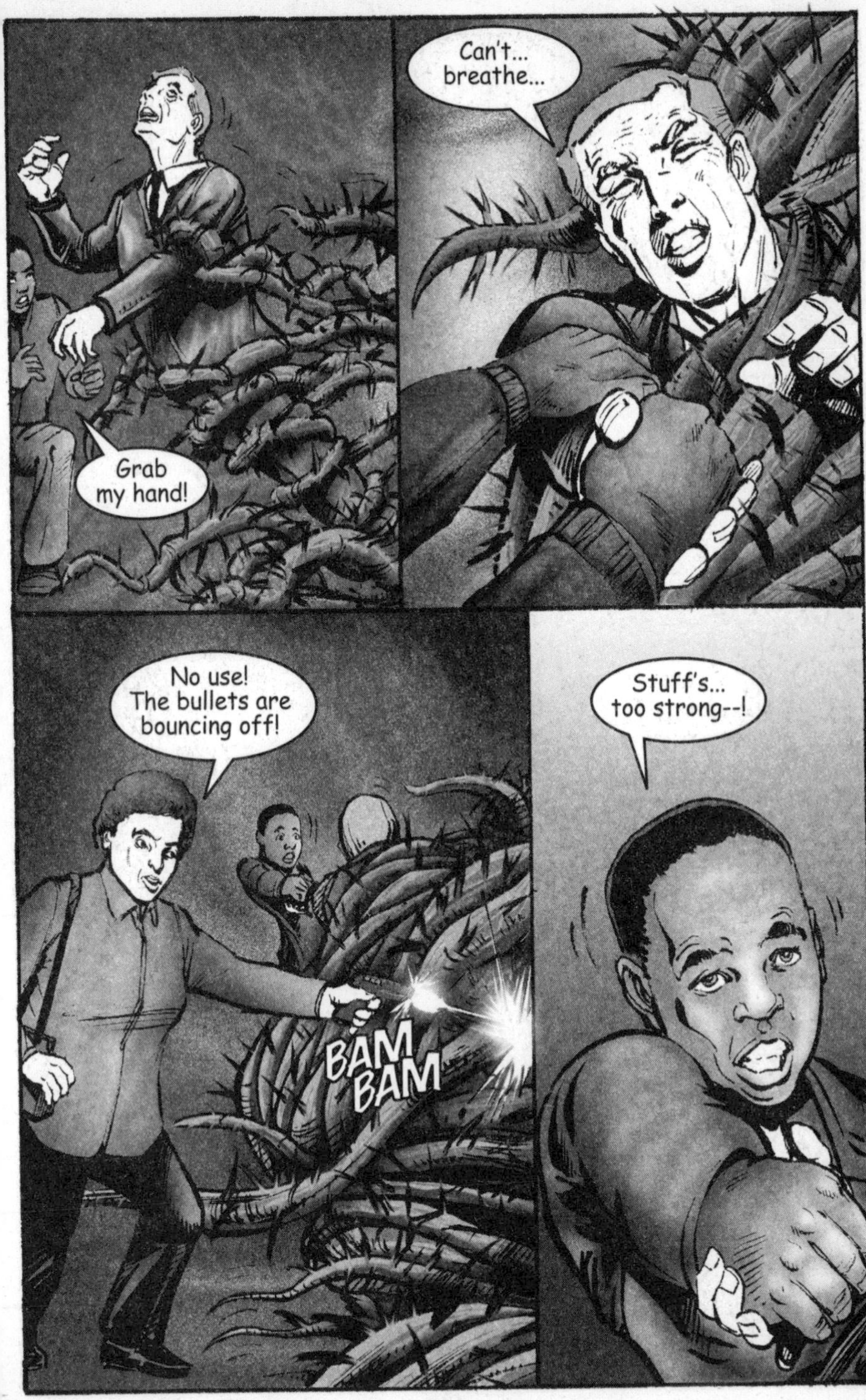
Grab my hand!
Can't... breathe...
No use! The bullets are bouncing off!
BAM BAM
Stuff's... too strong--!

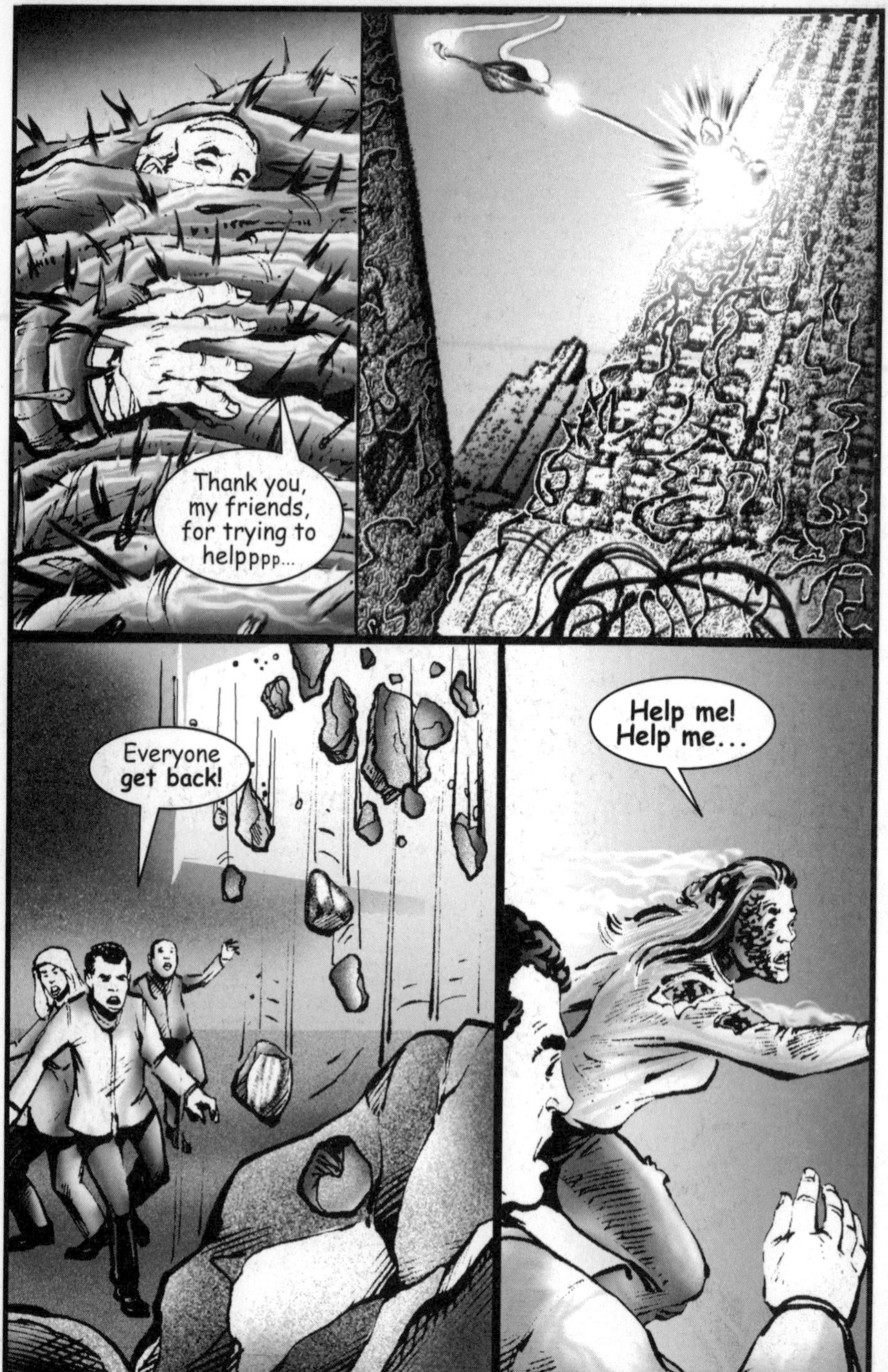
Thank you, my friends, for trying to helpppp...
Everyone get back!
Help me! Help me...

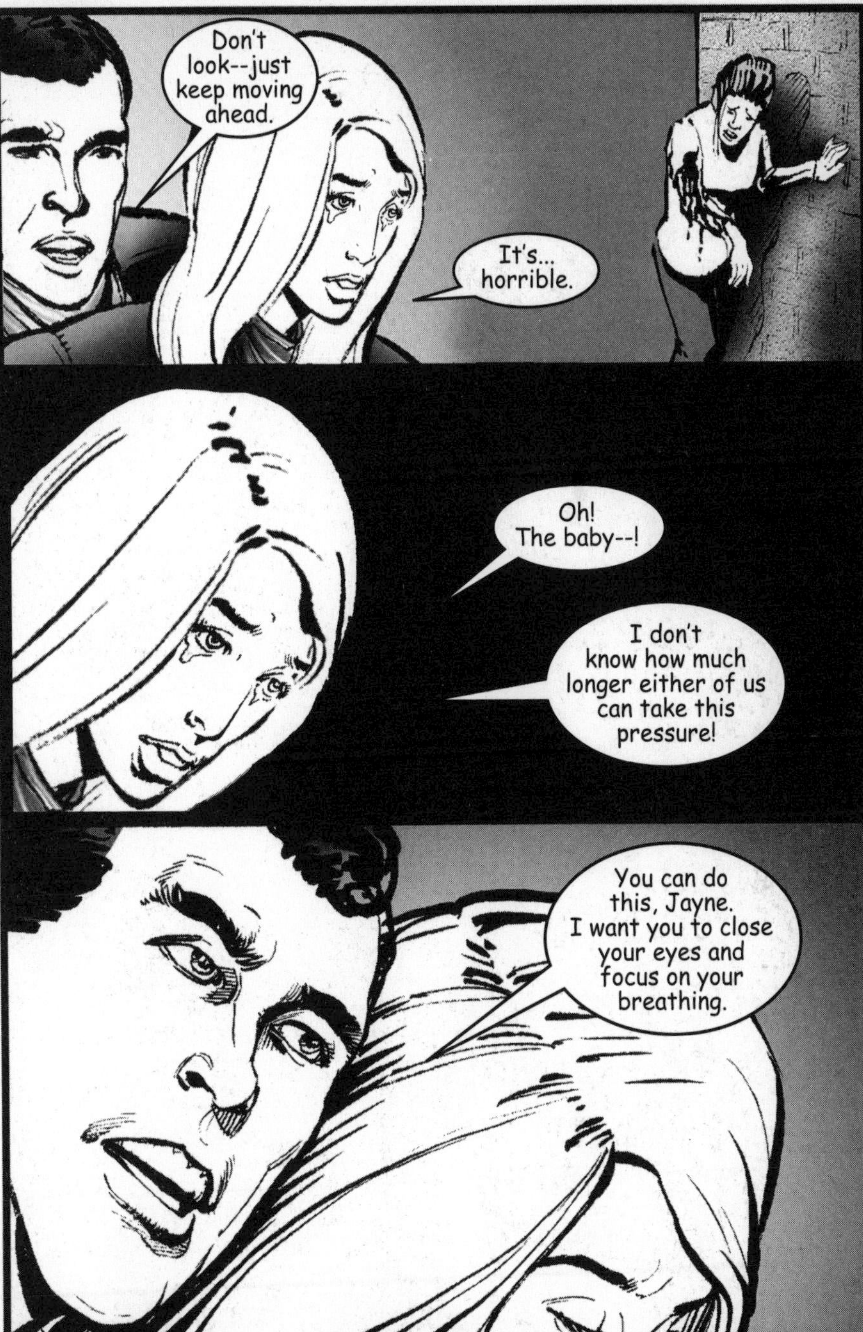
Don't look--just keep moving ahead.
It's... horrible.
Oh! The baby--!
I don't know how much longer either of us can take this pressure!
You can do this, Jayne. I want you to close your eyes and focus on your breathing.

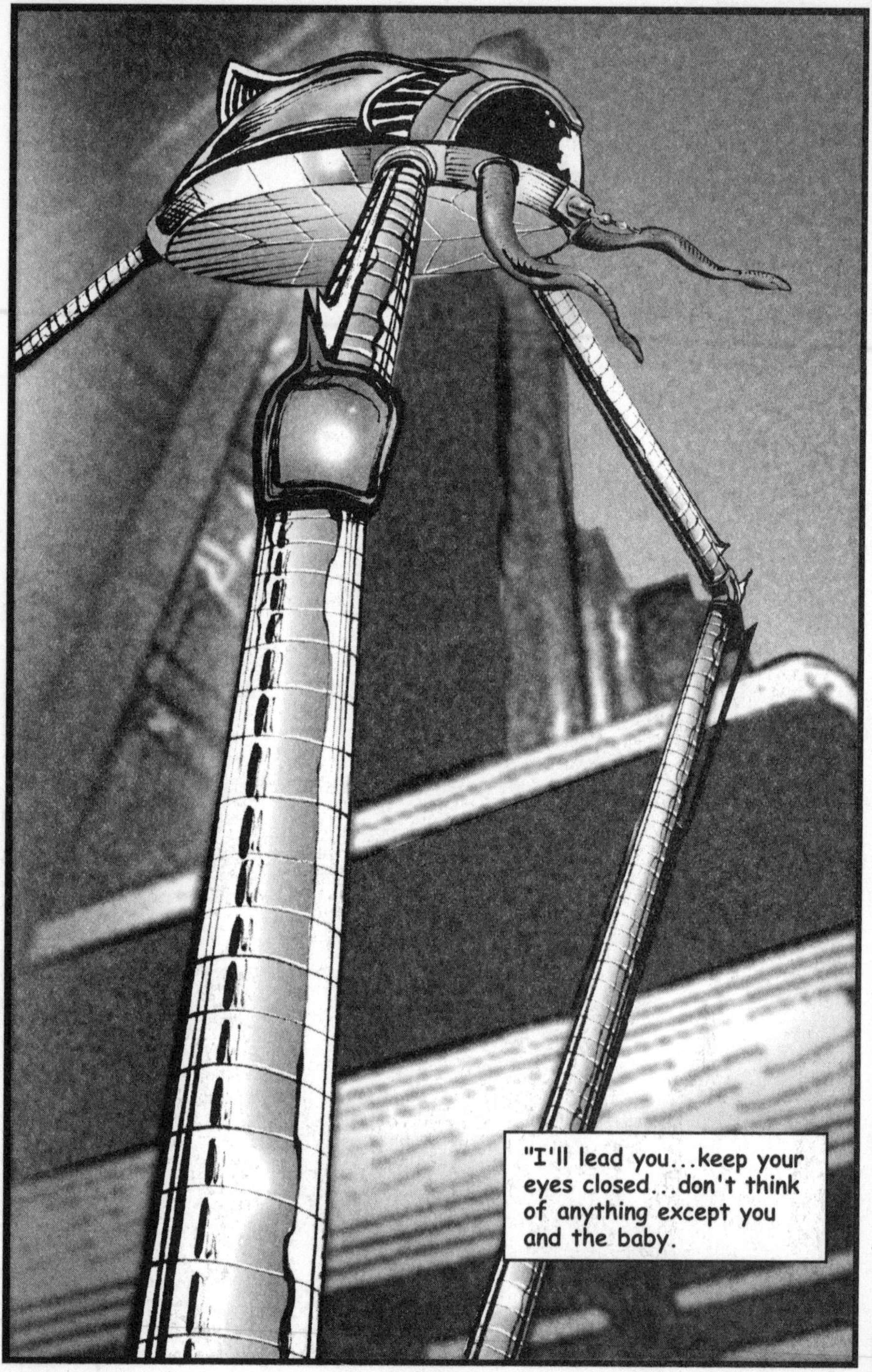
"I'll lead you...keep your eyes closed...don't think of anything except you and the baby.

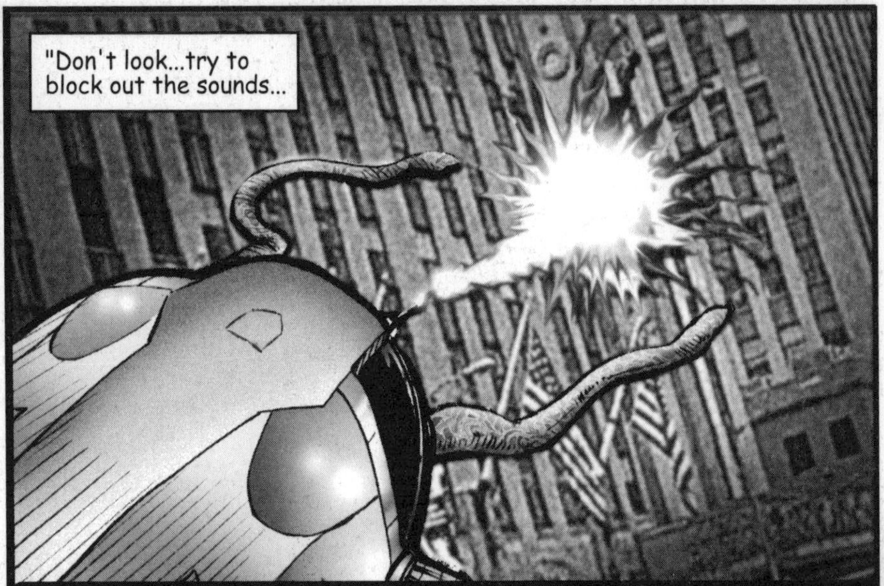
"Don't look...try to block out the sounds...

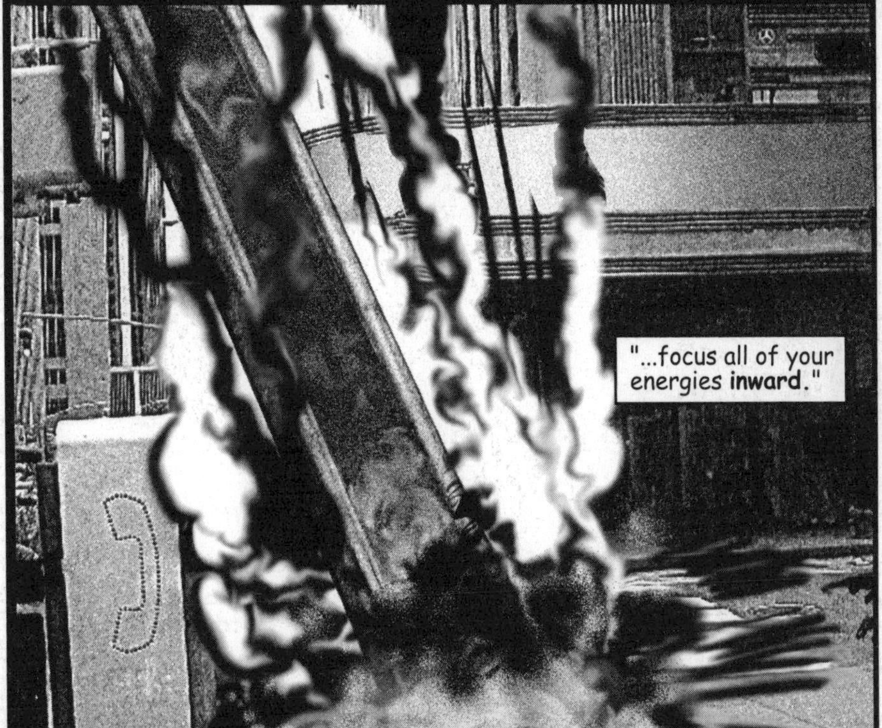
"...focus all of your energies **inward**."

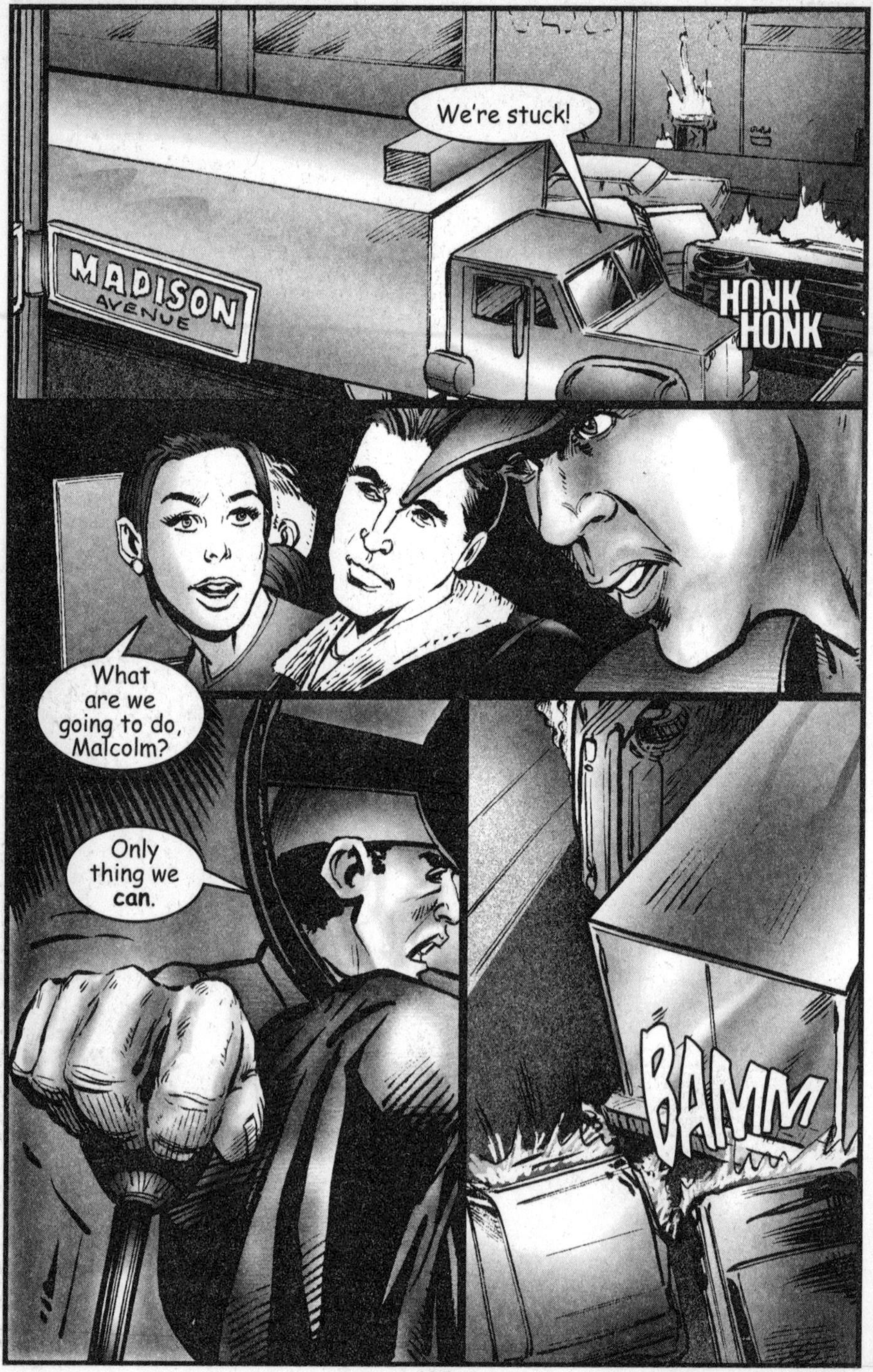
We're stuck!
MADISON AVENUE
HONK HONK
What are we going to do, Malcolm?
Only thing we can.
BAMM

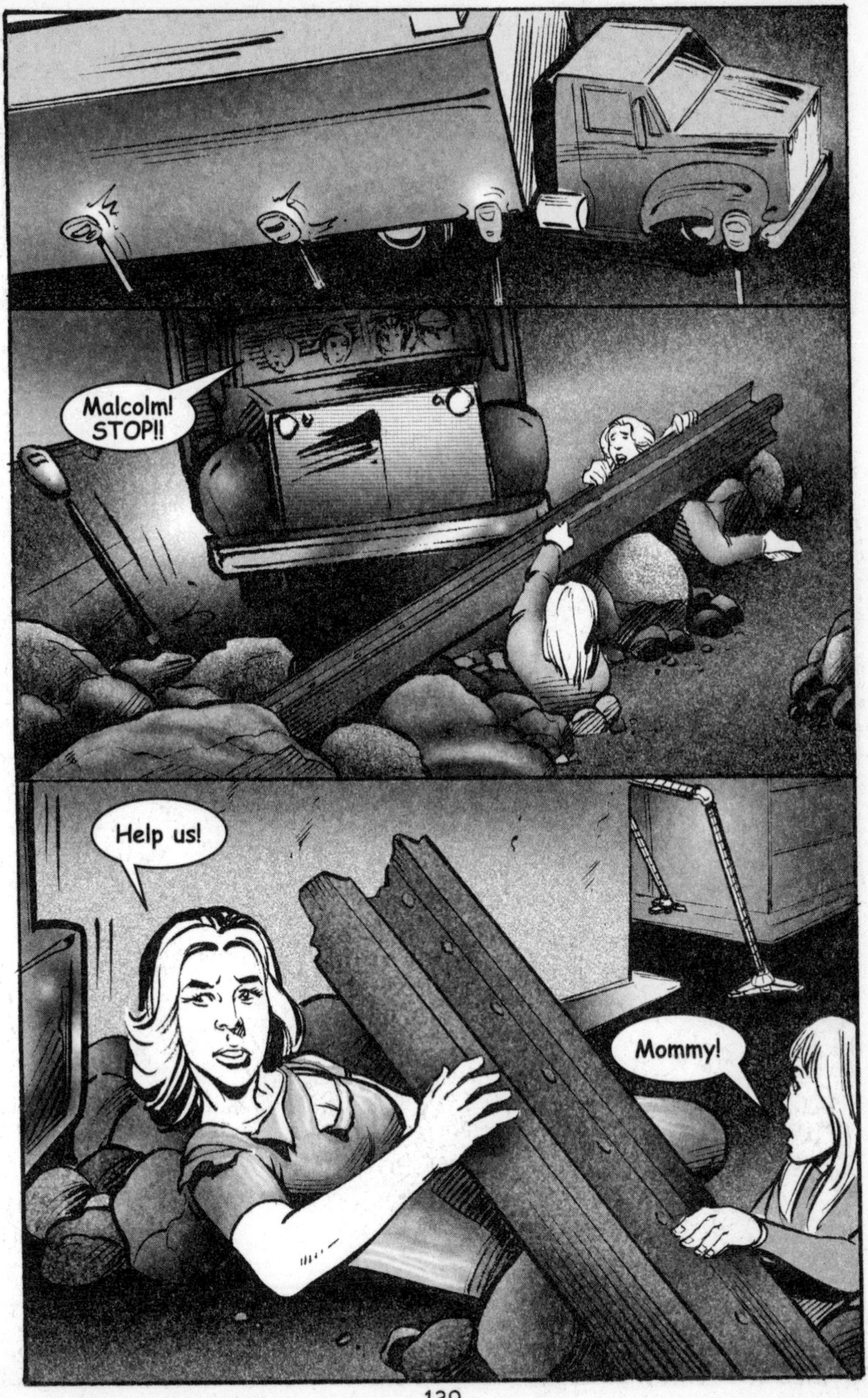
Malcolm!
STOP!!
Help us!
Mommy!

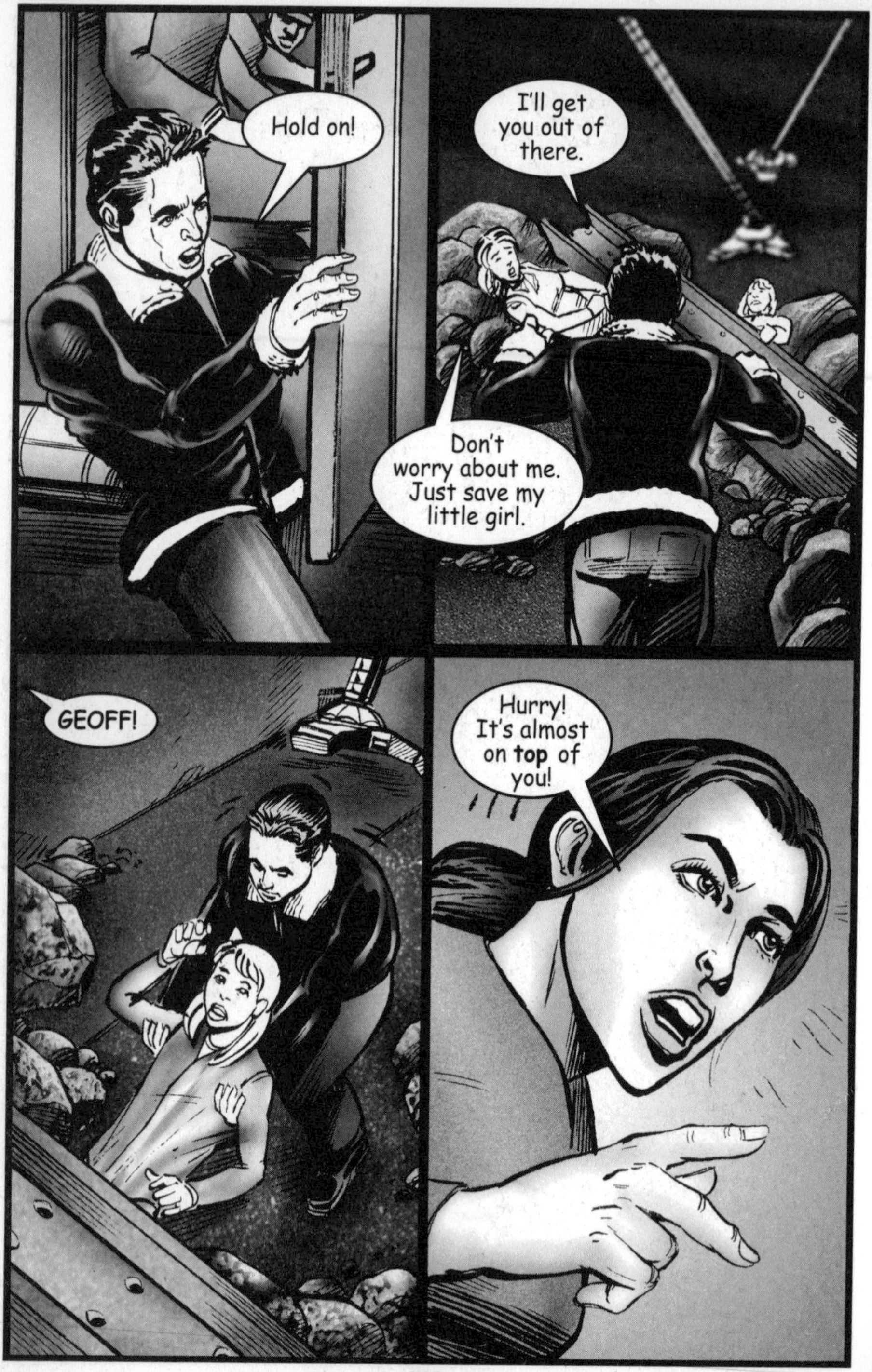
Hold on!
I'll get you out of there.
Don't worry about me. Just save my little girl.
GEOFF!
Hurry! It's almost on **top** of you!

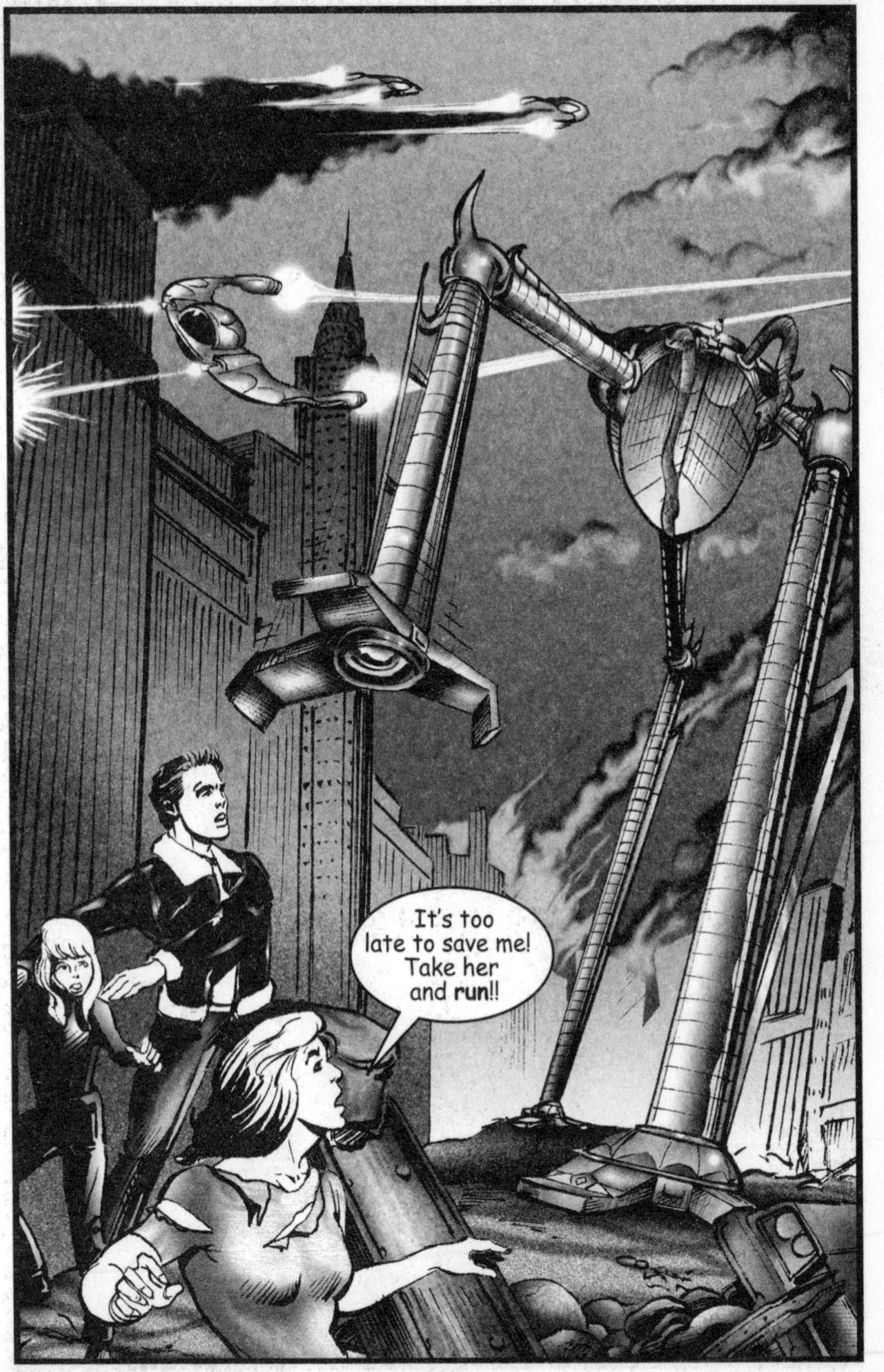
It's too late to save me! Take her and **run**!!

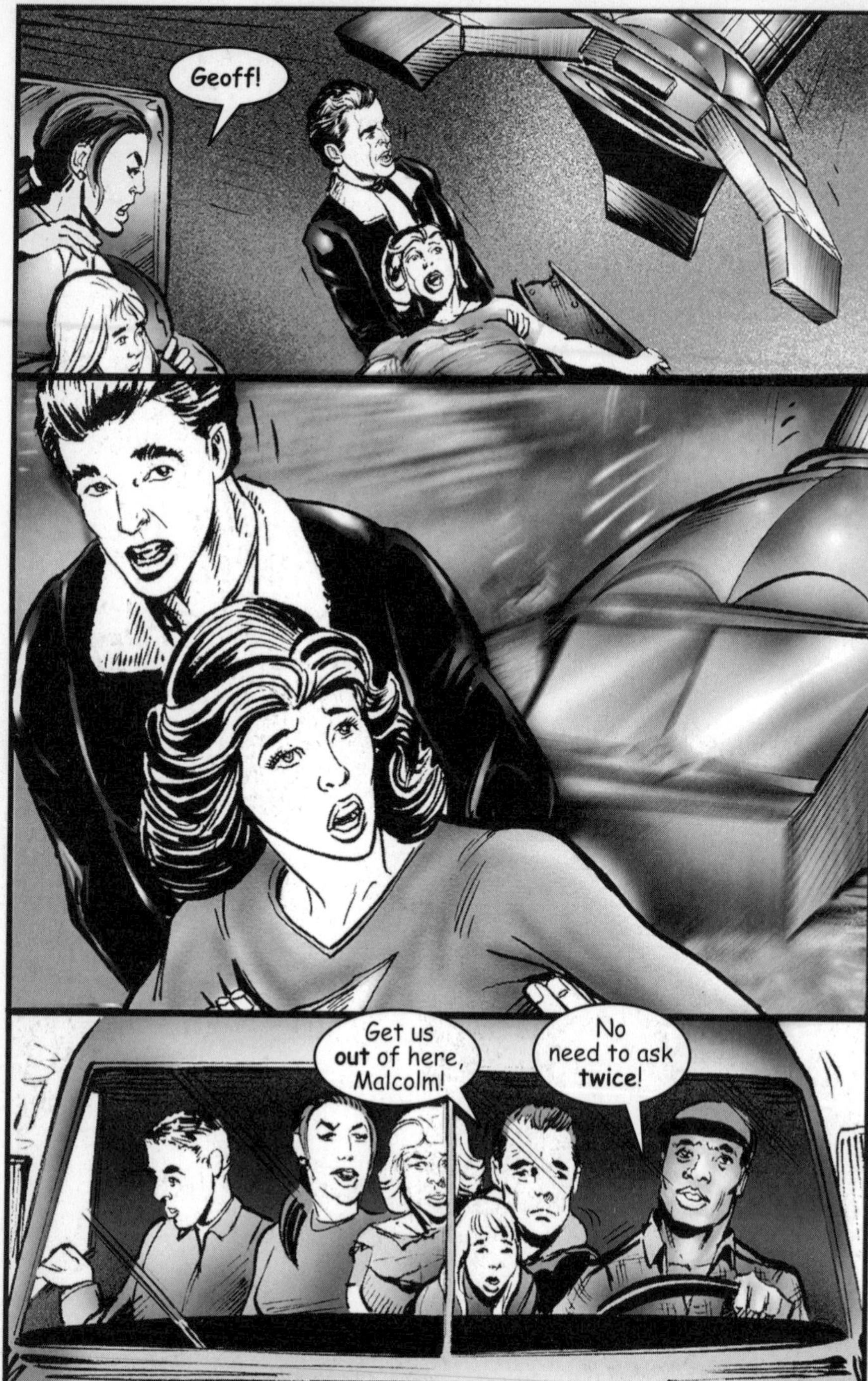
Geoff!
Get us **out** of here, Malcolm!
No need to ask **twice**!

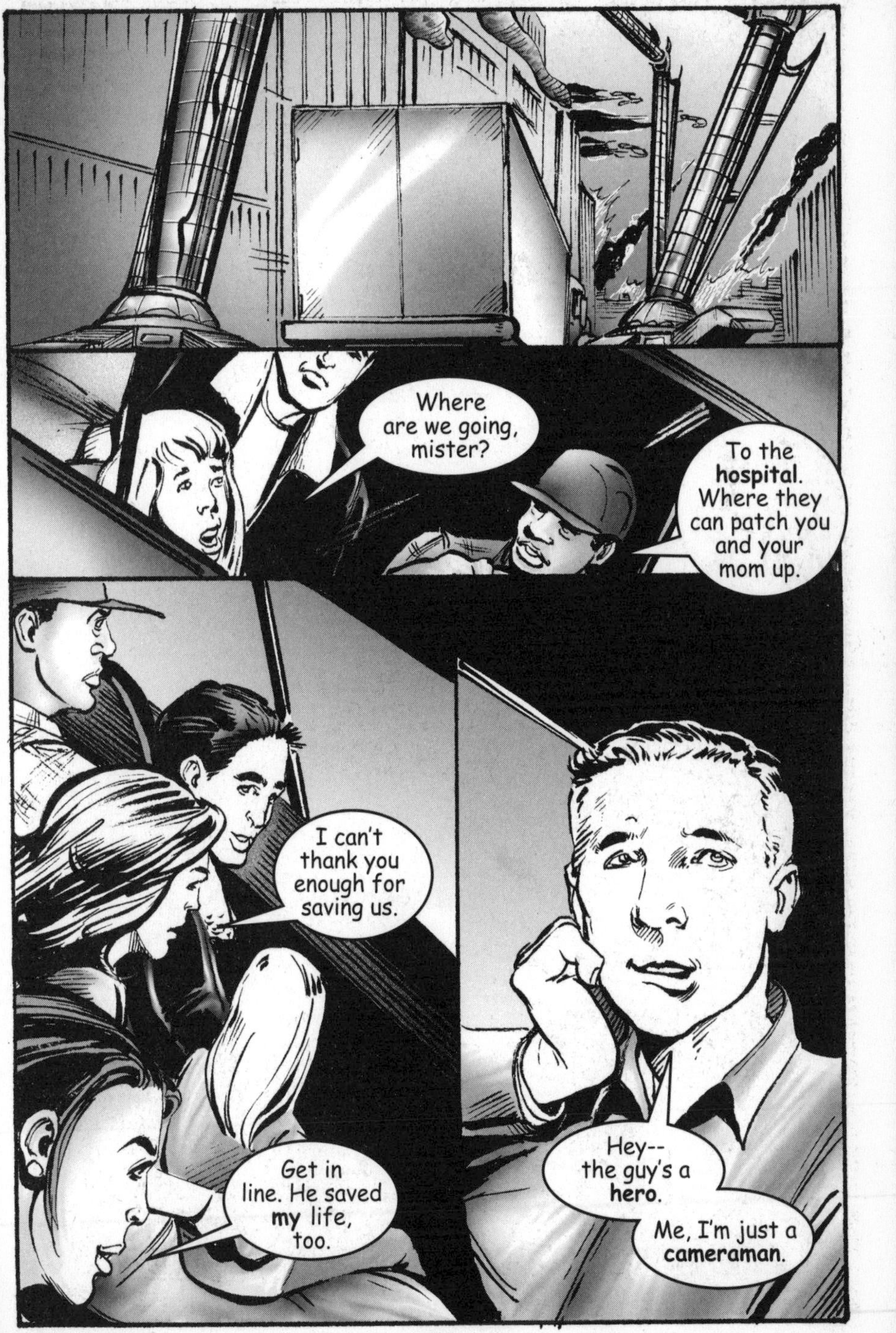
Where are we going, mister?
To the hospital. Where they can patch you and your mom up.
I can't thank you enough for saving us.
Get in line. He saved my life, too.
Hey-- the guy's a hero.
Me, I'm just a cameraman.

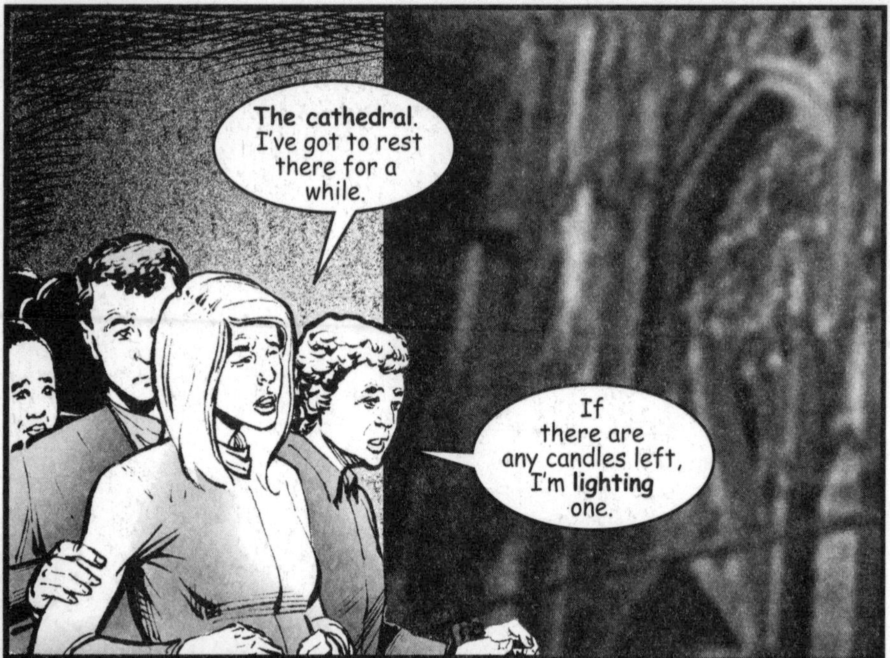
The cathedral. I've got to rest there for a while.
If there are any candles left, I'm lighting one.

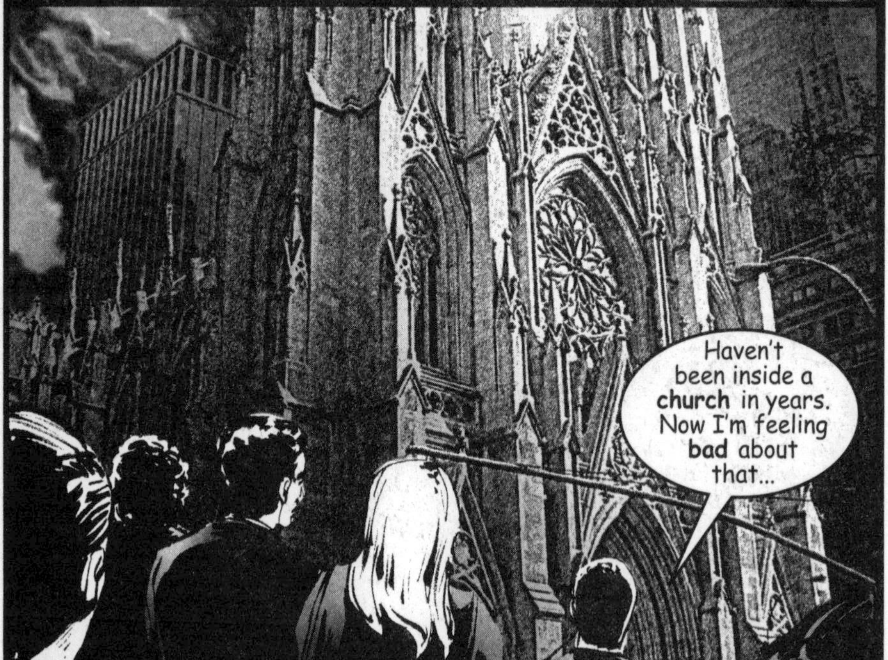
Haven't been inside a church in years. Now I'm feeling bad about that...

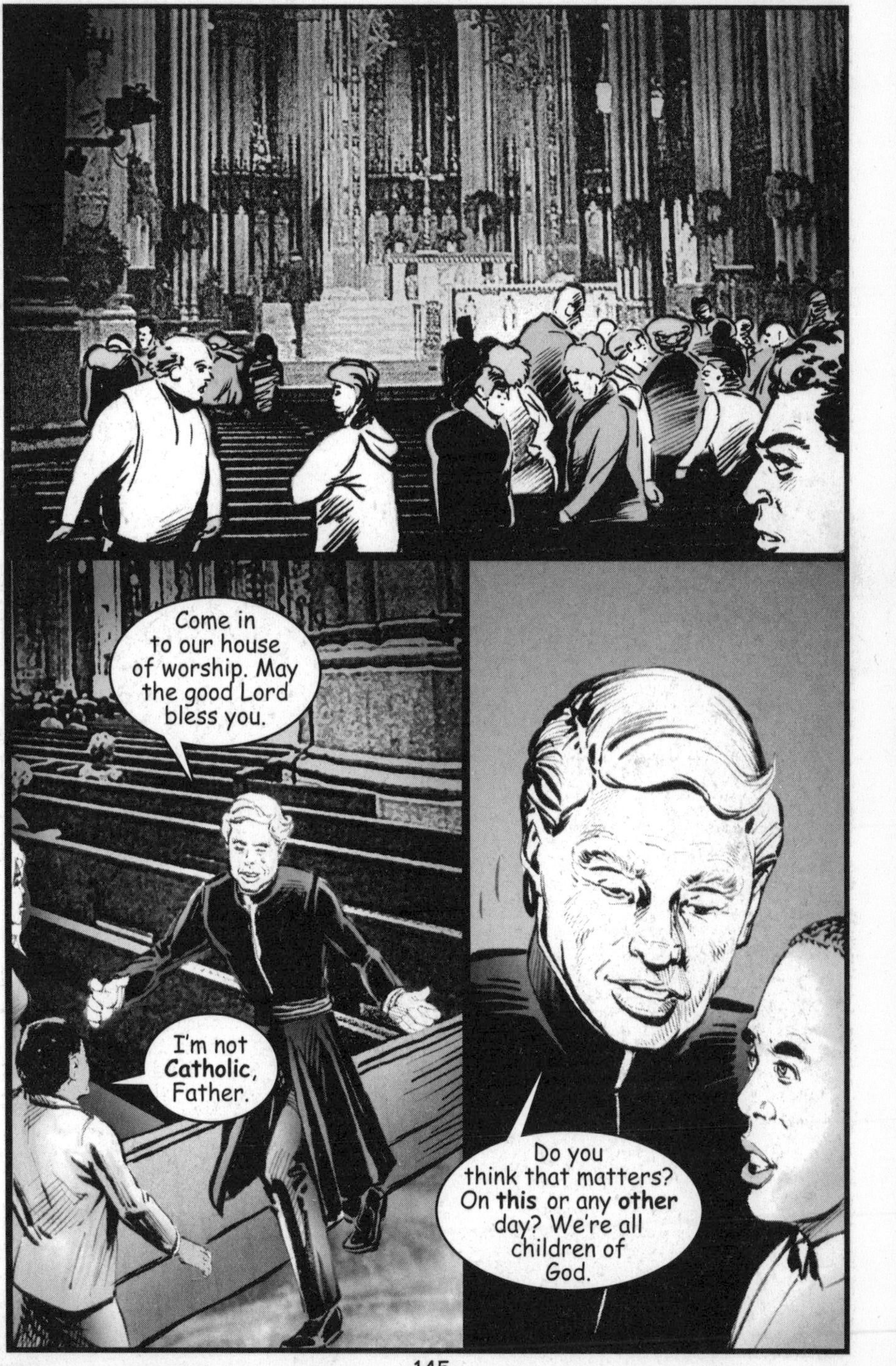
Come in to our house of worship. May the good Lord bless you.
I'm not **Catholic**, Father.
Do you think that matters? On **this** or any **other** day? We're all children of God.

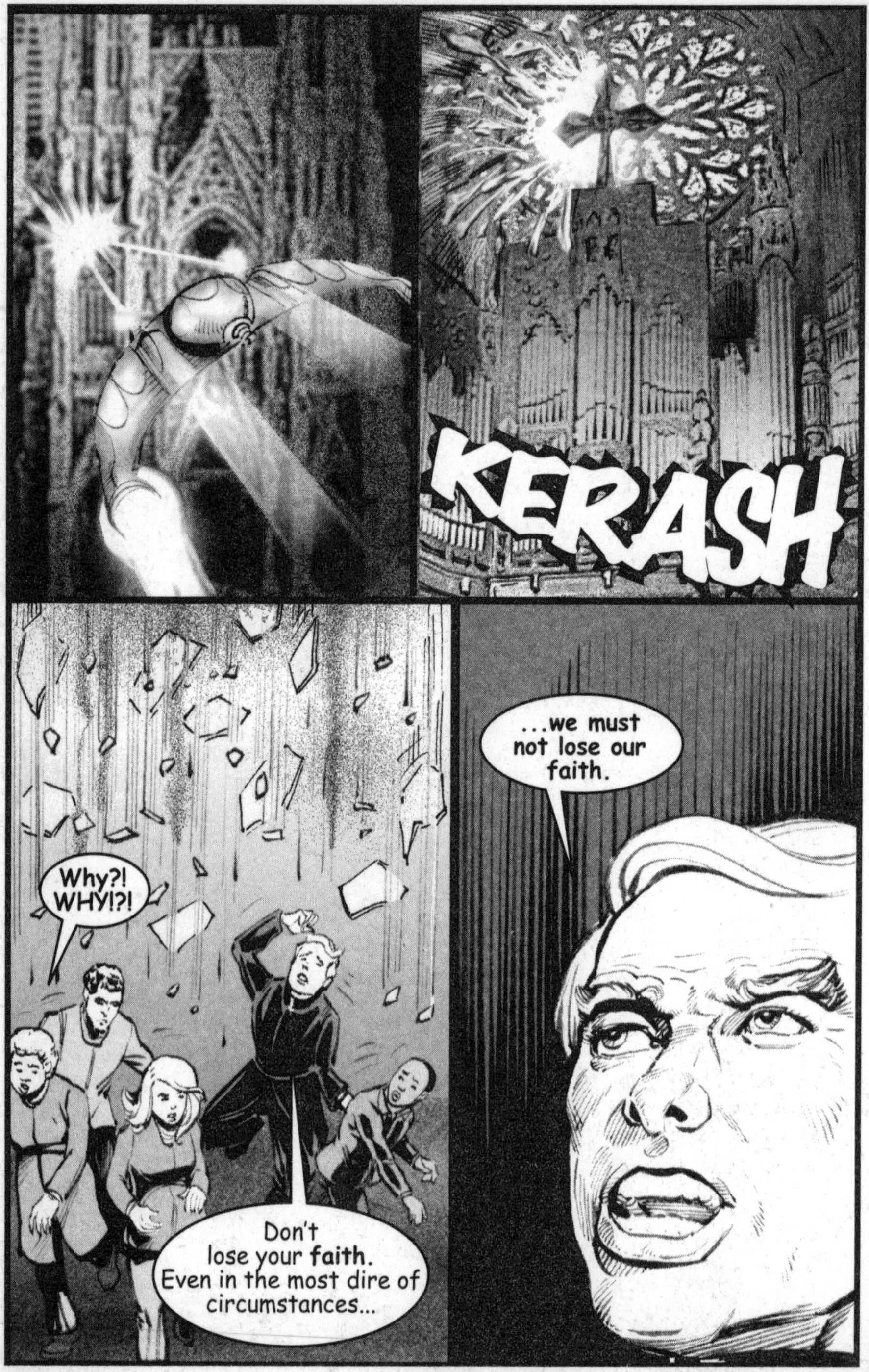
KERASH
Why?! WHY!?!
Don't lose your faith. Even in the most dire of circumstances...
...we must not lose our faith.

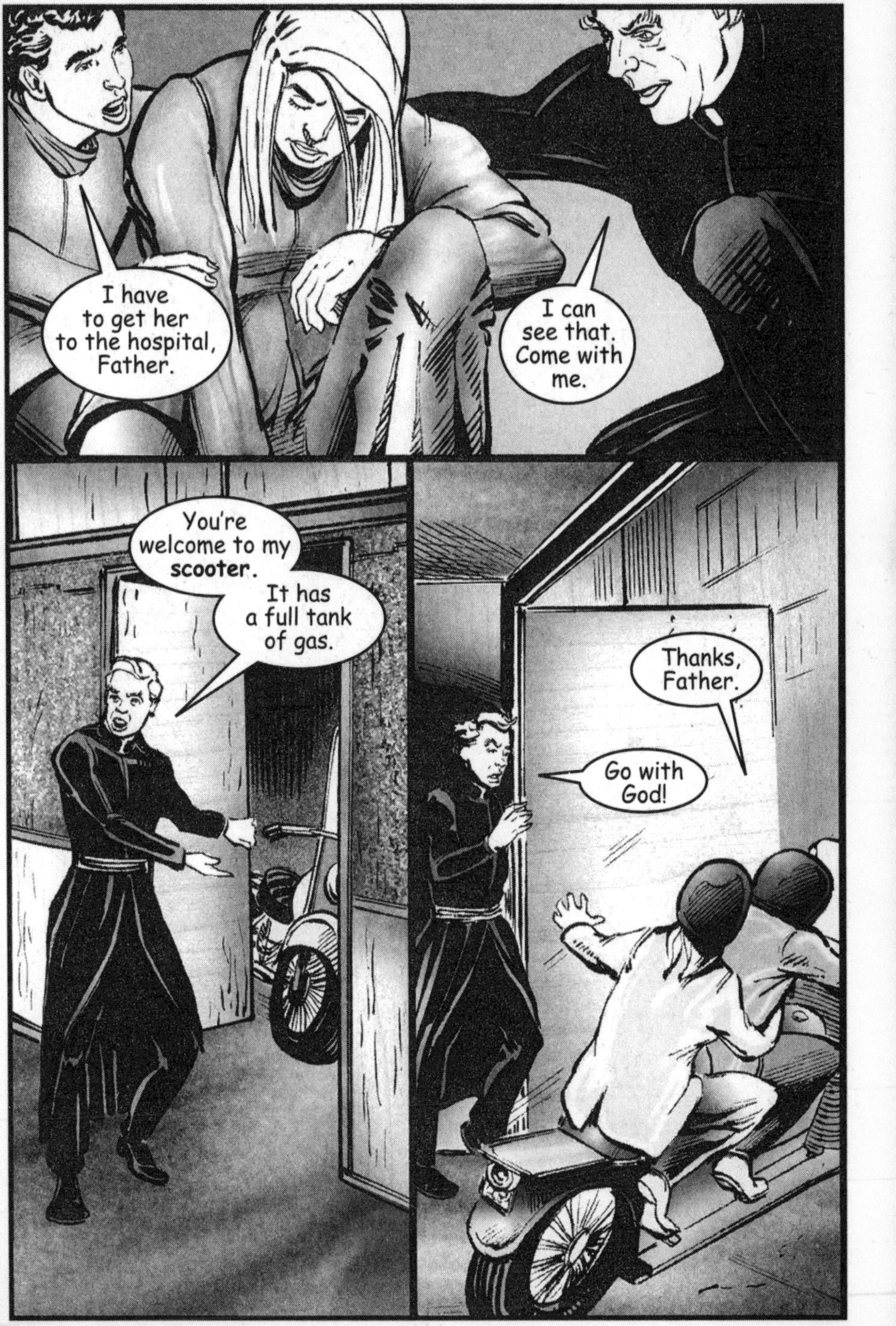
I have to get her to the hospital, Father.
I can see that. Come with me.
You're welcome to my **scooter**.
It has a full tank of gas.
Thanks, Father.
Go with God!

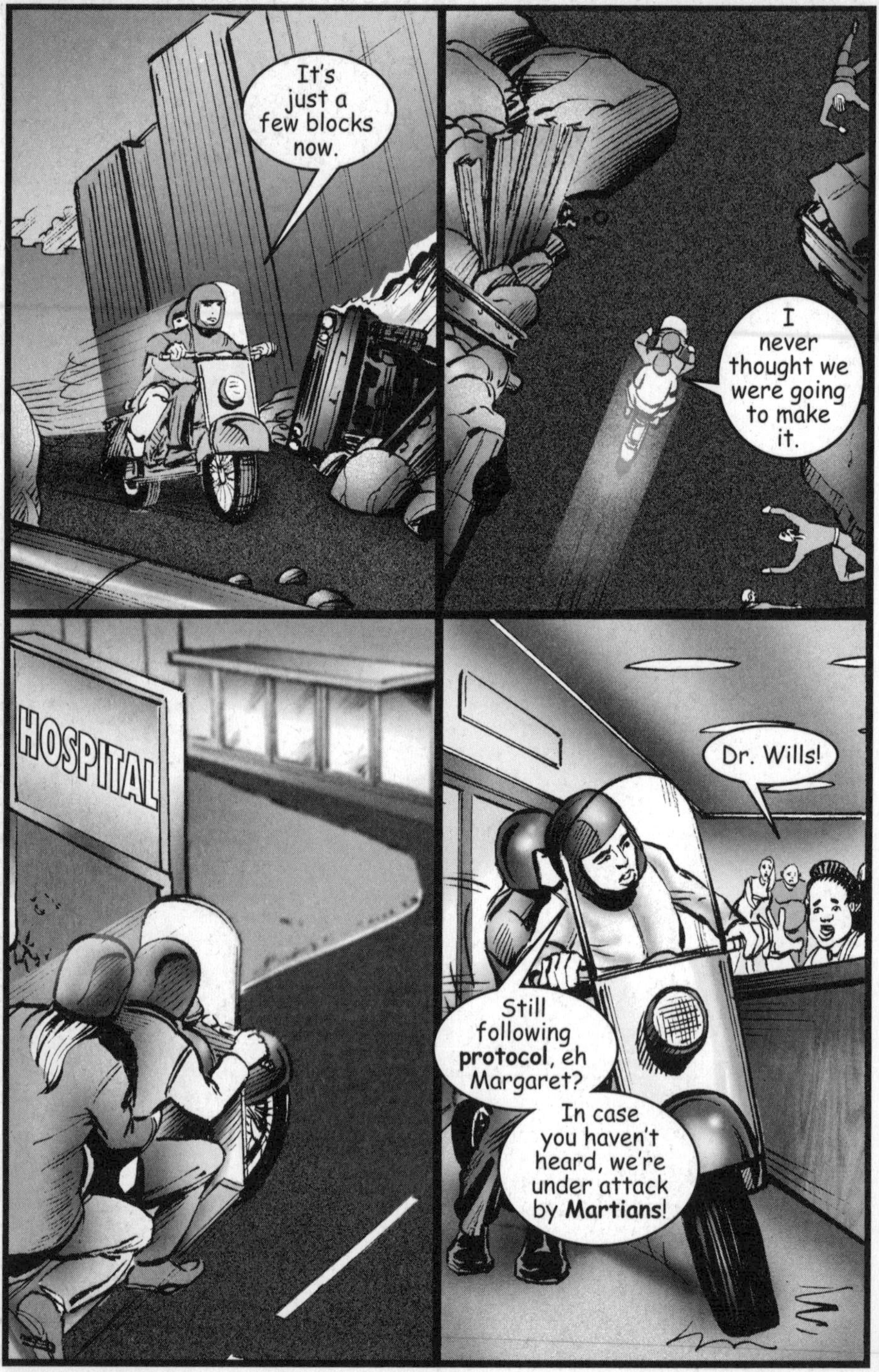
It's just a few blocks now.
I never thought we were going to make it.
HOSPITAL
Dr. Wills!
Still following **protocol**, eh Margaret?
In case you haven't heard, we're under attack by **Martians**!

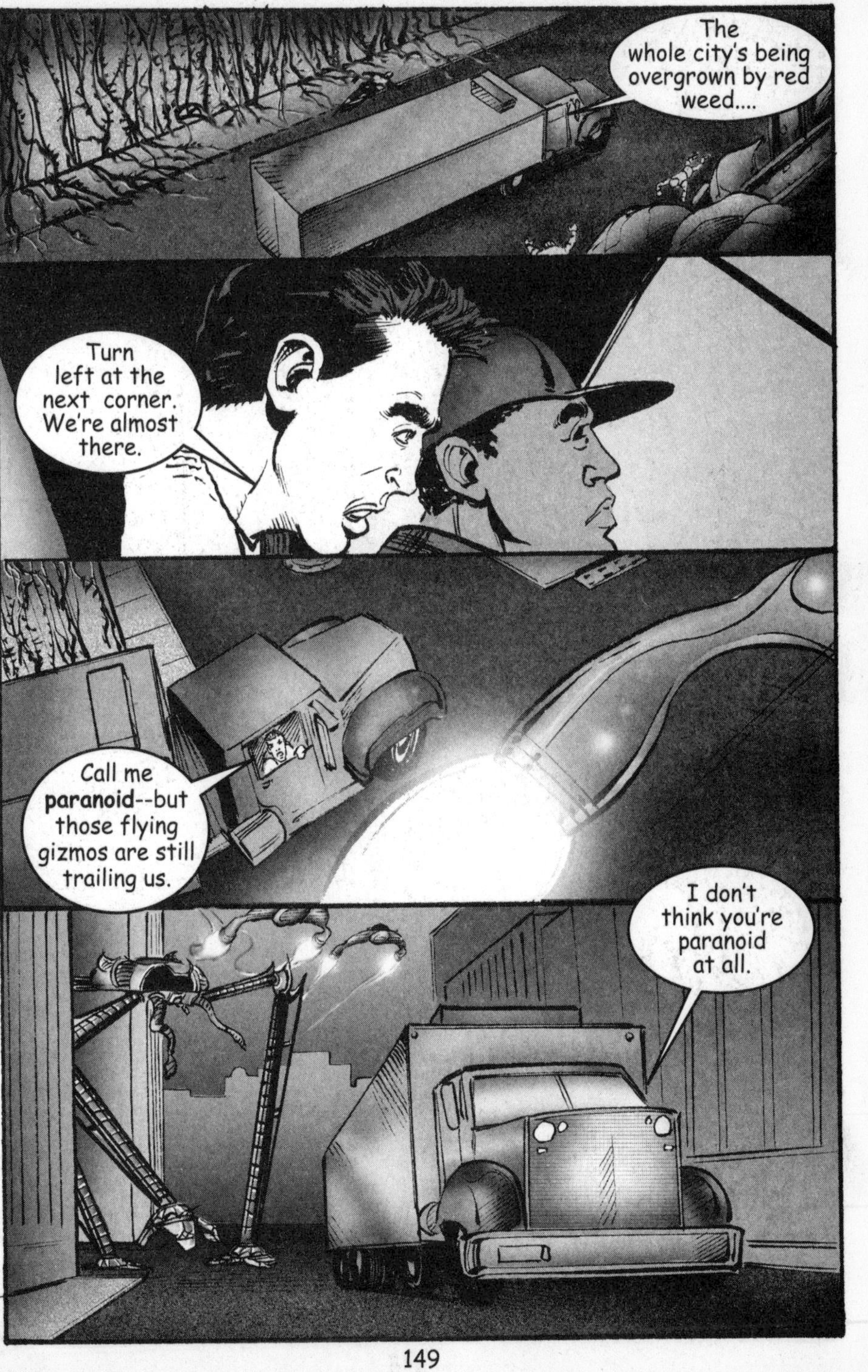
The whole city's being overgrown by red weed....
Turn left at the next corner. We're almost there.
Call me **paranoid**--but those flying gizmos are still trailing us.
I don't think you're paranoid at all.

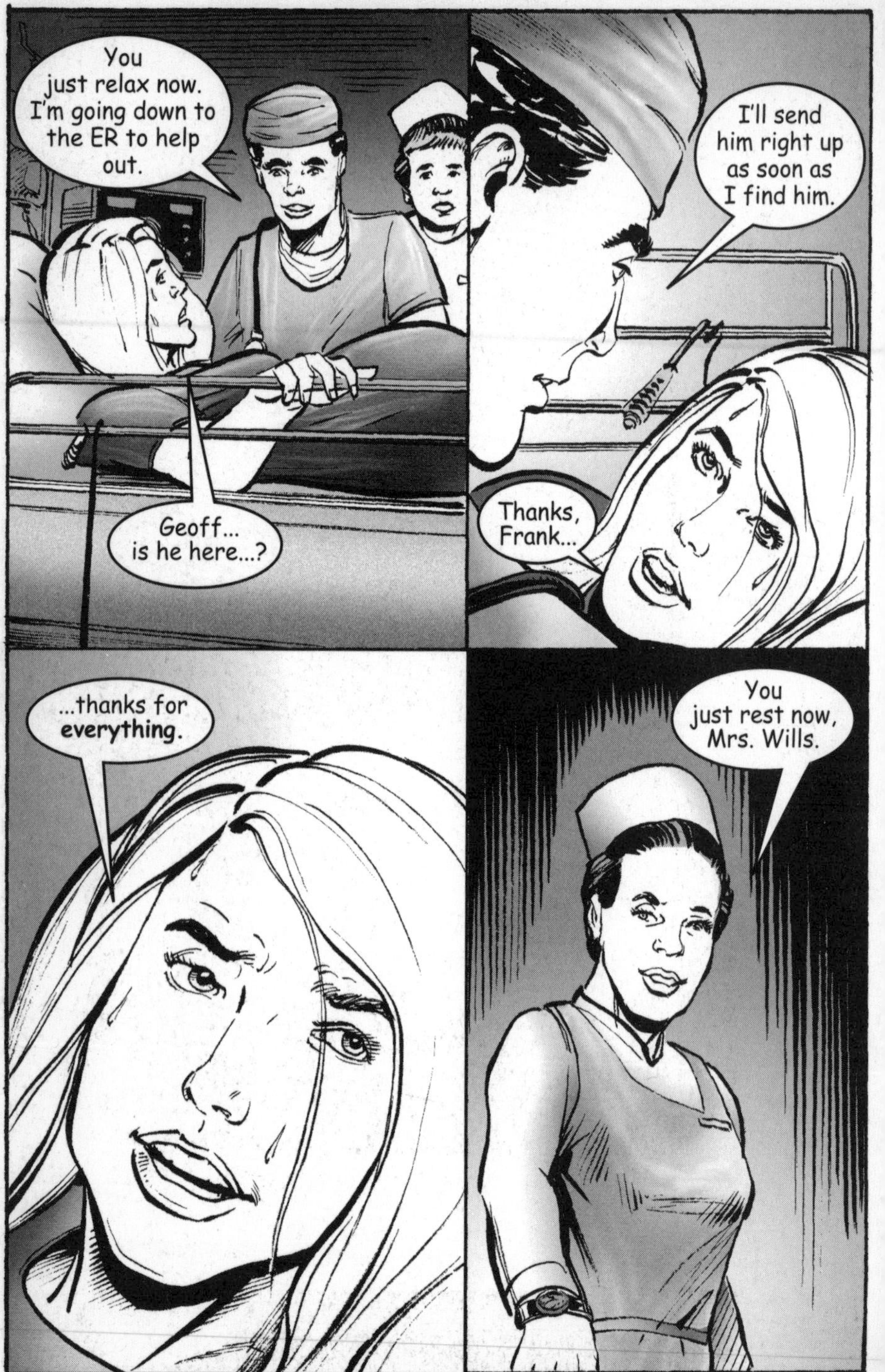
You just relax now. I'm going down to the ER to help out.
Geoff... is he here...?
I'll send him right up as soon as I find him.
Thanks, Frank...
...thanks for **everything**.
You just rest now, Mrs. Wills.

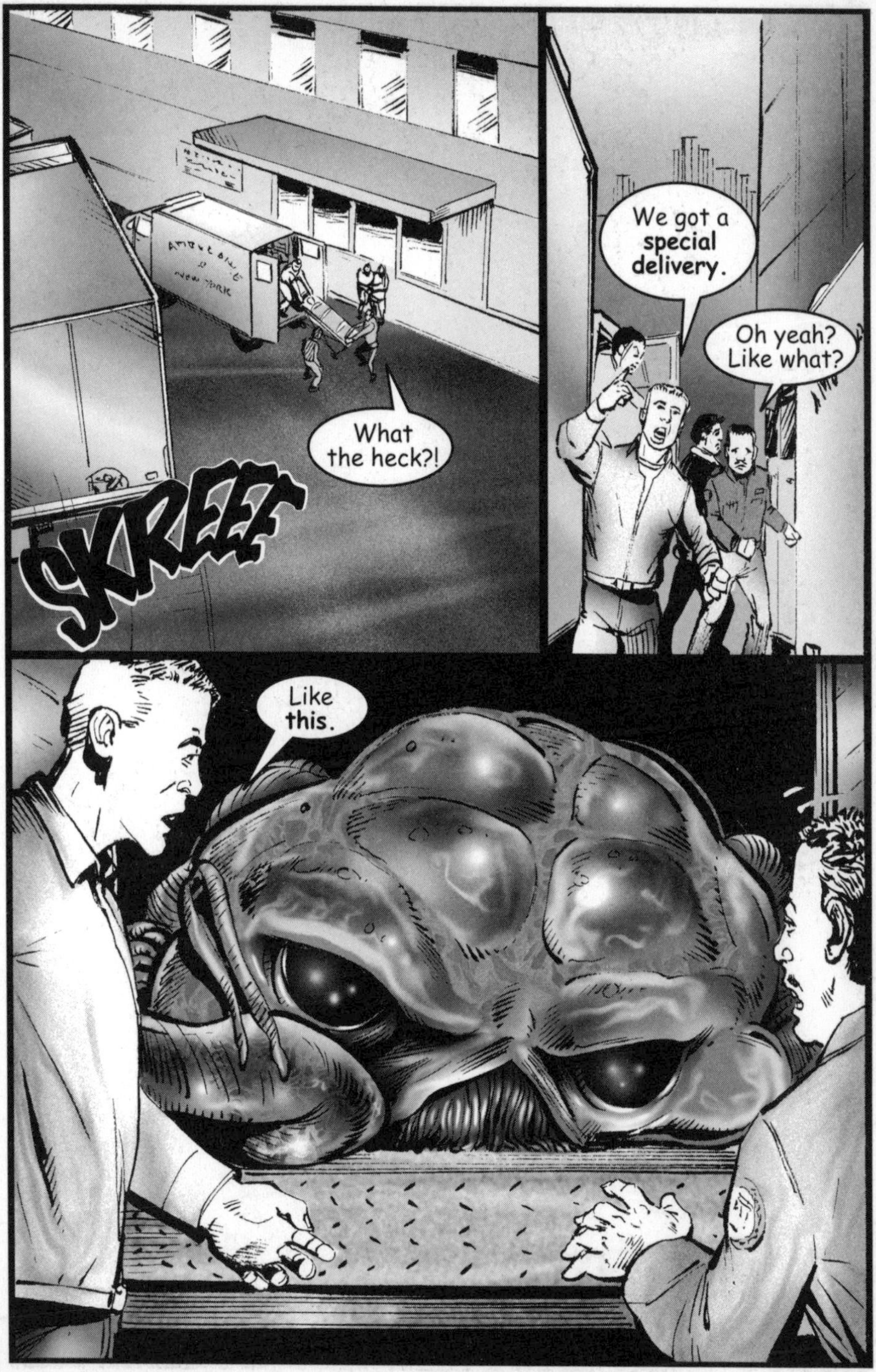
What the heck?!
SKREEE
We got a special delivery.
Oh yeah? Like what?
Like this.

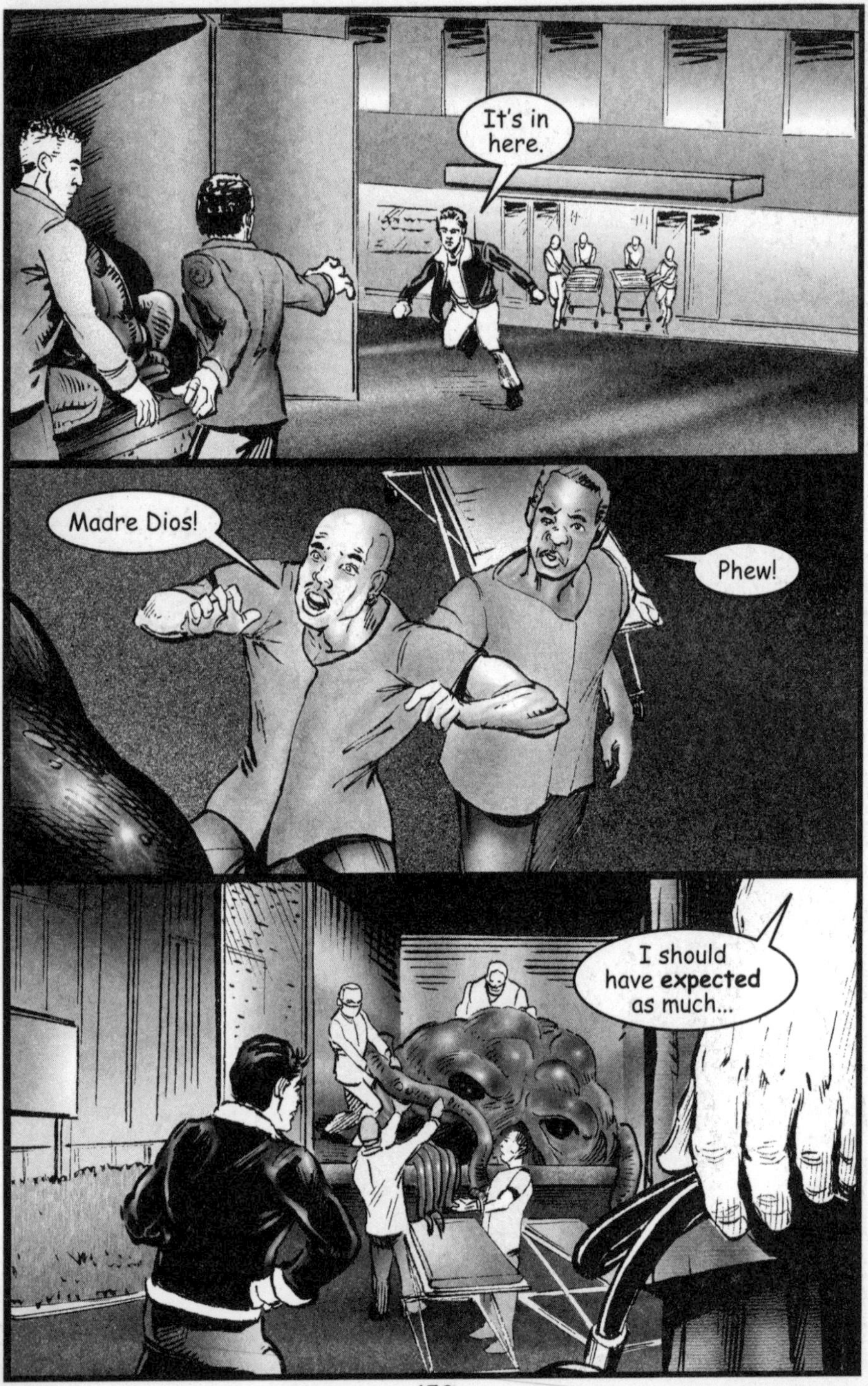
It's in here.
Madre Dios!
Phew!
I should have **expected** as much...

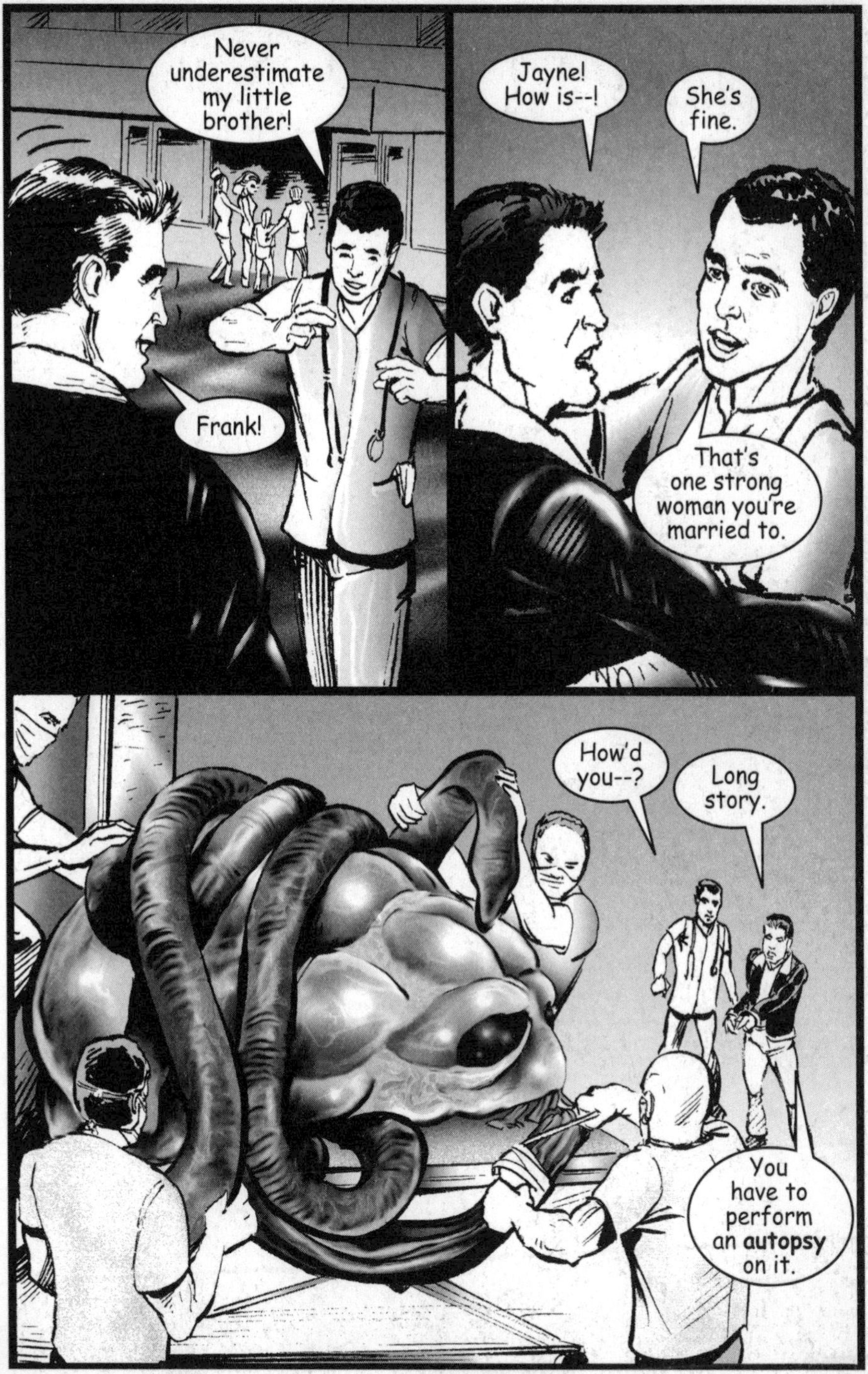
Never underestimate my little brother!
Frank!
Jayne! How is--!
She's fine.
That's one strong woman you're married to.
How'd you--?
Long story.
You have to perform an **autopsy** on it.

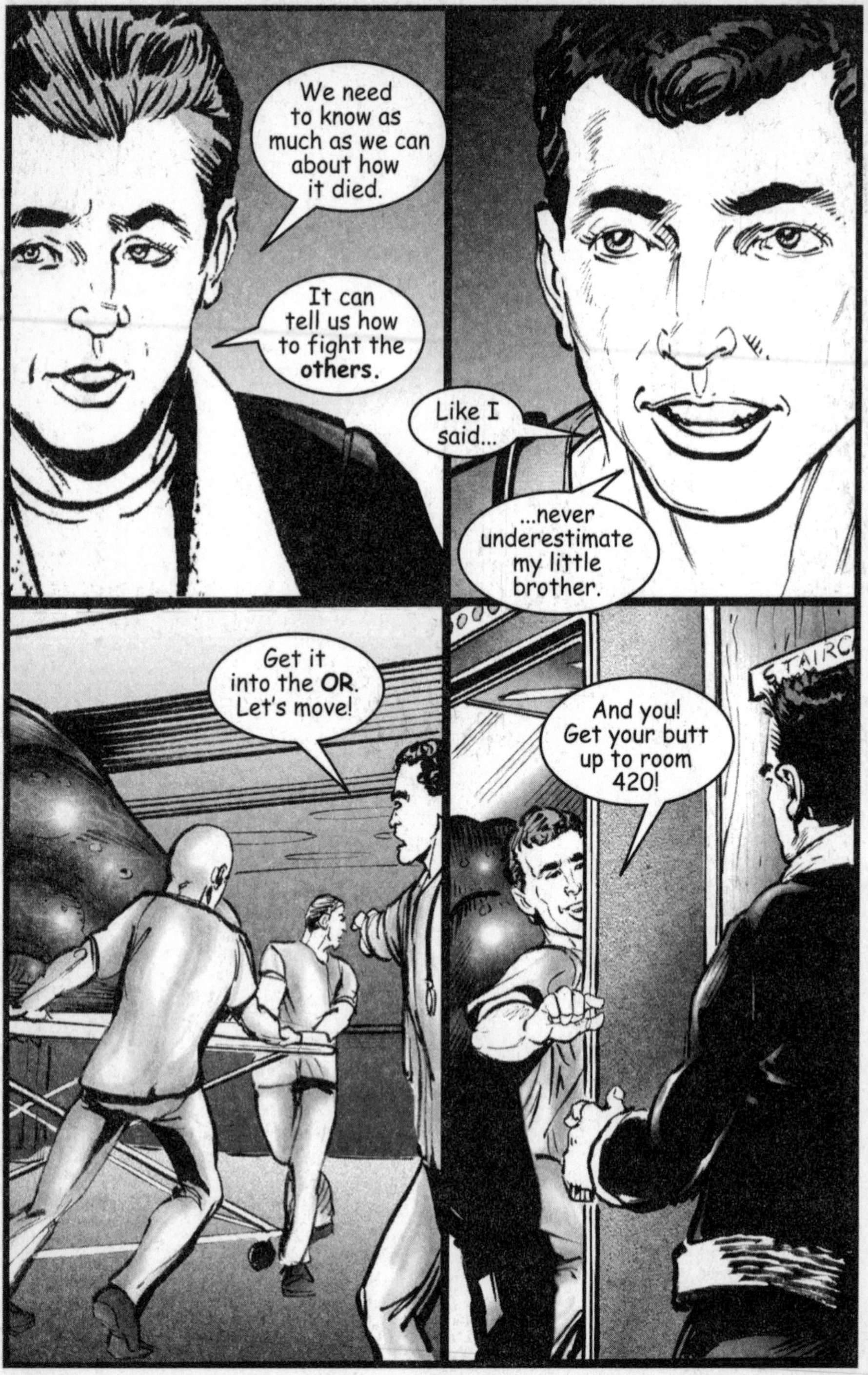
We need to know as much as we can about how it died.
It can tell us how to fight the **others**.
Like I said...
...never underestimate my little brother.
Get it into the **OR**. Let's move!
And you! Get your butt up to room 420!
STAIRC

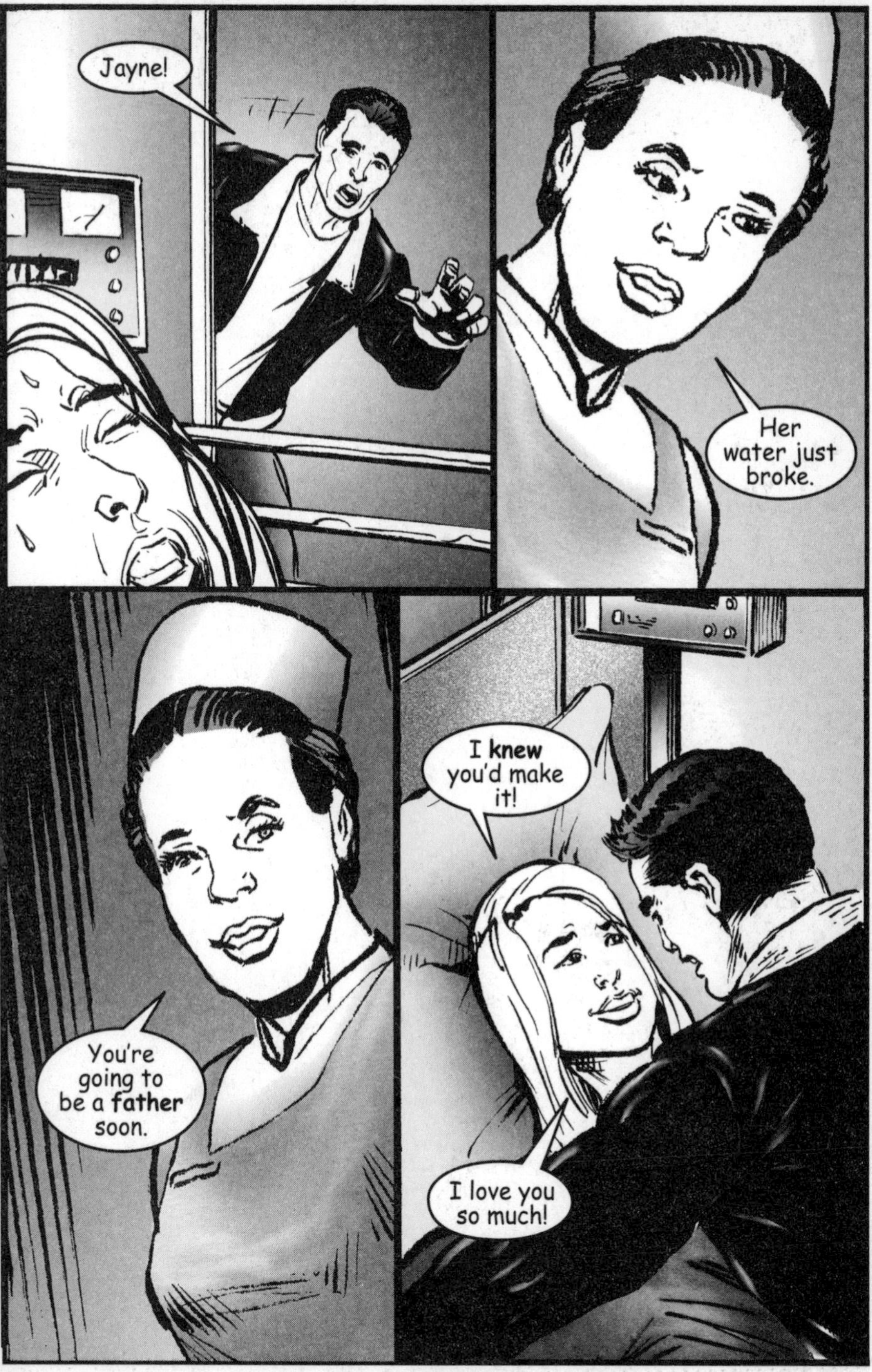
Jayne!
Her water just broke.
You're going to be a **father** soon.
I **knew** you'd make it!
I love you so much!

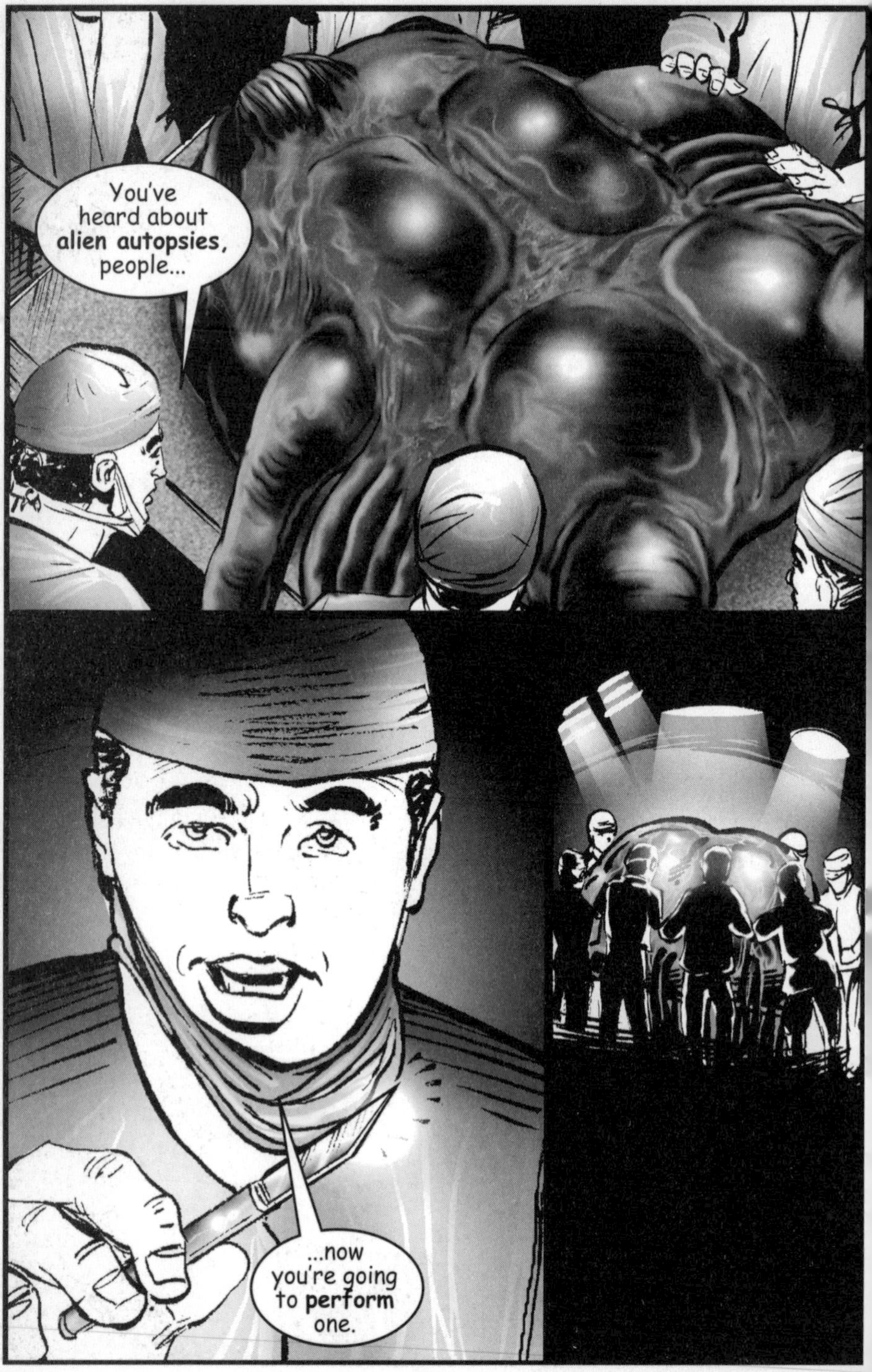
You've heard about alien autopsies, people...
...now you're going to perform one.

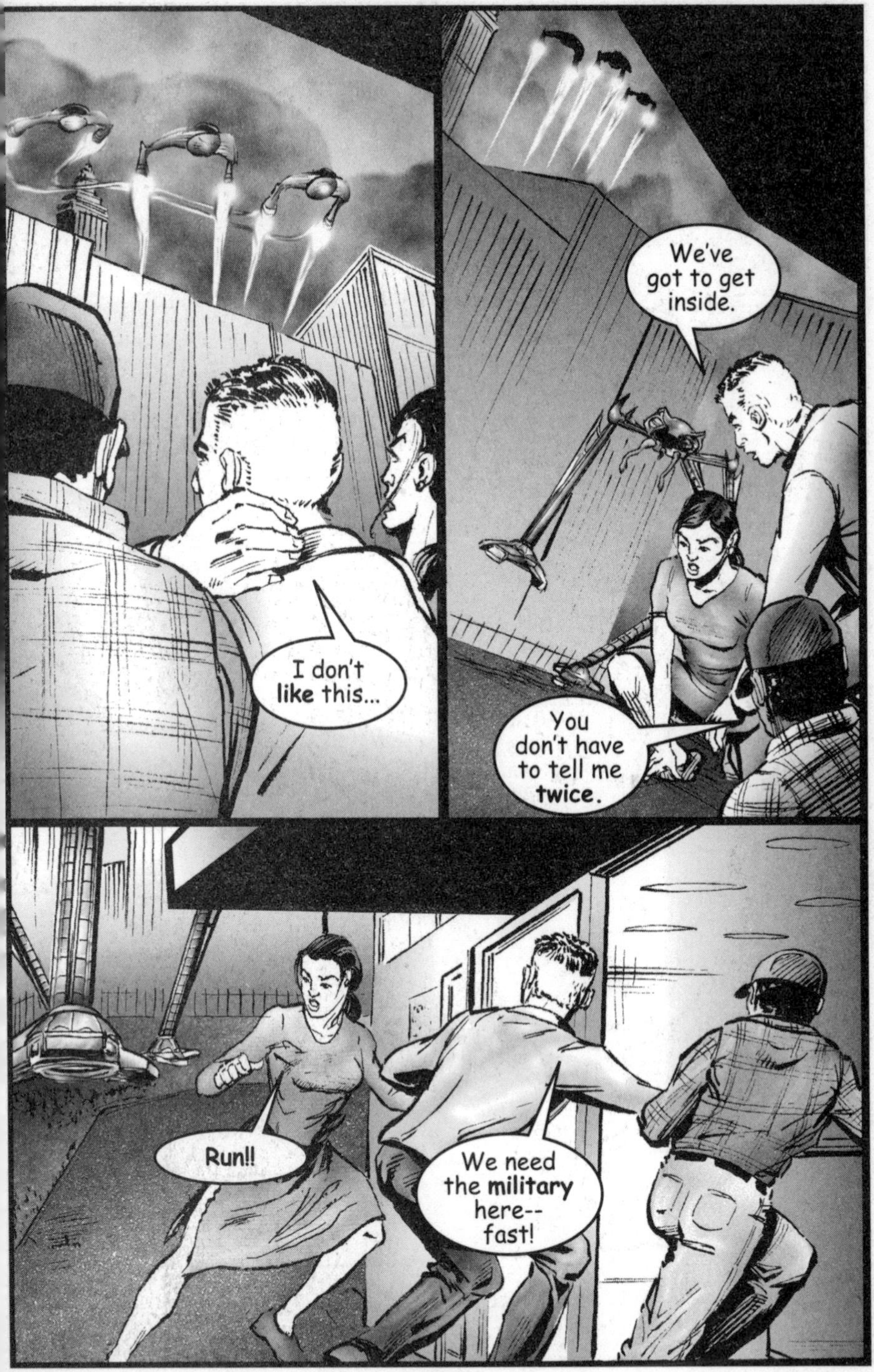
I don't **like** this...
We've got to get inside.
You don't have to tell me **twice**.
Run!!
We need the **military** here-- fast!

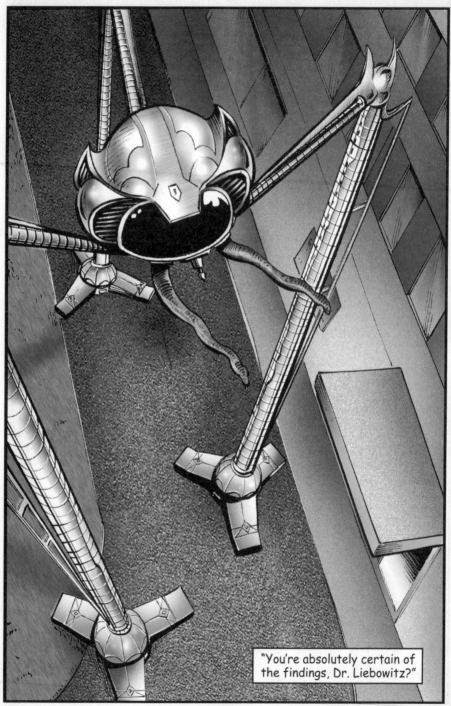

"You're absolutely certain of the findings, Dr. Liebowitz?"

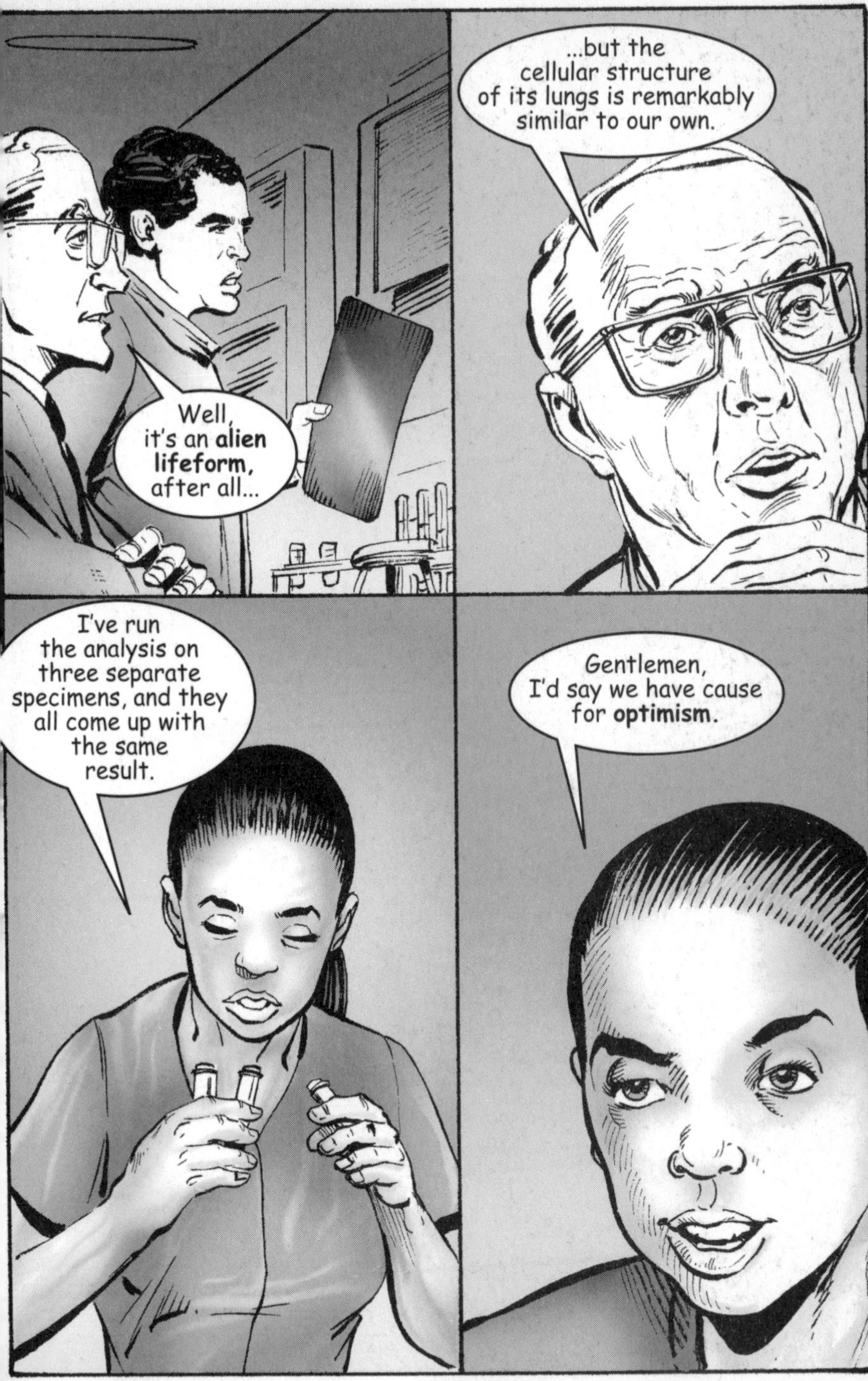
Well, it's an **alien lifeform,** after all...
...but the cellular structure of its lungs is remarkably similar to our own.
I've run the analysis on three separate specimens, and they all come up with the same result.
Gentlemen, I'd say we have cause for **optimism**.

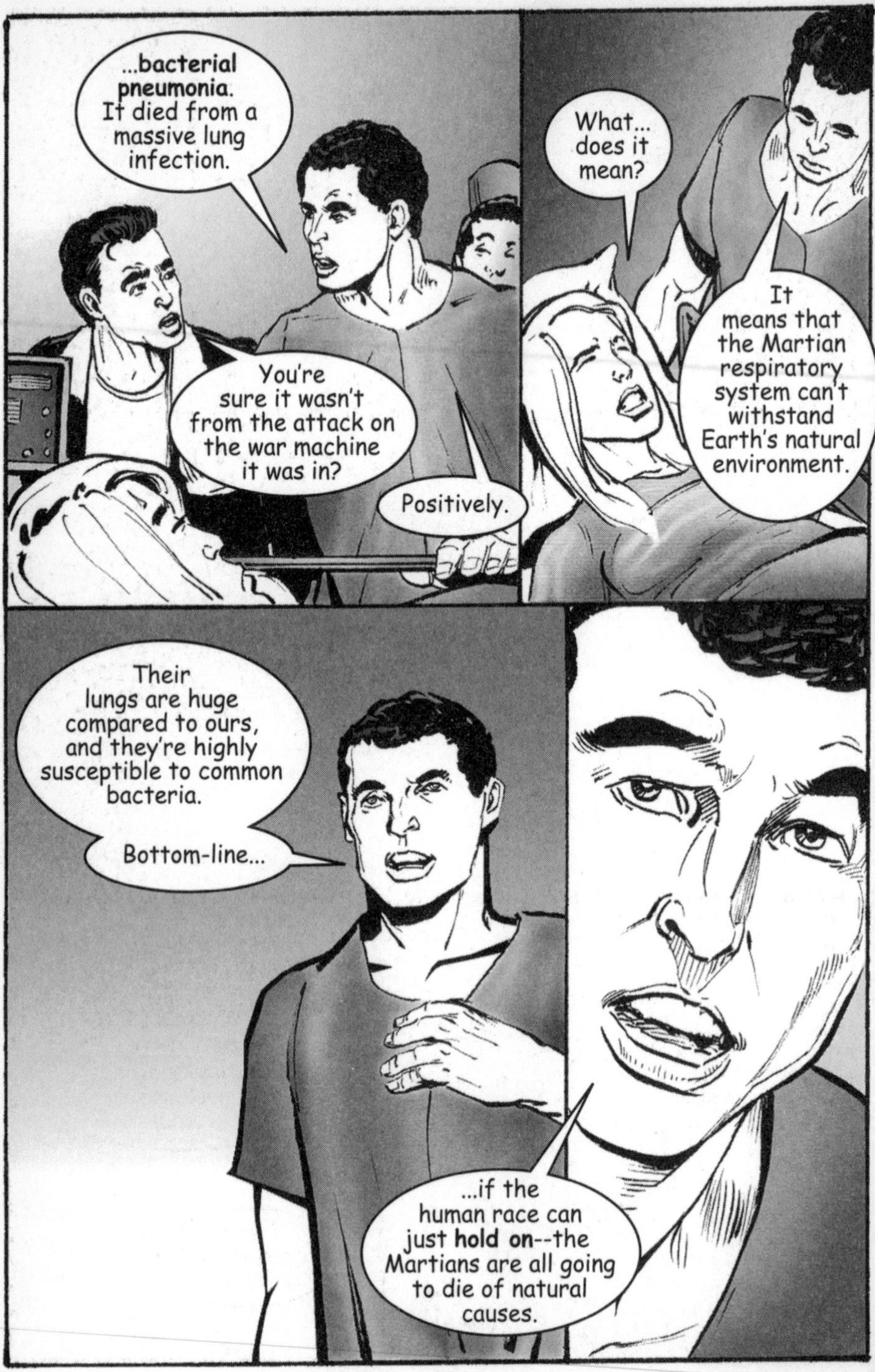
...**bacterial pneumonia**. It died from a massive lung infection.
You're sure it wasn't from the attack on the war machine it was in?
Positively.
What... does it mean?
It means that the Martian respiratory system can't withstand Earth's natural environment.
Their lungs are huge compared to ours, and they're highly susceptible to common bacteria.
Bottom-line...
...if the human race can just **hold on**--the Martians are all going to die of natural causes.

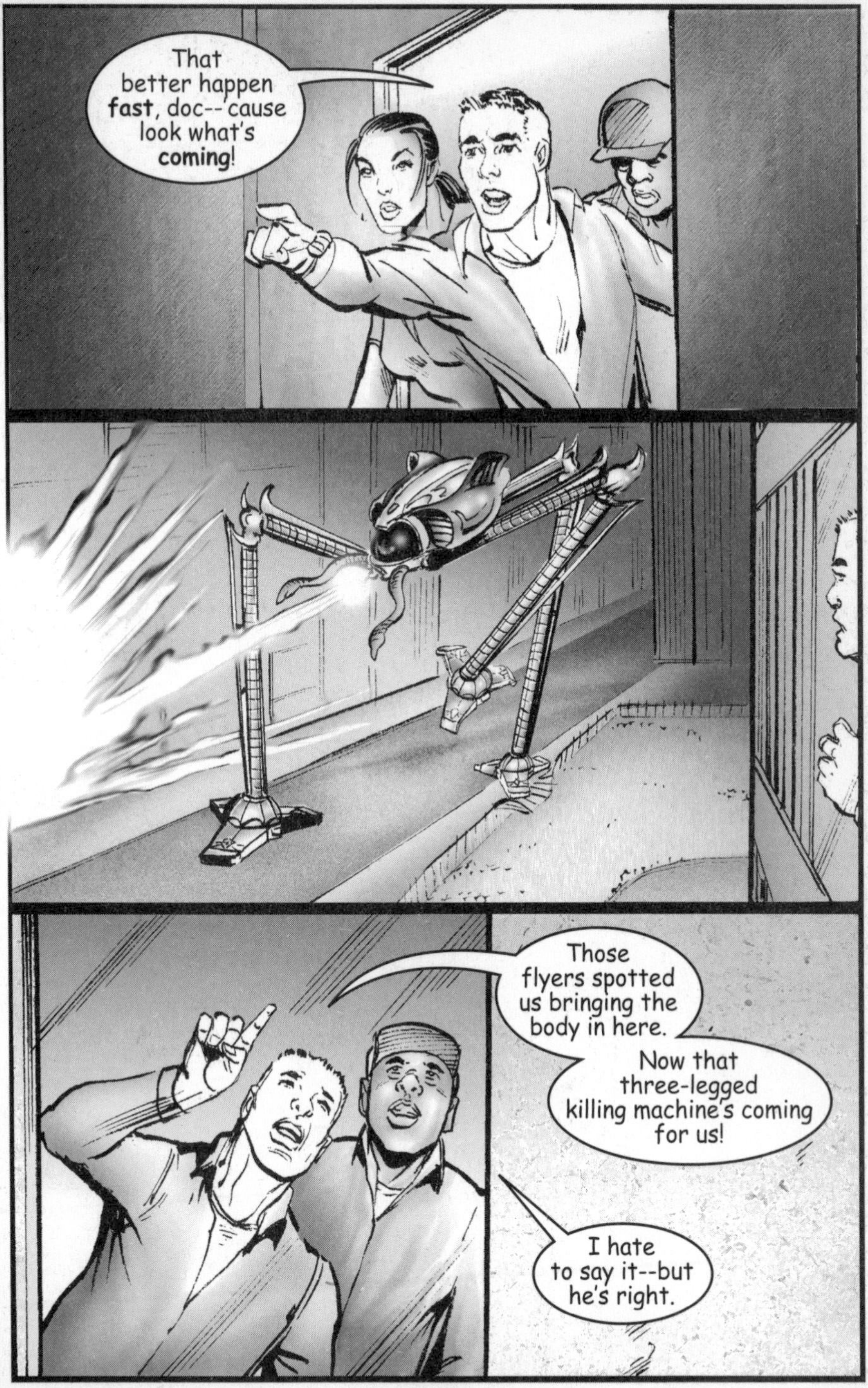
That better happen **fast**, doc--'cause look what's **coming**!
Those flyers spotted us bringing the body in here.
Now that three-legged killing machine's coming for us!
I hate to say it--but he's right.

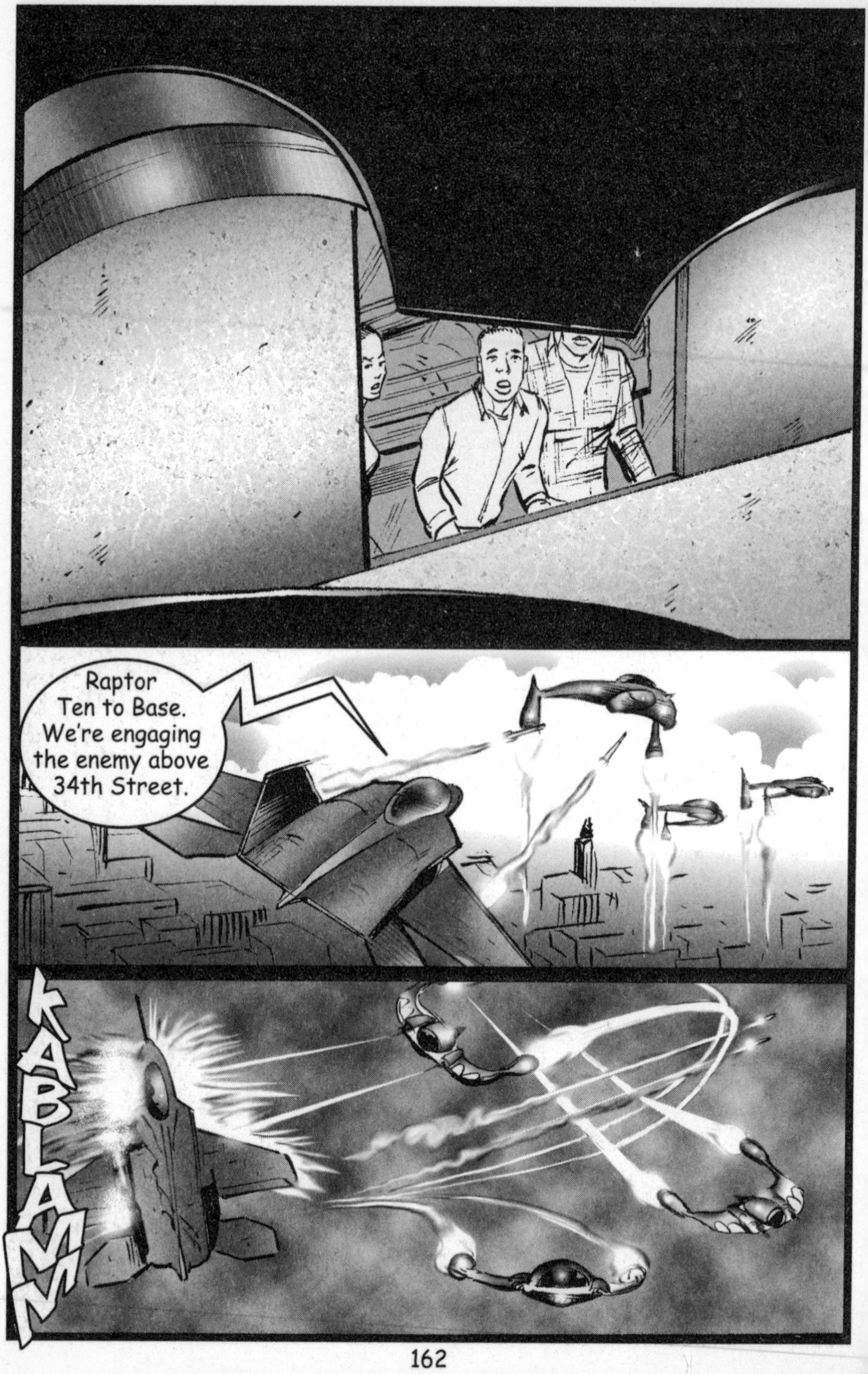
Raptor Ten to Base. We're engaging the enemy above 34th Street.
KABLAMM

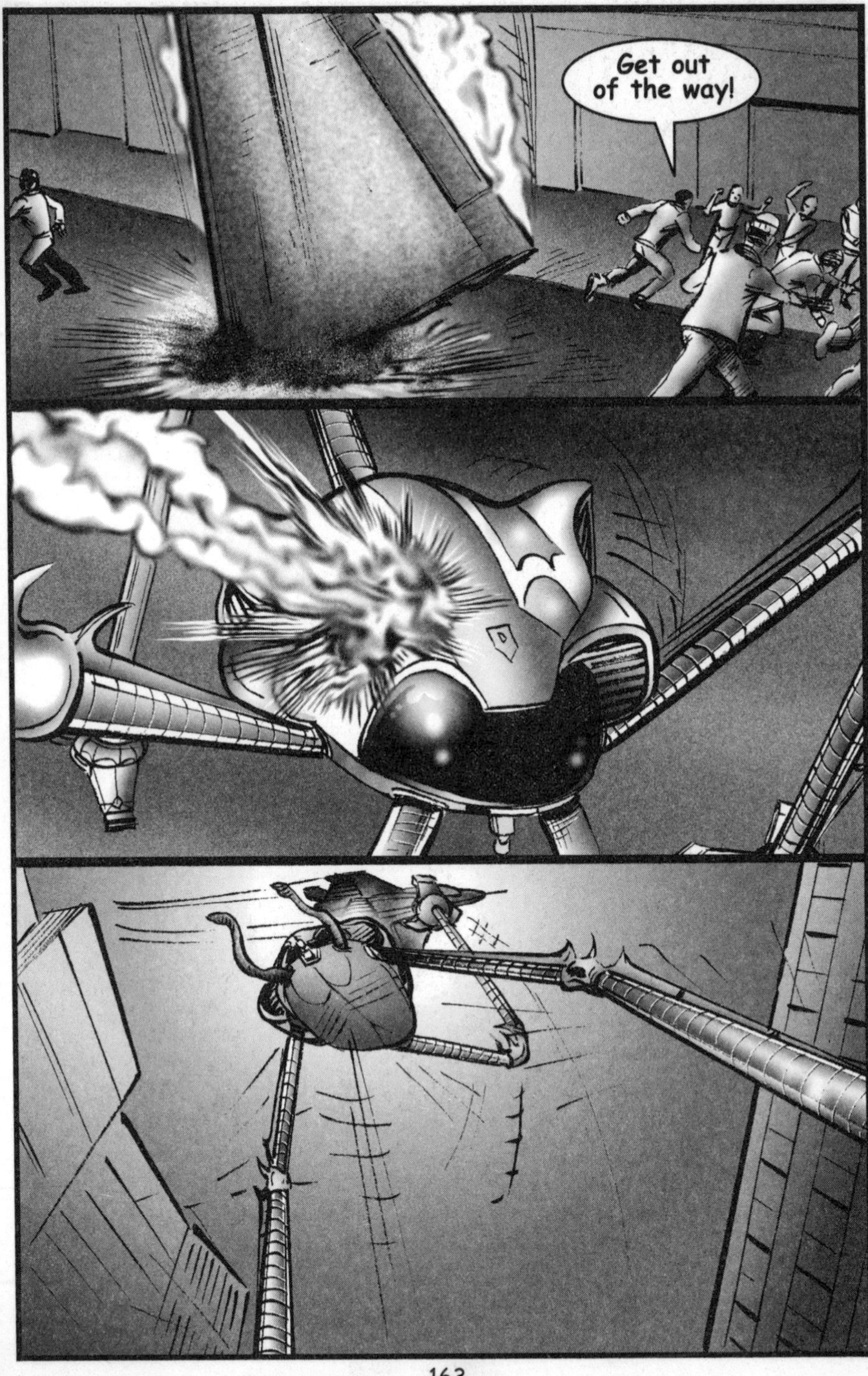
Get out of the way!

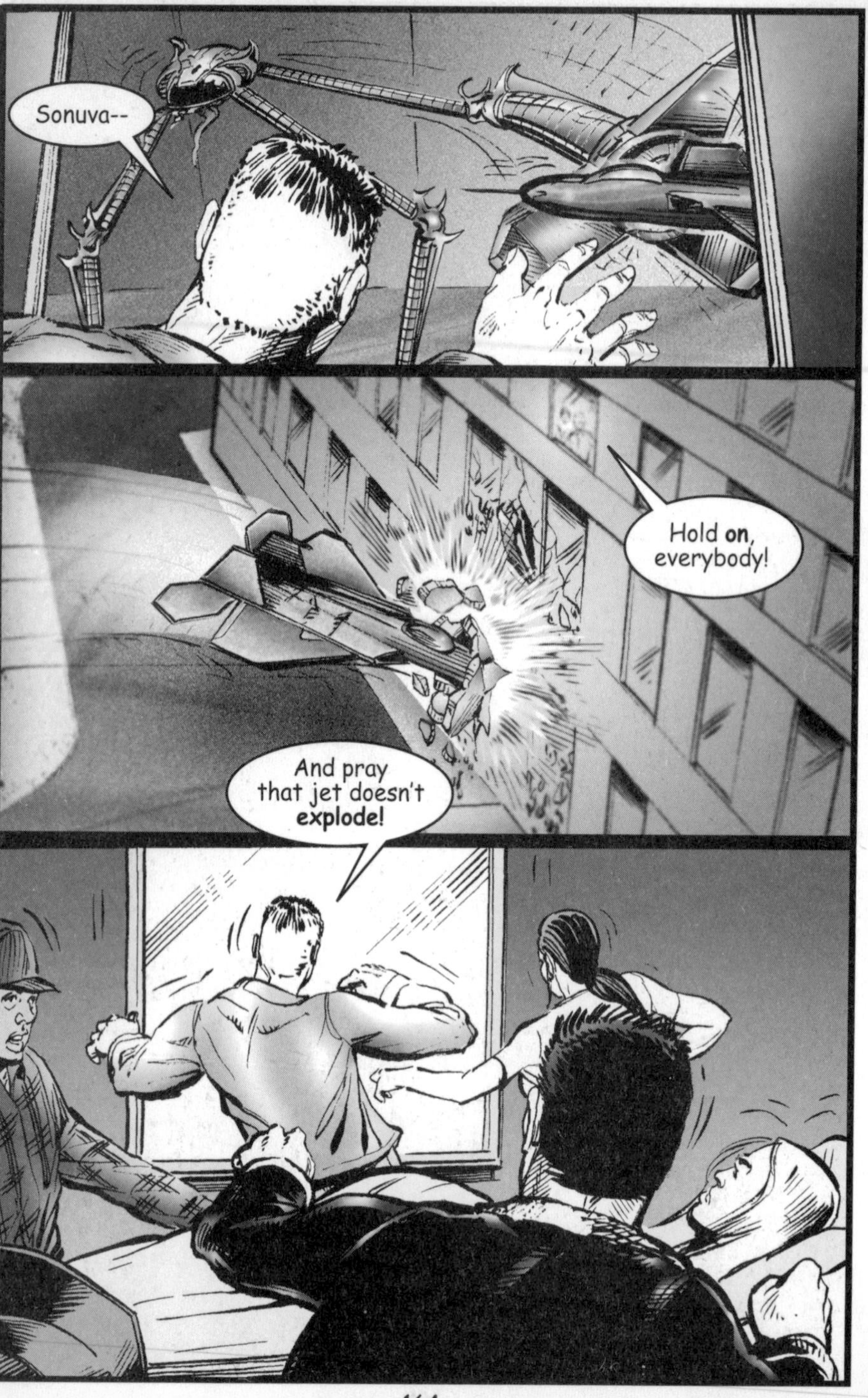
Sonuva--
Hold on, everybody!
And pray that jet doesn't explode!

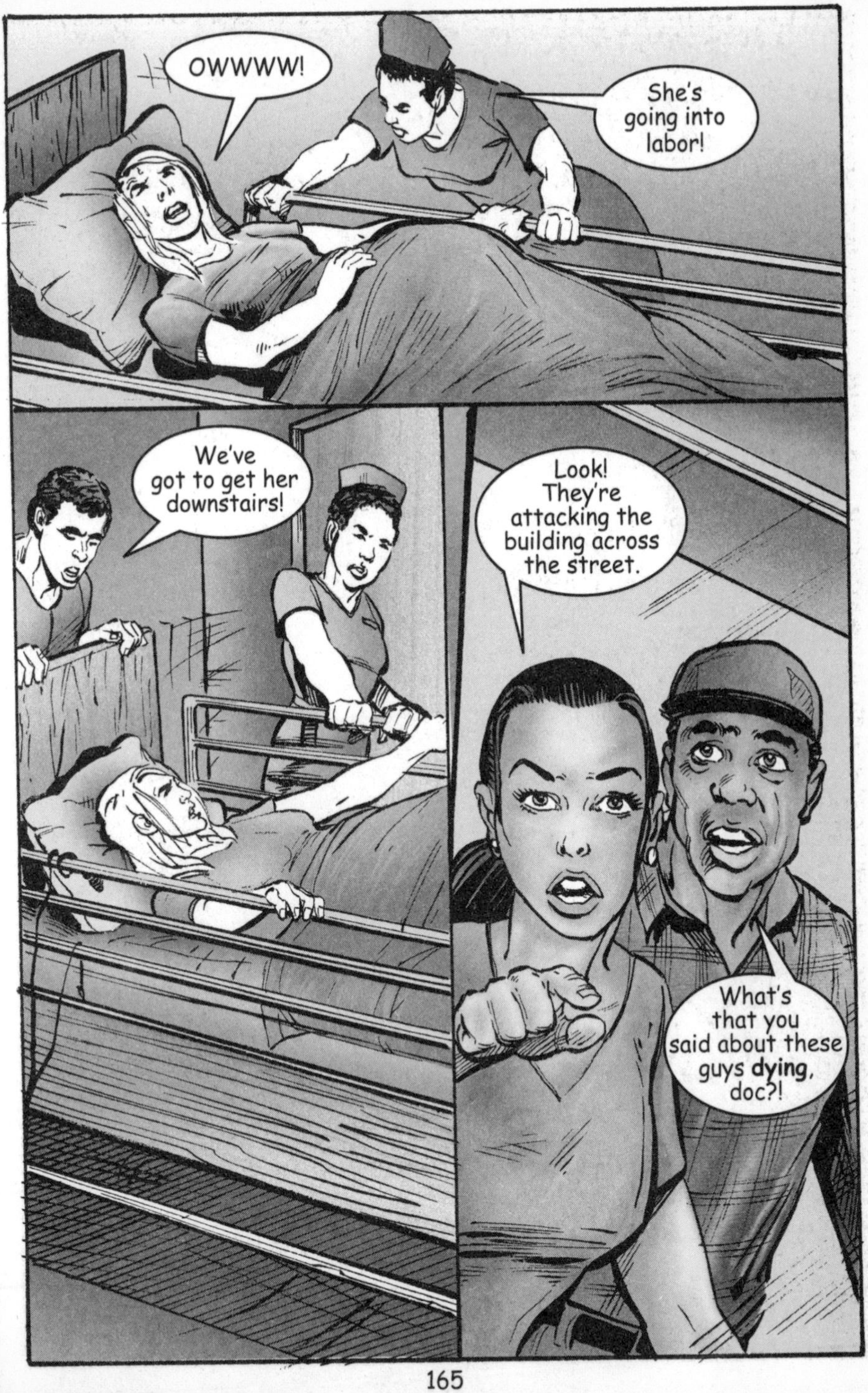
OWWWW!
She's going into labor!
We've got to get her downstairs!
Look! They're attacking the building across the street.
What's that you said about these guys **dying**, doc?!

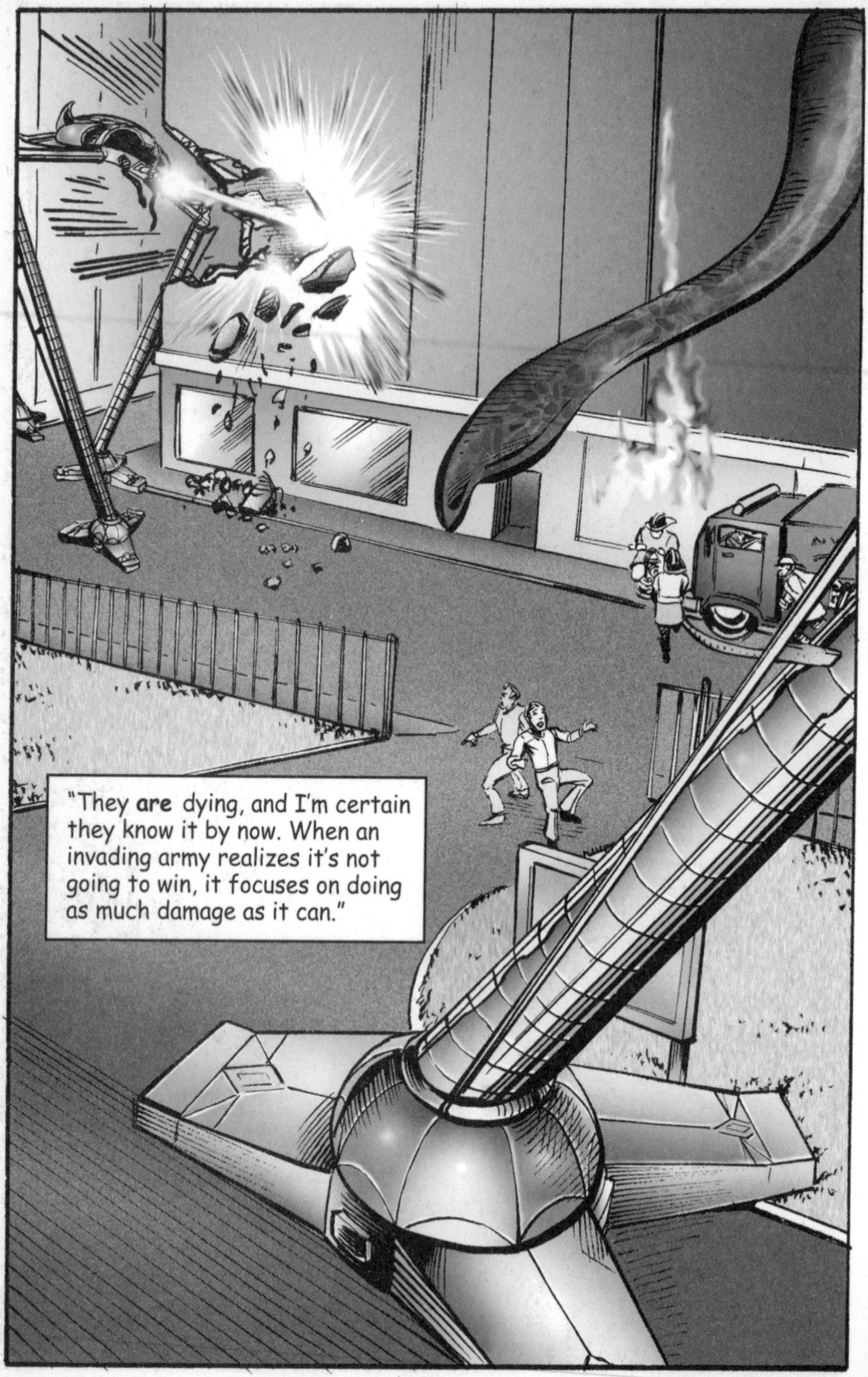
"They **are** dying, and I'm certain they know it by now. When an invading army realizes it's not going to win, it focuses on doing as much damage as it can."

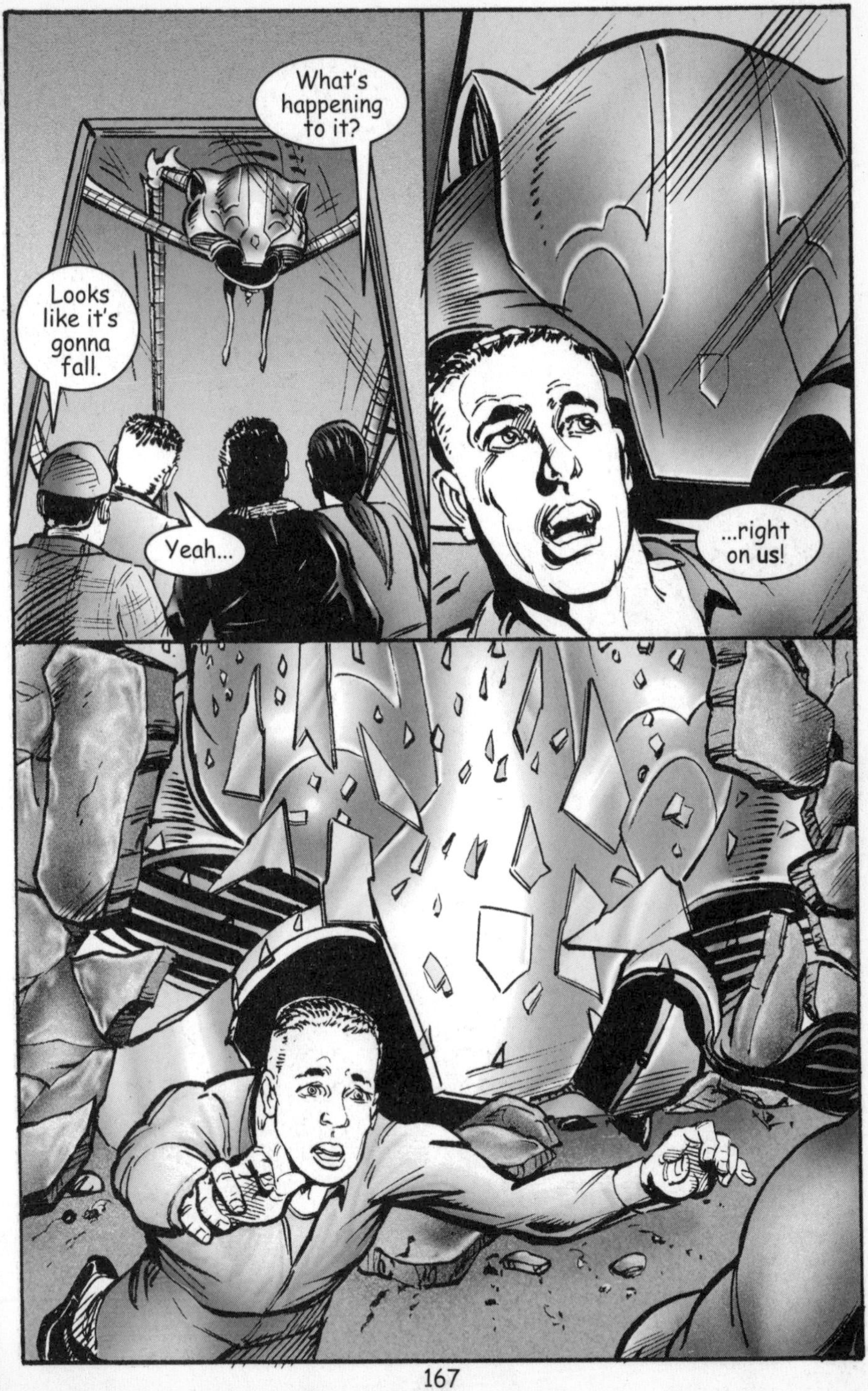
What's happening to it?
Looks like it's gonna fall.
Yeah...
...right on us!

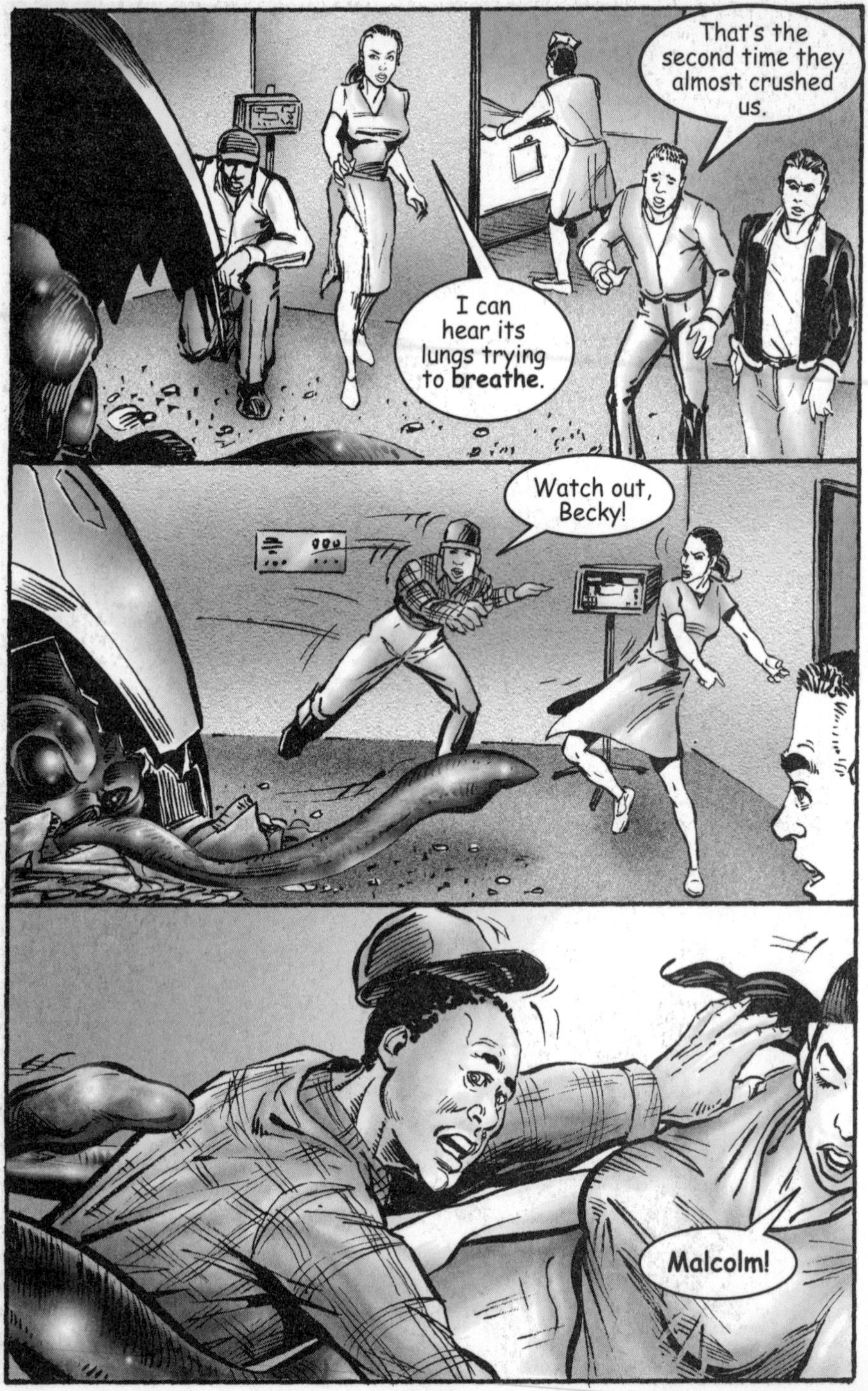

I can hear its lungs trying to **breathe**.
That's the second time they almost crushed us.
Watch out, Becky!
Malcolm!

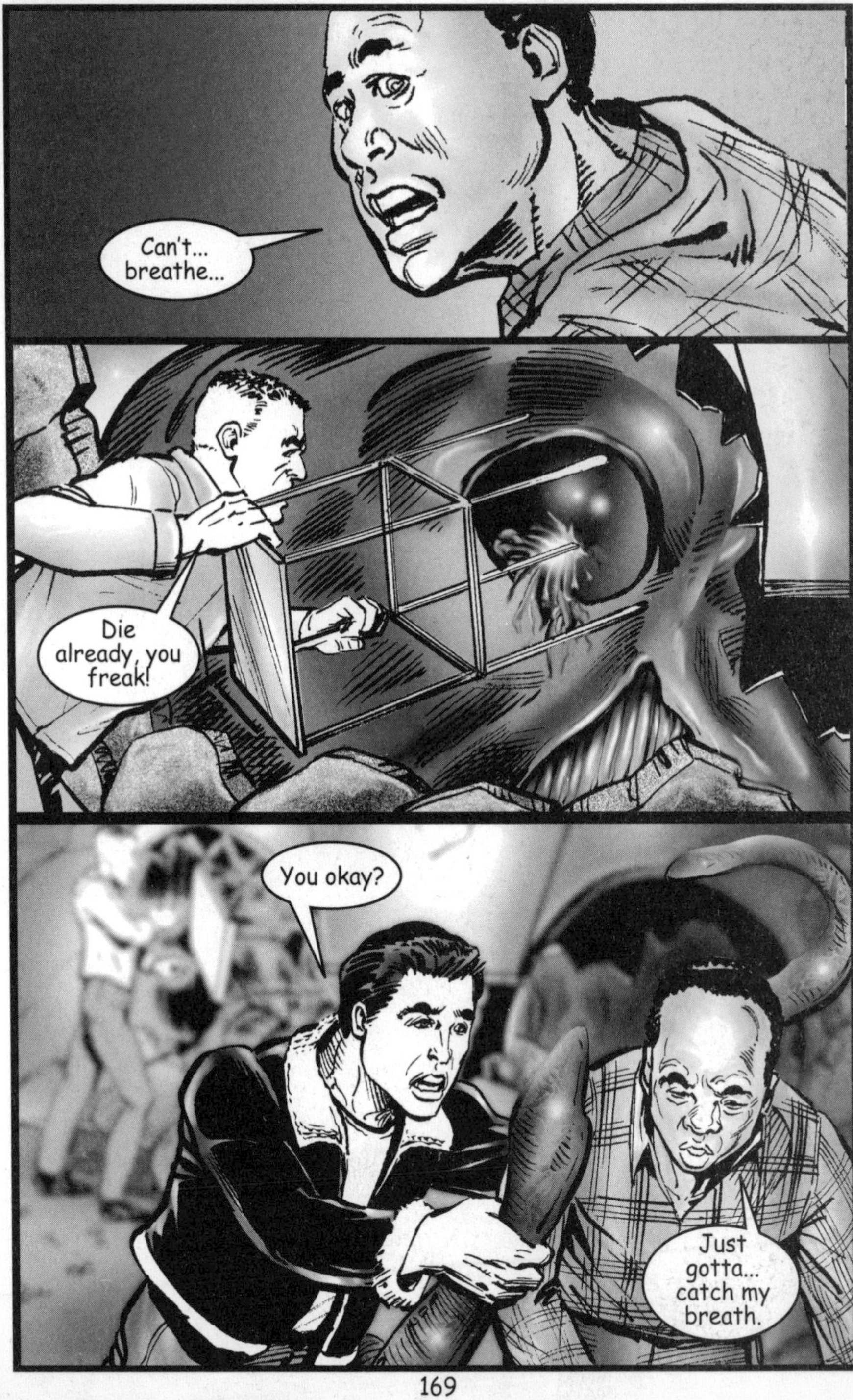
Can't... breathe...
Die already, you freak!
You okay?
Just gotta... catch my breath.

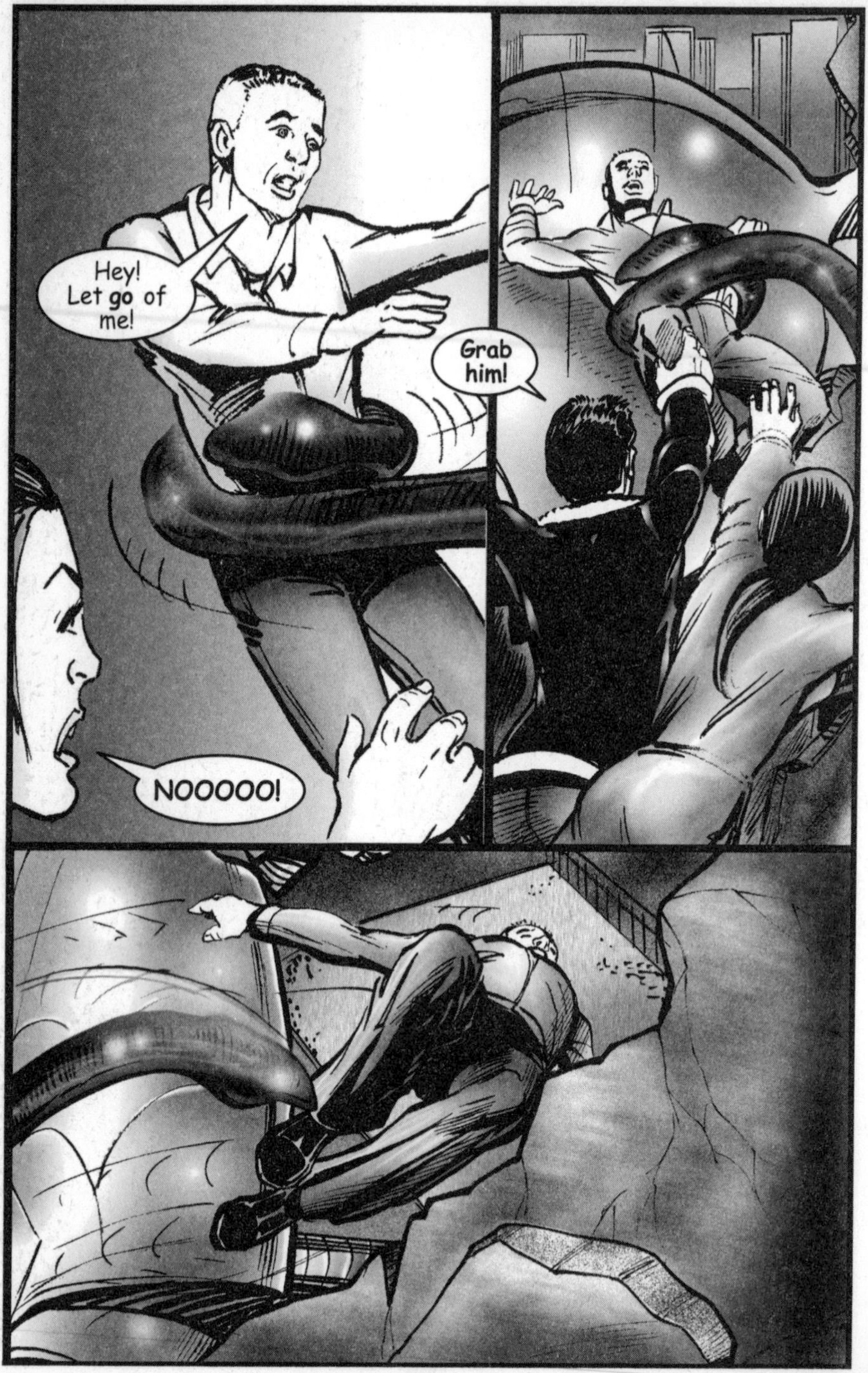
Hey! Let go of me!
NOOOOO!
Grab him!

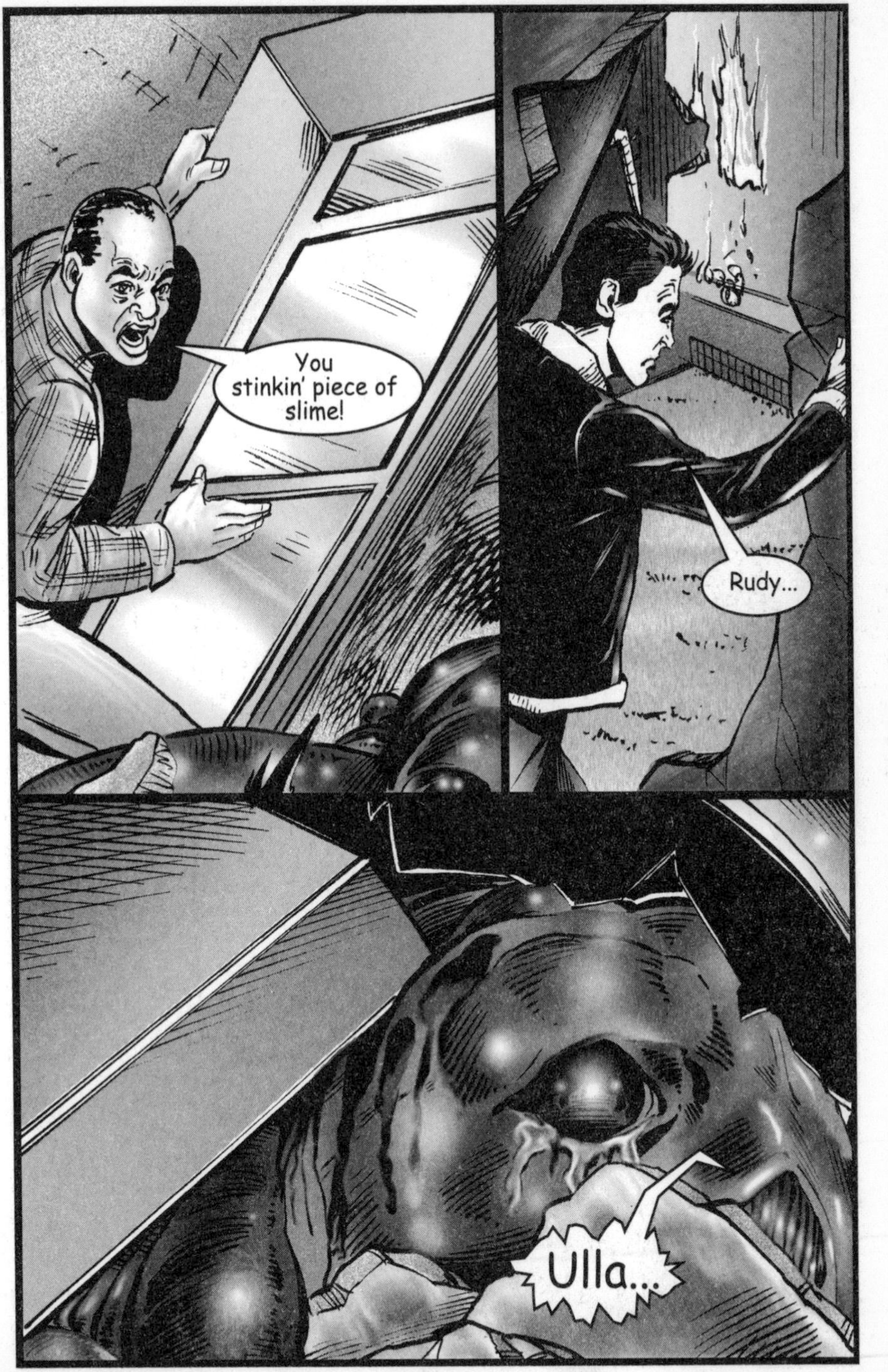
You stinkin' piece of slime!
Rudy...
Ulla...

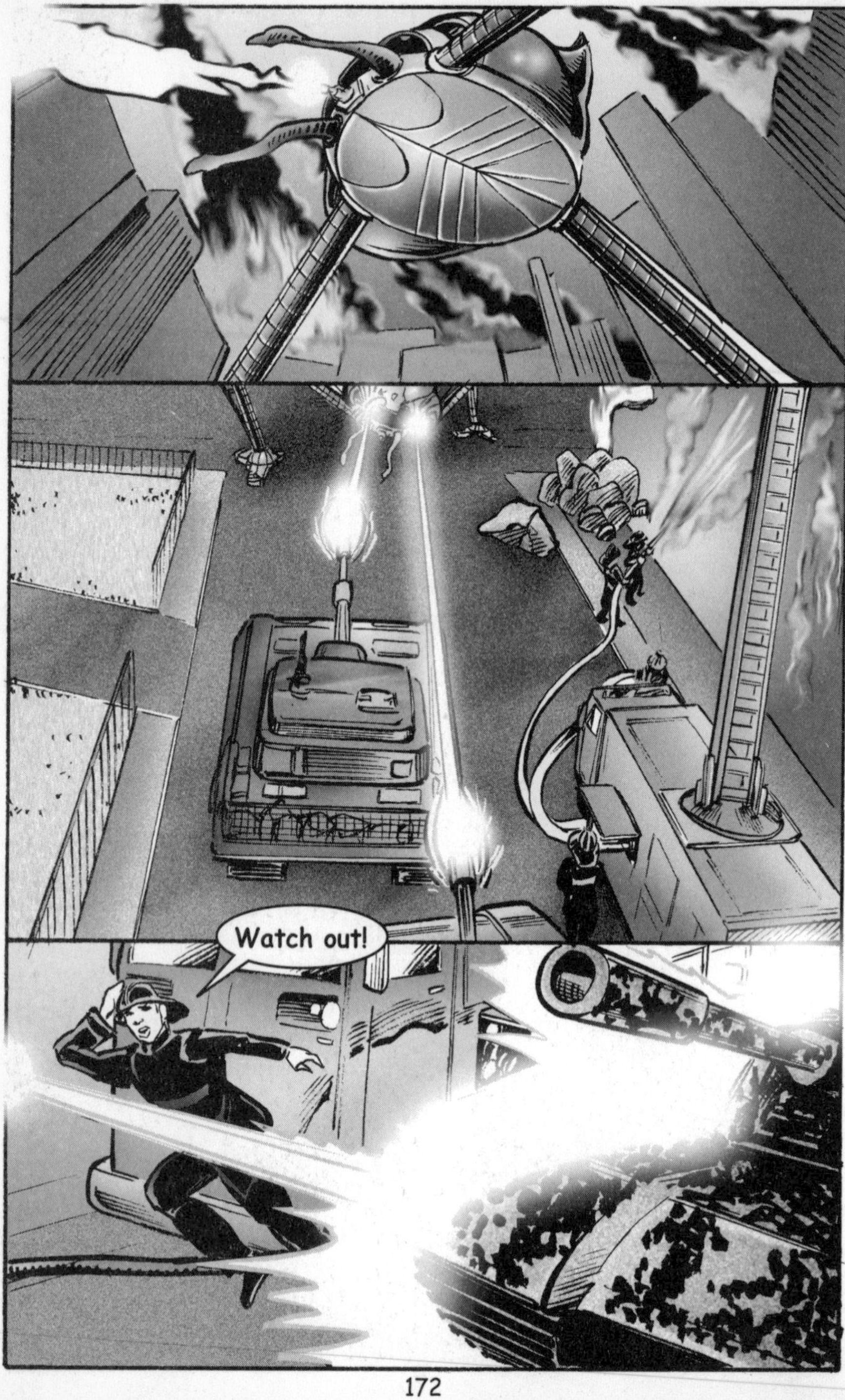
Watch out!

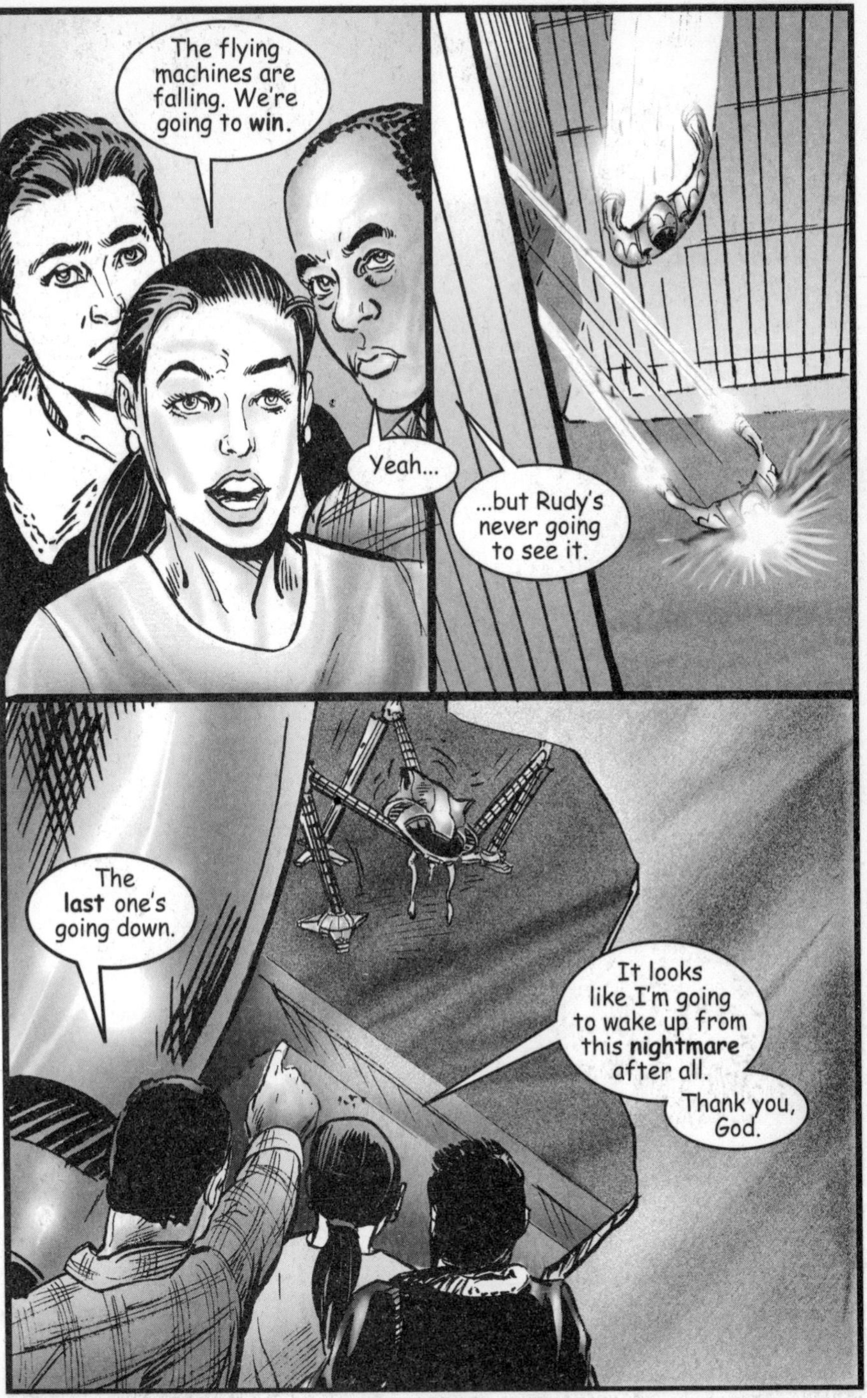
The flying machines are falling. We're going to **win**.
Yeah...
...but Rudy's never going to see it.
The **last** one's going down.
It looks like I'm going to wake up from this **nightmare** after all.
Thank you, God.

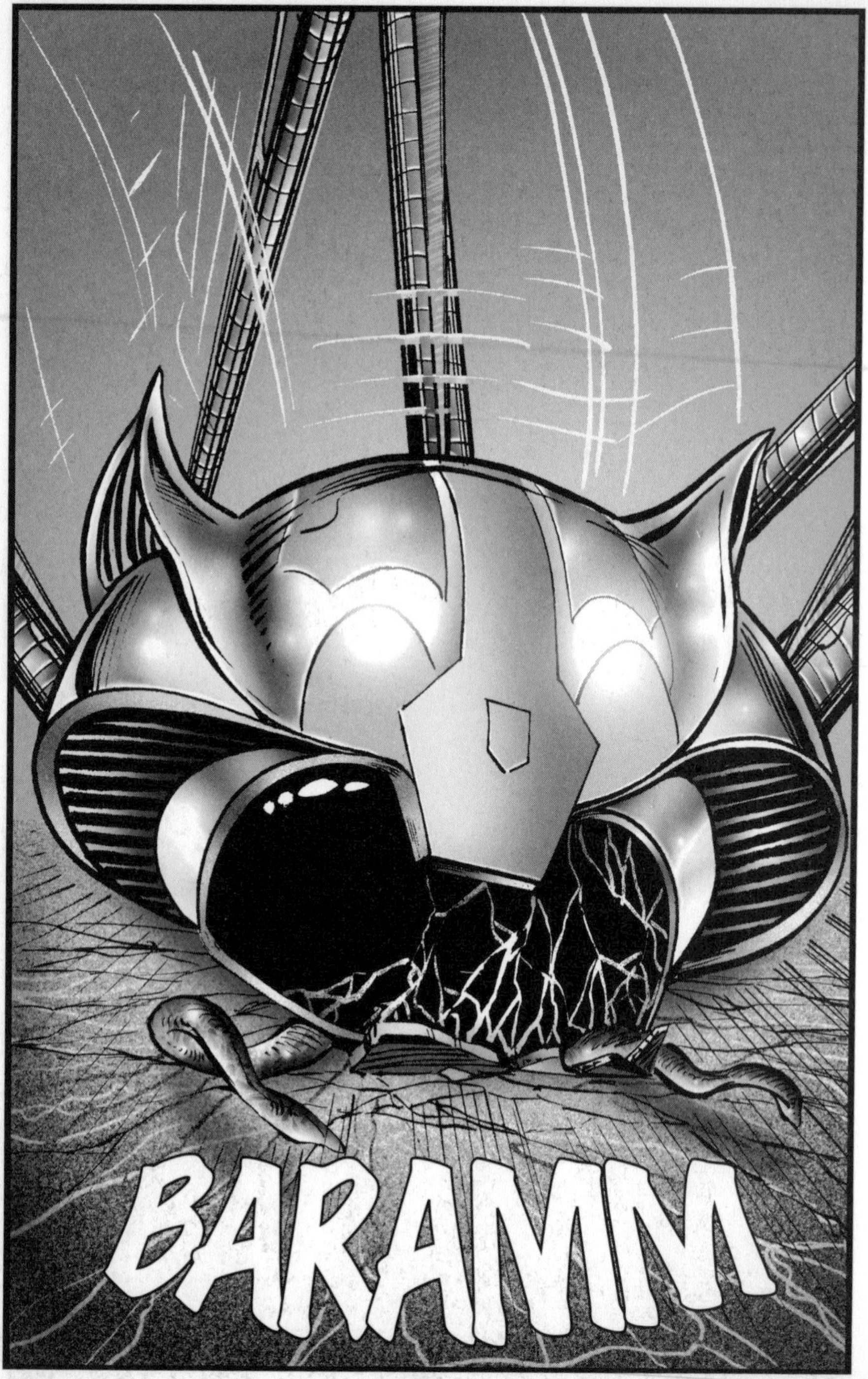
BARAMM

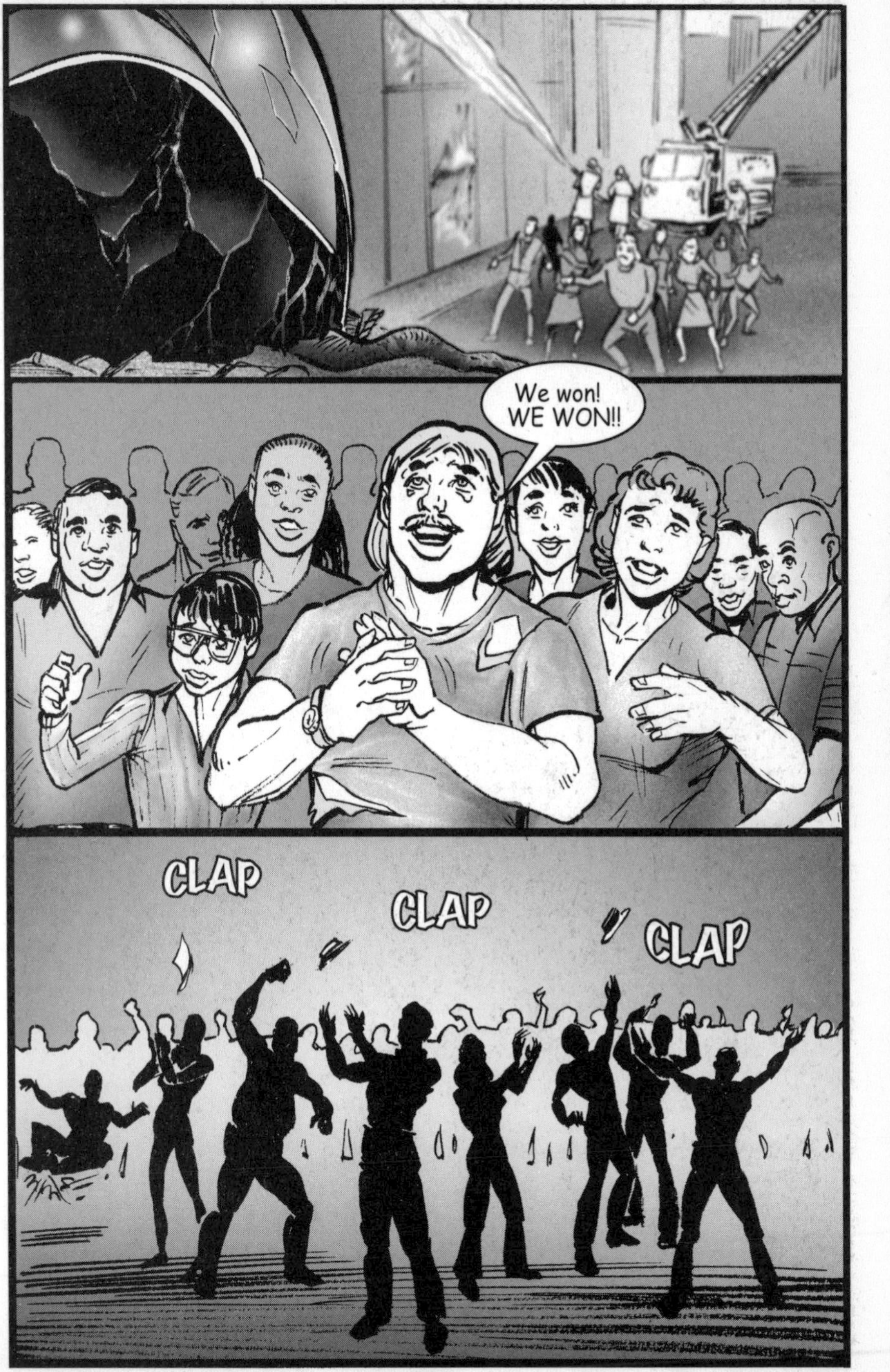
We won!
WE WON!!
CLAP
CLAP
CLAP

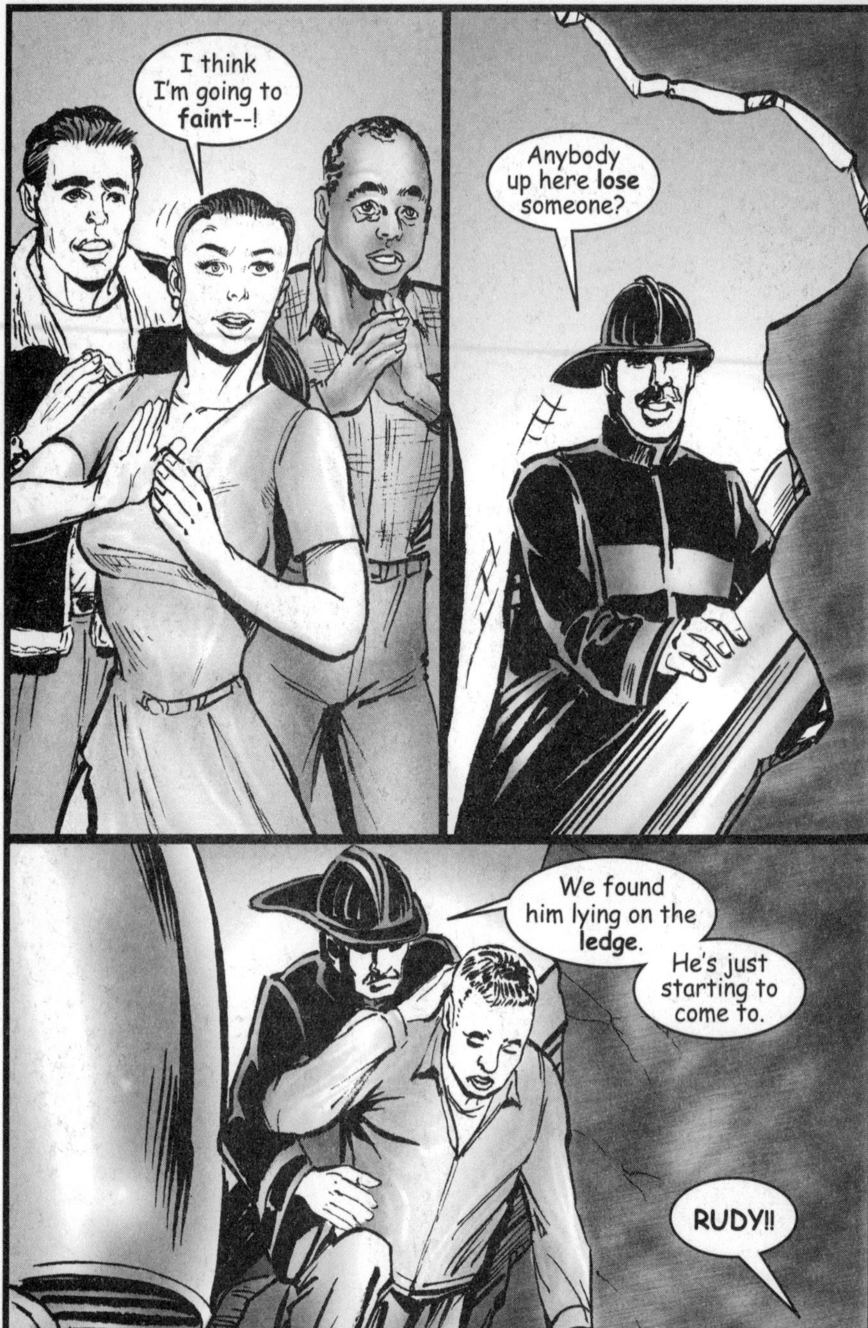

I think I'm going to faint--!
Anybody up here lose someone?
We found him lying on the ledge.
He's just starting to come to.
RUDY!!

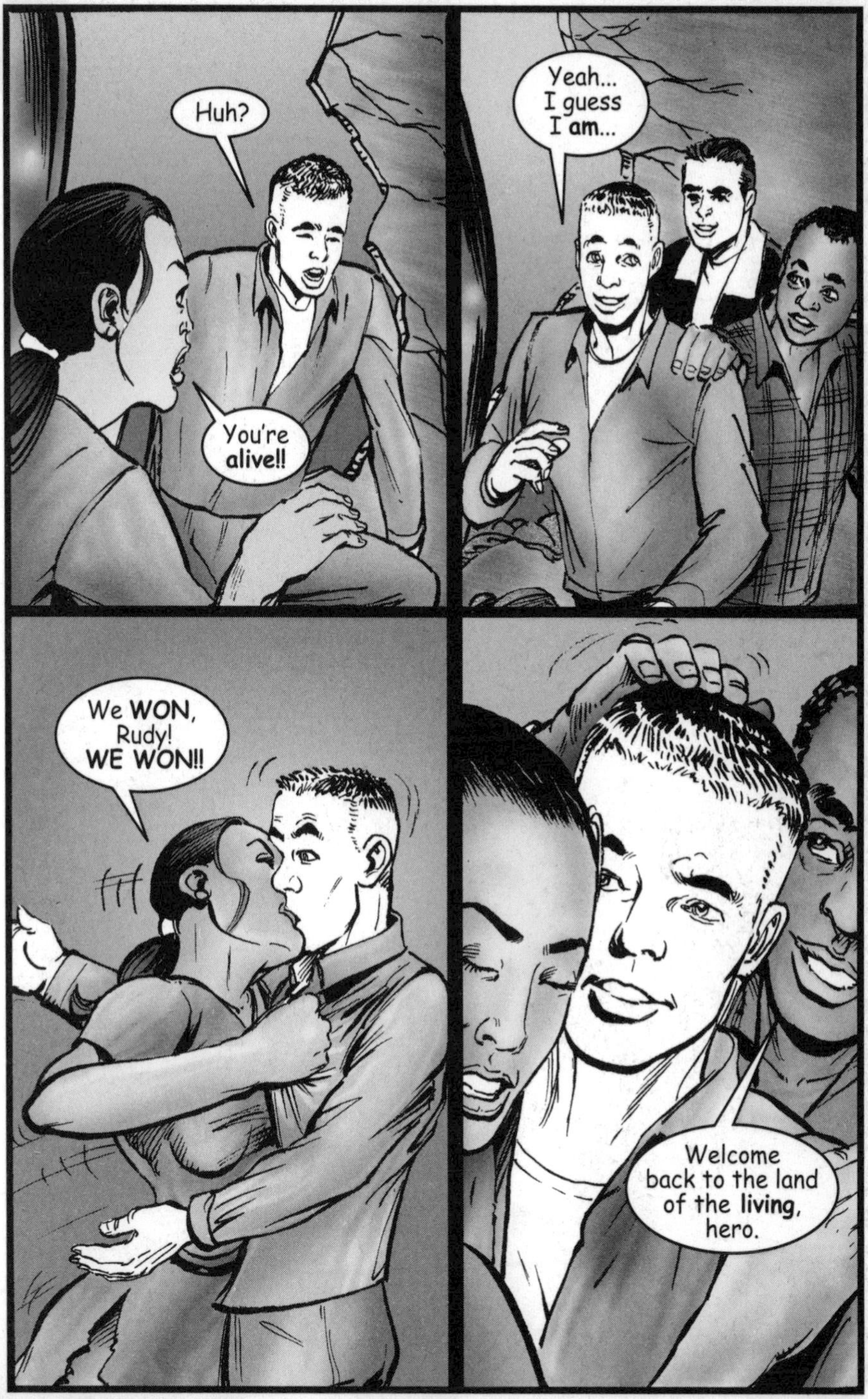
Huh?
You're alive!!
Yeah... I guess I am...
We WON, Rudy! WE WON!!
Welcome back to the land of the living, hero.

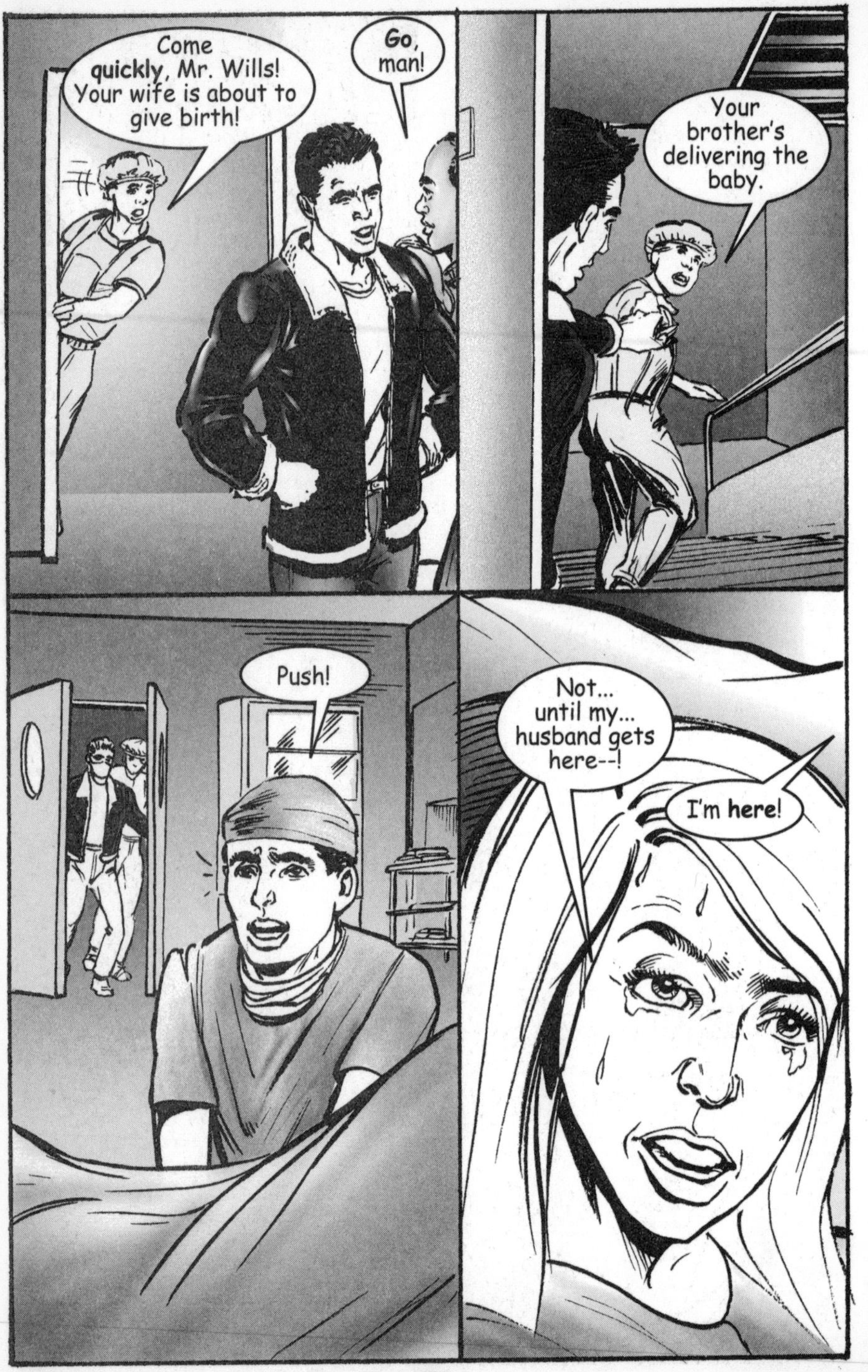
Come quickly, Mr. Wills! Your wife is about to give birth!
Go, man!
Your brother's delivering the baby.
Push!
Not... until my... husband gets here--!
I'm here!

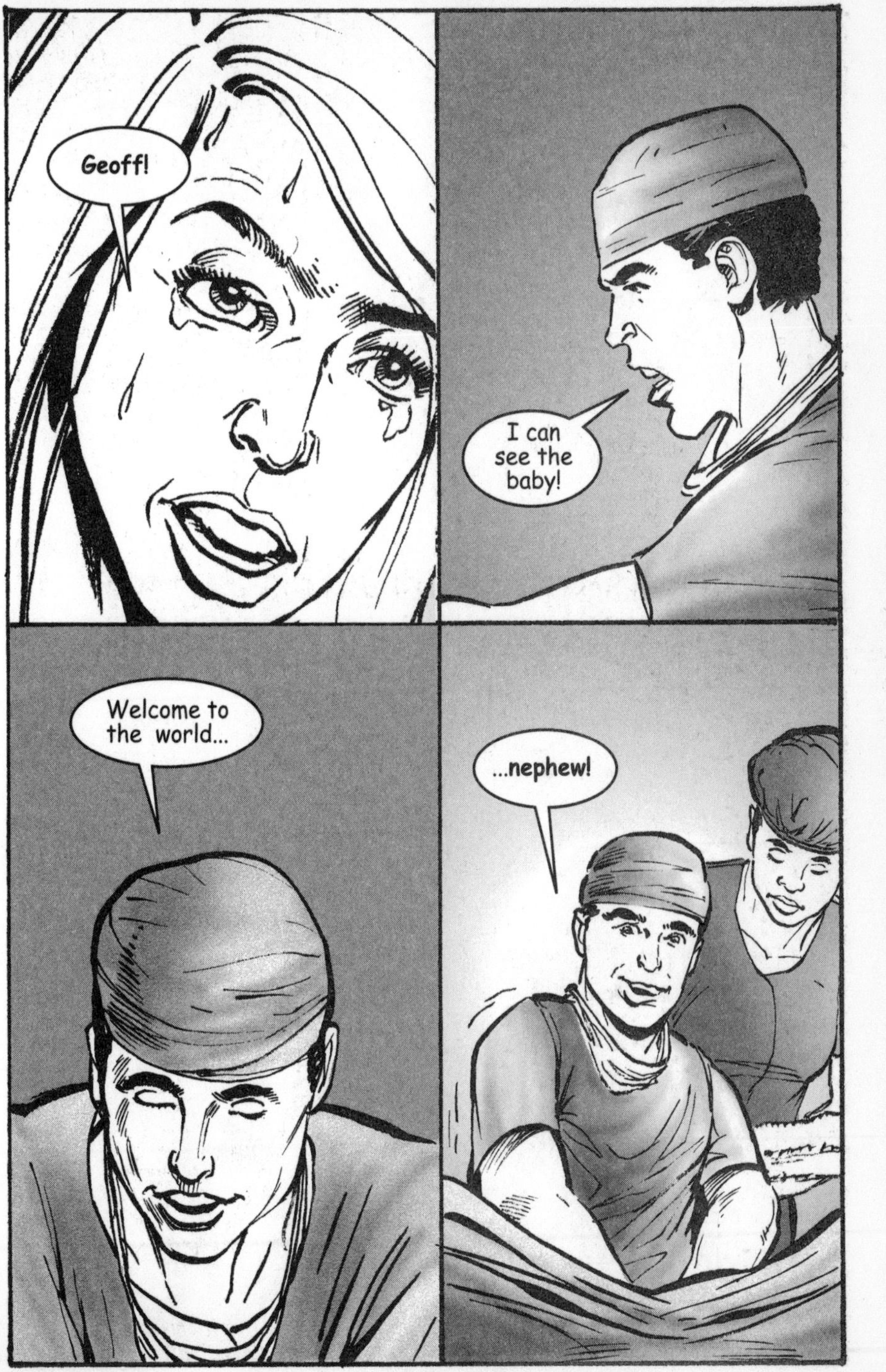

Geoff!
I can see the baby!
Welcome to the world...
...nephew!

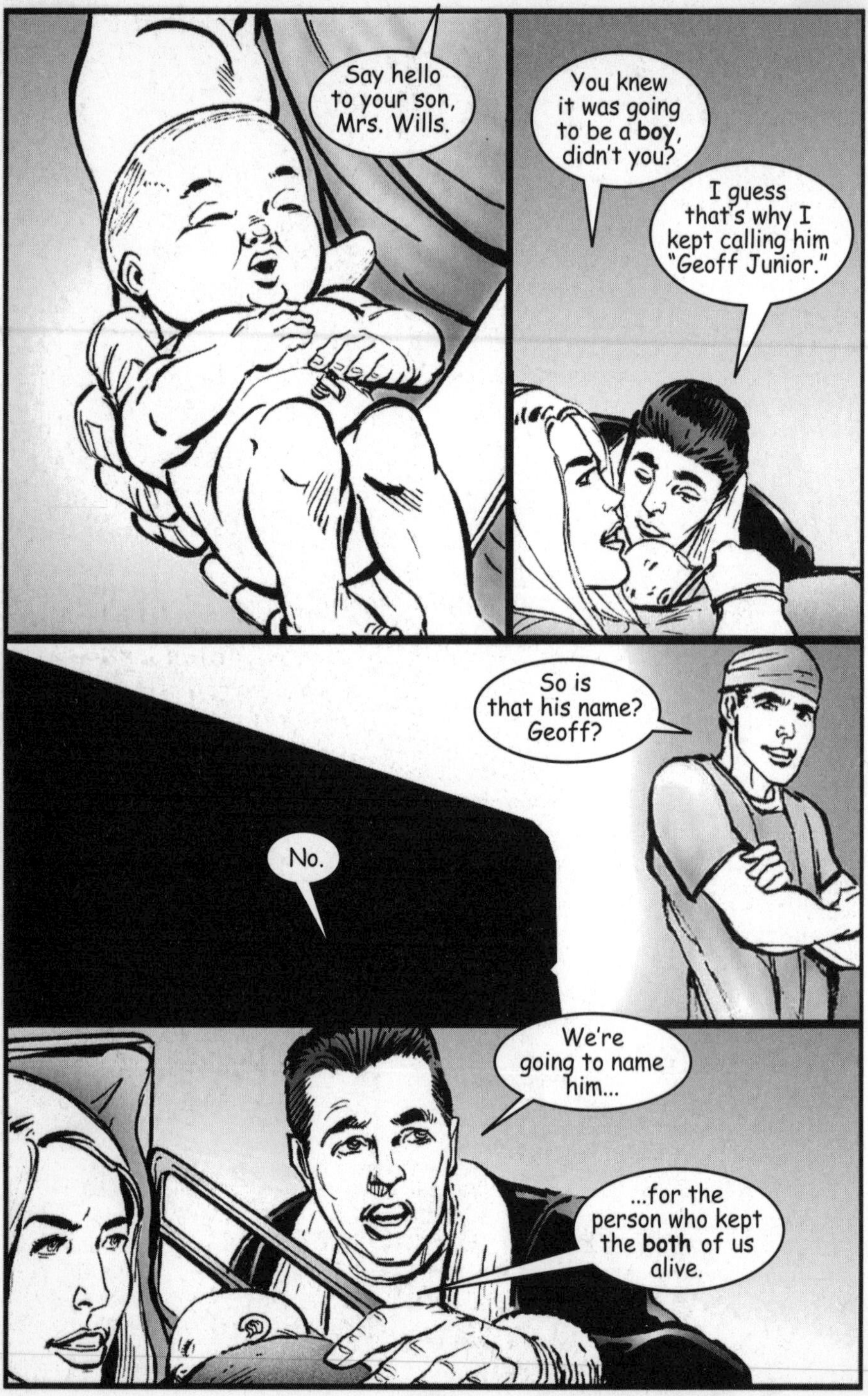
Say hello to your son, Mrs. Wills.
You knew it was going to be a **boy**, didn't you?
I guess that's why I kept calling him "Geoff Junior."
So is that his name? Geoff?
No.
We're going to name him...
...for the person who kept the **both** of us alive.

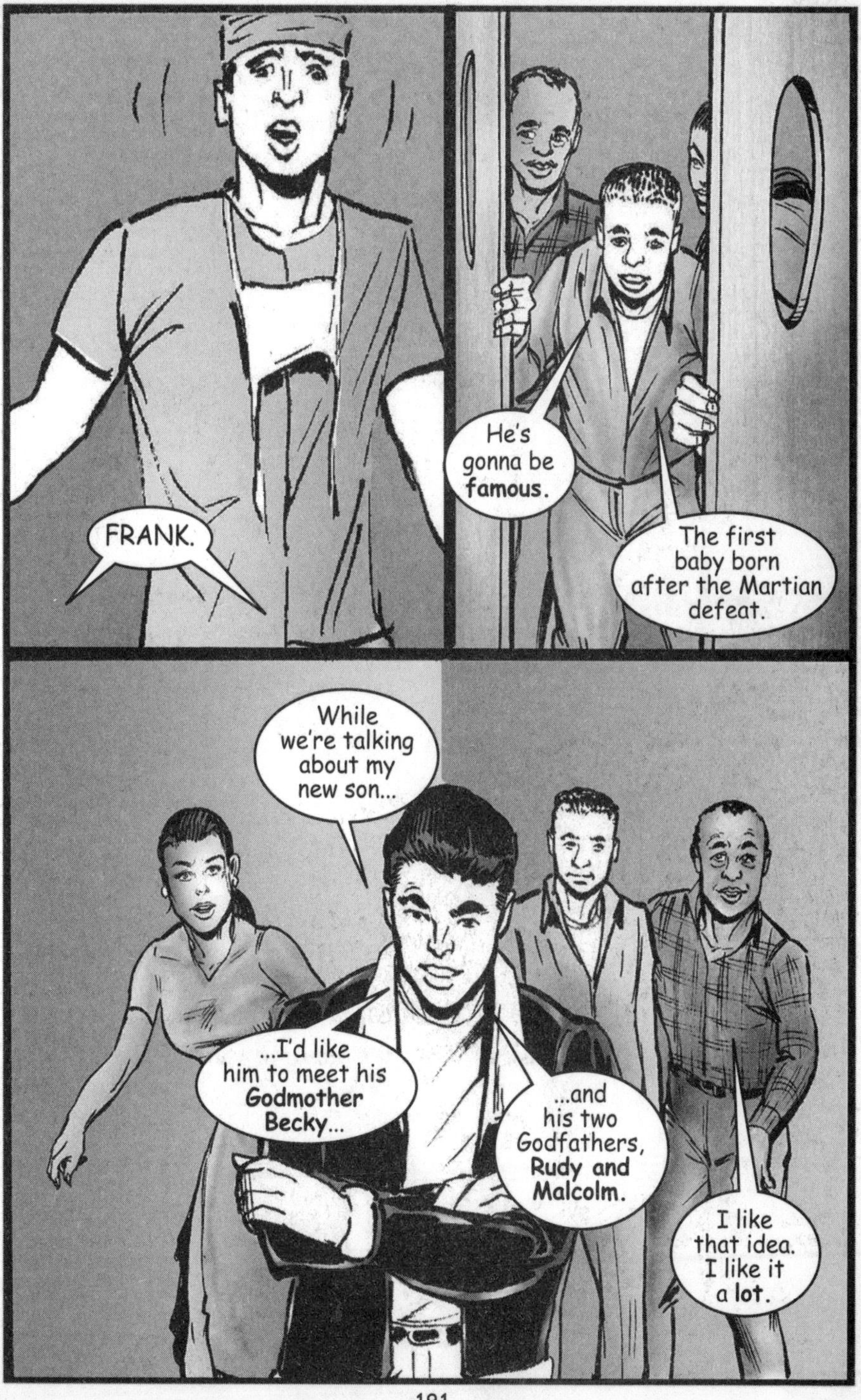
FRANK.
He's gonna be **famous**.
The first baby born after the Martian defeat.
While we're talking about my new son...
...I'd like him to meet his **Godmother Becky**...
...and his two Godfathers, **Rudy and Malcolm**.
I like that idea. I like it a **lot**.

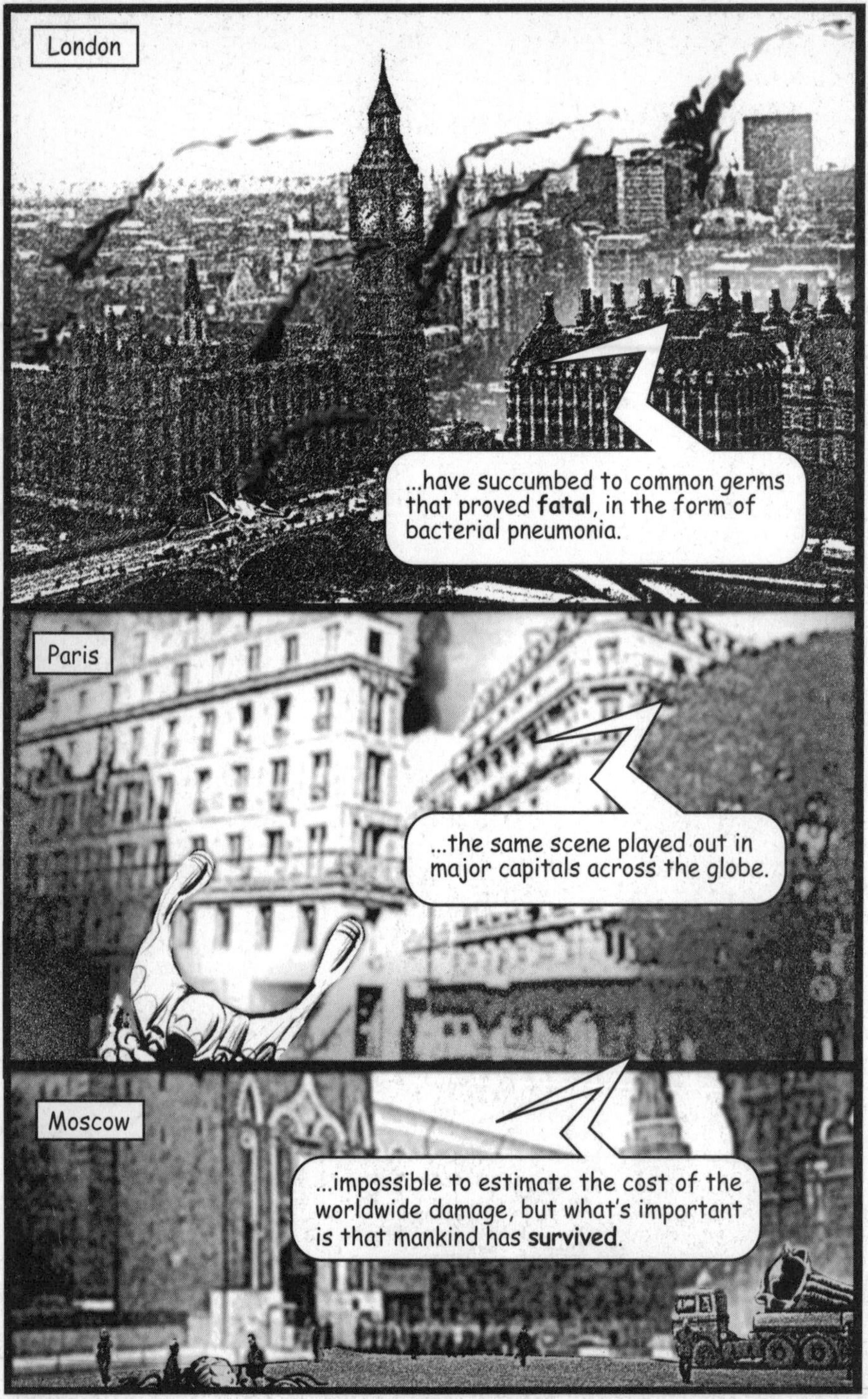
London
...have succumbed to common germs that proved **fatal**, in the form of bacterial pneumonia.
Paris
...the same scene played out in major capitals across the globe.
Moscow
...impossible to estimate the cost of the worldwide damage, but what's important is that mankind has **survived**.

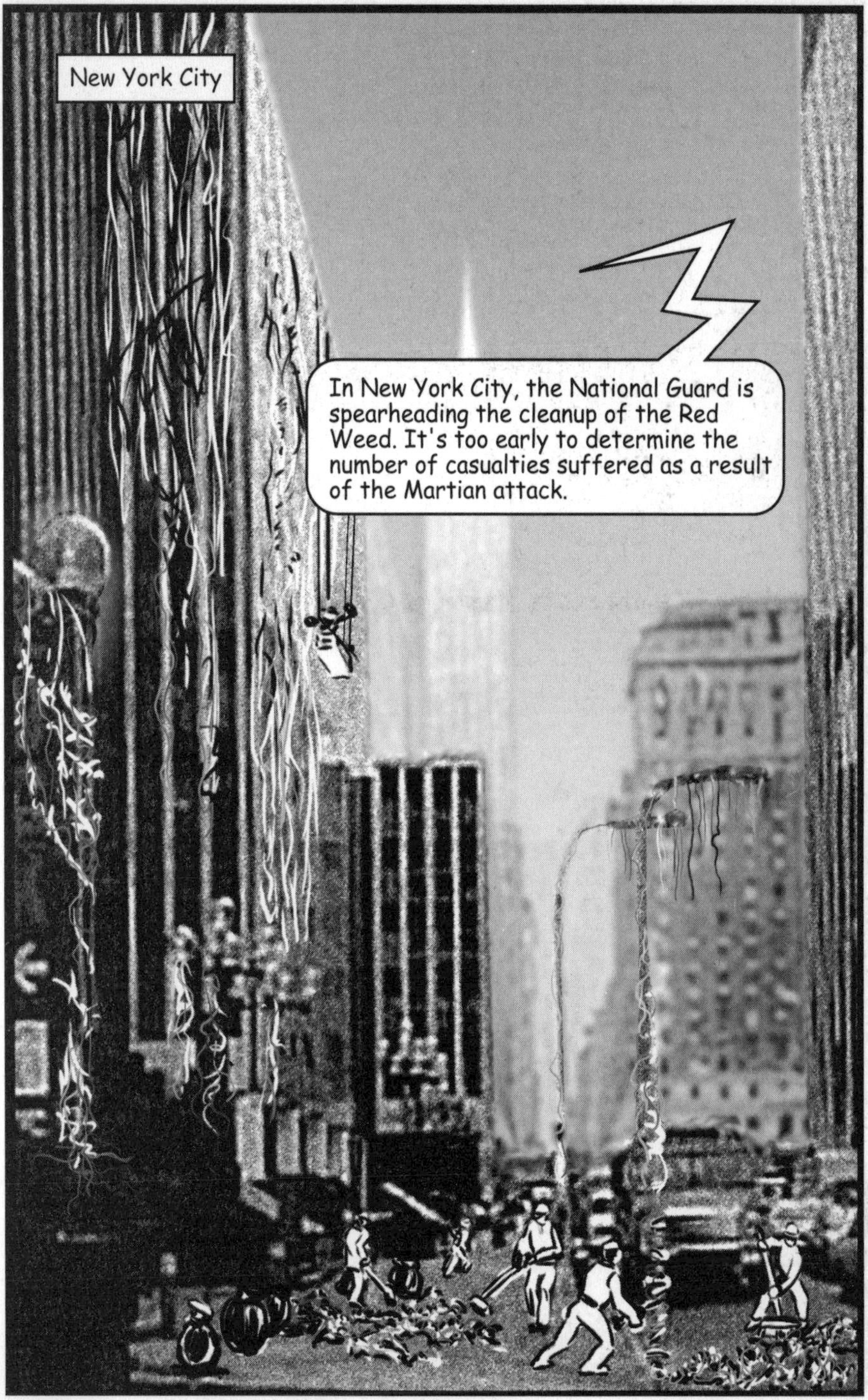
New York City
In New York City, the National Guard is spearheading the cleanup of the Red Weed. It's too early to determine the number of casualties suffered as a result of the Martian attack.

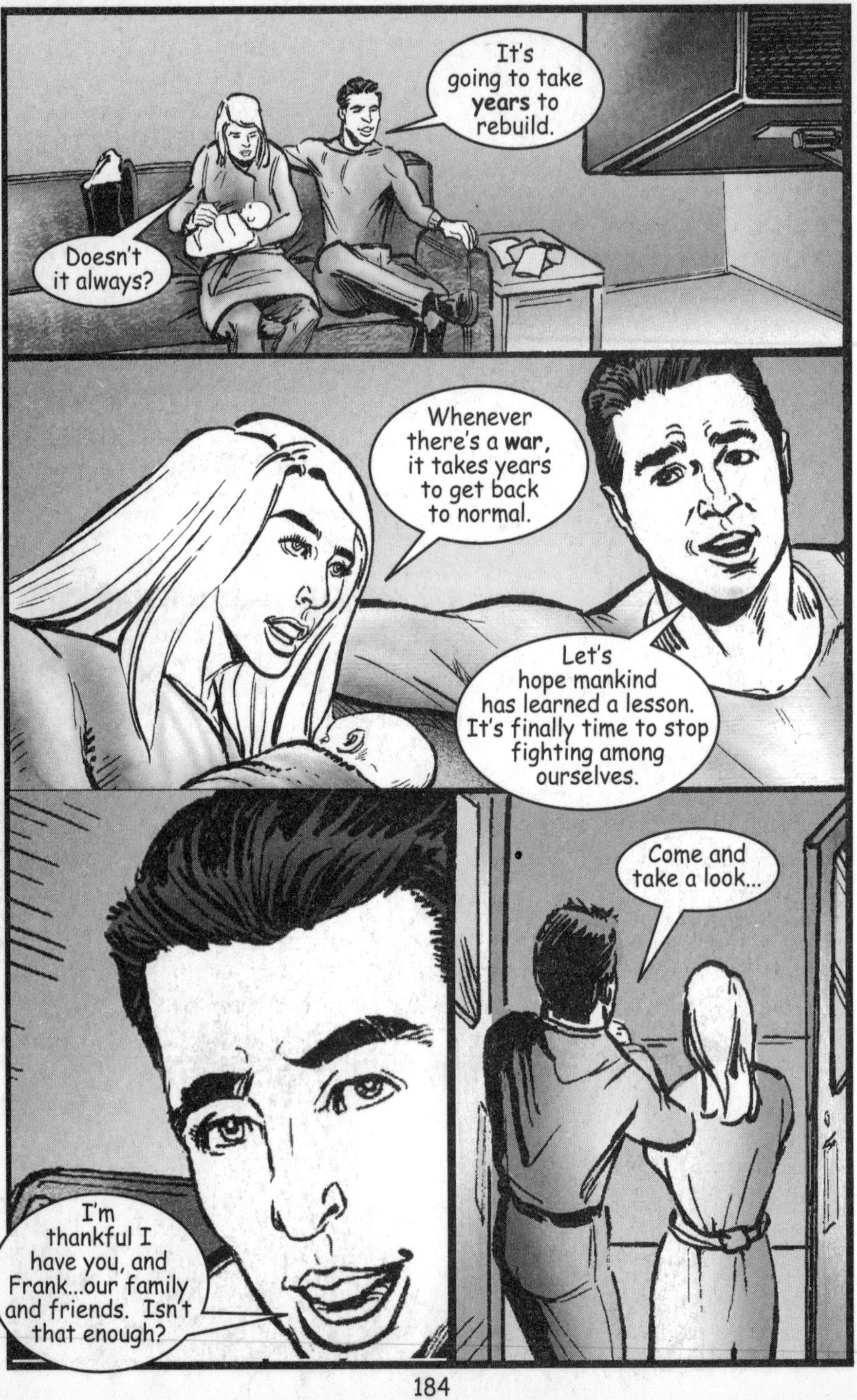
It's going to take **years** to rebuild.
Doesn't it always?
Whenever there's a **war**, it takes years to get back to normal.
Let's hope mankind has learned a lesson. It's finally time to stop fighting among ourselves.
I'm thankful I have you, and Frank...our family and friends. Isn't that enough?
Come and take a look...

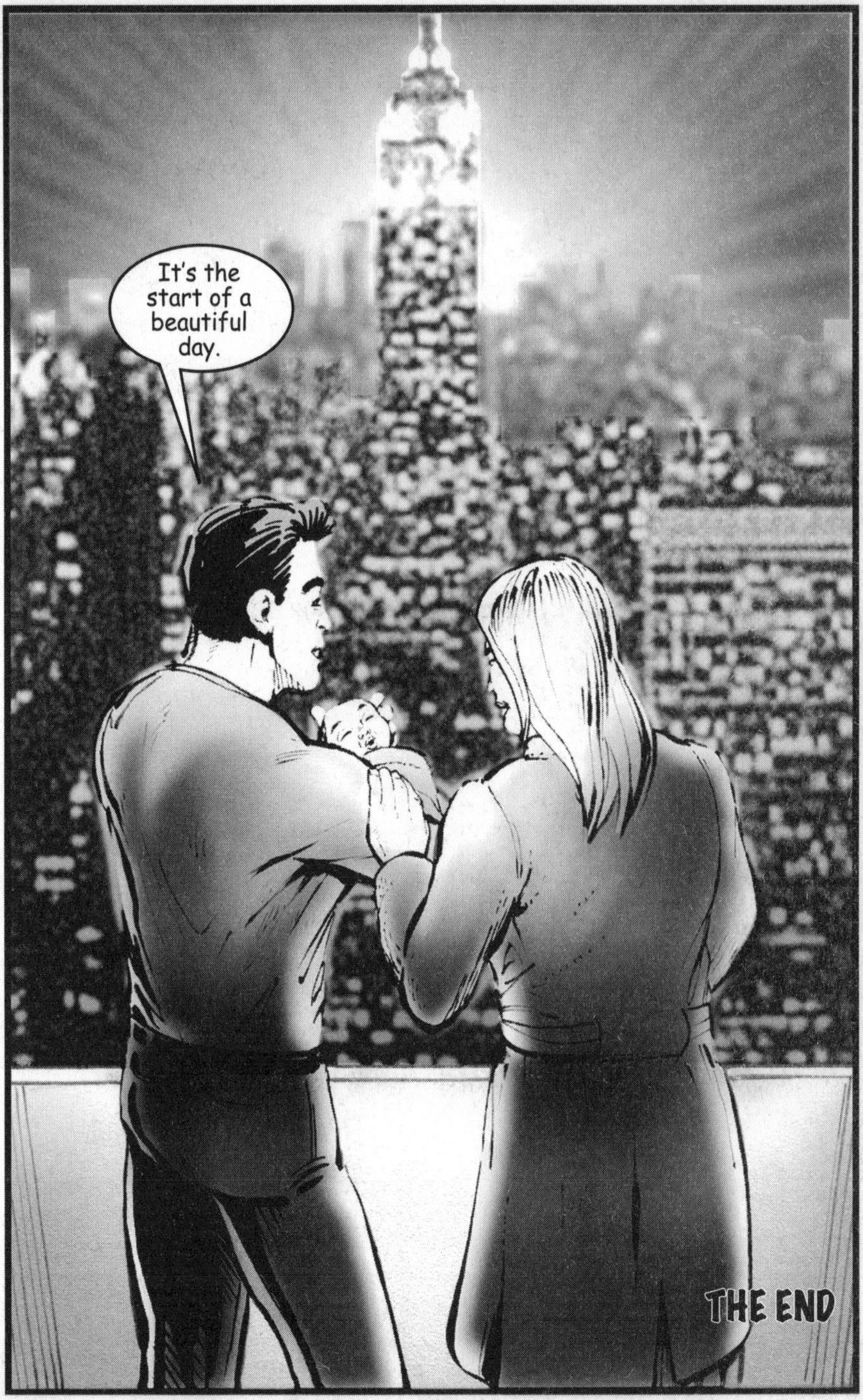
It's the start of a beautiful day.
THE END

To Pamela, Patti, Bettina, Adele, Arlene, Leona, Ruth, May, Bertha and Palomba--I wish to thank all of the wonderful women who have provided their unconditional love and support throughout the years.

S.S.

This is for the people who have believed in me over all the years and made the biggest difference in my life. Props go to Dick Giordano and Peter David, who have always been my biggest supporters in my comic-book career and my life around it. In my segue to working in Hollywood, credit goes to Bill and Tereza Campbell, Mira Furlan and Goran Gajic, Andrea Thompson, Jeff Walker and my acting teacher, the late Marc Lenard. You all believed I should be on the west coast and I finally listened. And, of course, to my sons Devin, Jordan and Matthew, who have made the trip through life worthwhile. To all these people, I dedicate this book.

A.S.

To Nancy, Edith, Sheri and Bonnie for all your genetics, spiritual support and patience.

D.C.